T0358431

VARIORUM COLLECTED STUDIES SERIES

Byzantium and the Other:
Relations and Exchanges

Angeliki E. Laiou

Angeliki E. Laiou

Byzantium and the Other:
Relations and Exchanges

Edited by Cécile Morrisson
and Rowan Dorin

Routledge
Taylor & Francis Group

LONDON AND NEW YORK

First published 2012 by Ashgate Publishing

Published 2016 by Routledge
2 Park Square, Milton Park, Abingdon, Oxon OX14 4RN
711 Third Avenue, New York, NY 10017, USA

First issued in paperback 2017

Routledge is an imprint of the Taylor & Francis Group, an informa business

British Library Cataloguing in Publication Data
Laiou, Angeliki E.
    Byzantium and the other : relations and exchanges.
    – (Variorum collected studies series ; CS1005)
    1. Byzantine Empire – Foreign relations – 1081–1453.
    2. Byzantine Empire – Commerce. 3. Crusades.
    I. Title II. Series III. Morrisson, Cécile. IV. Dorin, Rowan.
    949.5–dc23

Library of Congress Control Number: 2012936462

VARIORUM COLLECTED STUDIES SERIES CS1005

ISBN 13: 978-1-138-11571-2 (pbk)
ISBN 13: 978-1-4094-3206-7 (hbk)

CONTENTS

This volume contains xvi + 322 pages

PUBLISHER'S NOTE

The articles in this volume, as in all others in the Variorum Collected Studies Series, have not been given a new, continuous pagination. In order to avoid confusion, and to facilitate their use where these same studies have been referred to elsewhere, the original pagination has been maintained wherever possible. Articles XIII and XIV have necessarily been reset with a new pagination, and with the original page numbers given in square brackets within the text.

Each article has been given a Roman number in order of appearance, as listed in the Contents. This number is repeated on each page and is quoted in the index entries.

PREFACE

Daß wir erschraken, da du starbst, nein, daß
dein starker Tod uns dunkel unterbrach,
das Bisdahin abreißend vom Seither:
das geht uns an; das einzuordnen wird
die Arbeit sein, die wir mit allem tun.

Rilke, *Requiem für eine Freundin* (1908)

Angeliki Laiou (1941-2008) was among the leading Byzantinists of her generation.[1] Armed with a penetrating intellect and graced with an uncommon clarity of thought and expression, she broke new ground in the field of Byzantine social and economic history. Fruitfully drawing on the insights of other historical periods and scholarly disciplines, but always sensitive to the specificities of the Byzantine experience, she published pioneering studies of topics ranging from family structure to economic ideology.

The articles gathered here bear witness to these qualities, as well as to her readiness to revisit her own earlier work in light of new insights and discoveries. They testify equally to the tragedy of her swift and unexpected passing, which left Byzantine Studies bereft of one of its most eloquent defenders and robbed her colleagues and students of a beloved friend and mentor. It is on behalf of these colleagues and students that we have undertaken the task of preparing three collections of her articles to be published posthumously in the Variorum series.[2] Though the vitality of her presence is now but a treasured memory, it is our hope that these volumes will ensure that her scholarly legacy remains alive and well.

We are particularly grateful to David Jacoby for suggesting this project in the first place, to John Smedley for shepherding it through the publication process with patience and good humour, and to Vassili Thomadakis for his support and encouragement. We would also like to thank David Jacoby for generously agreeing to write the Introduction to this volume, and Gilbert Dagron, Michael McCormick, Nevra Necipoğlu, and the staff at Dumbarton Oaks for their assistance.

CÉCILE MORRISSON & ROWAN DORIN

---

[1] For a detailed account of her life and achievements, as well as a full bibliography, see the obituary by Cécile Morrisson and Alice-Mary Talbot in *Dumbarton Oaks Papers* 63 (2011): 1-14.

[2] *Women, Family and Society in Byzantium*, *Byzantium and the Other: Relations and Exchanges*, and *Economic Thought and Economic Life in Byzantium*.

ACKNOWLEDGEMENTS

Grateful acknowledgement is made to the following persons, institutions, journals and publishers for their kind permission to reproduce the papers included in this volume: Vittorio Klostermann GmbH, Frankfurt am Main (for article I); The Robbins Religious and Civil Law Collection, and The Regents of the University of California, Berkeley, CA (II); Dumbarton Oaks Research Library and Collection, Washington D.C. (III, VII, VIII, X, XIII); Editions Lethielleux, Paris (IV); Aristide D. Caratzas (V); Casa Editrice CLUEB, Bologna (IX); Glauco Brigati, Genoa (XI); Bertrand Hirsch, Publications de la Sorbonne, Paris (XII); and the Metropolitan Museum of Art, NY (XIV).

Every effort has been made to trace all the copyright holders, but if any have been inadvertently overlooked the publishers will be pleased to make the necessary arrangement at the first opportunity.

INTRODUCTION

The doctoral thesis of Angeliki Laiou, published in a revised version as *Constantinople and the Latins. The Foreign Policy of Andronicus II, 1282–1328* (Cambridge, Mass., 1972), her first book, signaled the beginning of her lasting interest in two closely interrelated topics: first, the encounter between Byzantines and foreigners, both at the individual and collective level, whether within or outside the Empire, and secondly, the economic history of Byzantium. These major topics remained at the focus of her research over the years. She repeatedly returned to them, each time exploring different aspects of their complexities, as illustrated by the fourteen papers assembled in this volume.

The first group of papers examines Byzantine definitions, perceptions, attitudes, institutional issues, and mechanisms of integration regarding foreigners and strangers residing in the Empire. The perception of 'self' and 'other' among intellectuals and the bureaucracy of Constantinople underwent an important development in the period preceding the twelfth century. By then the relative weight of religion and state service as defining group identification and differentiation from foreigners had been largely replaced by a cultural and especially a linguistic criterion. With respect to the state, political considerations, namely hostility and friendship toward Byzantium, defined respectively foreign-ness and Byzantine identity, as illustrated by the Venetians. In dealing with foreigners Byzantium strove to bring them into a status of dependence to the emperor by oaths and quasi-legal devices. Acculturation and assimilation, primarily by mixed marriages, were the path to the full integration of individual foreigners within the Byzantine system and to the loss of their foreign-ness (article I).

The foreigners' self-perception of their own identity, rights and place within the Byzantine system and the Byzantine perception in that respect differed according to the circumstances. Byzantine admission of the specific self-identity of foreigners residing and operating within the empire, namely Georgians and Armenians, and imperial service furthered their assimilation. This is illustrated by Gregorios Pakourianos, imperial subject and orthodox Christian, though considering himself Georgian. On the other hand, the insertion of crusaders within the Byzantine system gave rise to disagreement and was unsuccessful. The emperors considered the legal link between themselves and crusaders as entailing the latter's subordination, whereas the crusaders viewed it as creating bilateral feudal obligations that granted them certain rights, amplified by their status as fighters in the service of the Christian faith. The gap between these two interpretations was an important factor of dissension and occasional conflict between the two sides in the twelfth century (article II).

The Empire used its judicial system and taxation to integrate or assimilate various ethnic groups and foreign individuals. While maintaining the principle that all residents were subject to the same state law, the Byzantine judicial system displayed flexibility at the practical level regarding the application of foreign custom and individual arrangements in private legal transactions, as illustrated with respect to Georgians and Jews. The special tax delivered by the Milingoi and Ezeritai in the Peloponnese were in fact the payment of a tribute and a recognition of imperial sovereignty which, while integrating these peoples within the Byzantine political system, reinforced in their midst ethnic solidarity running counter integration. Foreign merchants permanently residing in the Empire created a different challenge. The emperors imposed Byzantine law on these foreigners and maintained it in cases opposing them to imperial subjects. The breach of this principle in 1198 resulted in the Palaiologan period in the loss of Byzantine jurisdiction and taxation within the extraterritorial enclaves of Venice and Genoa in Constantinople (article III).

The Western crusades compelled the Empire to confront new political and ideological issues, examined in the second section of this volume. The Normans of South Italy and Sicily were paramount in the development of plans for a crusade against Byzantium and in the formation of the Byzantine response. The Norman attacks on the Empire led by Robert Guiscard in 1081 and especially the one by Bohemond of Taranto in 1101 generated Byzantine fears of an assault on Constantinople. Proper plans to that effect were elaborated following the failures of the crusades against the Muslims in 1101 and 1147–49. However, three factors delayed the attack, namely the resolve of the crusaders to carry out the crusade, the opposition to war against Byzantium, considered a perversion of crusading, and effective Byzantine activity to thwart the enterprise. The successful propaganda campaign waged by Emperor Alexios I Komnenos and the astute diplomacy of Emperor Manuel I, which exploited the rifts between the Normans, the Papacy and the German emperors, were decisive in that respect. However, by 1203 Manuel's policy had collapsed under his successors and the Western opposition to an attack on Constantinople had considerably diminished, paving the way for the city's conquest in 1204 (article IV).

The Byzantine encounter with the crusading movement also raised the issue of war and its justification. The Byzantine approach is examined in the light of Anna Komnene's *Alexiad* which, though lacking a systematic statement, nevertheless provides a fairly coherent idea about 'just war', as fought by her father Alexios I. War is justified as a measure of self-defense, aimed at recovery of lost territory, the result of breached agreements, and as a pursuit of peace, based on the idea that the Empire sought peace but was forced into war. Most of Anna Komnene's ideas were supported by Aristotelian and Roman concepts already found in earlier Byzantine writings (article V). The Byzantines considered 'just war' a secular concept, the state being competent to declare war. Foreign to them was the western 'holy war' ideology of the crusades elaborated in the twelfth and thirteenth centuries, which implied a fight for the Christian faith by God's army, ordered by the Church and entailing the remission of sin and martyrdom as a reward for death in battle. At the socio-political level the opposition between the two different ideologies of war reflected the contrast between upward mobility largely through the civil service of a bureaucratic state headed by the emperor, versus a knightly military class partly achieving wealth, power and social status through war. The clash between these ideologies contributed to the breakdown of the Christian alliance and to the sack of Constantinople during the Fourth Crusade, which turned the rift between eastern and western Christendom into a permanent feature (article VI).

The ideology of 'holy war' also impacted upon the encounters between western colonizers and native populations from the eleventh century onward, and was reflected by the social structure of conquered territories. Expansion based on Christian ideology was an important factor in creating a predisposition toward a profound formalized and institutionalized intolerance toward the subjugated non-Christian population involving three options, namely assimilation, annihilation or separation. In Slavic lands heavy German immigration and uncompromising religious approach resulted in the extermination or expulsion of some Prussian tribes and the assimilation of others. In the Latin kingdom of Jerusalem the colonists erected a closed, exclusionist and defensive system to preserve their identity, leaving the fabric of the native society unchanged. No true assimilation occurred, and the two societies lived side by side, each with its own culture and language. In contrast, economic expansion fueled by trade and carried out by merchants and sailors is illustrated in Crete, where the Christian population, composed of Greeks and Latins, became an integrated society following the acculturation and assimilation of the foreign Western elite (article VII).

The impact of the crusades and the existence of the crusader states in the Levant also extended to economic issues, both within the Empire and in the latter's commercial relations with other regions. The first paper in the third section of this volume deals with the problems involved in the provisioning of the crusaders and their cash payments in various currencies during their journey across Byzantine territories. These problems were solved by a combination of state intervention and free market operations. A reorientation of Byzantine trade relations with the Seljuks and Egypt took place, and the Byzantine attitude toward the Italians evolved over time. In addition, the crusades and the crusader states were instrumental in the development and spread of institutions facilitating trade in the entire eastern Mediterranean. These included exchange and negotiation mechanisms and the expansion of the law of salvage, first elaborated in Byzantium (article VIII).

The Byzantine reaction to the early phase of Genoese expansion in the Black Sea is expressed in a letter sent by the Patriarch of Constantinople, Georgios Kyprios, to Theodoros Mouzalon, the Grand Logothete from the 1280s. It states that Byzantine merchants are compelled to sail with their goods on the ships of the Genoese and presumably also to sell them their merchandise. In addition, the Genoese have neutralized the imperial fleet patrolling the Black Sea, thus preventing it from ensuring the safety of navigation. Angeliki Laiou argued that the letter signals a new attitude of the emperors and the Byzantine elite toward the merchants, elaborated after 1261, which involved support for their activities and the defense of their interests. Twenty years after Georgios Kyprios Patriarch Athanasios I advocated control over the grain trade feeding Constantinople to protect consumers and gave practical advice to prevent the privileged Italians from acquiring a monopoly in this trade. The new attitude toward the Empire's merchants is illustrated by a short-lived attempt to protect their interests by the lowering of the *kommerkion* or trade tax in Constantinople in the late 1340s (article XI).

The influence of the Italians on the Byzantine economy and, more generally, on the destiny of late Byzantium raises the question how much the Byzantines knew about Italy and how much they cared about that region, its people and its politics. The investigation of the three major narrative historians of the fourteenth century reveals an evolution in this respect. George Pachymeres uses 'Italian' as a generic name for Westerners and Catholics and has some knowledge of politics in Italy and of Genoese commercial policy. Some fifty years later John Kantakuzenos and Nikephoros Gregoras revert to the generic name 'Latin'. In the meantime the Empire had lost Asia Minor and there was a growing Byzantine interest in Italy and the Italians, especially in Genoa on which the fate of Constantinople rather than the Empire depended. This shift reflects the weakness of Byzantium and its inclusion in the broader Mediterranean world in which the Italian maritime powers were the main players, the decline of the Byzantine navy being as a major factor in Genoese supremacy in the Black Sea in that period (article X).

Trade between Byzantium and the West also generated cross-cultural exchanges. Venice played a far more important role than Genoa in this respect, as a result of the accelerated expansion of its trade, the establishment of its colonies, and Venetian settlement in the eastern Mediterranean after the Fourth Crusade. The impact of trade on artistic exchange is reflected by the minor arts and by luxury items. A transfer of marble columns and plaques taken from a temple or a church from the Peloponnese to Venice occurred in 1292. The pivotal function of Crete in trade stimulated the island's economy and artistic symbiosis, illustrated by Venetian and Greek painters. Angeliki Laiou ascribes Corinth's decline after the twelfth century to a large extent to the weakening of its glass production and the flourishing of the Venetian industry, which was already exporting its products to Romania by 1276. The Venetian export of crystal objects and miniatures under crystal was yet another aspect of the substitution of Byzantium by Venice as major producer of precious objects (article IX).

Angeliki Laiou returned to several aspects of the Empire's economic policies and enlarged the scope of her investigation in a study devoted to the interplay between monopoly, protected trade, privileged free trade, and the liberalization of trade conditions from the eighth through the late fourteenth century. The Byzantine economy was never fully controlled or directed, yet the state acted until some time in the eleventh century as a restraining agent. This is primarily illustrated by silk economics. The prohibition to export certain foodstuffs was a protectionist policy safeguarding until the twelfth century the interests of the consumers in times of shortage. By then Italian merchants both exported and traded within the Empire. In the thirteenth and fourteenth centuries a progressive lowering of duties and the development of a common law of the seas promoted the establishment of an integrated Mediterranean market. The growing role of Byzantium and the Black Sea as sources of grain for the West prompted the Empire to establish some control over its trade, yet the Byzantine quasi-monopoly was replaced by free trade and competition, economic factors that eroded 'national' sovereignty (article XII).

The following study deals with a topic that has not enjoyed the attention it deserves, namely regional trade, based upon exchanges within a limited geographic range and involving commodities produced within that area. Regional trade and the networks fueling it in the Balkans in the Middle and Late Byzantine periods responded to demand that could not be adequately met by local exchange, either because it was too large or because it involved specific industrial products. Large concentrated demand for alimentary products was typically associated with the existence of large cities. Angeliki Laiou dwells upon the distribution of various commodities, including ceramics which offer important insights into regional trade networks. She especially explores the evolution of those related to Constantinople, Thessalonike, Thebes, Corinth, Athens, and Sparta. To emphasize the importance of regional trade she states in her conclusion that it "occupies a nodal place in a society's economic development. It is the point where both demand and production become differentiated and specialization sets in; where the productive forces of a large segment of the population become active; where demography, urbanization, and monetization meet and reinforce each other; it is the point at which products become commodities" (article XIII).

In the last study included in this volume Angeliki Laiou argued, with the support of chaos theory, that there was a dialectic relation between the political and territorial fragmentation of the Byzantine empire and economic unification in the eastern Mediterranean in the aftermath of the Fourth Crusade. The fragmentation initiated in the late twelfth century and accelerated by the Fourth Crusade reached a peak by the end of the fourteenth century. Multipolarity increased the areas of instability and the likelihood of war, to the extent that the small-scale units became unsustainable economically. Networks linking small units in temporary and shifting alliances were cemented by marriage alliances between Byzantium, Serbia, Bulgaria, Trebizond and the Albanians, yet did not halt the process of political and territorial atomization. The absence of large internally self-sufficient, protectionist political units furthered economic integration within an international market organized by and for the profit of Venice and Genoa (article XIV).

The fourteen papers collected in this volume, divided in three groups, duly reflect the intimacy of Angeliki Laiou with an extensive body of primary sources, both Byzantine and non-Byzantine, her analytical power, her novel approaches, partly based on theoretical models elaborated in the social sciences, and the broad range of issues and developments she investigated in original ways.

DAVID JACOBY

Jerusalem
September 2011

I

The Foreigner and the Stranger in 12th century Byzantium: Means of Propitiation and Acculturation

The categories of "foreigner" and "stranger," are by no means co-terminous. The concept of foreigner is predicated upon a collective self-awareness which depends on ethnic or political identification, signifying those who do not participate in the political group of the subject, the national group in modern societies. The term foreigner often has a juridical meaning. The concept of stranger is both broader and narrower: broader because it would normally encompass that of foreigner without being limited to it; and narrower, because it is dependent on a self-awareness whose boundaries can be much narrower than those of ethnicity : boundaries of clan, of class, of family, of small social groupings. The Byzantines too had different terms to describe the two concepts. The word ξένος meant someone "other" than self, self being a unit of social identification[1]. The word ἀλλότριος has the same significance as ξένος, i.e. someone outside the small grouping, often meaning outside the family[2]. The terms that denote foreigners, i.e. the other by reference to a political unit, are many: τὰ ἔθνη, ἀλλόφυλος, τὸ ἀλλόγλωττον, ἑτερόφυλον ἔθνος, are among them[3]. We will return to these terms.

---

[1] See, for example, Anna Comnena, *Alexias*, ed. REIFFERSCHEID, Leipzig, 1884; I,114; Anna Dalassena was very accommodating to the poor; her house was open τοῖς ἐξ αἵματος πενομένοις, but also to the ξένοι, who in this case are simply people who were not her relatives. In the poem of Digenes Akrites, the wife of Digenes' father asks her brothers to spare the "stranger," in a passage where the meanings stranger" and "foreigner" may be subsumed: ἡσχύνετο γὰρ φωραθείς, ὡς ξένος ἐφοβεῖτο (G II, 481 ff.); "μὴ, πρὸς θεοῦ, ἀδέλφιά μου, μὴ ἀδικηθεῖ ὁ ξένος, ὃς δι' ἐμὲ ἡρνήσατο συγγενεῖς καὶ τὴν πίστιν ..." E. TRAPP, *Digenes Akrites: Synoptische Ausgabe der ältesten Versionen*, Vienna, 1971; (G II, 533-534).

[2] Thus used by Choniates, who has John II say, on the occasion of the rebellion of his sister Anna and her husband, ἡ τάξις ἐπ' ἐμοί πως ἀντέστραπται· τὸ μὲν γάρ συγγενὲς πολέμιον εὕρηται, τὸ δ' ἀλλότριον φίλιον; cf. Nicetas Choniates, *Historia*, ed. VAN DIETEN, Berlin, 1975; 11.

[3] ἀλλόφυλος: Choniates, 117; ἀλλόγλωττον, Choniates 125, to be contrasted to "τὸ ὁμόφυλον ὡς ἀλλόγλωττον". Ἑτερόφυλον ἔθνος: Choniates, 300. The term "τὰ ἔθνη" is used frequently: see, for example, Choniates, 199, 532. On this term, see H. AHRWEILER, "Citoyens et étrangers dans l'Empire romain d'Orient", in *La nozione di "Romano" tra cittadinanza e universalità*, (Rome 1982), pp. 343-345. For a definition of "foreigner," see J. GILISSEN, "Le statut des étrangers à la lumière de l'histoire comparative", *Recueils de la Société Jean Bodin* 9 (1958), 10 ff. I have profited considerably from Jeannette Schmid's presentation at the Symposium (*infra* p. 147-167), and from the bibliographical references she provided, particularly H. TAJFEL, ed., *Differentiation Between Social Groups*, London, New York, San Francisco, 1978, and H. TAJFEL, *Human Groups and Social Categories*, Cambridge, London, New York, New Rochelle, Melbourne, Sydney, 1981.

I will concentrate here on the Byzantines' view of the "foreigner" in the twelfth century, with only a passing glance at their view of the "stranger." Furthermore, my discussion will center on a particular point of view. That is the view from the center, the capital, Constantinople. It will be the view of the intellectuals who were also members of the civil bureaucracy, occasionally members of the high clergy, the first reporting or representing, to some extent, but only to some extent, the views of the government, including the Emperors. The inquiry is therefore clearly biased, although the sense of the bias is not necessarily evident. It can, perhaps, be assumed that this group of intellectuals/bureaucrats, which possessed high (but not the highest) social status and created ideology had a well developed conscience of their own group identity, and thus of the difference between themselves and the other[4]. The other strata of the population may have had different concepts of both the foreigner and the stranger, but these will be mentioned only briefly here. Finally, the fact that my inquiry will be limited to the twelfth century needs a little elaboration. The twelfth century was a time of important developments as far as our topic is concerned. The Byzantines lived in a world where contact with foreigners, in the most simplistic definition of the term, not only was constant, but was taking place under new conditions. Western Europe was then in an expansionary phase, undergoing its own process of self-definition; its contacts with Byzantium were aggressive in the political and economic sphere[5]. At the same time, hostile contact with the Turks, the Petchenegs and others was endemic, as also was friendly contact with some foreigners both within the Byzantine Empire and outside it. A little after the turn of the century, the process culminated with the conquest of Constantinople by western European troops, a traumatic event which once again would force a clearer self-definition. Furthermore, the 12th century is marked by the existence of highly educated, perceptive intellectuals, whose writings allow us to try to examine their view of the world and of themselves. What I will discuss is both perceived exclusion and the means of inclusion.

In the twelfth century, traditional Byzantine views of the world, of the place of the Byzantines in it, and therefore of the place of the foreigner, still survive. The Byzantine Empire is, as it always was, still the center of the Universe,

---

[4] For the cognitive element in self-identification, see HENRI TAJFEL, *Differentiation between Social Groups: Studies in the Social Psychology of Intergroup Relations*, New York, 1978, 28 ff.).

[5] Among various works on the subject, I note H. HUNGER, *Graeculus Perfidus, ITAΛOΣ ITAMOΣ*, Unione Internazionale degli Istituti di Archeologia, Storia e Storia dell'Arte, Rome, 1987, with earlier bibliography. See also A. P. KAZHDAN, ANNE WHARTON EPSTEIN, *Change in Byzantine Culture in the Eleventh and Twelfth Centuries*, Berkeley, Los Angeles, London, 1985, 167-196. G. DAGRON's "'Ceux d'en face': les peuples étrangers dans les traités militaires byzantins," *Travaux et Mémoires*, 10 (1987), 207-232, although it stops before the twelfth century, is very useful for its perceptive analysis of a similar topic.

which is oriented by reference to Constantinople[6]. It is still buffeted by hostile foreigners from all sides. "Ἔως με καὶ δυσμὴ μαχόμενον ἔβλεψεν, τὰ πρὸς ἄμφω τὰς ἠπείρους ἔθνη μετῆλθον," says the Emperor John II Comnenus on his deathbed, and in Anna Comnena's narrative the transitional sentence when she shifts from one front of war to another is often a sentence which suggests that the foreigners on either side of the Empire and on the northern frontier do not let the state (and her imperial father) rest[7]. In the perception of the Byzantines, Constantinople remains the center of the world, against which the world measures itself. In the late twelfth century, in a reversion of the model, the city becomes, in the by then jaundiced view of Choniates, a model of evil to the rest of the world, promoting civil war by example: "Fratricide came out of the Queen of Cities, as though from a model, a *typos*, a common law, and it invaded the ends of the earth, so that not only the Persians and the Tauroscythians (Russians), the Dalmatians and the Pannonians, but also the other dynasts of nations (ἔθνη) filled their countries with rebellions and murder, raising their swords against their own people"[8]. What are the factors defining a foreigner, and how do they develop? On the other side of the same coin, what is the definition of self for the Byzantines of this period?

An old, general terminology is still in place: Byzantium is surrounded by people who are called "ἔθνη", or "βάρβαροι", (that is, peoples who are acknowledged as having their own distinguishing traits). Such peoples are also called ἀλλόφυλοι or ἑτερόφυλοι, of "other races", self being the norm[9]. They are identified by specific ethnic names, whether ancient and traditional (Persians, Mysoi, Huns, Latins), or modern: Turks, Bulgarians, Hungarians (Οὔγγροι), Italians, Sicilians, Normans[10]. They are ascribed various ethnic characteristics, again traditional and time-honored: all westerners, for example, are said to be quick to anger, rash, arrogant, much too warlike[11]. These descriptions mostly come from the ethnographic stock of antiquity, which gives them a certain respectability. Contemporary ethnographic observation is kept to a minimum, for the Byzantines

---

[6] DAGRON, *op.cit.*, 221–224 for the period of Leo VI.
[7] Choniates, 42–43 . In the *Alexias*, see, for example, I, 117 ff.
[8] Choniates, 532: ἐκ γὰρ τῆς τῶν πόλεων βασιλίδος ὥσπερ τινὸς ὑπογραμμοῦ καὶ τύπου καὶ κοινοῦ θεμιστεύματος τῆς ἀδελφοκτονίας ἐξιούσης καὶ διαδραμούσης τῆς γῆς τὰ πέρατα, οὐ Πέρσαι μόνον καὶ Ταυροσκύθαι καὶ οἶδε οἱ Δαλμάται καὶ μετέπειτα Πάννονες, ἀλλὰ καὶ λοιποὶ ἕτεροι παρ' ἔθνεσι δυναστεύοντες στάσεων καὶ φόνων τὰς ἑαυτῶν πατρίδας ἐνέπλησαν, καθ' ὁμογενῶν τὰ ξίφη σπασάμενοι. For English translation, see HARRY J. MAGOULIAS, *O City of Byzantium, Annals of Niketas Choniates*, Detroit, 1984, p. 292.
[9] Kinnamos IV.22, III.6; Choniates, 116–117, 86, 90, 133.
[10] Choniates, 52–53 (Turks), 368 ff, 394, 397, 398, 34, 436–37 (Vlachs, Mysoi, Serbs); for the Latins, see Choniates, 357 ff. and HUNGER, *op.cit.* For ethnic descriptions, see also PH. KOUKOULES, Θεσσαλονίκης Εὐσταθίου τὰ Λαογραφικά, II, Athens, 1950, 375ff; on the Latins, 375–378; on the Paiones, 383–385.
[11] See HUNGER, *op.cit.*, pp. 39 ff. for earlier references. Cf. Choniates 166, and 102, 253 on the Armenians.

labored under the burden of an old tradition, going as far back as Herodotus. The historiographic commonplaces by which old traits are ascribed to old and new peoples function in a way similar to the use of classical designations for comtemporary peoples, that is, calling the Turks Persians or the Petchenegs Scythians. This is a way of taming the barbarians, by inscribing them in the category of known peoples, for whom there are also known and venerable remedies[12]. Only rarely and briefly do ethnographic observations appear, specifically in the case of the Petchenegs[13]. The nomadic element is stressed, perhaps because nomadic peoples traditionally function as the quintessential foreigner / barbarian. Being on the other side of civilisation, they preserve a fascination, and are given some specific attention. Still, there is nothing like the ethnographic recording of contemporary Western Europe, for example, the description of the Welsh by Gerald of Wales[14].

So the 12th-century Byzantines could and did use traditional designations for foreigners. These were, as we have seen, stereotypical descriptions and as such incorporated past experiences and past traditions[15]. Nevertheless, the Byzantines were not limited to traditional ways of conceptualising what constituted a foreigner – and what constituted a Roman. Indeed, their view had changed since the tenth century in one very important way. No longer was religion seen to create a community the members of which were held together by common bonds, which transcended whatever other elements differentiated them. Gilbert Dagron has called Christianisation a "savonette à ethnies," a factor which blunted ethnic differentiation, and created one Christian community, fundamentally different from that of the world of the pagans or non-Christians, and dividing the world into Christian and non-Christian. In the first half of the twelfth century, reflecting perhaps the late eleventh-century situation, this concept still had a life, at least in rhetorical statements[16]. Anna Comnena could report her father as saying that Christians should not fight each other, and certainly not during major holy days[17]. But in the passages of Kinnamos and Choniates, religion plays a very minor role in defining the foreigner. Peoples long Christianised, like the Bulgarians, the Serbs, the Hungarians, Western Christians are

---

[12] For the Byzantine use of classical designations, see, among others, DAGRON, op.cit., pp. 213, 217 ff.
[13] Choniates, 93–94.
[14] On the nomads, see also KOUKOULES, op.cit., II, 381, and ROBERT BARTLETT, Gerald of Wales, 1146–1223, Oxford, Clarendon Press, 161.
[15] On stereotypes, see A. VAN KNIPPERBERG in TAJFEL, Differentiation, 171 ff., TAJFEL, in ibid., 5–6, and H. TAJFEL, Human Groups and Social Categories, Cambridge, 1981, 104 ff.
[16] DAGRON, op.cit., 220.
[17] Alexias, X.9 (vol. II, 87–88). Similarly, Anna Dalassena's and Isaac Comnenus' confiscation of the holy vessels of the Church was justified by the argument that these would be used to free Christians who had been captured by the Turks, so that the Christians would not be 'defiled': Alexias, I, 157.

called barbarians just as easily and in the same way as are the Turks or the Petchenegs[18]. As an example of this phenomenon, one may take the letter of Theophylact of Ochrid to Gregorios Taronites, celebrating the latter's victory when
he "defeated the arrogance of two nations (ἔθνη)"[19]. Theophylact praises him
for having brought down, with a single victory, the tower of "Persian" folly and
the mountain of "Frankish" folly (ἀπόνοια, in both cases). The Turks and the
Franks are always mentioned together and in a parallel way in this text, and the
differentiation between them, although it exists, is subsumed in the similarities: "Because of you, the most godless Turk bends his head and looks only at
what is at his feet, he who yesterday cast his insolent eyes (τὰς σοβάδας κόρας
τῶν ὀφθαλμῶν), everywhere, and thought of destroying the entire earth and the
sea. Now, his only hope of salvation lies in treaties ... And the Frank [Bohe-
mond] who once had an iron neck, now is shown to be softer than wax, and does
obeissance to you, and through you to our mighty Emperor ... For the Turk, forced by your hand, has been persuaded despite himself to make treaties and,
among other things, to turn the Frank over to our victorious Emperor ... All
those who bear the name of Christ and who counsel and wish the best for the
Empire of the Romans, owe a debt to you."[20] Only occasionally does religion differentiate specifically between Christians and non-Christians: thus, the Turks
are called ἀλλόφυλοι καὶ ἀσεβεῖς[21]. And on occasion the church reminded
people, including the Emperor himself, that the Turks should not enter churches, whether Santa Sophia or others[22]. On occasion, too, Nicetas Choniates
could reproduce a view of the Byzantines and the Turks which had the Bible as
a point of reference, and as a model of prose: the Turks were the sons of the servant Hagar, and he asked the Lord how long He would suffer the legitimate
heirs, the sons of a free woman, His "holy people" (τὸ σὸν ἅγιον ἔθνος) to be
destroyed by the Hagarenes[23]. But this signifies very little. For the same historian records, without adverse comment, the triumphs celebrated in Constantinople by Byzantine Emperors after their victories against Christian nations,
and the part played by the Virgin or the saints in such victories; thus invalidat-

---

[18] Kinnamos IV.22, III.6, Choniates 86, 90, 133, 436–437, 296, 368, 465 ff. (Asen) 474 (northern
barbarians, i.e. Scythians and Vlachs); Westerners: Choniates 479.
[19] P. GAUTIER, Théophylacte d'Achrida, Lettres. Thessalonika 1980, letter 81. The letter
refers to the liberation of either Bohemond, or his cousin, Richard of Salerno, from the emir of
Sivas: p. 427 (date of the letter: summer of 1103).
[20] Ibid., pp. 429–431. Cf. Alexias I, 13–14, where both Toutakh and Roussel de Bailleul are called barbarians; and ibid., I, 54: "οἱ βάρβαροι δοῦλοι τοῦ αὐτοκράτορος."
[21] Choniates, 118. Note also that the Emperor did not allow the defeated Vlachs to be handed
over to the Turkish allies, so that they would not renege on their Christian faith: Choniates, 504.
[22] Choniates, 422; also Choniates 123, 175 and Kinnamos V.3.
[23] Choniates, 116–117. These words of Choniates are not borrowed from a specific Biblical
reference, at least not verbatim. On the other hand, Biblical references abound in the lament for
the fall of Constantinople to the crusaders in 1204: Choniates 576 ff.

ing any special weight we might be tempted to give to Manuel's prayer in Santa Sophia before he left for his ill-fated encounter with the Turks at the battle of Myriokephalon[24]. Prayers, triumphs, the intercession of the saints played a part in all Byzantine wars of the period, whether these were undertaken against pagans or against peoples Christianised long ago[25]. The Christian world-view, differentiating between pagans and Christians, a world-view which had adherents in the tenth century, was no longer operative. Hostile foreigners were, for all intents and purposes, undifferentiated, or differentiated only as to the manner in which one could best deal with them[26].

Religion in the Middle Ages served as a powerful means of self-identification, and as an important distinguishing trait between one large group and the others, the foreigners. If it did not play this role in twelfth-century Byzantium, what did the Byzantines substitute?

We have, here, an early effort toward a secular definition of ethnicity and of the foreigner. As in Western medieval Europe, there is a duality between one's community and the foreigner, but since the duality no longer functions in religious terms, a secular basis for distinction is sought. The basic distinction the Byzantines made was between the "Romans", i.e. themselves, and the others, the non-Romans. The term "Roman", however, as used in the twelfth century, lacks a specific and consistent content. It certainly lacks any ethnic content. It can function as a means of inclusion as well as of exclusion. Thus, the army which was collected by the Byzantines to fight against the Hungarians (1167) is called a "Roman" army; but Kinnamos who reports its composition says that it was made up of Cumans, Turks, Germans, Serbs, Italian mercenaries and "Romans", the term here designating a subset of the Roman army. This "Roman" army fought against the Hungarians, here qualified as "barbarians", whom they eventually slaughtered[27]. It need hardly be pointed out that the Roman forces included pagans, while the barbarian Hungarians were Christians. Similarly, Manuel I, taking the road to his defeat in Myriokephalon, collected as large an army as he could; to the existing forces, he added foreigners (ξενικὸν οὐκ ὀλίγον), recruited especially among the "Latins" and the "Paristrian Scyths" (Petchenegs). This medley of peoples, who in other circum-

---

[24] Choniates, 178.
[25] Choniates, 157, on thanksgiving to the Virgin for victories against the Hungarians; cf. 18–19 and 92–93 (against the Serbs and the Hungarians). Cf. Kinnamos IV. 21.
[26] E.g., Choniates, 199 on Turks and westerners. On ἔθνη, meaning those peoples not subject to the Emperor, and therefore not a part of the οἰκουμένη, see Hunger, op.cit., 34, with references to Keroularios. See also J. GAUDEMET, "L'étranger au Bas Empire", in Recueils de la Société Jean Bodin, 9 (1956), 217 ff., 129 ff., on religion as a criterion for "Romanness" in the 4th-5th centuries.
[27] Kinnamos VI.7: τοσοῦτος μέντοι βαρβάρων φόνος ἐγένετο ...; ὃ πάμμεγα τοῖς βαρβάροις τούτοις ἐπὶ ἁμάξης ἐφέρετο ...

stances would be called barbarian, is called the army of the Romans[28]. It might
be added that the Byzantines were perfectly capable of perceiving distinctions
between peoples in practice, if not in ideology: a seasoned soldier like John II
organized his army by race, so that they would support each other as "friends,"
and fight better[29].

The general phenomenon is well known, and one can give a general explanation. The Byzantines, in good statist fashion, used the term "Roman" with a
political meaning: a "Roman" was a Christian subject of the Byzantine emperor, or, at least, someone who temporarily or regularly acted for his interest
and on his side. This answer is, indeed, correct, and underlies the argument that
Byzantium, in the twelfth century, shows an impressive capacity for assimilating
foreigners, and a growing liberalism in its attitude toward foreigners[30]. This is
particularly true in the specific context of the assimilation of foreign generals or
aristocrats. The explanation, however, which assumes that the Byzantines had
a political or statist definition of the foreigner, is neither sufficient, nor entirely
accurate. For there were, in the twelfth century, peoples who were Byzantine subjects, but who were considered barbarians, internal barbarians, for example the
Bulgarians: Byzantine subjects, not strangers at all, but still foreigners in a
sense. Pertinent in this respect is the well-known text of Theophylact, bishop of
Ochrid, which discusses his flock, Christians and certainly subjects of the
Byzantine Emperor, but clearly differentiated from the "Romans", and alien to
himself: "Here I am," he says, "serving not a rich, clean, beautiful queen, but the
barbarian dirty *slaves* who stink of the pelt of sheep, and are as poor in substance as they are rich in nastiness... Rescue me from this shameful servitude,
you, who have the power to do so"[31]. From his position of "exile," he wrote to the
bishop of Vidin, telling him that the Cumans, who were attacking his area from
the outside (and were pagans) were better than the Bulgarians who inhabited
his own diocese[32]. The distinction between Roman and foreigner is not simply a
statist distinction: it is also a *cultural* distinction, and becomes increasingly so
in the course of the twelfth century, as the intellectuals, at least, strive to define
themselves. Under the pressure of political events, the older concepts, the older

---

[28] Choniates, 178 ff., and *Alexias* I, 209 ff., 250; II, 190. Kinnamos II, 7 (p. 48) mentions as a
Roman soldier Poupakes, "a Turk by birth", who fights against the "barbarians" (i.e., the Turks).
For a slight twist on such concepts, see *Alexias* I, 84–85 where the Germans are called a 'barbarian people who have always served the Roman Emperor'.
[29] Choniates 29–30.
[30] KAZHDAN-EPSTEIN, *op.cit.*, 180, 184. Cf. AHRWEILER, *op.cit.*, 343–345, 348–349; D. A. ZAKY-
THINOS, "Byzance, état national ou multinational," *ΔXAE*, ser. 4, vol. 10 (1980–81), 29–52.
[31] GAUTIER, *Lettres*, letter 5 (ca. 1088–89), p. 145: πλὴν ὅσον οὐ βασιλίδι δουλεύω πλου-
σίᾳ, καθαρίῳ τε καὶ καλῇ καὶ συνόλως Ἀφροδίτῃ χρυσῇ, ἀλλὰ δούλοις βαρβάροις ἀκαθάρ-
τοις κινάβρας κωδίων ἀπόζουσιν καὶ πενεστέροις τὸν βίον, ἢ ὅσον τὴν κακοήθειαν πλούσιοι
... Λύσατέ με τῆς αἰσχρᾶς ταύτης δουλείας οἱ τοῦτο δυνάμενοι ...
[32] *Ibid.*, letter 57 (1093–1094 or 1095), pp. 323–325.

statist definitions, become dysfunctional, and what remains at the end is a cultural distinction between Romans (increasingly identified as Hellenes) and barbarians. That distinction had always been there, but it emerges with clarity by the end of the twelfth century. Linguistic identification now becomes paramount, language functioning as an indicator of culture, of participation in Greek culture. Self-identification is based on language, a shared classical past, an appreciation of the classics and the virtues of the Greeks.

We can trace the evolution of the concept through a number of texts. Anna Comnena, speaking of John Italos, who was, like his father, Italian by birth but a Byzantine subject, says that he went to Constantinople, and studied with Michael Psellos, whose erudition she admired greatly. But Italos, "because of his barbarous and untutored ways, was unable to comprehend the profound truths of philosophy, nor was he at all capable of accepting his teachers, even in the act of learning, but, full of arrogance and barbaric folly, thought he was better than anyone else, even before he had been taught..."[33]. This is contrasted to Michael Psellos who, through his own native intelligence and with the help of God and his mother, was able to acquire all the wisdom of the Hellenes and the Chaldaeans. By the mid-twelfth century, when the term "Hellene" becomes more common, the situation is clearer. George Tornikes, Metropolitan of Ephesos and of Greek origin, (i.e. from Greece proper) distinguishes between barbarians and Hellenes, those who are "slaves by nature" (τοῖς φύσει δούλοις)) and those who are free (ἐλεύθεροι) (it is implied that they are free also "by nature"); those who speak a barbarous tongue, have barbarous mores and serve the God of war, and those whose tongue and behaviour is Greek, and who are disciples of the Muses and of Hermes: Μή μοι τοῖς βαρβάροις τὸν Ἕλληνα μηδὲ τοῖς φύσει δούλοις τὸν ἐλεύθερον συναπόγραφε ὁ φιλέλλην καὶ φιλελεύθερος [34]. The concept of Roman / Hellene as free by nature and of the barbarian as a slave by nature, perhaps deriving from Aristotle's *Politics,* becomes common in this period.

The development culminates with Nicetas Choniates. This historian is as inconsistent as anyone in his use of the term "Roman", and quite subtle in his attitude toward foreigners; an intelligent man, he did not assume the pose of presenting all foreigners, collectively and individually, in a negative way. Furthermore, writing as he was in difficult times, he often presents the Byzantines,

[33] *Alexias*, I, 177–178. Nor did Italos ever learn Greek perfectly: *ibid.,* 180–181. Cf. *Alexias* II, 93, for her well known statement that she could not name the crusaders, because barbarian tongues are ἄναρθροι.
[34] J. DARROUZÈS, *Georges et Démétrios Tornikès; Lettres et discours*, Paris, 1970, letter 10. He urges John Kamateros, logothete and sevastos, not to prefer a barbarian to a Greek. Cf. p. 235. On the distinction between Greek and barbarian as founded in nature, see Aristotle, *Politics*, I.2. 13–15; I.2, 18–19; cf. Hunger, *op.cit.,* 34–35.

or at least, the inhabitants of Constantinople and their rulers, in a worse light than he does foreigners. Indeed, sometimes the foreigner serves, as he had for Tacitus, for an adverse commentary on contemporary mores: a mirror through which the Byzantines could view their decline. However, Choniates' conceptualisations extend beyond such matters. For he, too, has a view of the collective self, with different connotations from the statist definition of the term "Roman." Events close at home forced him to differentiate between his own people and the foreigners. The accession of foreigners to positions of power in the Byzantine Empire; the expulsion of the Venetians by Manuel I; the capture of Thessaloniki by the Normans, and, finally, the Fourth Crusade were all dramatic events. It is therefore not surprising that they forced self-definition. Choniates is much more conscious than Kinnamos of the ethnic background of highly-placed people, and of the differentiation between them and "true" Romans. He contests a basic principle underlying the concept of Romanity and the practice of the Byzantine state, i.e. the inclusion of foreigners into Byzantine service: thus, his well-known criticism of Manuel I, that he despised the "Romans" as thieves, and used foreigners in his administration, and that the Romans were forced to pay taxes to half-barbarous little men, is inscribed into his larger developing cultural self-definition. The foreigners of whom he speaks are ἀπὸ γενῶν ἑτερογλώττων (from races who speak other languages); they have no culture, nor can they speak any Greek: "they have no education, and they search for the traces of the Greek tongue as the peaks and the rocks seek out the reverberating echo of the shepherds' flute"[35]. Similarly, Andronikos I is blamed for appointing as his personal guard barbarian men, totally uncultured, and, for the most part, ignorant of the Greek tongue[36]. Culture is sometimes thought to posit a superiority not only in the arts of peace but in the arts of war, as when Andronikos Kontostefanos makes an oration to his troops before the battle with the Hungarians, and tells them, among other things, that they (here qualified as Romans) are superior to the barbarians in reason and culture, and thus in their knowledge of strategy[37].

Given the historical circumstances, it is not surprising that Choniates' most clear-cut definition of "foreigner" is undertaken in connection with Western Europe. This is understandable for other reasons as well. For it was the western Europeans who were most visible at Constantinople. It was they who were closest to the "Romans", they with whom the "Romans" had had close historical and ecclesiastical ties, they whom Constantine VII had considered alone

---

[35] Choniates, 204–205, 209. Cf. M. Psellos, *Chronographie*, II, 35. On language as an important defining characteristic, cf. Choniates, 322.
[36] Choniates, 322: Ἑλληνίδος φωνῆς.
[37] Choniates, 154–155.

worthy of marrying Byzantine princesses[38]. It was, therefore, with them that the problem of differentiation had always been the most difficult. Choniates' reaction is a refuge into cultural differences. The capture of Thessalonika by the Normans he ascribes to profound hatred against the Greeks: "ἀνὴρ μισορρώμαιος καὶ τοσαύτην ἀποθησαυρίσας ἐν ἑαυτῷ καθ' Ἕλληνος ἀνδρὸς τὴν ἀπέχθειαν..."[39]. The fall of Constantinople in 1204 urges the historian to press this Hellenic identification still further, as he does the differentation with the western barbarians. Constantinople, "the beautiful city of Constantine," had been the common pride (ἐντρύφημά τε καὶ περιλάλημα) of all the nations; it was captured and looted by wind-sown western races, mostly unknown and nameless[40]. These westerners were barbarians, ignorant of the Graces and the Muses[41]. The lament addressed to the statue of Helen of Troy, melted down by the crusaders, reflects the cultural identification: Helen was "the prize of Greeks and Trojans." Fully aware of the fact that the Franks considered themselves to be descendants of the Trojans, Choniates considers for a moment the possibility that they melted down the statue in revenge for the burning of Troy; but he cannot believe it, for he knows that these men are above all rapacious and money-grubbing. Besides, he says, "how can these unlettered and totally ignorant barbarians have read and known the epic verses written for you – 'it were no shame for the Trojans and the well-greaved Achaeans to have suffered so long over such a woman. For she resembles the immortal Goddesses'"[42]. In this passage, the identification is clear: the Byzantines, i.e., Choniates' Byzantines, who knew Homer, and cherished the ancient statues, are the descendants of the ancient Greeks; the foreigners are barbarians, and the westerners cannot even be the descendants of the Trojans, i.e. they have no respectable classical antecedents. The Byzantines stand alone, as they did in the past – but not as the Christian oikoumene; rather, as the cultural heirs of ancient Greece. This becomes clear, too, when Choniates speaks of the crusaders' progress into Greece – the area normally known as the κατωτικὰ μέρη. The text is replete with classical cultural references: there is Corinth, glorious of old; Pylos, the birth-place of Nestor; Lakonia; Alpheios, the "Greek river" (Ἕλλην ποταμὲ Ἀλφειέ), which is being beseeched not to allow victory to the barbarians[43]. The self-iden-

---

[38] Constantine Porphyrogenitus, *De Administrando Imperio*, ed., transl. Gy. MORAVCSIK, R.J.H. JENKINS, Washington, D. C., 1967, p. 70: διάταξις φοβερά ... ἐναπογέγραπται ... τοῦ μηδέποτε βασιλέα Ῥωμαίων συμπενθεριάσαι μετὰ ἔθνους παρηλλαγμένοις καὶ ξένοις ἔθεσι χρωμένου τῆς Ῥωμαϊκῆς καταστάσεως, μάλιστα δὲ ἀλλοπίστου καὶ ἀβαπτίστου, εἰ μὴ μετὰ μόνων τῶν Φράγγων ...
[39] Choniates, 301.
[40] Choniates, 585: ἠθάλωται πυρὶ καὶ ἡμαύρωται ... παρὰ γενῶν ἑσπερίων σποραδικῶν, ἀφαυρῶν τὰ πλεῖστα καὶ ἀνωνύμων ... Cf. Choniates, 576.
[41] Choniates, 598.
[42] Choniates, 652–653.
[43] Choniates, 610–611.

tification is now complete and obvious: the "Romans", for Choniates still speaks of Romans, are in fact the descendants of the Hellenes. What is paramount in this self-definition is the Greek language and classical culture. The foreigners are those who do not participate in this culture, Christian though they may be. This self-definition is the result of a crisis.

It may be argued that the crisis, in its multiple forms, created a situation in which the concept "Roman" no longer provided sufficient means of self-identification to the members of the group we are examining. This is perhaps connected with the entrance of non-Greek speakers, or people of non-Greek culture into the "Roman" ruling class; those who spoke Greek and partook of a high Hellenic culture, i.e., the members of the upper bureaucracy, civil and ecclesiastic, would thus necessarily focus on language and culture as an important element of differentiation and group identification[44]. The insufficiency and non-functionality of the term "Roman", a statist term, is certainly also connected with the growing inadequacy and eventual dissolution of the twelfth-century state. Furthermore, the development of terminology carries with it a somewhat increased exclusivity. We start with a broad, flexible, open-ended concept of "Romans" (in the statist sense) versus non-Romans. This, then, develops into a differentiation between Greeks and barbarians. The older concept was potentially highly inclusive. The new concept is more restrictive, but remains weak, and still allows the assimilation of some foreigners. It is true, as Hunger has argued, that once one qualifies the foreigners as "barbarians", they are then assumed to have certain characteristics by nature, that is, the nature of a barbarian[45]. But at the same time, acquiring Greek culture, or becoming part of the Byzantine social fabric, can act as a purifier, cleansing people of their barbarity. The boundaries of foreignness become stricter, but are still elusive.

In order to underline the fluidity of the Byzantine concept, one might usefully contrast it with a strain in western European attitudes toward foreigners, that strain which is exemplified by the historical accounts of the First Crusade, and the *Song of Roland* (early twelfth century). In these writings, the differentiation of self and other is stark. The *Song of Roland* is much the clearest text, as works of literature often are. In the poem there is an express parallelism between the behavior and society of the Christians and the Muslims – a parallelism which is structural and conceptual. The political process, for example, is exactly the same in both camps. There is a process of consultation, a feudal court, with

---

[44] See TAJFEL, *Differentiation*, 5, on stereotypes as providing rationalisations for keeping others at bay.

[45] For the ancient Greek distinction between barbarians and Hellenes, see HUNGER, *op.cit.*, 20–21, and J. JUETHNER, *Hellenen und Barbaren; aus der Geschichte des Nationalbewusstseins*, Leipzig, 1923, 70.

which the poem opens: first in Saragossa, i.e. the Muslim court, then in Charlemagne's court; Charlemagne has twelve peers, as does the kings of the Saracens; Charlemagne meets a brave enemy in the Egyptian sultan Baligant. The means of battle are essentially the same, the heroes having special horses, swift steeds with pedigrees and names, and individual swords, with a pedigree, a history and a name. The Christian Trinity is paralleled by the fictitious Muslim trinity. In short, here are two societies, very similar to each other, conceived in feudal terms. But there is one difference, which hovers above the similarities, and makes the two societies clearly antithetical. That is, of course, religion, which creates a stark and unbridgeable differentiation, encapsulated in a line of the poem, "Christians are right, Saracens are wrong." That means that the Saracens do not and cannot exist in a natural world, with its own moral and legal differentiations. They cannot be rightful lords or good knights; they cannot be pious. What they can be and are by definition is the negative aspect of a duality; they are the evil in a world separated by religion into good and evil. Even their names bear witness to this fact: thus there is Falseron, whose name carries a character evaluation, and whose description is that of an ugly man, with a huge head and a fearful aspect. Often, such characters are pitted against specific Christians, in fights with powerful symbolic overtones.

The parallelism of the two societies posits a duality: the other, the foreigner, who is also the enemy, is a negative image of self. The contact between the two is a cosmic conflict of good and evil. For example, Roland, the hero, a man surrounded by light, is pitted against Chernuble, "the ruler of that land men call the Hills of Darkness... In that land, they say,/ The sun shines not, nor rain nor gentle dew/ Fall from the heavens, and not a grain of corn/ May ripen; no stone is there that isn't solid black; some say it is the Devil's habitation"[46]. In a generalised way, the war between what might have been two feudal forces becomes a cosmic battle between good and evil, the forces of light and the forces of darkness, the true God and the false deities, as can be seen in the reaction of nature itself to the fighting: "And meanwhile, far away in France, a storm/ Of rushing wind and thunder swept the land,/ And rain and hail were mingled, and the earth/ Trembled, and over all was fearful darkness,/ Save where the sky was split by thunderbolts,/ From Sens to Saint Michael of the Sea./ From East to West there is no house in France/ Unshaken and men cry 'It is the end!/ The end of all the world!' They do not know the truth. Alas! It is the sorrowing/ Of

---

[46] The translation used here is partly from F. B. LUQUIENS, *The Song of Roland*, MacMillan paperback ed., 1964, p. 35, and partly from R. HARRISON, *The Song of Roland*, Mentor paperback ed., 1970, p. 82. For the French original, see T. ATKINSON JENKINS, *La Chanson de Roland*, Boston, New York, 1924.

land and sea and sky for Roland's death!"[47] To this duality there is only one solution: return to unicity, by the destruction of the enemy: either physical destruction, i.e. extermination, or moral destruction, i.e. conversion.

The Song of Roland is, as I have suggested, the clearest statement of this attitude; and it is also the most powerful, because of its literary value. But the views it expresses are in complete accord with those of the writers who wrote on the First Crusade. The Turks, for them, were "an accursed race, a race utterly alienated from God, a generation forsooth which has not directed its heart and has not entrusted its spirit to God ..."[48] Compare this with the description of Abysme in the *Song of Roland*: "spotted with many sins, believing not in God, the son of Mary, loving ... treason and murder of his fellow man"[49]. The ultimate statement is perhaps made in the *Gesta Francorum*, where the bravery of the Turks is posited and then negated: "What man ... would dare to write of the skill and prowess and courage of the Turks?... Yet, please God, their men will never be as good as ours ... If only they had stood firm in the faith of Christ ... and had been willing to accept One God in three persons ... you could not find stronger or braver or more skillful soldiers; and yet, by God's grace, they were beaten by our men"[50]. The translation of this attitude into action is to be found in the *Annales Augustani*: "Hierosolima a duce Gotefrido et sequacibus eius est capta; religio christiana per provintias dilatatur; barbari omnes aut extincti aut fugati sunt"[51]. As for the army of Charlemagne in the *Song of Roland*, it is composed of all those who were, in the early twelfth century, Catholic Christians, and its enemies were those who were, historically or in actuality, not orthodox Christians: Frenchmen – Normans, Burgundians, Bretons – Flemings and some Germans (Bavarians, Burgundians, Frisians); against an army composed of the Egyptian, African and Spanish contingents, Persians and Turks – all Muslim; but also Slavs (Christian or not, is not clear) and Petchenegs, still pagan; Avars

---

[47] Luquiens, p. 50. I have changed his "Xanten" into "Sens". See *Chanson de Roland*, note to line 1428.

[48] Robert the Monk. *Recueil des Historiens des Croisades: Historiens Occidentaux* III, Paris, 1866, p. 727. Translation from E. Peters, *The First Crusade*, Philadelphia, 1971, p. 2. On this topic, see W. Tavernier, *Zur Vorgeschichte des altfranzösischen Rolandsliedes*, Berlin, 1903.

[49] Luquiens, p. 52.

[50] *Gesta*, 21. To be compared with the *Song of Roland*: "Were he but a Christian, he'd be a rightful Lord". (fust chrestiens, asez oüst barnet, 1.899; cf. Solimannus ... vir nobilissimus, sed gentilis ... Albert of Aix, *Recueil des Historiens des Croisades: Historiens Occidentaux* IV, 314). Intelligent leaders could use such widespread attitudes to good effect. Thus, Bohemond captured some Petchenegs who served in Alexios I's army and took them to Italy where he displayed them, calling them "Παγάνους ἄνω καὶ κάτω" in order to show that Alexios was using infidels against the Christians and thus give force to his argument for a virtual crusade against Byzantium: *Alexias* II, 168.

[51] Ed. G. H. Pertz, *MGH SS* 3: 135. cf. Benjamin Z. Kedar, *Crusade and Mission: European Approaches toward the Muslims*, Princeton, 1984, p. 65.

and Huns, long defunct; Hungarians (already Christianised); Armenians, Bulgarians, and Byzantines.

The duality which we find in these texts is powerful, the self-identification is clear, the foreigner is the enemy, easy to identify and easy to describe, as a negative image of self, with religion as the main identifier of self. In Byzantium of the twelfth century, this was never the case, if it ever had been the case in the past. There is no equivalent to the *Song of Roland* in literature or historiography, nor is there an equivalent to the uncompromising western concept of the foreigner. In Choniates, the duality of Roman-barbarian, or Roman-Hellene is present, but it dissolves under pressure: the barbarians of various sorts have strange mores, and are desrcibed as beasts of various kinds; but the Emperor Andronicus I is also a beast, a θήρ[52]. This may be the result of Choniates' own alienation, or of societal malaise: the positive correlation of "Roman" and good attributes no longer holds[53]. A clear example of this alienation is provided by Choniates' description of civil strife in the Empire: καὶ κατ' ἀλλήλων ἐκπεπολέμωτο τὸ ὁμόφυλον βαρβαρωθὲν καὶ τῆς συγγενείας νόμους ἠγνοηκός[54]. At the same time, Frederick Barbarossa, enemy of the Emperor and of the Byzantines, is an admirably pious man, and duly admired by Choniates[55]. The power of religion is rarely invoked, and martyrs are rarely accommodated; an exceptional case is that of Theodore Gavras, whom Zonaras calls a martyr because he fell in battle against the Turks[56]. In the romance of Digenes Akrites, dualities become resolved, the hero himself is the embodiment of the conciliation of two cultures, and what remains is a disturbingly individualistic definition of self and a broad but not inflexible definition of the foreigner. The hero is "ἐθνικὸς μὲν ἀπὸ πατρός, ἐκ δὲ μητρὸς ῥωμαῖος"[57]. When he builds his palace, no "Roman, Saracen, Persian or inhabitant of Tarsus" dares come near; his identification with the Romans is slight indeed.

The Byzantine concept of foreigner in the twelfth century was subject for one thing to political considerations: this was to some extent connected to the concept of self as Roman, i.e. to the statist definition, which officially considered as Romans those newcomers (whether they be peoples or individuals) who served the Byzantine Empire or became subjected to it[58]. It also varies according to the sources and the nature of the source: official state documents sometimes contain a different concept of the foreigner than do narrative sources, which can

---

[52] Choniates, 254, 272, 283.
[53] On the emotional component of group membership, see TAJFEL, *Differentiation*, 28.
[54] Choniates, 263.
[55] Choniates, 416–417.
[56] Zonaras 3, 739.
[57] E. TRAPP, *Digenes Akrites*, G. IV. 1002.
[58] Cf. GAUDEMET, *op. cit.*, 218 ff. for similar attitudes in the late Roman Empire.

present a more hostile picture of the foreigner. This may be due to differences between conceptualisation and actual behavior[59]. It is also connected with cultural biases, or with a cultural definition of the foreigner, and therefore becomes clearer by the end of the twelfth century. In both kinds of sources one must distinguish between friendly and unfriendly foreigners.

The ambivalence and relative open-endedness of the Byzantine official concept of foreigner may be seen in connection with the Venetians who, because initially they were formally a part of the Byzantine Empire, had in any case an ambivalent position[60]. In the privileges granted to them, the Venetians are sometimes treated as foreigners and sometimes as Byzantines. The first privilege, granted by Basil II at the end of the tenth century, calls them *extraneos*: contrasting them to those who were *sub manu nostra*, even though the Venetians were still subjects of the Byzantine Emperor[61]. In the chrysobull of 1082, they are considered as *recti* (or *fideles*) *duli imperii mei*. They have the right to inhabit and receive revenues from landed property in Constantinople and Durrazzo – although the right to own it is not explicitly stated[62]. The reason why the Venetians are now considered Byzantines is political: it is the help the Venetians gave Alexius I against Robert Guiscard. This mark of Venetian devotion is repeated some generations later: John II says "*fidelium gesta Veneticorum nullus de hominibus ignoravit*"[63]. More than one hundred years after the fact, in 1187, Isaac II Angelus still remembers, as the clearest token of Venetian devotion to the Byzantine Empire, their help against Guiscard. His predecessors, he says, because of this, made them into *one body with Romania*, under *one head, the Emperor*[64]. This, however, is rhetorical, since the Venetians are later called *amici fideles*, who have for the Byzantine Empire *fides, servitus* and *amor*, suggesting that they are not, in fact, the same as Romans[65]. In 1189, the same Emperor, at a moment when he is courting the Venetians and negotiating the restoration of the property confiscated by Manuel I, produces another rhetorical statemtent: "*verumtamen, quia non ut alienigenas, immo ut aborigines*

---

[59] The point was made by Jeannette Schmid in discussion.

[60] On this topic, see R. S. Lopez, "Foreigners in Byzantium," in *Bulletin de l'Institut belge de Rome* 44 (1974), pp. 341–352, and P. Schreiner, "Untersuchungen zu den Niederlassungen westlicher Kaufleute im Byzantinischen Reich des 11. und 12. Jahrhunderts", *Byzantinische Forschungen* 7 (1979), pp. 175–191.

[61] J. and P. Zepos, *Jus Graecoromanum* I, Athens, 1931, 260; F. Thiriet, *Le Romaine vénitienne au moyen âge*, Paris, 1975, p. 34 and R. - J. Lilie, *Handel und Politik*, Amsterdam, 1984, 3, n. 6.

[62] S. Borsari, "Il Crisobullo di Alessio I", *Annali dell' Istituto Italiano per gli Studi Storici*, Naples, 1970, 115; G. Tafel and G. Thomas, *Urkunden zur Älteren Handels- und Staatsgeschichte der Republik Venedig*, Venice, 1856, I, pp. 43 ff. Cf. Lilie, 11, Thiriet, *op. cit.*,39.

[63] *JGR* I, 139; Cf. Kinnamos, Bonn, 281; Borsari, 116.

[64] *JGR* I, 437 (1187).

[65] *JGR* I, 438.

Romanos genus Veneticorum nostra serenitas reputat"[66]. The reason is, by now, familiar to us: *"Tantumque pro Romania dolent, quantum et ipsi Romani, tantamque erga eam habent devotionem, quantam et erga terram qua eos emisit"*. They are Romans, at least *ab origine*, because of their devotion to the Byzantine cause. By 1199, the situation is even more complex: the privilege of Alexios Angelos distinguishes (I think for the first time) between Venetians and Greeks (*Grecos*), in connection with judicial disputes; it makes specific arrangements for the resolution of judicial disputes between Venetians and Greeks; it provides (at the request of the Venetians) for the disposition of the property of a Venetian who might die in the Byzantine Empire, which must be handed over to his heirs, even if he dies without a testament, or to his *fideicommissarii*; and it mentions a novel (lost) of Manuel I, which regulated judicial matters *"inter extraneos et indigenas"*[67]. There is, thus, a vacillation of the official position, in which the Venetians are treated both as foreigners and as quasi-Byzantines. The vacillation is reflected in the fact that for one hundred years the privileges granted to the Venetians did not make specific dispositions for things such as ownership of property, rights of succession, judicial procedure, i.e., those things which might distinguish between a foreigner and a Byzantine subject. The chrysobull of 1199 treats the Venetians as foreigners in a new, more formal way, which may have something to do with the Venetians' own need for regulated relationships; the judicial dispositions are perhaps connected with the development of laws regarding foreigners in western Europe[68].

The ambiguity of the official position is reproduced in the narrative sources, but with significant differences. Kinnamos, describing a highly charged political situation (Manuel's opposition to Frederick Barbarossa in Italy in the 1160s), has a Byzantine envoy, Chalouphes, say to the Venetians: "Since out of the rest who exist under his sway (ὑπὸ τὴν παλάμην τελοῦσι αὐτοῦ) he (Manuel) is particularly confident of your gratitude," thus making the Venetians almost into subjects of the Byzantine Empire[69]. For the rest, Kinnamos distinguishes clearly the Venetians from the "Romans". He focuses on their hostile actions against the Byzantines. He has Manuel I saying to them that they had "poured into the Romans' state as vagabonds (ἀλῆται) gripped by poverty"[70]. He does not actually call them barbarians, but he describes them as follows: "ἔστι δὲ τὸ ἔθ-

---

[66] *JGR* I, 454.

[67] *JGR* I, 479.

[68] Cf. M. BOULET-SAUTEL, "L'aubain dans la France coutumière," *Recueils de la Société Jean Bodin*, II Brussels (1956), 65 ff., and GILISSEN, *ibid.*, 46 ff. There is a debate concerning the exact effect of the privilege on the juridical status of the Venetians: see LILIE, *op. cit.*, 47–48, 105.

[69] Kinnamos, 230: cf. "sub manu eius" of the chrysobull of 992. cf. Choniates 173: ἰσοπολίταις οὖσι Ῥωμαίοις.

[70] Kinnamos, 285.

νος ἤθει μὲν διεφθορός, βωμολόχον εἴπερ τι καὶ ἀνελεύθερον", ἀνελευθερία being, as we have seen, a trait of the barbarians[71]. He shows that, before 1171, they had freedom of movement in the Byzantine Empire; that they married Byzantine women, and lived outside the quarter given them by the Emperor which suggests that they had rights similar to those of the Byzantines – but the historian finds this improper[72]. Therefore, the ambiguity probably derives from the fact that the historian had to reproduce both the attitude of hostility and the fact of contact.

There remains the case of Choniates, who was laboring under two important conditions: he finished writing his history after the fall of Constantinople in 1204, and, writing and living in the late twelfth century, he had been used to a situation where large numbers of Venetians had settled in the Byzantine Empire, and acculturation had already taken place. He therefore sees them in an interesting light. He says that, after 1082, they settled in Constantinople and everywhere in the Romania; and they retained only their name, "in other ways being of similar race and altogether Romans" (τὰ δ' ἄλλα σύμφυλοι ὄντες καὶ πά-νυ Ῥωμαῖοι). Thus, they were no longer strangers, and perhaps not foreigners. The passage is not friendly to them, finding them insolent and tricky, but does show assimilation, and suggests that long domicile brings it about, although not necessarily in legal terms[73]. Indeed, according to Kinnamos, Manuel I had created a new category of foreigner, based on long domicile. These were the "bour-gesioi", to be distinguished from merchants who were merely passing through[74]. The Venetians Choniates is talking about as being very similar to the Romans are those who had lived there for a long time: he mentions some of them, who were his friends, and rescued him and other Byzantines from the hands of the French crusaders, in 1204. We have, here, a case where the foreigner is seen not as a monolithic entity but with specific individual traits. This points out an important configuration: at a group level, Choniates is intensely hostile to the Venetians. At the level of individual interaction, he is perfectly happy to dine with specific Venetians and to seek their protection. The one position does not negate the other; they simply belong to different levels of interaction[75].

Interestingly enough, Choniates does call the Venetians barbarians, in one instance. It is an instance with little significance in terms of political ideology, but of some importance in terms of cultural attitudes. It refers to the time, dur-

---

[71] Kinnamos, 280. cf. 170, 98.
[72] They owned houses in Thebes and Halmyros in the mid-twelfth century: THIRIET, op. cit.,47.
[73] Choniates, 171.
[74] Kinnamos, 283.
[75] Choniates, 588 and contrast 538 ff. TAJFEL, Differentiation, 41 ff.

ing the campaign against Roger of Sicily, in which the Venetian fleet fought as allies of the Byzantines. There was a brawl between the Venetians and the Byzantines, and then the Venetians dressed a black man in imperial clothes, put him on the imperial ship which they had captured and mocked Manuel, who was himself dark. Choniates calls them "barbarian" on both ocasions: on the first occasion because they behaved like beasts in their refusal to stop the fighting, and in the second case because they behaved improperly[76]. In both cases, the objection is cultural, and this is what differentiates the Venetians from the Byzantines and makes them into foreigners, barbarians, not good Byzantines.

This brings us to another topic, that is, to the question of the means through which foreigners became acculturated or assimilated in Byzantine society, and the perceived limits of such acculturation. We have seen one mechanism at work in the case of the Venetians. It is the port-of-trade situation, which, in the case of merchants who became settled (the "bourgesioi"), leads into acceptance and some acculturation. In more general terms, there a variety of mechanisms were at work at different stages. One must distinguish between the accommodation of foreigners, i. e., the acceptance of difference, coupled with mechanisms which mediate the difference, and acculturation or assimilation.

Let us take first the means of accommodation. The purpose of accommodation is not to change the nature of the foreigner, but rather to turn unfriendly foreigners into friendly ones, and to bind them to the Byzantine state in a hierarchical way, i.e. make them into unequal allies. This is achieved by the creation of a quasi-legal contractual relationship. Where an entire people is concerned, the process involves treaties, but much more importantly, it involves oaths, which seal a treaty, and are more powerful than a treaty. Oaths played a major role in Byzantine relations with foreigners in this period, as they did in relations between the Byzantines themselves[77]. They were important, first of all, in regulating relations between states, i.e. between Byzantium and foreign potentates, or foreigners who expected to become potentates. Significantly, there does not seem to have been a differentiation between Christian and non-Christian foreigners as far as the expected potency of the oath is concerned. Thus, in 1161, after a Turkish defeat in the hands of John Kontostefanos, the Sultan (Kilidj Arslan) made a treaty of alliance with Manuel. The Emperor

---

[76] Choniates, 77, 86.
[77] N. SVORONOS, "Le serment de fidelité à l'empereur byzantin et sa signification constitutionnelle, in *idem, Études sur l'organisation intérieure, la société et l'économie de l'Empire byzantin*, (London, Variorum Reprints, 1973), pp. 109 ff., discusses the oath of fidelity to the Byzantine Emperor as an indicator of the development of personal links under the Comneni, a development reinforced by the Latin conquest.

"bound him with mighty oaths," before returning home[78]. Oaths were, it would seem, an important and perhaps necessary component of agreements or treaties, sealing them in ways more powerful than the agreement itself: thus, Manuel was offered an agreement by the King of the Czechs, but he did not entirely trust him: so he sent some envoys to the King (Vladislav II), and "ordered the agreement to be confirmed by oath, and the other unhesitatingly did this at once. Not only that, but he reiterated with additional oaths what... he had previously pledged"[79]. This is clearly the σωματικός ὅρκος which, in Byzantine treaties with the maritime Italian cities is a necessary condition for the validation of the treaty. The oath must be taken *in person* by the representatives of the foreign power that negotiates the treaty; when the treaty is further ratified by the government of the city (i.e. the Doge, of the head of the government, and the people), this is done in the presence of imperial envoys[80]. The oath is made on the Gospels and a cross, and is included in an ὀρκωμοτικὸν ἔγγραφον, i.e. is secured by a process similar to oath taking in Byzantium[81]. The Byzantine Emperor does not ever himself take an oath when dealing with foreign governments; he promises and grants through a chrysobull whatever privileges are being granted, but the oath seems to be demanded only of others. Where non-Christian potentates are concerned, we do not, as far as I know, have the texts of their oaths. We may, however, assume that they were asked to take the most serious oath prescribed by their religion and/or customs. This assumption is based on Bas. 22.5, which says that one swears according to his own religion, and is further supported by a curious text of the 12th century, which details the oath a Jew must take in litigation against a Christian[82].

---

[78] Kinnamos IV. 24, p. 201; F. DÖLGER, *Regesten der Kaiserurkunden des Oströmischen Reiches von 565-1453*, II, Munich, 1925, 1444.

[79] Choniates, 16, 17. Kinnamos., V.8, Bonn, 224: ὅρκοις τὰ δεδογμένα πιστοῦσθαι ἐκέλευε, καὶ ὃς αὐτίκα μηδὲν μελλήσας ἐπιτελῇ ταῦτα ἔθετο. οὐ μὴν ἀλλὰ καὶ ὅσα πάλαι, καθάπερ ἔφην, ὑπέσχετο δευτέροις ἐπικαταλάμβανεν ὅρκοις. Oaths are given by the Russians (Kin.V.10, 232), the Hungarians, who routinely break them (V.10, 231; V.8, V.12, V.16, 268, Chon.151), the princes of Antioch (V.13), the King of Jerusalem (Chon. 165), Frederick Barbarossa and Manuel I (Chon.401-402). They seal a treaty (Kinnamos V. 16, 248, with the Hungarians), or an agreement: the Serbian king swore terrible oaths (φρικώδεσιν ὅρκοις) to mend his ways and not to do anything to displease Manuel I (Chon. 136).

[80] F. MIKLOSICH and J. MÜLLER, *Acta et Diplomata Graeca Medii Aevi*, Athens, 1865, III, 3 ff., 25 ff. Anna Comnena mentions that her father, when he wrote to Henry IV, said that the manner in which Henry's oath must be taken had already been indicated to him and would be further clarified by the imperial envoy, who would instruct Henry on all the points to be sworn to: *Alexias* I, 121. She calls both the Pope and Robert Guiscard 'barbarians', for breaking their oaths: *Alexias*, I. 47.

[81] MIKLOSICH – MÜLLER, *op. cit.*, III, 15, 30-31; in Latin in *JGR* I, 460: the representatives of Pisa swear on Gospel, etc., and are also delegated to swear on the soul of the Podestà of Pisa; those of Genoa on the soul of the head of the government of Genoa: MIKLOSICH-MÜLLER, III, 30-31; on swearing on icons, the cross, etc., see PH. KOUKOULES, *Βυζαντινῶν Βίος καὶ Πολιτισμός*, Athens, 1949, 3, 353 ff; On the ὀρκωμοτικὸν ἔγγραφον, see MIKLOSICH-MÜLLER, III, 45-46.

[82] *JGR* I, 373-375, and E. PATLAGEAN, "Contribution juridique à l'histoire des Juifs dans la Méditerranée médiévale: les formules grecques de serment", in EADEM, *Structures sociales,*

It is, perhaps, pertinent to note that oaths were taken seriously by the Byzantines in the twelfth century, at least in a formalistic way, and that oath-breaking was as formal a business as oath-taking seems to have been. Perhaps because, in the period of the Comneni, oaths to the Emperor by some or all of his subjects had acquired a new importance, there was legislative interest in oath-taking, and juridical interest in oath-breaking. Alexius I passed a general law which affirms in an unequivocal way that minors who make an agreement and confirm it with a corporal oath may not break their oath, and that no private individual, nor his successor Emperors may allow them restitution. The decision was the result of a debate among jurists, and was resolved by the Emperor in an act which affirmed the power of the oath beyond what the law had required until then[83].

An oath taken to the Emperor was even harder to break. The prime example is given by the oath which Manuel I exacted from his subjects (or, to be exact, his aristocratic subjects) on the matter of his succession. The story is instructive: Manuel, having no sons, betrothed his daughter Maria to Bela / Alexis of Hungary, and made "everyone" swear that they would accept Alexis and Maria as his successors. While everybody took the oath, his cousin Andronikos declined, saying, among other things, that if the Emperor subsequently married again and had a son, "we would then swear to give the Empire to this new imperial offspring, and our recent oaths to his daughter will by necessity be broken (μὴ εὐορκεῖν). This, indeed, is what happened. Manuel remarried, had a son, and at that point "transferred" the oaths from Alexis and Maria to his son. The oaths were given in a formal ceremony (διὰ τῆς τελεσιουργίας τῶν ὅρκων ... τὴν σκηπτουχίαν ... μεταθέμενος), in the church of Vlachernai, in the presence of the Emperor and his son. The oath was inscribed in a document (βιβλίον τοῦ ὅρκου), and included a general statement of defense of the Emperor's honor: this is not unlike a feudal contract, although we do not, of course, know whether the document included any reciprocal obligations on Manuel's part. In the end, Andronikos, who had taken this oath, killed Manuel's son Alexios. But nevertheless, he thought his oath sufficiently serious to ask the Patriarch (Basil Kamateros) and the synod to invalidate the oath he and others had taken. The Patriarch did so, but Choniates reports this action very negatively: ὡς εἰ δεσμεῖν ἀδιαφόρως καὶ λύειν τὰ πάντα εἰλήφασι πρὸς θεοῦ[84].

famille, chrétienté à Byzance, London, Variorum Reprints, 1981, Study XIV. Cf. *Alexias* I, 76–77, and I, 23.

[83] *JGR* I, 292–296. Cf. *ibid.*, 279 ff.

[84] Choniates, 137, 169–170, cf. *ibid.*, 228 ff., 276; Svoronos, *op.cit.*, 109–111, says that the oath was taken by all the subjects; I doubt that, since the names of those who took it seem to have been inscribed in a "biblion". He mentions two previous cases, one where the oath was taken by Senate, army, and people at the request of Leo VI, to acknowledge the succession of his son, and

Foreigners, then, were bound to the Empire, in a formal way, by oaths, this being a link whose juridical importance was considerable in this period. They were thus brought into an orderly, hierarchical relationship with the Byzantine state; this is a process of normalisation, of inscribing the "other" into an order created and recognized by "self". It is a process undertaken by the state; the historians who describe it give it negative value, by the stereotypical judgement that all foreigners break their oaths.

If accommodation was sought with regard to those outside the Empire, assimilation was considered desirable for those within it. Marriage was an important mechanism of acculturation. In Byzantium of the twelfth century this is visible mostly among the aristocracy, or in the case of foreigners who were good soldiers or administrators and thus entered state service. I assume that the mechanism worked in similar ways in the case of those merchants who married into Byzantine families. Women became the mediators, in a number of important ways, mediating both peace and alliance between two states, and the acceptance of individual foreigners in Byzantine society. Mixed marriages took two primary forms. Foreigners married or sought to marry Byzantine women, or foreign women came into Byzantium to marry Byzantines[85]. That second configuration is known primarily, although not only, within the imperial family. John Comnenus married a Hungarian, Manuel Comnenus married first a German and then a princess from Antioch, his son Alexius married Agnes of France, and Isaac Angelos married a Hungarian princess. I do not know of any cases where Byzantine men married foreign women and went to live abroad. When we look at imperial families, we find that the male offspring commonly married westerners, and the female ones married Byzantines, with only a few exceptions. That is, the dominant partner, the male, was the one to marry outside, thus bringing his wife and her people into the Byzantine fold. The first exception is the betrothal of Manuel I's daughter Maria to Bela of Hungary and her later marriage to Renier of Montferrat.

one instituted by the Grand Domestic Ioannes Axouch who exacted it from all (SVORONOS p. 110). In fact, that is not so. What Axouch did was to urge John II to ask each of the "megistanes" who commanded parts of the army, and the army they commanded, to acclaim Manuel; and they – presumably the megistanes, and especially the relatives of the Emperor, who could rebel, – took an oath on the Gospels (τῶν θείων... λογίων) to confirm the acclamation. The seriousness of oath-taking and oath-breaking is attested by Balsamon, who argues for allowing Christians to take oaths; and who also asserts (G. RALLES and M. POTLES, Σύνταγμα τῶν θείων καὶ ἱερῶν κανόνων, Athens, 1854, IV.249) the high value given in his day to oaths "on the head of the Emperor", since those who broke such an oath were greatly punished, while others who had promised to go on pilgrimage to Jerusalem and broke their oath were not at all punished (cf. Ralles-Potles, I, 13.18) (Ralles-Potles, IV.167–8, which posits differentiation of punishments; and also the legitimacy of oaths; p. 249 distinguishes between σωματικὸν ὅρκον and ἔγγραφον ὅρκον. On oaths, cf. P. GOUNARIDES, "Ορκος και αφορισμός στα Βυζαντινά δικαστήρια", Symmeikta VII (1987), pp. 41–57.

[85] See for example, the efforts of Frederick Barbarossa to form a marriage alliance with Byzantium: Kinnamos IV.1.

When foreign princesses married Byzantines, the purpose of the marriage was clearly political: the only thing that mattered was that the women be of good lineage. In the panegyrics, invariably the ancient race of the woman was praised, and sometimes the political aspect of the marriage was highlighted with the statement that it signaled the union of Old and New Rome[86].Women were thus means through which foreign (as well as domestic) alliances were made. These women, who changed their name and presumably their religion upon their marriage, were expected to become Byzantine. If Choniates remembered, as late as 1203, that the Empress Bertha/Irene, was ἡ ἐξ Ἀλαμανῶν δέσποινα, if the Empress Mary of Antioch was considered a foreigner, nevertheless in general it was assumed that they would become Byzantine[87]. At the same time, Byzantine women who married abroad were assumed to have become lost to their family and fatherland. When Theodora Comnena married Henry II Jasomirgott of Babenberg, her mother lamented: "I saw my beloved daughter defiled / when she married a western beast / and mourned her while she was still alive"[88].

More interesting in terms of acculturation are the marriages between men who were foreigners and Byzantine women, within the Byzantine Empire, if only because a number of people were affected: soldiers who came to the Byzantine Empire and were successful, or sons of foreign potentates who for one reason or another found themselves in Byzantium, such as Bela, son of Stephen IV of Hungary whom Manuel I betrothed to his daughter Maria specifically in order to lay claim to the throne of Hungary[89]. These men were expected to change allegiances[90]. Marriage with a Byzantine woman was supposed to change foreigners from enemies into friends, and even to alter their barbarous nature[91].

As part of the process of acculturation, men married to upper class Byzantine women changed their names, just as did foreign princesses who came to Byzantium. Thus, Bela became Alexios, and Ivanko also became Alexios (adopting the name of his wife's grandfather)[92]. Manuel Comnenus gave Renier of Montferrat the name John after John II, his own father[93].

[86] W. Hörandner, *Theodoros Prodromos: Historische Gedichte*, Vienna, 1974, no. 7; Choniates, *Orationes et Epistulae*, ed. van Dieten, Berlin, 1972, p. 40; cf. *ibid.*, p .36.
[87] Choniates, 544, 53–54; 146–147.
[88] *RHC, Hist. Gr.* II, 768: Καὶ τὸ τερπνὸν θυγάτριον λελυμασμένον εἶδον, / Ὁπόταν θὴρ ἑσπέριος ἐκείνη συνηνώθη, / Καὶ ζῶσαν ἀπεθρήνησα κατὰ νεκρὰν τὴν παῖδα.
[89] Kinnamos V. 5. At a lower social level, there is the case of John ἐκ Πούτζης, who married a faded and undesirable aristocratic woman. Choniates, 56.
[90] See Choniates, 214–215.
[91] Choniates, 473; cf. Kinnamos V. 13.   [92] Choniates, 509–510.
[93] Choniates 171, 200, 230; Eustathius of Thessalonika, ed. Kyriakides, p. 20, gives him the name Ioannes. William of Tyre, *RHC Historiens occidentaux*, II, 412–413, is formal: Li patriarches Theodoses les esposa. Li Empereres chanja le non à Renier et il mist le non de son

This change of name, especially if the new name was that of the wife's paternal grandfather, is symbolic of the man's acceptance into his wife's family: he became a son of the Emperor as surely as Bela / Alexios became a son of Manuel I in a formal ceremony. Non-Christians who were baptised may also have been given a name which tied them into their sponsor's family: the one clear example is that of the Turk John Axouchos, who was taken into the imperial family and was given the name John, in an act which symbolically made him an adopted son of the Emperor.

Whether the same symbolic action occurs in the case of men who married Byzantine women not of the immediate imperial family cannot be easily determined. However, the general effect of mixed marriages is clear, and is most clearly presented in the Romance of Digenis. The foreigner marrying into a Byzantine family has first to negate his own: the Arab Emir abandons his family and his religion to marry a Byzantine woman. He then turns around and persuades his mother and his people to convert, in an act redolent with symbolism as he becomes the godfather of his mother and also of his people, in a reversal of roles: πατὴρ δέ σου γενήσομαι ἐν πνεύματι ἁγίῳ[94]. In the poem, it is love which unites people of different races: "καὶ καταμάθῃ ἀκριβῶς ἔρωτος τὰς δυνάμεις, / πῶς ἀλλοφύλους ἤνωσεν εἰς μίαν φέρων πίστιν"[95]. The Emir changes his clothing on re-entering the Romania after his trip to see (and convert) his mother; a symbolic representation of the change of name and manners that was expected of a foreigner who marries a Byzantine[96]. Marriage therefore involves a change in political allegiance and religion, and has as symbolic appurtenances a change of name and change of clothing and manners. There is a further symbolism in this: for commonly it was the woman who became incorporated into the husband's family, and a man took his wife's family name only when he was inferior in social terms. Thus, the foreigner who marries into a Byzantine family retains an inferior position, assimilated though he becomes.

The incorporation of the Emir into the new family and culture is not accomplished immediately. The brothers of the Emir's wife have accepted him but, it seems, under conditions. When he wants to leave for his own country, to see his mother, i.e., to return to his family and origins, his situation as a foreigner and a stranger is reaffirmed. The girl's brothers insist that he may leave, but without his wife. They are clearly afraid of her becoming, in her turn, a stranger in a strange land. The Emir, their brother-in-law, becomes again an enemy, a

père; si fu apelez Jehans. Cf. K. Varzos, Ἡ Γενεαλογία τῶν Κομνηνῶν, Thessalonika, 1984, no. 153 (II. 449).

[94] E. Trapp, Digenes Akrites, G II, 495–500, G III, 834.

[95] Spoken by the mother of the Emir, Digenes Akrites G III, 929–930; cf. G. IV, 1460 ff.

[96] Digenes Akrites G III, 865.

παράνομος ἐχϑρός. As for the Emir himself, he is conscious of his condition as a foreigner. The poet says, ᾐσχύνετο γὰρ φωραϑείς, ὡς ξένος ἐφοβεῖτο; the girl pleads with the brothers, μή, πρὸς Θεοῦ, ἀδέλφιά μου, μὴ ἀδικηϑεῖ ὁ ξένος, ὃς δι᾽ ἐμὲ ἠρνήσατο συγγενεῖς καὶ τὴν πίστιν[97]. There are, in fact, some limitations to the acceptance of foreigners who become Byzantines through marriage. Certainly, the first generation remains under scrutiny, almost on probation. A number of the Byzantine magnates said, in connection with Manuel's efforts to have Bela/Alexios recognised as the future Emperor, that "it was not at all in the interest of the Emperor's daughter, or of the Roman people, to have the branch of an olive tree of different kind (ἑτεροφύλου) grafted on a cultivated olive-tree and prefer him to others in assuming the imperial power"[98]. Ivanko may have changed his name to Alexios on his marriage, but some Byzantines thought it was impossible for him to change his barbarous nature and his hostility toward the Byzantines, and they were right[99]. Conrad of Montferrat married Theodora, sister of the Emperor Isaac Angelos. He was, says Choniates, of Italian race (τὸ γένος Ἰταλειώτης), brave, wise, and a renowned soldier, certainly a much braver soldier than his brother-in-law. But eventually, a real or imagined slight made him forget all about his wife, to go to Palestine, to his ὁμόφυλοι, says Choniates[100]. He was clearly unassimilated, but then, he had been in Byzantium only a short time.

Jean-Claude Cheynet has recently argued, on the basis of sigillographic evidence, that two generations (father to son) suffice for the development of Byzantine forms in the names of foreigners[101]. If that is a mark of assimilation, it suggests that assimilation took place very rapidly. Indeed, with someone like John Axouchos, one generation, his own, sufficed. Certainly, two generations, especially if there was marriage to a high-class family, were sufficient indeed. Long service under the Emperor, and a long period of living in the Romania could make first-generation foreigners acceptable, although their roots were not forgotten. John Axouchos (*megas domestikos*), a brave soldier and wise statesman, was, Choniates informs us, "a Turk by birth", who, when Nicaea was taken in the late eleventh century, was given as a present to Alexios I, and grew

---

[97] *Digenes Akrites* G. II, 481 ff., 533–534. The son himself is both Roman and non-Roman: ἐϑνικὸς μὲν ἀπὸ πατρός, ἐκ δὲ μητρὸς Ῥωμαῖος: G IV 1002 ff.

[98] Choniates, 137.

[99] Choniates, 510–511, 518.

[100] Choniates, 382 ff., 394–395. Cf. *Alexias*, II, 20: Anna Comnena, commenting on the *megas hetaireiarches* Argyros Karatzas, says: Σκύϑην μὲν ὄντα, φρονιμώτατον δὲ καὶ ἀρετῆς καὶ ἀληϑείας ἐπιμελούμενον.

[101] J.-C. CHEYNET, "Du prénom au patronyme: les étrangers à Byzance (X⁰-XII⁰ siècles)," in *Studies in Byzantine Sigillography*, ed. N. OIKONOMIDES, Washington, D.C., 1987, pp. 57–66.

up with Alexios' son John[102]. This is the only time his origins are mentioned by Choniates, and Kinnamos does not mention them at all. For the rest, both historians of the period are very well disposed toward him, and make no further connection between his actions and his antecedents[103]. As a further example, one may mention the family of the Kamytzai. The first known Kamytzes was a Turkish soldier, sent by the Sultan to Alexios I in 1083 with 7 000 mercenary troops[104]. A son or nephew, Eustathios Kamytzes, appears in the Alexiad as fully assimilated, to the extent of fighting the Turks and giving God thanks for his victory; he also appears at the synod of Vlachernai[105]. No mention of his antecedents is made. He became *pansebastos sebastos*. A Constantine Kamytzes married Maria Angelina, granddaughter of Alexios I[106]. This is not to say that the Byzantines forgot consistently to mention the antecedents of assimilated foreigners: the descendants of Peter of Aliphas[107], the Patralifai, had, according to Cheynet's standard, become assimilated; but Choniates still identifies them by their race: ἐκ τοῦ τῶν φράγγων γένους ὁρμώμενοι[108]. Three processes are at play here. First, in terms of behavior, one finds that assimilation of foreigners through marriage was possible. This process affected the ruling class, which brings us to the second point: people like Choniates were a little reticent to accept the inclusion of foreigners in the governing élite, for this was threatening to their own social status. Thirdly, however, since these were, by definition, individual cases, attitudes were to some extent derived from the behavior (real or perceived) of individuals rather than of groups[109].

There were, as we have pointed out, some limits to the assimilation of foreigners. It took place very quickly, especially through marriage. But, at least at first, it implied an inferior position of the foreigner in the family, and the first

---

[102] Choniates 9. Pakourianos' origins are mentioned as "Armenian" only once by Anna Comnena: *Alexias*, I, 137 ff.

[103] Choniates, 9.82. Kinnamos, 47 ff. We do not know whom he married, but if he was, indeed, *pansebastos sebastos* (Varzos II, 118), he must have married into the imperial family. His son, Alexios Axouchos, married Maria, a granddaughter of the Emperor John II (Choniates, 103–104; Varzos no.123). For other marriages of children of John Axouch into the imperial family, see Varzos no. 57, 53. Alexios was much less loyal than his father, and in fact plotted with both Latins and Turks, and built himself a palace which was decorated with paintings depicting the deeds of the sultan (Kinnamos, VI. 6). But neither Kinnamos nor Choniates ascribe this faithfulness to his origins.

[104] *Alexias*, I, 168. Cf. Varzos, *op. cit.*, no. 91, vol.I, 650.

[105] *Alexias*, II, 119, 190, 243–244, 246–249, 255, 276. P. Gautier, "Le synode des Blachernes (fin 1094); étude prosopographique," *REB* 29, 1971, 259, identifies him as son or nephew of the Turk.

[106] Varzos, no.91.

[107] *Alexias*, II, 119.

[108] Choniates, 83. It was possibly their descendants, i.e. the third generation, who married into the Comnenian family: Varzos nos. 126, 168.

[109] On this point, see Tajfel, *Differentiation*, 41 ff.

generation was only rarely assimilated fully. By the second generation, assimilation was far advanced, although some people might remember and mention the non-Byzantine antecedents of a family.

It is, perhaps, necessary to say a few words about the attitude of the people to all of this. There has been no work on the subject, and it is sorely needed. My suggestion is that their self-identification was much weaker than that of the aristocracy and the *literati*. True, one regarded outsiders with suspicion, whether these were strangers (i.e. from another locality, for example, Cappadocia), or foreigners. Thus, in the same cosmopolitan twelfth century, the governor of Athens was suspicious of some men from Rome, considering them as spies. It took an intervention of a holy man, and, more importantly, imperial letters of safe conduct to change his mind[110]. At the same time, people seem to have had rather limited patience with their rulers and with those who created the ideology I have been discussing, and little to do with their concerns. There are a number of examples of groups of people who changed allegiances and went over to the Turks in the course of the twelfth century, because of a general alienation from imperial rule[111]. The Turks were not strangers to them, and perhaps seemed less foreign than their Constantinopolitan rulers. There are also examples of acceptance of Latin rule after 1204, at least in the beginning.

By way of conclusion, the following points may be made:

In the twelfth century, traditional and stereotypical definitions of self and the other remain. The content of the stereotypes, however, has changed with time, and it differs according to the social status of the observer. The relative weight of religion as a factor defining the foreigner is now much less than it was two centuries earlier. The statist perception of self as including all those who serve the Roman state is also weakened, at least in the writings of the intellectuals and members of the bureaucracy. Progressively, this perception is replaced by a cultural differentiation, in which language plays a primary role. The new definition is a mark of weakness, partly due to disenchantment with the late twelfth-century state, and is evidence of a need to find and affirm clear distinctions. It is still a relatively flexible concept, to the extent that it is accepted that the cultural characteristics of self can be acquired; but it is much less flexible than the older concept.

Insofar as the actions, not the ideology, of the state is concerned, the situation is somewhat different, and the definition of a foreigner is open-ended: the same

---

[110] "Vita Meletii iunioris", by Nikolaos of Methone, ed. V. VASILIEVSKIJ, *Pravoslavny Palestinski Sbornik* 17 (1886), vol. VI, pp. 32–33.
[111] Choniates, 37–39; cf. pp. 494–495.

people or peoples may be considered foreigners when acting in a hostile manner to the Byzantine state, and Byzantines when they are friendly. This has been seen in the example of the Venetians.

In dealing with foreigners, the Byzantines tried to bind them to their own society in ways which created dependence, and brought the foreigner into an orderly system. Groups of foreigners might be brought into the system through oaths, a ceremonial and quasi-legal mechanism, which did not at all affect their status as foreigners, or the stereotypical perceptions of them. Individual foreigners were dealt with differently. The ideal was to acculturate and assimilate them, and thus have them shed their foreign traits, an ideal achieved primarily through mixed marriages. We have seen that there is a certain ambivalence and ambiguity in both the concept and the position of the foreigner. That is the result of changing realities at a time when old concepts still had force, and newer ones had not been fully elaborated; it is also the result of the fact that our sources reflect the views and actions of diverse entities, primarily the state and the educated élite. With the dissolution of the state in 1204 an important turning point was reached, after which political realities in the Eastern Mediterranean would change fast and profoundly; and that would force a further elaboration of the concepts of self and foreigner.

II

L'étranger de passage et l'étranger privilégié à Byzance, XIe-XIIe siècles

Le thème de ce colloque n'est pas des plus faciles. En fait, les étrangers, comme les marginaux, sont des groupes qui, presque par la nature des choses, ont laissé beaucoup moins de témoignages de leur propre condition d'étranger que ne l'ont fait ceux qui appartenaient pleinement à la société d'accueil. Il reste que la perception que se font les étrangers de leurs droits fait partie intégrante de la place des étrangers dans la société, et le contrepoint de l'idée que se fait la société d'accueil. S'il y a un écart entre les deux perceptions, on peut supposer qu'il y aura aussi des conflits, dont l'étendue et l'importance sera plus ou moins grave selon l'importance numérique et la puissance des groupes étrangers. D'autre part, nous nous trouvons en face de questions qui touchent au sens d'identité des étrangers. Les droits reconnus aux étrangers en tant que tels auraient comme résultat non pas une tendance à l'assimilation de ces groupes, mais plutôt l'admission de leur particularité, tandis que les droits reconnus en dépit de la condition d'étranger seraient des mécanismes d'assimilation.

Dans ce qui suit, je voudrais développer deux thèmes: l'idée que se faisaient les étrangers de Byzance et de leur propre place dans la société byzantine; et, aussi, les droits que cette société leur accordait, toujours selon le point de vue des étrangers. Mon enquête sera centrée sur deux groupes différents, les géorgiens et arméniens--étrangers privilégiés--et les croisés--étrangers de passage. En ce qui concerne le premier groupe, nous disposons d'un texte clef, le *Typikon* (charte de fondation) de Grégoire Pakourianos pour le monastère de Bac kovo (Pétritzos), qui date de la fin du XIe siècle.[1] Or Grégoire Pakourianos était un homme très riche, extrêmement puissant, et même lié à la famille impériale par des liens de mariage, son neveu étant le gambros de Nicéphore Comnène, frère de l'empereur Alexis Ier Comnène.[2]

---

[1] Le *Typikon* a été rédigé en décembre, 1083. J'utilise ici l'édition de P. Gautier, "Le Typikon du sébaste Grégoire Pakourianos," *RÉB*, 42 (1984), pp. 5-145. En préparant cette communication, j'ai beaucoup profité des discussions avec MM. N. Oikonomidès et A. Kazhdan.

[2] P. Gautier, *Théophylacte d'Achrida, Lettres* (Thessalonique, 1986), p. 99.

Originally published in *Identité et droit de l'autre*, ed L. Mayali (Berkeley: Robbins Collection, 1994), 69–88. Copyright 1994 by the Regents of the University of California, The Robbins Religious and Civil Law Collection, School of Law (Boalt Hall), University of California at Berkeley.

L'identification ethnique de ce personnage, qui, à la fin de sa vie, occupait un des plus grands offices de l'Empire byzantin, celui de grand domestique d'Occident, est confuse, dans les sources ainsi que dans l'historiographie moderne. Il se prononce "Ibère," mais Anne Comnène le qualifie d'Arménien: "homme de petite taille, selon le poète, mais bon soldat, provenant d'une famille illustre arménienne."[3] En plus, son monastère était fondé exclusivement pour des "Ibères," mais Pakourianos dit qu'il a fait rédiger son *Typikon* en grec, géorgien et arménien; dans son *Typikon*, il parle aussi de ceux de ses parents et de ses "gens" qui étaient "de la religion des Arméniens" (κἂν τῆς θρησκείας τῶν ᾿Αρμενίων τυγχάνωσιν).[4] Matthieu d'Edesse mentionne un certain Phers (Phersès), membre de l'entourage de David le Curopalate et, selon la généalogie établie, frère du grand-père de Grégoire Pakourianos, et dit qu'il était parmi les troupes de l'Arménie.[5] Sa description de Pakourianos est d'un intérêt particulier pour notre thème. Matthieu d'Edesse, en décrivant le siège d'Ani, en 1064, parle des "infâmes chefs *romains* que l'empereur avait établis préfets de l'Arménie, Pakrad, père de Sempad, (et) Grégoire, fils de Pagouran, *géorgien* de nation...";[6] donc, selon lui, Pakourianos était un Byzantin d'origine géorgienne.

Les historiens qui se sont occupés de Grégoire Pakourianos le considèrent parfois géorgien,[7] parfois membre d'une aristocratie "Arméno-Ibère."[8] Le *Oxford Dictionary of Byzantium* note les différences d'opinion, en concluant qu'il appartenait, selon toute probabilité, à une aristocratie "arméno-géorgienne, chalcédonienne de confession." En fait, nombre de chercheurs ont signalé que la désignation "Ibère" dans les sources byzantines peut se rapporter à la fois à une ethnie (géorgienne) et à une confession (chalcédonienne, en opposition à la confession monophysite des Arméniens).[9] Cette question subtile a peu d'importance pour nous.

---

[3]   *Typikon*, pp. 21, 31; Anna Comnena, *Alexias*, ed. A. Reifferscheid (Leipzig, 1884), vol. 1, p. 67.
[4]   *Typikon*, pp. 128-129.
[5]   *Chronique de Matthieu d'Édesse (962-1136)*, trad. E. Dulaurier (Paris, 1858), Partie I, ch. XXII, p. 32.
[6]   *Chronique*, Partie II, ch. LXXXVIII, p. 123.
[7]   P. Lemerle, *Cinq études sur le XIe Siècle Byzantin* (Paris, 1977), p. 158, qui rappelle, en même temps, les liens très étroits de Pakourianos avec l'Arménie.
[8]   A.P. Kazhdan, *Armjane v sostave gospodstvujushchego klassa vizantijskoj imperii v XI-XII vv* (Erevan, 1975), p. 47 et #16.8-10.
[9]   *Oxford Dictionary of Byzantium*, *s.v.* "Iberians," "Iberia"; A.P. Kazhdan,

Par contre, la généalogie de Pakourianos présente beaucoup d'intérêt, puisque il nous faut savoir à quelle génération de "Byzantins" il appartenait.[10] La chronique de Skylitzès nous apprend que Basile II avait amené de la Géorgie (ca. 1001) trois nobles géorgiens, les frères Pakourianos, Pheudatos et Phersès.[11] P. Lemerle croit que ce Pakourianos était le grand-père de Grégoire. D'autre part, le *Typikon* de Grégoire Pakourianos nous apprend que son père, nommé, lui aussi, Pakourianos, était "archonte des archontes."[12] Le titre grec traduit les titres "ishkan ishkanats" et "eristav des eristavs," portés par des nobles de l'Arménie et de la Géorgie. En Géorgie, l'eristav détenait, au nom du roi ou du prince, un territoire qui pouvait être assez vaste. Il pouvait, à son tour, dépendre d'un eristav des eristavs, (en effet un gouverneur de province), titre et fonction ancienne, et attestée toujours au XIe siècle.[13]

La généalogie des Pakourianoi établie par P. Lemerle fait de notre Grégoire Pakourianos le petit fils du Pakourianos qui avait été amené à Byzance par Basile II. C'est une hypothèse bien plausible, même si aucune source ne pose explicitement une parenté entre les deux hommes. Si on accepte cette généalogie, il faut poser la question, comment le père de Grégoire continuerait à porter un titre géorgien après la soumission de son propre père à Byzance? On pourrait proposer, soit que Pakourianos père avait gardé des terres en Géorgie, et avec elles le titre (et la fonction?) de ἄρχων τῶν ἀρχόντων, soit qu'il portait le titre par courtoisie. Il me semble que la première hypothèse est la meilleure, puisque Grégoire parle de son père comme s'il remplissait les fonctions de son office: "τοῦ

Armjane, pp. 143-144, avec référence à V.A. Arutjunova-Fidanjan, *Armjane-Khalkidonity na vostochnykh granitsakh vizantijskoj imperii XIv* (Erevan, 1980).
[10]   Plusieurs efforts ont été fait pour établir la généalogie des Pakourianoi. Voir, par exemple, V.A. Arutjunova-Fidanjan, *Tipik Grigorija Pakuriana* (Erevan, 1978), 35ss, et Lemerle, *Cinq études*, 158ss, avec la bibliographie antérieure.
[11]   *Ioannis Scylitzae Synopsis Historiarum*, ed I. Thurn (Berlin and New York, 1973), pp. 339-340; Lemerle, *Cinq études*, p. 159.
[12]   *Typikon*, p. 21.
[13]   Pour l'Arménie, voir Constantin le Pophyrogénète, *De Administrando Imperio*, edd. Gy. Moravcsik et R.J.H. Jenkins (Washington, 1967), vol. I, 43.30 et commentaire, vol. II, p. 157; pour la Géorgie, B. Martin-Hisard, "Les biens d'un monastère géorgien (IXe-XIIIe siècle)," in: V. Kravari, J. Lefort, C. Morrisson, *Hommes et richesses dans l'empire byzantin, VIIIe-XVe siècle*, II (Paris, 1991), pp. 117 n. 5, 145, et M. Lordkipanidze, *Georgia in the XI-XII Centuries* (Tbilisi, 1987), pp. 167-168.

ἄρχοντος μὲν τῶν ἀρχόντων ὄντος τε καὶ διαπρέποντος."[14]
Il serait, donc, seigneur géorgien et sujet byzantin, dualité fort intéressante pour l'histoire administrative du XIe siècle ainsi que pour notre thème.[15] Avec Grégoire Pakourianos, l'intégration de la famille dans le cadre byzantin s'est accentuée. Rappellons-nous les paroles de Matthieu d'Edesse, qui le qualifie de chef romain, géorgien de nation.[16] Pakourianos lui-même était bien conscient de ces deux attributs. Ce serviteur fidèle des Empereurs byzantins, qui appartenait à la troisième génération établie à Byzance, s'identifiait toujours à sa race géorgienne.[17] Il avait, cependant, une perception exaltée de l'empire byzantin; il n'avait pas épargné son sang ni celui de ses proches et de ses gens, "pour la défense de l'empire Romain dans l'est et dans l'ouest,"[18] en se battant contre les ennemis de "la divine croix et de la Romanie."[19] Sa victoire (qui n'est pas autrement attestée) contre les Petchenegues est une victoire remportée contre "les terribles et sauvages ennemis, dressés non seulement contre la Romanie mais encore contre toute la race des chrétiens."[20] Pour lui, l'empire Byzantin est le grand empire chrétien (il souligne, d'ailleurs, son orthodoxie et celle des Géorgiens en général) et le défendre est défendre l'état (les empereurs aussi) ainsi que la foi. C'est une idée quelque peu archaïque, qui, par son insistance sur la religion, se

---

[14] *Typikon*, p. 21.
[15] Je trouve ici un certain rapport avec ce que nous connaissons du titre "toparque" au onzième siècle, qui peut qualifier ou bien des chefs étrangers qui possèdent des territoires qui peuvent être revendiqués de l'Empire, ou bien des Byzantins qui jouissent d'une indépendance considérable, surtout à cause de gouverner un territoire éloigné du centre: J.-C. Cheynet, "Toparque et topotèrètès à la fin du 11e siècle," *RÉB*, 42 (1984), pp. 214-224. Un parent de Pakourianos, Achsartanos, était toparque en Orient: *Typikon*, p. 37. Aux données généalogiques de la famille des Pakourianoi, on peut ajouter deux sceaux de la collection de Dumbarton Oaks. L'une, du onzième siècle, appartient à Apasintos Pakourianos, peut-être le magistros Apasios, frère de Grégoire, et l'autre à Aspietos Pakourianos: 55.1.3211, 55.1.3980. Je remercie M. John Nesbitt de m'avoir communiqué cette information.
[16] Sa brillante carrière de soldat et fonctionnaire ayant été détaillée par Paul Lemerle, il n'y a certainement pas question de la reprendre ici.
[17] *Typikon*, pp. 21, 31.
[18] Ma traduction; cf. Gautier, *Typikon*, pp. 32-33.
[19] *Typikon*, p. 35.
[20] *Typikon*, pp. 42-43; Lemerle, *Cinq études*, p. 172.

rapporte au Xe siècle plutôt qu'au XIe.[21]

Il est aussi possible que ce concept de l'Empire byzantin soit un concept traditionnel parmi les membres de l'aristocratie géorgienne et arménienne qui sont passés au service de Byzance à la fin du Xe siècle, sous le règne de Basile II, comme l'avait fait le grand-père de Grégoire Pakourianos. Je pense à un texte récemment commenté par Jean-Pierre Mahé, l'*Histoire de la Sainte Croix d'Aparank'*, composée à la fin du Xe siècle par le moine Grigor, dans un monastère au sud-ouest du lac Van, donc voisin à la région d'où provenaient les Pakourianoi, texte que d'ailleurs je ne connais que d'après ce commentaire.[22] Or ce moine arménien se faisait une idée eschatologique de l'Empire byzantin: "(les contrées de leurs ennemis) deviennent désertes et leurs chemins deviennent aveugles, comme il se doit pour ceux qui résistent à la volonté miséricordieuse de la céleste providence et de la droite de Dieu"; l'empire "déployé à l'image du ciel...sur la vaste surface de toute la terre, rassemble en son ample sein d'innombrables multitudes, comme un troupeau unique en un unique lieu, un unique synode en une unique église, l'unique épouse en la chambre nuptiale...."[23] Mahé relève aussi l'attitude favorable du chroniqueur envers les seigneurs et princes arméniens qui ont quitté leurs domaines (après la défaite de Bardas Skléros, en 979) pour entrer au service de Basile II; aussi l'attitude de ces "dynastes locaux" qui, "tout en restant très attachés à leur patrie,...sont fiers de pouvoir servir à Constantinople, bien assurés d'ailleurs de la permanence immuable de leurs familles, installées sur leurs terres depuis le Déluge."[24] Nous avons vu que Pakourianos s'identifie en "Ibère," mais il connaissait la langue arménienne (c'est en arménien qu'il a signé son *Typikon*), il possédait des biens dans la région d'Ani et à Taïq, sa carrière a commencé à Ani et Kars.[25] On peut le considérer comme représentant d'une aristocratie caucasienne, où la différence entre arménien et géorgien n'était pas

[21]   Angeliki E. Laiou, "The Foreigner and the Stranger in 12th Century Byzantium: Means of Propitiation and Acculturation," *Fremde der Gesellschaft*, ed. M.-T. Fögen (Frankfurt, 1991), pp. 74 ff.

[22]   J.-P. Mahé, "Basile II et Byzance vus par Grigor Narekac'i," *TM*, 11 (1991), pp. 555-573.

[23]   *Ibid.*, p. 563.

[24]   *Ibid.*, p. 571.

[25]   Lemerle, *Cinq études*, 165s. Sur la fortune de Pakourianos, voir les remarques de Michael Hendy, *Studies in the Byzantine Monetary Economy, c. 300-1450* (Cambridge, 1985), pp. 212-216.

poussée, et la conscience des différences ethnique n'était pas forte. D'ailleurs, son grand-père était allé à Constantinople dans des circonstances très proches de celles qui ont poussé les nobles arméniens vers l'Empire, et, en plus, il était chalcédonien, ce qui, d'ailleurs, est normal pour un géorgien. Il serait donc probable que Grégoire Pakourianos ait absorbé des idées propres à cette aristocratie militaire arménienne: une idée de l'empire byzantin qui soulignait l'aspect chrétien-religieux, et un attachement à l'empereur, source de pouvoir et de richesses.

Quels étaient les droits auxquels prétendaient les membres de cette aristocratie? D'après le témoignage du *Typikon* de Pakourianos, les droits qui sont en premier ordre sont les droits sur la propriété. La constatation n'a rien de remarquable, puisque c'est dans la nature de cette sorte de source d'insister sur la possession des biens qui seront légués à la nouvelle fondation monastique. Il y a, toutefois, des particularités. D'abord, les versions grecque et géorgienne du *Typikon* conservent mention d'un nombre très considérable de chrysobulles ou d'autres documents impériaux de donation, ou de privilèges sur les domaines déjà donnés par l'Empereur.[26] Il s'agit de la liste la plus détaillée que nous ayons de l'époque byzantine. Est-ce que c'est par hasard qu'elle a été enregistrée ici, ou est-ce que ce seigneur byzantin, qui se sentait aussi géorgien, a fait un effort spécial pour protéger ses biens par appel aux documents de donation? Tout au moins, on peut dire, avec Lemerle, que les biens très considérables de Grégoire Pakourianos et de son frère provenaient presque tous de donations impériales, et avaient auparavant été des biens du fisc.[27] Pakourianos insiste aussi qu'il avait reçu ces biens comme biens patrimoniaux, et qu'ils lui appartenaient en pleine propriété: ἐκ τῶν δὶ εὐσεβῶν χρυσοβούλλων δωρηθέντων ἡμῖν κτημάτων πατρικῆς κατασχέσεως λόγῳ ἐπὶ ἀναφαιρέτῳ καὶ τελείᾳ δεσποτείᾳ καὶ ἀληθεῖ ἐξουσίᾳ.[28]

---

26 *Typikon*, pp. 125-131; 150-200 documents selon Lemerle, *Cinq études*, p. 153.

27 Lemerle, *Cinq études*, 181ss.

28 *Typikon*, p. 35. Je comprends les mots "πατρικῆς κατασχέσεως λόγῳ" comme l'équivalent de la phrase "κατὰ λόγον γονικότητος," c'est à dire, "détenus en biens patrimoniaux." Pour le sens "possession" du mot κατάσχεσις, voir *Typikon*, p. 35, 1. 270. On constate avec intérêt qu'il y a une formule très proche de la notre dans une charte géorgienne de la fin du 9e siècle: "J'ai demandé au roi des biens patrimoniaux qui m'appartenaient héréditairement et il me les a accordés....": Martin-Hisard, "Les biens," p. 141.

Certes, lui même et son frère détenaient et exerçaient sur ces biens tous les droits reconnus par la loi byzantine pour les biens patrimoniaux. Son frère lui a laissé, à titre de legs, le village Sdravikion qu'il avait reçu de l'empereur; il a laissé par testament d'autres biens en titre de donation à un monastère qui serait fondé éventuellement. Quant à Grégoire Pakourianos, il a fait des achats de terres et de bâtiments, il a porté des améliorations sur les terres qui lui appartenaient, il a, finalement, fait de grandes donations au monastère qu'il a fondé. Bref, il détenait, sur ses biens, tous les droits prévus par les lois, et aussi des privilèges fiscaux comme, d'ailleurs, d'autres membres de l'aristocratie byzantine. Par extension, on peut supposer qu'il avait tous les droits civils des Byzantins. Son *Typikon* fait mention des accusations contre lui, et peut-être de procès qui ont été intentés contre lui.[29] Il n'est pas possible de repérer ni les cas, ni les dispositions, ni les tribunaux devant lesquels ils ont été jugés. Tout ce que nous savons, c'est que Pakourianos avait obtenu des documents impériaux tranchant les cas, ce qui pour le XIe siècle, et pour un membre de l'aristocratie n'est pas surprenant. Donc, Grégoire Pakourianos réclamait et détenait tous les droits d'un Byzantin. Quant à ses privilèges, ils étaient dûs à son rang plutôt qu'à ses origines étrangères, au moins du point de vue de l'État: le XIe siècle, en fait, a vu l'extension de donations de biens et de droits incorporels, qui se sont beaucoup augmentés sous Alexis Ier et ses successeurs.

Mais Grégoire Pakourianos lui même se faisait une idée un peu particulière de ses droits sur ses biens. Il insiste à plusieurs reprises sur le fait qu'il avait obtenu ses propriétés foncières, ainsi que d'autres cadeaux, à cause de son service à l'empereur et à l'Empire byzantin:

"J'ai reçu (le village de Pétritzos), par...chrysobulle de nos très puissants et saints empereurs, en récompense du sang versé dans les nombreux et grands combats que j'ai livrés depuis ma jeunesse jusqu'à cette période de ma vieillesse, parce que je n'ai jamais épargné mon sang, ni celui de mes parents qui m'accompagnaient, ni celui de la grande foule de

mes gens, pour complaire au pouvoir de sa majesté, combats

---

[29] *Typikon*, p. 127, ll. 785-88.

livrés sur son ordre en Orient et en Occident pour la défense de l'Empire grec....Si donc je dis que bien peu de mes parents et de ceux qui me servaient avec un pieux attachement sont morts dans leur lit de mort naturelle, je ne mentirais pas, car tous ont versé leur sang sous les coups d'épées des ennemis de la divine Croix et de la Romanie.... Je puis dire que (pour construire les églises et le monastère) je n'ai pas eu recours à l'argent d'autrui ou à des pratiques injustes, ou encore à des corvées, des réquisitions ou des prestations abusives de mes parèques...mais à des labeurs et des efforts justes et strictement personnels."[30]

Et encore: "(je n'avais) besoin d'aucun bien matériel--car grâce à Dieu..., et grâce à la protection et au bonheur de nos puissants et saints empereurs et de mon zèle extraordinaire je n'avais besoin de rien...."[31] Simple rhétorique d'un fier et rude soldat, qui tient à démontrer qu'il ne doit rien à personne, qu'il a payé avec son propre sang pour tout ce qu'il détient? C'est possible, mais ce n'est pas suffisant. En 1083, nous sommes encore au début du système de la *pronoia*, de l'échange de terres contre service militaire. Mais Pakourianos accuse déjà une idée très développée du lien étroit entre service militaire et donation de biens fonciers--même s'il s'agit ici de biens en pleine propriété plutôt qu'à titre viager. Je suis persuadée que cette perception est particulière à des gens de provenance étrangère qui dépendaient absolument de la volonté impériale et réclamaient la récompense de leurs services.[32] Et je trouve là une explication, et pas la plus faible, de l'extension de la *pronoia* sous les Comnène. Si cela est vrai, les droits des étrangers de la classe militaire auraient eu une influence profonde sur la société

---

[30] *Typikon*, pp. 33-35.
[31] *Typikon*, pp. 40-41. Il a aussi reçu des vêtements précieux et impériaux en récompense, sans doute symbolique, de sa victoire contre les Petchenegues et après sa libération des mains des Coumans; donation symbolique--voir le fait qu'une partie des vêtements avaient été portés par l'empereur lui même--mais à laquelle il tenait beaucoup: *Ibid.*, p. 43.
[32] Il est vrai que, dans la même époque, les empereurs donnent à des soldats purement Byzantins des terres en récompense de leur service militaire: voir, à titre d'exemple, les chrysobulles d'Alexis Ier en faveur de Léon Képhalas: P. Lemerle, A. Guillou, N. Svoronos, D. Papachryssanthou, *Actes de Lavra*, I (Paris, 1970), no. 44 (1082) et 48 (1086). Il me semble, tout de même, que la conscience de ce lien entre donations de terre et service est plus aigüe parmi les étrangers, dont la dépendance de la faveur impériale était plus grande.

byzantine. Est-ce nécessaire de rappeler ici le témoignage plus tardif de Choniatès sur l'asservissement des Romains à des maîtres (c'est à dire, des propriétaires fonciers) étrangers?

Si Pakourianos se faisait une idée particulière (et pesante) du rapport entre service et droit de propriété, il reste que, comme nous l'avons déjà constaté, les droits que lui accordait le pouvoir impérial étaient ceux qu'il accordait à tous les Byzantins, exception faite des droits (par exemple, l'*exkousseia*) qui étaient des privilèges de rang; mais là aussi, il n'y a pas de distinction entre Byzantins et étrangers, sauf, peut-être, en ce qui concerne l'étendue de ces droits. Donc, nous nous trouvons devant des mécanismes d'assimilation. C'est dire que Grégoire Pakourianos, caucasien d'origine, avait les droits d'un byzantin, même s'il leur donnait un contenu particulier. Est-ce qu'il avait aussi des droits qui, à ses yeux et aussi aux yeux du pouvoir central était spécifiques à ses origines? Le *Typikon* n'en révèle qu'un seul. Grégoire Pakourianos a obtenu, par chrysobulle impérial, "la faculté de transmettre mes biens à qui je veux de mes parents et de mes gens, même s'ils sont de la religion des Arméniens."³³ Or il s'agit là d'une exception à la règle, encore invoquée au XIe siècle, qui dit que les hérétiques (comme les Arméniens anti-chalcédoniens) n'avaient pas le droit de transmettre leurs biens même à leurs propres enfants. Il s'agit sans aucun doute d'un privilège accordé à Pakourianos à cause de ses origines qui faisaient que son entourage était en partie composé d'Arméniens "hérétiques."³⁴

Pour ce qui concerne le thème de l'étranger à Byzance, Grégoire Pakourianos est un cas limite. Il était, après tout, sujet de l'Empire, et chrétien orthodoxe. Est-ce qu'on peut vraiment le considérer comme étranger? Je crois, en effet, qu'il fait partie d'un groupe intéressant, de gens qui fonctionnaient et qui était considérés en partie Byzantins et en partie étrangers. Pour la preuve, il faut chercher en dehors du *Typikon* et en dehors des rapports avec l'empereur et l'état. Pakourianos est loin d'être le seul représentant d'un groupe étranger qui a émigré à Byzance et s'y est installé. Au contraire, comme il est bien connu, depuis le règne de Basille Ier et pendant

³³ *Typikon*, pp. 128-129.
³⁴ Voir la décision synodale du Patriarche Alexis Stoudite: G. Ficker, "Erlasse des Patriarchen von Konstantinopel Alexios Studites," *Festschrift der Universität Kiel zur Feier des Geburtstages des Kaiser und Königs Wilhelm II* (Kiel, 1911), no. 5.

tout le dixième siècle il y a une immigration considérable de
militaires géorgiens et arméniens qui ont fait fortune à Byzance tels,
par exemple, le fondateur et les premiers higoumènes du monastère
d'Iviron. Quelques documents du XIe siècle permettent de croire
que certains d'entre eux gardaient, en quelque forme, le statut d'é-
tranger. La compilation des décisions du juge Eustathe Rhômaios, la
Peira, contient le cas du fils du patrice David l'Ibère, c'est à dire, le
Géorgien.[35] David avait rédigé un testament selon lequel, si son fils
mourait sans enfants et intestat, ses biens iraient aux oncles du jeune homme, c'est à dire, aux frères de David. Le fils étant mort à
l'âge de 20 ans, quelqu'un, vraisemblablement sa mère, a intenté un
procès. Le *vestes*, Eustathe Rhômaios, a décidé que la veuve de
David avait droit au tiers de ses biens, et le reste irait à ses beaux-
frères. Dans son argumentation, Eustathe a dit que le fils aurait eu la
possibilité de faire disposition testamentaire sur la totalité des biens:
mais, "puisque le fils était ethnikos, ceci a été reglé par dispense"
(διὰ δὲ τὸ εἶναι τὸν υἱὸν ἐθνικόν, τοῦτο ᾠκονόμηται). Joëlle
Beaucamp, qui a commenté ce cas, observe, à juste titre, que David
l'Ibère avait cherché à garder ses biens dans sa propre famille, et en
empêcher le passage à une autre famille par l'intermédiaire d'une
femme. Elle note aussi que normalement le patrimoine de David aurait passé à sa femme, et que la dispense a été accordée parce que le
fils était étranger: "ce qui signifie qu'un Byzantin n'aurait pas été
dispensé de la loi."[36] Puisque je suis tout à fait ignorante des
coutumes de succession géorgiennes, il ne m'est pas possible
d'interpréter les dispositions testamentaires de David, de proposer,
par exemple, qu'elles reflètent des structures de parenté où le
patrimoine est réparti parmi la descendance mâle d'un ancêtre.[37]
D'ailleurs, d'autres textes de la même époque iraient contre une
telle interprétation. Grégoire Pakourianos lui-même nous dit que sa
propre mère avait dépensé tous les biens de la famille en faveur de
ses filles, qui ont été richement dotées, à l'exclusion de Grégoire et
son frère: "Notre père, mort jadis prématurément, nous laissa tout
petits et tout jeunes. Et toute sa fortune, notre mère, par un
comportement bien féminin, la donna en dot pour les besoins de ses

---

[35] *Peira* 54.6.
[36] J. Beaucamp, "Au XIe siècle, Byzance: Le jeu des normes et comportements,"
in C. Piault, ed., *Familles et biens en Grèce et à Chypre* (Paris, 1985), p. 203.
[37] Cf. J.-P. Mahé, "Structures sociales et vocabulaire de la parenté et de la col-
lectivité en arménien contemporain," *REArm*, 18 (1984), pp. 327-345.

filles, nos soeurs, et nous laissa sans ressources et les mains vides de tout héritage paternel ou maternel. Nos soeurs, avec leur dot, sont allées se marier en diverses contrées. Moi j'ai longtemps erré en Arménie, en Géorgie, en Syrie, puis en Romanie, pour gagner ma vie."[38] Cela aussi, s'il est vrai, est contre les lois byzantines, mais dans un sens contraire à celui décrit dans la *Peira*.

En tout cas, ce qui nous intéresse ici n'est pas de dégager le système successoral géorgien à travers des textes byzantins, mais plutôt le fait que Eustathe Rhômaios qualifie le fils d'un patrice d'origine Ibérienne en *éthnikos*, c'est à dire, étranger, homme appartenant à une autre éthnie, même s'il était, visiblement, sujet byzantin, comme l'était aussi sans doute son père. Il est aussi important de noter, que dans ce cas, Eustathe a reconnu, d'une certaine façon, les coutumes propres aux étrangers: si le droit byzantin demandait un certain comportement, Eustathe était tout de même conscient qu'il y avait d'autres coutumes (ou même un autre droit?), auxquels il attribuait une certaine légitimité. Donc, en pleine Constantinople, un juge averti reconnaissait des droits propres aux étrangers. Malheureusement, il n'est pas possible de savoir s'il s'agit là d'une exception ou non. En fait, une autre décision du même juge va tout à fait en sens contraire. Il s'agit du passage 14.16 de la *Peira*. Un autre patrice, qui n'est pas nommé, a rédigé un testament par lequel il a légué tous ses biens à sa deuxième femme. Sa fille du premier lit a reçu "beaucoup moins de sa belle-mère." Eustathe a invalidé le testament, parce que "le testateur, quoique barbare, est venu à l'empire romain, et a été honoré par un grand office, et a reçu beaucoup de donations, et donc il est nécessaire qu'il suive les lois romaines et qu'il ne fasse pas testament dans la manière des éthnikoi (des étrangers). Et si lui-même ne connaissait pas les lois avec exactitude, il y avait cependant des gens à qui il aurait fallu s'adresser pour qu'ils lui l'apprennent." Donc, selon cette décision, la condition d'étranger ne dispense pas de l'obligation de connaître les lois actuelles, et on ne reconnaît pas de droit propre aux étrangers. Tout de même, il est évident que des gens d'origine étrangère, installés à Constantinople, se reconnaissaient à eux mêmes le droit de préserver leurs propres coutumes ou leurs propres lois, au moins en ce qui concerne la gestion des biens de famille. On peut aussi sup-

---

[38] J'utilise ici une combinaison des traductions de Lemerle (*Cinq études*, p. 147) et de Gautier (*Typikon*, p. 92).

poser que l'état byzantin ne s'en mêlait pas, sauf si quelqu'un contestait les dispositions faites par des étrangers. Même en cas de contestation, les tribunaux byzantins acceptaient, quand cela était commode, les coutumes étrangères.[39]

Il est bien probable que les gens auxquels Eustathe Rhômaios avait affaire étaient des étrangers d'immigration récente, peut-être ces Arméniens et Géorgiens arrivés ou amenés à Constantinople pendant le règne de Basile II. Au cours du XIe siècle, beaucoup d'entre eux se sont assimilés, en ce qui concerne le droit public. Le testament de Symbatios Pakourianos n'est pas facile à distinguer des testaments d'autres aristocrates byzantins.[40] Ceci ne veut pas dire qu'ils ont forcément perdu tout sens d'identification avec leur éthnie d'origine.[41] C'est surtout dans le domaine de la famille et de la vie privée qu'on constate un attachement plus ou moins fort à ses origines, et la conscience d'appartenir à un groupe particulier. Regardons, d'abord, les prénoms. Sainte Marie la Jeune était arménienne d'origine, son père étant venu à Constantinople à la fin du IXe siècle. Elle s'est mariée au *drungarios* Nicéphore, selon toute évidence d'origine grecque. Ils ont eu quatre fils, dont deux avaient des prénoms grecs et les deux autres des prénoms arméniens. Il a déjà été remarqué, par P. Peeters, que c'est comme si le couple avait décidé d'alterner les prénoms de leurs descendants.[42] À la fin du XIe siècle, Symbatios Pakourianos avait un demi-frère avec le nom byzantin de Sergios; puisque nous ne savons rien de leurs mères, ce n'est pas possible de dire quelque chose d'intelligent sur le choix des prénoms. Grégoire Pakourianos, lui, portait un nom grec de forme, mais plus courant parmi les Géorgiens et les Arméniens; son frère s'appelait Apasios, comme son parent par

---

[39] Voir les dispositions faites par Dèmètrios Chomatianos sur un cas de divorce "à l'étrangère" (ἐθνικὸν), A. Laiou, "Contribution à l'étude de l'institution familiale en Empire au XIIIe siècle," in *Gender, Society and Economic Life in Byzantium* (London: Variorum Reprints, 1992), V, pp. 315-316, et 321-322.

[40] J. Lefort, N. Oikonomidès, D. Papachryssanthou, *Actes d'Iviron*, II (Paris, 1990), no. 44; cf. no. 47, testament de sa femme, Kalè (Maria) Basilakaina.

[41] Pour d'autres exemples de ce phénomène, voir Laiou, "The Foreigner and the Stranger," pp. 94-95, et P. Gautier, *Michel Italikos, Lettres et Discours* (Paris, 1972), pp. 72 et 51-52 (sur les origines "orientales," i.e. arméniennes, du Patriarche Michel Kourkouas).

[42] P. Peeters, "Une sainte arménienne oubliée, Sainte Marie la Jeune (+902-903)," *Recherches d'histoire et de philologie orientales*, I (Bruxelles, 1951), p. 133.

alliance, Apasios, frère du toparque Achsartanès.[43] Les mariages de
ces gens étaient parfois avec des personnes d'origine grecque
(Symbatios Pakourianos, Sainte Marie la Jeune, la fille du protospathaire Etienne l'Ibère, qui a épousé le patrice Xiphias,[44] un neveu
ou petit cousin de Grégoire, qui était le gambros de Nicéphore
Comnène et destinataire de la lettre 68 de Théophylacte d'Achrida),
parfois avec leurs compatriotes: la soeur de Marie la Jeune a épousé
Vardas Vratzès, c'est à dire, l'Ibère; au moins une des soeurs de
Grégoire Pakourianos a épousé un Géorgien. Il en va de même pour
l'entourage de quelques unes de ces personnes. Symbatios
Pakourianos et sa femme avaient un entourage composé de personnes qui sont appelées leurs "gens" ou "hommes," dont le seul nom
parvenu jusqu'à nous est celui d'Apelgaripès, nom arabe bien sûr,
mais porté par une famille ibérienne, bien attestée à Byzance depuis
le Xe siècle.[45] Quant à notre Grégoire Pakourianos, il avait tout un
entourage de Géorgiens, et sans doute aussi d'Arméniens, dont nous
ne connaissons qu'un seul nom, celui d'un certain Vardanès.[46]

D'ailleurs, le *Typikon* de Grégoire Pakourianos donne une idée
assez claire de la dualité qui régissait la vie et la conscience de
quelques-uns des étrangers les plus privilégiés de Byzance.
Aristocrate byzantin, bénéficiaire de tout ce que pouvait donner l'é-
tat byzantin, serviteur loyal des empereurs, Grégoire Pakourianos
était byzantin dans sa personne publique et géorgien de conscience.
L'empire byzantin, la Romanie, est admirable: le vrai et seul empire,
l'état chrétien pour lequel on verse son sang; Constantinople est la
Nouvelle Rome, et Pakourianos se sert d'un des monastères établis
là comme modèle pour le sien.[47] Mais les Byzantins, c'est autre
chose. Il parle de trois ethnies dans son *Typikon*: les Bulgares, qu'il
appelle le "peuple turbulent" (ἀνίδρυτον ἔθνος); les Grecs, qu'il appelle "la race très orthodoxe et très pieuse des Romains" (τῷ ὀρθο-
δοξοτάτῳ καὶ ἐνθεοτάτῳ τῶν Ῥωμαίων γένει), et les Géorgiens,
"la race très illustre des Géorgiens" (τῆς τῶν Ἰβήρων παμφανεσ-
τάτης φυλῆς).[48] Les Géorgiens sont ses "gens" (ἄνθρωποι), ses

---

43 *Typikon*, pp. 37, 39.
44 K. Sathas, Μεσαιωνικὴ βιβλιοθήκη, V (Paris, 1877), p. 200.
45 J. Lefort, N. Oikonomidès, D. Papachryssanthou, H. Métrévéli, *Actes d'Ivi-ron*, I (Paris, 1985), pp. 16-17; cf. Kazhdan, *Armjane*, no. 9.6, p. 34.
46 *Typikon*, p. 37.
47 *Typikon*, p. 21.
48 *Typikon*, pp. 21, 31, 33.

clients; ils sont des gens bien disciplinés, accoutumés à la vie militaire et dure, et capables donc de suivre la discipline monastique.[49] Ils ont leurs propres habitudes en ce qui concerne la nourriture: une cuisine: "que nous apprécions depuis notre enfance et par tradition ancestrale."[50] Ce sont des gens simples, qui ont bien et loyalement servi Pakourianos ainsi que l'Empire;[51] pour Pakourianos ils éprouvent une ἔνθεος ἀγάπη. Les Grecs, d'autre part, sont envahissants, péroreurs, accapareurs (βίαιοι, περίλογοι, πλεονέκται), et c'est pour protéger ses compatriotes de la cupidité des Grecs qu'il défend absolument que des moines ou des prêtres grecs s'installent dans son monastère; seul est permis un notaire grec.[52] Il y a, donc, une dualité bien claire: l'Empire byzantin, et l'Empereur d'une part, dont Pakourianos est le serviteur fidèle; d'autre part l'ethnie géorgienne à laquelle il appartient. Domaine public, domaine privé; et la langue sert comme signe de cette dualité: Pakourianos a rédigé son *Typikon* en grec et en géorgien; seule la version grecque a-t-il considéré comme ayant autorité, et elle est la seule qu'il a signée, mais en caractères arméniens, car, paraît-il, il n'a jamais appris à écrire le grec (et le géorgien non plus).[53]

Les droits reconnus aux étrangers "internes"[54] au XIe siècle étaient donc assez clairs, surtout dans le domaine public; et dans ce domaine les droits étaient, à quelques exceptions près, et avec des nuances, les mêmes que l'on reconnaissait aux Byzantins. Il n'y a

[49] *Typikon*, pp. 21, 33.
[50] *Typikon*, pp. 22-23.
[51] *Typikon*, pp. 33, 35.
[52] *Typikon*, pp. 104-105.
[53] Jean Tornikès, qui appartenait à la même génération que le grand-père de notre Grégoire Pakourianos, était, comme lui, de l'entourage de David le Couropalate, et ensuite est entré dans le service de Basile II, a employé l'arménien dans une inscription, et a commandé la production de manuscrits en géorgien: *Actes d'Iviron*, I, pp. 8-9; Kazhdan, *Armjane*, pp. 48-49. Ce n'est pas certain qu'il pouvait écrire l'une ou l'autre de ces langues, ou le grec.
[54] Hélène Ahrweiler emploie le terme "semi-étrangers" pour désigner des groupes pareils à celui qui est en cause ici: "Citoyens et étrangers dans l'Empire romain d'Orient," *La nozione di "Romano" tra cittadinanza e Universalità, Da Roma alla Terza Roma, Documenti e Studi*, Studi II (1982), pp. 346-347. N. Oikonomidès désigne en "néobyzantins" les immigrés surtout arméniens dans les contrées orientales de l'Empire, au cours du Xe siècle: "L'organisation de la frontière orientale de Byzance au Xe-XIe siècles et le *Taktikon* de l'Escorial," *Actes du XIVe Congrès International des études byzantines*, I (Bucarest, 1974), 297 ss.

donc pas, dans ce domaine, d'écart considérable entre les prévisions de l'état byzantin et les aspirations du groupe d'étrangers que nous avons examiné. Disons-le autrement: les arrangements faits par ces étrangers selon leurs coutumes "barbares" ou étrangères ne s'écartaient pas du droit byzantin plus que ne le faisaient des arrangements faits entre des Byzantins purs et durs, par exemple, des contrats de divorce *communi consensu*, interdits par la loi mais néanmoins connus de la pratique.[55] Une preuve supplémentaire n'est peut-être pas nécessaire; il serait, cependant, utile de citer un cas intéressant, ayant affaire à un bien qui avait été donné à un certain Etienne Ivèritzès, protospathaire, par <u>pittakion</u> impérial, et confirmé par un chrysobulle de Basile II. Étienne était géorgien d'origine, soit d'immigration récente sous Basile II, soit d'une immigration plus ancienne. Le texte présente un intérêt multiple. Il suffit de dire ici que le petit fils d'Etienne, le protospathaire et vestiaritès Jean Ivèritzès, a contesté une vente faite par son grand-père en 1001, en disant, entre autres, que ce n'était pas une vente mais une hypothèque. La contestation a duré au moins vingt ans, de 1028 à 1049, mais pas une seule fois on ne parle d'actes ou de dispositions qui allaient contre les lois byzantines. Toute l'argumentation est faite selon le droit byzantin, et la seule indication, pas du tout sûre, d'ailleurs, qu'il y avait quelque chose hors de l'ordinaire est l'assertion du juge que la signature d'Etienne Ivèritzès avait une orthographie particulière--mais c'est une assertion générale, sur l'idiosyncrasie orthographique des signatures.[56]

Pour ce qui est des étrangers de passage, d'autre part, les concepts et les conditions étaient différentes. Je pense, ici, à deux groupes, les marchands italiens et les croisés. Dans les deux cas, leurs droits étaient établis et réglés par des instruments formels. Dans le cas des marchands italiens, ces instruments étaient des traités, dans celui des croisés il s'agissait d'accords ou de serments. Dans les deux cas, aussi, l'état byzantin avait l'intention d'inscrire les étrangers dans un rapport hiérarchique avec l'empereur, mais sans leur accorder les droits ou les privilèges dont jouissaient les Byzantins--ou les étrangers privilégiés. Quoique la situation fut nuancée en ce qui concerne les Vénitiens, à cause de leur apparte-

---

[55]   A.E. Laiou, *Mariage, amour et parenté à Byzance, XI-XIIIe siècles* (Paris, 1992), ch. IV.

[56]   Michel Psellos, in Sathas, Μεσαιωνικὴ Βιβλιοθήκη, p. 199.

nance historique à l'état byzantin, il est tout de même clair que ces étrangers gardaient un statut particulier, qu'il y avait, par exemple, des dispositions spéciales en ce qui concerne la compétence des tribunaux byzantins envers eux. Je rappelle ici la disposition du chrysobulle de Basile II (992), selon laquelle les marchands vénitiens seraient jugés seulement par le logothète *tou dromou*, chargé des affaires étrangères, ainsi que la Novelle perdue de Manuel Ier qui réglait les procédures judiciaires dans des cas "inter extraneos et indigenas."[57] Les droits des étrangers de passage étaient différents de ceux des sujets byzantins, soit qu'il s'agisse des privilèges soit qu'il s'agisse d'incapacités. L'état byzantin et les marchands étrangers n'ont pas réussi à se mettre d'accord pour ce qui concerne le statut de ces derniers; les marchands insistaient d'une part sur les privilèges exclusifs (privilèges commerciaux, concessions extra-territoriales) ainsi que sur les droits des sujets byzantins (le droit de résidence, par exemple), tandis que l'état byzantin, qui a commencé par des donations de privilèges essayait, sans succès, d'inscrire ces privilèges dans le cadre des droits et obligations des Byzantins. Il y a, donc, ici, un décalage entre la perception des marchands étrangers et celle des Byzantins.

Quant aux croisés, ces étrangers de passage par excellence, ils avaient, au début, une idée assez vague de leurs droits envers l'Empire byzantin, comme on peut l'apercevoir à travers les chroniques des deux premières croisades. Ils réclamaient, d'abord, des droits bien spécifiques de sauf-passage: le droit de traverser les terres byzantines sans danger, d'acheter des provisions facilement et bon marché, avec des justes mesures et poids, de changer de l'argent à des cours favorables.[58] Tout cela, l'état byzantin était prêt à le garantir, mais pas avant d'inscrire ces étrangers dans un système de rapports avec lui-même. Or pour les Byzantins, les croisés devaient être liés à l'état par le moyen de serments (première croisade), y inclus les serments incorporés dans le traité de Dévol, ou de traités

---

[57] A. Pertusi, "Venezia e Bisanzio nel secolo XI," dans *La Venezia del Mille* (Florence, 1965), pp. 127-128 et 157.31-35; cf. Laiou, "Foreigner," pp. 85, 86, 91.

[58] Raimundi de Aguilers, *Historia Francorum qui ceperunt Iherusalem, RHC* Occ., III (Paris, 1866), p. 237; Alberti Aquensis, *Historia Hierosolymitana, RHC* Occ., IV (Paris, 1879), pp. 306, 307, 311-312; *Gesta Tancredi, RHC* Occ., III, p. 707; Odo de Deuil, *De Profectione Ludovici VII in Orientem*, ed. V.G. Berry (New York, 1948), pp. 27-29.

(seconde croisade). Le sauf passage leur était garanti, mais les croisés devaient, de leur part, prêter serment de non-aggression contre l'empire,[59] et aussi de restituer à l'empereur toutes les terres qui lui avaient appartenu jadis, et que les croisés auraient arrachées des mains des Turcs.[60] C'était là, pour Alexis Ier, qui a été le premier à imposer ce lien par serment, une variante d'une politique bien byzantine qui employait les serments comme moyen d'assurer la fidélité d'une personne ou d'un groupe, et surtout de les obliger à des actes spécifiques. Ainsi, Grégoire Pakourianos, entre autres, avait prêté serment à Alexis Comnène (avant qu'il soit devenu Empereur, il est vrai) de l'aider dans sa révolte contre Botaneiatès; en échange, Alexis leur avait promis des dignités et des cadeaux.[61] C'est peut-être dans ce sens qu'Alexis a demandé aux croisés de devenir ses "gens" (ἄνθρωπον αὐτοῦ γενέσθαι), c'est à dire, ses clients, dans le même sens à peu près que Pakourianos parlait de ses "gens."[62] D'autre part, les croisés ont compris le serment qu'on leur demandait et qu'ils ont fini par prêter, comme un serment d'hommage et fidélité propre au système féodal auquel ils étaient accoutumés.[63] Cela explique le fait que les chroniqueurs de la

---

[59]   Odo de Deuil, p. 26: "*ut rex imperatori de suo regno nullam civitatem aut castrum auferret.*"

[60]   Odo de Deuil, p. 26: "*immo restituerit ei si ab aliquo quod sui iuris esset Turcos excluderet*"; Anna Comnena, X. 10, = II 91: "ὁ Γοντοφρέ...ἐπωμόσατο ὅνπερ ἀπῃτεῖτο ὅρκον, ὥστε ὁπόσας πόλεις καὶ χώρας ἢ φρούρια φθάσει κατασχεῖν ὑπὸ τὴν βασιλείαν Ῥωμαίων τὸ πρῶτον τελοῦντα, πρὸς τὸν ἐπ' αὐτῷ τούτῳ παρὰ τοῦ βασιλέως ἀποστελλόμενον ἀρχηγὸν παραδιδόναι." Geoffroi de Bouillon; cf. X. 10, XI. 3.

[61]   Anna Comnena I, pp. 67-68.

[62]   Anna Comnena, X. 8 = II 81: ils ont dû prêter le serment habituel des Latins: X.11 = II 96, X. 8 = II 81. Pour la bibliographie sur la question des rapports entre Alexis Ier et les croisés voir, en dernier lieu, J.H. Pryor, "The Oaths of the Leaders of the First Crusade to Emperor Alexius I Comnenus: fealty, homage=*pistis, douleia*," *Parergon*, n.s., II (1984), pp. 111-142 et n. 1. Pryor a sans doute raison quand il dit que pour Anne Comnène le mot "ἄνθρωπος" ne désigne pas forcément un vassal (pp. 116-118).

[63]   Albert d'Aix, pp. 307, 311: Geoffroi de Bouillon devient le vassal d'Alexis Ier: "*non solum se ei in filium sicut mos est terra, sed etiam in vassalum junctis manibus reddidit*" (sur la question de l'"adoption" des chefs de la croisade par Alexis Ier, voir F.-L. Ganshof, "Recherches sur le lien juridique qui unissait les chefs de la première croisade à l'empereur byzantin," *Mélanges offerts à M. Paul-E. Martin* [Genève, 1961], pp. 57-58); *Gesta Francorum et aliorum Hierosolymitanorum*, RHC Occ., III, p. 125: Alexis promet un fief à Bohémond; Raymond d'Aguilers, p. 238; Odo de Deuil, pp. 71, 79. Je ne peux pas suivre

première croisade sont plutôt spécifiques en ce qui concerne les promesses des croisés (et ce qu'ils représentent comme les promesses d'Alexis), tandis qu'Anne Comnène demeure vague. Après, donc, leur accord avec Alexis, les croisés croyaient qu'ils avaient tous les droits des vassaux, y inclu le droit d'aide réciproque. Selon les *Gesta Francorum* et la Chronique de Fulcher de Chartres, Alexis avait, lui aussi, prêté serment qu'il accompagnerait les croisés (mais nous savons que les empereurs byzantins ne prêtaient pas serment pour confirmer leurs accords), et qu'il leur avait promis *auxilium et consilium*.[64] Ces deux chroniqueurs avaient donc compris qu'il existait un contrat *bilatéral* féodal entre l'empereur et les croisés, ce qui, pour Byzance de cette époque, est impossible d'admettre, et que Anne Comnène n'avait pas du tout compris. C'est pourquoi les croisés ont cru pouvoir employer le droit de défiance (*diffidatio*), puisque Alexis ne leur avait pas prêté d'aide (*auxilium*) pendant le siège d'Antioche.[65] Pour l'Empereur, d'autre part, ses

Pryor, qui suggère que les croisés n'avaient pas fait hommage à Alexis. Son argumentation est forcée, puisqu'elle reste parfois sur un effort de mettre en doute toutes les sources occidentales qui parlent d'hommage, et parfois sur la proposition contestable que les seigneurs des croisés en Europe auraient été fâchés si les croisés avaient fait hommage à Alexis (e.g., pp. 114, 131). D'ailleurs, je ne suis pas du tout persuadée que le serment de fidélité qui, à l'époque carolingienne, pouvait ne pas entraîner l'hommage, gardait toujours, à la fin du 11e siècle, une existence autonome, séparable du lien vassalique, comme le propose Pryor, sans pouvoir le prouver. En fait, à la fin du 11e siècle, l'hommage était moins rigide que ne le croit Pryor, et en même temps était une conséquence presque obligatoire du serment de fidélité. Même dans le cas de l'hommage en marche, qui était en premier lieu un serment de paix et de concorde, l'élément vassalique était présent: J. F. Lemarignier, *Recherches sur l'hommage en marche et les frontières féodales* (Lille, 1945), 74ss, 82ss, pp. 122-123 (je suis reconnaissante à M. Adam Kosto qui m'a signalé cet ouvrage important). En même temps, il est sûr que les croisés n'avaient pas fait hommage lige, malgré l'argumentation de J. Ferluga, "La ligesse dans l'Empire byzantin," *ZRVI*, 7 (1961), pp. 97-123. L'analyse de F.-L. Ganshof ("Recherches sur le lien juridique") est toujours la meilleure, mais la question est à reprendre.

64 *Gesta Francorum*, p. 125: "*Imperator quoque omnibus nostris fidem et securitatem juravit etiam quia veniret nobiscum pariter cum suo exercitu per terram et per mare.*" Cf. Fulcherii Carnotensis, *Historia Hierosolymitana*, *RHC* Occ., III, p. 332: "*erat enim omnibus hoc necesse, ut sic cum imperatore amicitiam consolidarent, sine cuius auxilio et consilio nostrum iter nequirimus expedire.*" Cf. N. Svoronos, "Le serment de fidélité à l'empereur byzantin et sa signification constitutionnelle," *Revue des Études byzantines*, 9 (1951), p. 138.

65 Bolderic de Dol, *RHC* Occ., IV, pp. 72-73; Raymond d'Aguilers, p. 267, et, surtout, Albert d'Aix, p. 434: "*[ut investigarent] auxilium quod pollicitus est cur*

obligations avaient été acquittées par les grands cadeaux qu'il avait faits aux croisés. Il n'avait sûrement pas l'idée que les croisés avaient des droits envers lui, ou qu'il avait d'autres obligations envers eux.

En plus, et c'est peut-être là l'aspect le plus important de la question, les croisés s'accordaient des droits en tant que chrétiens engagés dans la guerre pour la foi chrétienne. Ces droits n'étaient pas du tout spécifiques, mais ils étaient tout de même des droits qui leur étaient très chers, et qu'ils croyaient que l'empire byzantin aurait reconnus. Or c'est exactement ces droits que les Byzantins ne comprenaient pas du tout, et c'est dans ceci que les croisés ont été déçus. Ils s'attendaient au bon et joyeux accueil, à ce que l'empereur se réjouisse quand ils ont brûlé un village byzantin hérétique (bogomile) en Macédoine,[66] qu'il aille avec eux contre les infidèles.[67] C'est à cause de ces droits vagues que la question de provisions devint si importante--pour les Byzantins c'était un problème de gestion, pour les croisés un droit incontestable. Et c'est ces droits de Chrétien que les Byzantins ne comprenaient pas.

Les croisés, donc, se reconnaissaient les droits de guerrier chrétien et, éventuellement, les droits réciproques de la vassalité, dans une forme encore inconnue à Byzance. Par conséquence, il y avait un décalage très important et qui devint grave entre l'idée de droits que se faisaient les croisés et celle de l'état byzantin. En fin de compte, les Byzantins étaient bien accoutumés aux étrangers internes tel Grégoire Pakourianos. Ils se sentaient bien à l'aise avec eux, et ils avaient développé des mécanismes pour les inscrire dans le système byzantin, même s'il restait des étrangers qui gardaient une certaine distance à l'égard la société byzantine. Par contre, les Byzantins étaient beaucoup moins à l'aise avec les étrangers de passage, dont ils ne comprenaient pas tout à fait la mentalité. On peut même dire que cette observation vaut pour nombre d'empires: a elle vaut certainement pour l'empire ottoman et pour l'empire chinois dans l'ère moderne. Le décalage entre les droits que réclamaient ces étrangers (marchands et croisés) et ceux que leur

---

in tanta necessitate exhibere neglexerit...injunctum est etiam illis ut eidem imperatori indicarent quomodo ab omni promissione et sacramento principes exercitus soluti haberentur, eo quod omnia quae promiserat auxilii ex timidorum et fugitivorum suggestione mentitus est."
[66] *Gesta Francorum*, p. 124.
[67] Odo de Deuil, pp. 68, 70.

reconnaissaient les Byzantins est une des causes importantes des malentendus qui se développèrent au cours du XIIe siècle.

III

Institutional Mechanisms
of Integration

The Byzantine state and church employed many means that tended to integrate or assimilate various ethnic groups. Christianization, the use of the Greek language, service in the army or the administration, intermarriage all played their part in this effort, and all have been studied by scholars. Less well known are the effects of two institutional mechanisms, justice and finance. This paper will seek to establish the degree to which the judicial system was used as an integrating mechanism and the degree to which deviating behavior was practiced and permitted. Similarly, fiscal measures, that is to say, taxation, can either affect people independently of ethnicity, or target specific groups by reference to their ethnic origin or religion. Given the importance of fiscality in the Byzantine Empire, the role of taxation in this respect is of particular interest. With regard to both justice and fiscality, an effort will be made to investigate, on the one hand, the degree of control that the Byzantine state considered necessary and, on the other, the reactions of the people over whom such control was exercised.

Justice

The functioning of the judicial system provides useful insights into institutional mechanisms of integration, the state's position toward the treatment of outsiders or internal groups with a certain cohesion of their own, and the response of such groups. I use the words "functioning of the judicial system" advisedly, for it is possible that theory and practice conform, and in some cases they do. But it is also possible for theory to state one position, and for practice to diverge from it—and this was also sometimes the case. I will try here to present a number of courses of action that were followed and then disengage from this information a set of general principles. I will look into the matter with two different types of groups in mind: first, the "internal foreigners," i.e., ethnic groups with certain traditions and/or legal customs of their own, and secondly, foreign merchants, who slowly acquired extraterritorial privileges, including judicial privileges, and whose position was therefore a special one; but it helps, I think, to elaborate general principles of behavior on the part both of the state and of the outside group that is in some ways becoming an inside group, while very clearly retaining its identity.[1]

Let us first look at ethnic groups resident within the empire. I start with three general statements. First, I am dealing here with ethnic groups, not with heretical groups, which were subject to the same courts as the Orthodox population, but labored under special legal incapacities. Secondly, as far as the Byzantine state was concerned, there was no formal distinction between the various ethnic groups and the generic Byzantine subject insofar as their position vis-à-vis the judicial system was concerned. There is one exception to this statement, and that is the Jews. For an undetermined period of time before the reign of Manuel I Komnenos, the Jews (of Constantinople) were subject to special jurisdiction, i.e., to that of the *strategos* of the Stenon.[2] During Manuel's reign, however, they were brought under the jurisdiction of the normal courts of the empire, as they were meant to be since late Roman times. We will return to the treatment of the Jews. With the stated exception of the Jews, then, everyone else was,

---

[1] For further documentation on what follows, see A. Laiou, "L'étranger de passage et l'étranger privilégié à Byzance, XI–XIIe siècles," in *Identité et droit de l'autre*, ed L. Mayali (Berkeley, 1994), 69–88; eadem, "The Foreigner and the Stranger in 12th Century Byzantium: Means of Propitiation and Acculturation," in *Fremde der Gesellschaft*, ed. M.-Th. Fögen (Frankfurt, 1991), 71–97; eadem, "Law, Justice and the Byzantine Historians," in *Law and Society in Byzantium, Ninth-Twelfth Centuries*, ed. A. E. Laiou and D. Simon (Washington, D.C., 1994), 151–85.

[2] G. Ralles and M. Potles, Σύνταγμα τῶν θείων καὶ ἱερῶν κανόνων, 6 vols. (Athens, 1852–59), I, 41. The *strategos* of the Stenon seems to have been responsible for the surveillance of the Black Sea, and the reference therefore must be to the Jews of Constantinople. For the *strategos tou Stenou*, see N. Oikonomidès, *Les listes de préséance byzantines des IXe et Xe siècles* (Paris, 1972), 35, and H. Ahrweiler, *Byzance et la mer; La marine de guerre, la politique et les institutions maritimes de Byzance aux VIIe–XVe siècles* (Paris, 1966), 102, 122, 403. On the Jews, see pp. 168–71 below; P. Magdalino, *The Empire of Manuel I Komnenos, 1143–1180* (New York-Cambridge, 1993), 384; A. Sharf, *Byzantine Jewry from Justinian to the Fourth Crusade* (London, 1971), 156, and D. Jacoby, "Les juifs de Byzance: Une communauté marginalisée," in Οι περιθωριακοί στό Βυζάντιο (Athens, 1993), 10–54.

in theory, subject to the same courts, whether these were clearly secular courts, such as that of Eustathios Romaios in the eleventh century, or ecclesiastical courts with civil jurisdiction, such as those of John Apokaukos and Demetrios Chomatianos in the thirteenth century. Theoretically, too, the courts were supposed to apply the same laws to everybody, heretics always excepted. Surely this in itself is a powerful mechanism of integration since the intent is to subject everyone to the same laws and the same court procedures. I should add that the Byzantine judicial system did, of course, provide for courts with specific jurisdiction over different areas or groups of people: these were people who could claim, through the *prescriptio fori,* to be judged by a court other than the court of their domicile or of the place where the crime was committed.[3] Included in this category was the clergy, as a pre-eminent example; but also, eventually, senators, members of the guilds, and soldiers. However, none of these categories of persons included ethnic groups, jurisdiction over whose members was independent of ethnic status. The second general observation is quite simply that our information about the actual functioning of the courts, and even of the principles governing jurisdiction, for the period before the eleventh century, is rather limited. Thus, we have to try to extrapolate from a small number of known cases. To my knowledge, these consist of a few cases mentioned in the *Peira,* and one case judged by Chomatianos; the remaining cases are too ambiguous to be useful in this connection.

What I think we can extrapolate is the following: The general principle that the same law is applicable to all subjects of the Byzantine Empire would not have been disputed in theory. Practice, however, seems to have been different. In practice, the Byzantine courts for which we have information confronted the question of foreign customs in matters of civil law and took a varied and flexible position toward them. The functioning of the court of Eustathios Romaios is instructive. At the end of his career, Eustathios was *droungarios tes viglas,* i.e., chief justice. His was a Constantinopolitan court, judging, certainly, according to the laws, but applying in its judgments the flexibility that judges normally have, in choosing, for example, which of the possibly pertinent laws was the most appropriate to each case. As others also have argued, reality and social and personal

---

[3] On this, see R. Macrides, "The Competent Court, " in Laiou and Simon, *Law and Society,* 117–29.

164

relations influenced the decisions of the court; and inherent in the process of flexible application of the law, was also an element of making law, albeit informally and primarily on the level of practice rather than theory.[4]

In his court, Eustathios at least twice faced cases which involved foreigners. Both cases involve matters of inheritance, which I think is an important point.[5] In one case, the ethnic origins of the man in question are unstated, but he is said to be "of barbarian origin," or *ethnikos*. In the other case, the man is clearly of Georgian origin. In both cases, the wives and offspring of the two men are involved; the ethnic origins of the wives are not stated, but it is possible that these were women of "Byzantine" origin, i.e., not of an easily identifiable ethnic group. The two cases were resolved in very different ways. In one, the court took the strict position that the ethnic origins of the man, a recent immigrant to the Byzantine Empire, did not entitle him to special treatment with regard to the laws. The fact that he held imperial office and had received imperial gifts, "makes it necessary for him to follow the laws of the Romans." Therefore, the man's testament, which had included provisions that Eustathios considered to be "according to the customs of foreigners" was invalidated. Ignorance of the laws was not accepted as an excuse, any more than were foreign origins. One would be tempted to say that this proves that all Byzantine subjects, whatever their ethnic origin, were subject not only to the same courts but also to the same laws.

Things, however, were not so clear-cut. The very same compilation of judicial decisions includes discussion of another case, in which the testator, a Georgian by origin, had made testamentary provisions that were contested by, in all probability, his widow. In this case, Eustathios accepted a modified version of the provisions of the will, which were different from what Byzantine law would have prescribed. That is to say, he tempered somewhat the provisions, to bring them closer to what would have been legal, and changed them; but he knew perfectly well that this was an exceptional situation. His statement on the topic was that he had used accommodation—*oikonomia*—because the party in question was a foreigner.

A quite different kind of accommodation was made for the monks of the monastery of Iveron: in order to protect them from injustice stemming from the fact that they spoke a different language (and, presumably, did

[4] N. Oikonomides, "The 'Peira' of Eustathios Rhomaios: An Abortive Attempt to Innovate in Byzantine Law," *Fontes Minores* 14 (1986), 170, 184–85, 191.

[5] *Peira*, 14.16 and 54.6 in Zepos, *Jus* IV, 47, 224. On what follows, see my "Etranger," 78–80.

not know Byzantine law well), it was ordered that any cases, whether civil or criminal, brought by them or against them could be adjudicated only in the court of the *katepano* or the *doux* of Thessalonike, perhaps because such a court might be more equitable, or perhaps because there were advantages in having to deal with a single court. In any case, there is no doubt that Byzantine laws would have been applicable here, but, of course, the disputes would have involved not Georgians among themselves, but Georgians and other Byzantines.[6]

Even more interesting is a case that was adjudicated by Demetrios Chomatianos in the early thirteenth century. The case is, once again, one of family law, although it is concerned with divorce rather than with inheritance. Nevertheless, we are still in the realm of family relations rather than in the realm of public law. It is a rather complex case, which I have discussed elsewhere and will not repeat in detail here.[7] At its heart is the question whether a divorce that was issued by a process unknown to Byzantine law, and on the strength of local and foreign custom, should have its validity recognized by a Byzantine court many years later (eighteen to be precise). The case had originated in a village near Prizren, and the parties involved were Slavs. Everything about the divorce is redolent of local legal custom: it was pronounced before a group of the couple's relatives and other "honorable people," who served as witnesses—although we do not know whether they signed the document or not. It was signed by the husband and by the wife's parents. Whether still following local custom, or to further validate the document, it was confirmed by the bishop of Prizren, also present at the ceremony. There is no question that according to Byzantine law this contract was invalid. What is interesting is the mechanisms that were put into effect, both when it was issued and when it was contested. At the time is was issued, as I have already suggested, there was a procedure unknown to Byzantine law but clearly current among the local population, since it is described by Chomatianos as "a local foreign custom" (ἐθνικὸν ἔθος ἐγχώριον). Its validity remained unquestioned for eighteen years. When the husband, for his own reasons, decided to try to remarry his first wife, he seems to have brought into question the validity of the original divorce, perhaps because it was not

---

[6] J. Lefort, N. Oikonomidès, and D. Papachryssanthou, *Actes d'Iviron,* 2 vols. (Paris, 1990), II, no. 41 (1079).

[7] A. Laiou, "Contribution à l'étude de l'institution familiale en Épire au XIIIe siècle," *Fontes Minores* 6 (1984), 275–323.

according to the laws—at least that is what may be implied in one of Chomatianos' statements. Chomatianos himself, as well as the Despot of Epirus, first pronounced the divorce "invalid," because it had not taken place according to the laws. However, many years later, and with at least ten children involved, applying such a decision would have been disruptive in a multiplicity of ways. Therefore, Chomatianos accepted the validity of the divorce. The signature of the local bishop was taken as already having given certain validity to this strange document. But Chomatianos also made a general statement: "sometimes it is necessary to permit even barbarian, foreign customs" (ἔθεσιν ἐθνικοῖς).

This sentence may be taken to summarize the Byzantine practice at least during this period, on the position of ethnic groups with regard to justice and also the role that law and justice played as mechanisms of integration. To be sure, theoretically all were subject to Byzantine law and to the formal courts. This was a mechanism of integration, and undoubtedly it functioned as such to a large extent. Indeed, Byzantine law played this role even in areas outside the empire: one example is the spread of the law of the *Ecloga* into Slavic countries. Another, in a somewhat more remote connection, is the advice of the patriarch Photios to Boris/Michael of Bulgaria. In his letter, the patriarch enunciated principles of justice and government that he considered to be true for the Byzantine Empire and universally: the prince should follow good laws; he should apply to himself strict laws; but to his subjects he should apply lenient laws; he should have wise judges; and he should discern the opinion of his subjects so as to govern with their consent. Nowhere is the prince told to apply different laws to different ethnicities; rather he is instructed to apply the laws justly and leniently (a contradiction) to all.[8] What is true of civil law is also true of canon law, to some extent: since the canons of the first four ecumenical synods were universally accepted by the Eastern Churches, the same basic laws applied to all Christians, whatever their doctrinal positions, and whether they lived inside or outside the empire. That having been said, it is equally certain that Byzantine law and justice did not level all foreign customs.

The few documents we possess show clearly that various ethnic groups had their own customs and continued to retain them under Byzantine rule. That the visible customs are tied to family law is not surprising, for this

[8] PG 102, cols. 672–73, 676, 677.

is a domain in which there was always a tension between the public and the private. It is probable that such customs obtained also in other areas of the law. In the eleventh century, Skylitzes reports the case of a woman who was raped by a Varangian soldier. She killed him, and his comrades gave her his property in what looks like an application of their own custom;[9] but it was not very far from what Byzantine law would have prescribed during the same period, and perhaps because of this the chronicler does not comment on it. At quite a different level, census records and legal cases in thirteenth- and fourteenth-century Macedonia show that there were different patterns of inheritance, residence, and dowry among the Slavic and Greek elements of the population of Macedonia.[10] The point is that foreign customs were allowed to exist as long as they did not pose a problem either to public order or to important individuals, and as long as they were not vigorously contested. This flexibility is a very important trait of the Byzantine judicial system; it applied not only to foreign custom but also to individual arrangements that were outside the law, but acceptable as long as they did not create trouble; many examples exist, again primarily in the domain of private and family law. The discretion of the judge was quite extensive, and if this makes for a certain arbitrariness, it also makes for flexibility.

As far as the ethnic communities were concerned, the preservation of their customs may be seen as a form of group cohesion and preservation of identity, but possibly also as a form of resistance to the equalizing tendencies of formal law. Undoubtedly it allowed the continuous cohesion of various ethnic groups at the most important level—that of private life. Obviously, it was easier for communities to retain their customs for a long time than it was for lone individuals to continue doing so. In any case, we have here a nice example of the double aspect of Byzantine institutional attitudes toward internal foreigners: there is integration at one level, but also flexibility and a certain liberality at the practical level. Whether the flexibility, which operates fairly generally—this *oikonomia* in practice—is influenced by the existence of local customs of ethnic provenance is a large and intriguing question, which I will leave open to discussion. What the

---

[9] *Ioannis Scylitzae Synopsis Historiarum,* ed. I. Thurn (Berlin-New York, 1973), 394; cf. A. Laiou, "Sex, Consent, and Coercion in Byzantium," in *Consent and Coercion to Sex and Marriage in Ancient and Medieval Societies,* ed. A. Laiou (Washington, D.C., 1993), 156 ff.

[10] See, for example, A. Laiou-Thomadakis, *Peasant Society in the Late Byzantine Empire: A Social and Demographic Study* (Princeton, 1977), 182 ff.

Byzantine state and indeed the law courts could not so easily accept were judicial decisions made by an authority that they considered illegally constituted: judgments given, for example, by conquerors, whether these were Latins or Serbs.[11]

The case of the Jews may now be seen in this light and will serve as a way of testing the limits of the role of justice as a mechanism of integration in Byzantium. Formal legislation from the time of the first Christian emperors (late fourth century) made the position of the Jews vis-à-vis the judicial system quite clear. Two legal compilations of the tenth and the thirteenth centuries, the *Synopsis Basilicorum* and the *Synopsis Minor,* respectively, state the principles which governed the status of the Jews throughout the period under discussion: The Jews should be governed by the common laws; whether plaintiffs or defendants, they are to be judged by Christian judges, unless, by common agreement, they appear before Jewish judges in matter of civil contracts. These arrangements go back to Justinianic legislation that was incorporated in the *Basilics.*[12] That legislation states that a lawsuit between Christians and Jews is to be judged by the appropriate civil courts. The exception is for private contracts or, as the law puts it, "in civili negotio" (περὶ χρημάτων), between Jews. If two Jews agree to be judged by Jews regarding such matters, then the decision of the Jewish judges will be recognized. So, financial transactions between Jews could, but did not have to be judged by Jewish judges, and presumably according to Jewish law; I suppose that Jewish laws on usury, for example, would be applicable. But in all other cases, the Jews were subject to the state's laws, including, according to the same legislation, the laws on marriage.[13] Since the legislation predates the compulsory role of a church ceremony in the marriage, this must mean that Jews were subject

---

[11] See D. Simon, "Witwe Sachlikina gegen Witwe Horaia," *Fontes Minores* 6 (1984), 325–75, and A. Laiou, "In the Medieval Balkans: Economic Pressures and Conflicts in the Fourteenth Century," *Byzantine Studies in Honor of Milton V. Anastos,* ed. S. Vryonis, Jr. (Malibu, Calif., 1985), 137–62.

[12] *Syn. Bas.* I.3; *Syn. Min.* I.14 = *Bas.* I.1.36; *Cod.* I.9.8: "Iudaei Romano communi iure viventes in his causis, quae tam ad superstitionem eorum quam ad forum et leges ac iura pertinent, adeant sollemni more iudicia omnesque Romanis legibus conferant et excipiant actiones. Si qui vero ex his communi pactione ad similitudinem arbitrorum apud Judaeos in civili dumtaxat negotio putaverint litigandum, sortiri eorum iudicium iure publico non vetentur. Eorum etiam sententias iudices exsequantur, tamquam ex sententia cognitoris arbitri fuerint attributi." (A.D. 398.)

[13] *Syn. Bas.* I.2; *Syn. Min.* I.13 = *Bas.* I.1.35; *Cod.* I.9.7: Jews may not follow their own marriage laws, nor have more than one wife at the same time. (A.D. 393.)

to the rather limited late Roman/early Christian legislation on marriage, for example, the necessity of consent and the incest prohibitions. The law, which dates from 393 A.D., mentions monogamy specifically. The provision of the *Codex,* subsequently adopted in the *Basilics,* that heretics, including Jews, could not bear witness except when the opposing party was equally heretical, is a provision that derives from the incapacities of heretics rather than those of ethnic groups; it does not appear either in the *Synopsis Basilicorum* or in the *Synopsis Minor.*

The tenor of formal legislation, then, is that Jews were subject to the normal legislation and the normal courts, except for private transactions involving Jews only; I imagine that this would include family law and family property. Andrew Sharf argues that the decisions of Jewish courts of law "in civil cases between Jews had full legal force and were to be executed by the imperial magistrates as though they were their own."[14] Despite this formal legislation, at some point the custom developed of having the Jews (presumably those of Constantinople) judged only by the *strategos* of the Stenon, an official in charge of the Straits. When this developed and why is not known; it may date back to the mid-eleventh century, when the Jewish quarters in Constantinople appear formalized,[15] but it may equally well mean simply that the Jews were heavily engaged in trade and that their affairs were primarily commercial. In that case, the date of the custom is unclear, but we might assume that the *strategos'* court judged mostly commercial affairs, or judged the Jews as merchants. In any case, the custom was, for some reason, abolished by Manuel I, who ordered that "they should be judged by all and any courts, according to the laws."[16] In terms of our topic, this simply meant that the Jews, as far as the state was concerned, were subject to the same laws and the same courts as everyone else. However, it is probable that this obtained primarily in cases where one of the parties was not Jewish. As with other ethnic groups, arrangements between Jews might still be made by custom or by a Jewish court, and they would have been accepted as valid, unless they created problems.

---

[14] Sharf, *Byzantine Jewry,* 20–21.

[15] On the Jewish quarters in Constantinople, see D. Jacoby, "Les quartiers juifs de Constantinople à l'époque byzantine," *Byzantion* 37 (1967), 167–227.

[16] Ralles-Potles, I, 41. Sharf, *Byzantine Jewry,* 156–57, interprets the measure as part of a general effort by Manuel to strengthen central authority. Magdalino, *Manuel I,* 384, takes it as "evidence of hardening attitudes," but this seems to me to be going too far. Valsamon himself, our only source for this measure, describes it only in order to show that custom which was not validated by judicial decision could be and sometimes was abrogated— i.e., that custom does not acquire the force of law automatically through the passage of time.

None of this is meant to address the broader question of the position of the Jews within the empire—their economic role, or the religious or civil incapacities they may have labored under—much less is it meant to address questions of ideology.[17] My purpose is rather limited, and my examination has been equally limited. There is, however, one point on which we might stop for a moment, since it is closely connected with justice and the courts: that is the question of an oath specific to the Jews. That there was such an oath is certain, and to be expected, since Jews were able to appear in court, whether one governed by Roman or by Jewish law;[18] that it was specific is interesting but not unique to the Jews, since all those who had special customs were required to take a special oath, according to their rite: Bas. XXII.5.5 (= D XII.2.5) requires that each person swear according to his religion. The oath of the Jews, as we have it, is an oath in the name of God, attesting that the person swearing it is not lying in his testimony. Evelyne Patlagean has already suggested that this oath is quite similar, *mutatis mutandis,* to the oath a Christian might take.[19] During the reign of Manuel I, a Jew from Attaleia who had converted to Christianity and who had a property dispute with the Jewish community there, appealed to the emperor on the matter. He sought a ruling that the Jews either give him the property in question (it seems to have been his parents' property; the Jews had accepted his taking the landed property, but disputed the mobile property), or that they swear an oath, "not as they would like, but rather the oath that I will give them in writing." The oath in question was highly insulting, and in fact the emperor rejected it in favor of the earlier form, which bore no insulting connotations. Strangely enough, this curious little episode has been seen as evidence of a hardening of anti-Jewish sentiment in the reign of Manuel I.[20] In fact, there is nothing to support such an interpretation: the new, insulting oath was requested by a converted Jew; it was at first ostensibly accepted by the Jews, but in the end they bought their way out of it; it was not even demanded for any purpose

---

[17] For a general overview of such questions, see Jacoby, "Les juifs de Byzance."

[18] E. Patlagean, "Contribution juridique à l'histoire des Juifs dans la Méditerranée médiévale: Les formules grecques de serment," *Revue des études juives,* 4th ser., 4 (1965), 137–38.

[19] Patlagean, "Contribution juridique," 147; Zepos, *Jus* I, 375.

[20] Sharf, *Byzantine Jewry,* 156–57; Magdalino, *Manuel I,* 384–85. See the somewhat different analysis by Patlagean: she considers it a popular type of oath, insulting, to be sure; she considers Manuel's treatment of the Jews to have been favorable, but also sees a medieval tendency to treat Jews and foreigners in a similar way. "Contribution juridique," 144, 146.

other than the humiliation of former co-religionists; and the emperor rejected it. The only thing this affair proves is something we already know and understand by now: That the Jews, like other ethnic groups and indeed like the majority of Byzantines, had a certain freedom of action insofar as private legal transactions were concerned; that the Jewish community had certain rights over the inheritance of Jews; and, most importantly for us, that the Jews, when taking an oath, took a specific kind of oath, were bound by it, and its effectiveness was recognized by the Byzantine state. They were, therefore, a group subject to the common laws but with specific practices and particular legal customs that were recognized by the state; the Jews were subject to their own courts in private matters. The negative perception of this same principle may also be stated (it is that of Evelyne Patlagean): that while in formal law the Jew is as much subject to the laws as anyone else, in practice the Jew does not partake of the common law. A proof is thought to lie in the magical aspects with which his oath is surrounded and in the perceived tendency of making the position of the Jew under the law comparable to that of the western foreigner, therefore, a tendency to create discriminatory procedures.[21]

This, then, brings me to the question of the foreign merchants who were established in and lived on Byzantine soil. At first glance, this might seem to be outside our topic: were not these, after all, transient groups, whose members, at least individually, were not settled permanently in Byzantium, and for whom, therefore, the problem of assimilation or separation was not posed formally, although one might still wonder what processes of assimilation went on in practice? The last part of this question, i.e., the process of assimilation that went on informally, I will leave more or less out of the discussion. It has occasionally been treated by scholars, and we all know about the Genoese of Pera who worshipped virtually indistinguishably in Greek and Latin churches, not to mention the Venetians of Crete; these Venetians, within two generations from the time of conquest, had children who learned Greek from Greek mothers and/or nursemaids, and in their middle age, made wills leaving property both to Greek and to Latin churches.[22] These processes, although connected to our general topic, are outside the concerns of my own presentation. However, the foreign merchants do form a group the investigation of which is

---

[21] Patlagean, "Contribution juridique," 155–56.
[22] On the latter, see, for example, A. Laiou, "Venetians and Byzantines: Investigation of Forms of Contact in the Fourteenth Century," *Thesaurismata* 22 (1992), 29–43.

pertinent for the following reasons to the issues discussed here. First of all, they test the limits of the system. Secondly, one of the two most important groups of western merchants in the Byzantine Empire was the Venetians, who from the beginning were in an ambivalent situation since they were still Byzantine subjects when they began to receive judicial and fiscal privileges; thus they would in any case fall within the parameters of our topic. The Venetians being by far the most privileged foreigners in the twelfth century, it is quite fair to say that the privileges of other Italian merchants were patterned on those of the Venetians, so that what happened to those former subjects of the empire eventually affected other groups of foreigners. Thirdly, it should not be forgotten that during the twelfth century a number of foreign merchants became *bourgesioi,* i.e., acquired special status, in an effort on the part of the Byzantine state to bring them under effective control.[23] And finally, it seems to me that the evolution of the position of foreigners with regard to the law marks the abandonment of certain basic principles on the part of the Byzantines— and thus is a development of particular importance for our subject.

The cornerstone of the presence of foreign merchants in the Byzantine Empire in the period after the late tenth century is privilege, which *ipso facto* made them a group that the state did not attempt to assimilate. Before the first privileges were granted to Venetians by Basil II, the status of foreign merchants in Byzantium was not very clear, but its general lines can be discerned. Their economic activities, as well as their presence, were, of course, closely regulated by the eparch of the city.[24] Those who broke the regulations, whether they were Byzantine, or foreign merchants, were punished by the officials of the eparch; if they were judged at all, they presumably were judged at the court of the eparch. The privilege given to the Venetians by Basil II in 992 describes them as foreigners (*extraneos,* as opposed to those *sub manu nostra*). The emperor gives them the right to be judged solely by the court of the *logothete* of the *dromos,* i.e., the official in charge of foreign affairs. It was undoubtedly a privilege for the Venetians to have their commercial affairs and their ships examined by the officials of only one office.[25] But it is also stressed that "if a legal dispute

[23] Kinnamos, Bonn ed. (1836), 282; P. Schreiner, "Untersuchungen zu den Niederlassungen westlicher Kaufleute im Byzantinischen Reich des 11. und 12. Jahrhunderts," *ByzF* 7 (1979), 188–89.

[24] *Das Eparchenbuch Leons des Weisen,* ed. and trans. J. Koder (Vienna, 1991), chaps. 5, 6, 9, 20.

[25] Cf. the similar privilege given to the monks of Iveron, pp. 164–65, above.

arises either between themselves or between them and others, this will be examined and judged by the *logothete* of the *dromos* himself and not by any other judge."[26] The situation bears a certain similarity to that of the Jews, although the latter had a choice of private courts for civil matters among themselves, a choice that is not stated for the Venetians. Thus, although the Venetians are, for the purposes of this chrysobull, regarded not as Byzantines but as foreigners, the jurisdiction of the state over them is complete; even in cases involving only Venetians the imperial courts are the sole competent ones; and the privilege consists exclusively of having a single court judge the cases. This is, however, a formal way of looking at things. Undoubtedly the Venetians, who came and went, who had their own notaries and soon enough their own structures of authority in the Byzantine cities, judged cases among themselves in Venetian courts, probably in Venice, possibly and unofficially in the Byzantine Empire. That is normal and uninteresting. What is more interesting is what went on in mixed cases, of Byzantines and Venetians, and here we have limited information. We do know that in commercial transactions Venetians made contracts with Greeks *in Greek*.[27] One supposes that in such cases Greek notaries were used, and if a dispute arose the matter would have been adjudicated by a Byzantine court.

The development of all this is of some considerable interest. There are, in fact, two different strands. One is the effort of Manuel I Komnenos to bring western settlers under full imperial authority: he made them *bourgesioi*, presumably under a special regime.[28] Their precise status is not easy to discern. They certainly took an oath of loyalty to the emperor, presumably a personal oath which may have been not unlike the type registered in a document published by Sathas: this *horkomotikon* registers a promise of *douleia* to the emperor and the empire "as long as I live," in word and deed.[29] The *bourgesioi* seem to have had military obligations,[30]

---

[26] Zepos, *Jus* I, 261.

[27] A. Lombardo and R. Morozzo della Rocca, *Documenti del commercio veneziano nei secoli XI-XIII* (Turin, 1940), no. 11 (1151).

[28] Kinnamos, 282; Schreiner, "Untersuchungen," 188–89. S. Borsari, "Il commercio veneziano nell Impero bizantino nel XII secolo," *RSI* 76 (1964), 997 and n. 57.

[29] K. Sathas, Μεσαιωνική Βιβλιοθήκη, 7 vols. (Athens-Venice-Paris, 1872–94; repr. Hildesheim, 1972), VI, 652–53; Kinnamos, 282.

[30] *Urkunden zur älteren Handels- und Staatsgeschichte der Republik Venedig mit besonderer Beziehungen auf Byzanz und die Levante,* ed. G. L. Tafel and G. M. Thomas, 3 vols. (Vienna, 1856–57), I, 197 (1187).

but their legal and fiscal position is not known. Whether they were judged by Byzantine judges or by some sort of other court we do not know; we may surmise that formally they would be subject to Byzantine law, but informally they would be subject to their own courts, probably back home. The case of the Pisan Signoretto, already discussed by Schreiner, gives us some clues, the primary one among them being the fact that when a Latin was made *burgensis* (as this Pisan was) the Byzantine fisc claimed the right to inherit his property if he died intestate; but that right was very powerfully disputed by the man's heirs, who in any case claimed that he *had* left a testament, and who in the end secured a favorable ruling from the emperor.[31] It is clear that there were double loyalties and double obligations, which were interpreted variously by contemporaries. This was, after all, still a fairly mobile population, with very strong ties to the homeland, suggestive more of a dual citizenship than of anything else. If my interpretation of the status of *bourgesioi* is correct, we are dealing with an effort by the Byzantine state to bring the resident foreign western merchants under the same kind of arrangement that obtained with internal foreigners: make them subject to Byzantine jurisdiction and fiscal obligations (perhaps), even though under a special regime; that is, use fiscality, justice, and oaths to integrate these people into the normal functioning of the Byzantine state. Thus, Manuel I seems to have issued a Novel regulating the maximum duration of suits (three years for civil suits), and this governed also the duration of Venetian suits, at least until 1199.[32]

The position of the Venetians vis-à-vis the courts prior to 1198 and after 992 may be pieced together from the treaties of 1169 and 1170 between Genoa and the Byzantine Empire, and the chrysobull of 1198 for Venice.[33] The two treaties (in the form of chrysobulls) extend to the Genoese certain judicial arrangements which, according to these documents, were already operative for Venetians and other Latins; it is for this reason that the texts can be used to reconstruct the Venetian privileges. According to the chrysobulls of 1169 and 1170, referring now to the Genoese,

---

[31] G. Müller, *Documenti sulle relazioni delle città Toscane coll'oriente cristiano e coi Turchi* (Florence, 1879), no. 10, pp. 11–13.

[32] Zepos, *Jus* I, 479; R. Macrides, "Justice under Manuel I Komnenos: Four Novels on Court Business and Murder," *Fontes Minores* 6 (1984), 128–30; Laiou, "Foreigner," 86.

[33] Chrysobull of 1198: Zepos, *Jus* I, 469 ff. Treaty of 1169 (chrysobull of Manuel I): Zepos, *Jus* I, 417 ff. (in Latin); treaty of 1170 (chrysobull of Manuel I): F. Miklosich and J. Müller, *Acta et diplomata graeca medii aevi*, III (Vienna, 1865), 35 ff. (in Greek).

but encompassing the Venetians, the competent courts are still the Byzantine ones, on all matters pertaining to injuries caused by the Genoese to Greeks or others, "as is the case with the Venetians and other Latins": "de offensionibus . . . quas fortasse fecerint in terris domini Imperatoris, grecis vel aliis gentibus que non sint Januenses, debent judicari in curia domini Imperatoris, sicut Venetici et cetere Latine gentes." That is to say, the general Byzantine principle of the competent court being the court that had jurisdiction over the defendant (i.e., the court within whose geographical limits the defendant lived) was not quite followed, unless we imagine all the Latins to have been *bourgesioi.* On the other hand, the other principle is preserved, i.e., that the competent court is the one in whose jurisdiction the crime was committed.[34] In any case, it is further stated that if the plaintiff is Genoese and the defendant either Greek or foreign (non-Genoese), the case will be heard by the imperial court: "Sed et statim quod reclamationem fecerint contra aliquem Grecum vel aliam gentem coram Imperatore, invenient justiciam in curia Imperii sui." In the treaty of 1170, the phrase reads: "καὶ ὁπηνίκα ἐγκαλοῦσι κατά τινος 'Ρωμαίου ἢ ἀλλογενοῦς ἐνώπιον τῆς βασιλείας μου, ἵνα εὑρίσκωσι δίκαιον ἐν τῇ αὐλῇ αὐτῆς." Both chrysobulls state that if the Genoese harm anyone in any way, i.e., if they are the defendants, they must be judged, not by other foreigners (παρά τινος ἑτέρου ἀλλογενοῦς), but by the imperial *curia,* presided over by one of the relatives or men (ἀνθρώπων, hominibus) of the emperor. This is quite an extraordinary provision: insofar as mixed cases are concerned, the Genoese are subject to the imperial judicial system but not—as defendants—to the regular courts; rather, to a court of the emperor, specially constituted. This may be a further elaboration of the system of competent courts, which appears in the *Ecloga Basilicorum* of 1142, under which the emperor was the sole competent judge of senators; if so, this emphasizes the privileged position of the Italian merchants.

There is, then, a double position before the Byzantine legal system: In cases touching only themselves, the foreign merchants in the late twelfth century (prior to 1198) were, perhaps, subject to their own courts; in mixed cases, they were subject to Byzantine courts, but under a special régime, and perhaps under a very broad interpretation of the Byzantine laws.

---

[34] Note that Constantinople was perceived, in the *Ecloga Basilicorum,* as the common country of all who find themselves there, and thus, for judicial purposes, the common residence of all those who find themselves in Constantinople, with the exception of ambassadors: Macrides, "The Competent Court," 117–29, esp. 121.

176

One strand of the Byzantine reaction to the foreign merchants, therefore, was an effort to bring them under the system of imperial justice. This
effort was not destined to succeed. Instead, what eventually developed was
an extraterritoriality that created quite a new set of rules for privileged
western merchants and completely undercut the authority of the Byzantine
state. This was a creation of the Palaiologan period, but the bases were set
in the late twelfth century. A few years before the fall of Constantinople
in 1204, the principle that foreign merchants were to be judged by Byzantine courts—at least in all mixed cases—came to an end forever. This
is the tenor of the chrysobull of 1198, issued by Alexios III Angelos in favor
of the Venetians. It was a broad charter, giving the Venetians access to all
Byzantine markets and lifting all dues ("not even an obol shall be paid")
from all of their transactions. It also allowed, for the first time in a formal
way, Venetian judges to judge mixed civil cases if the defendant was
Venetian; if the defendant was Greek, the case would be judged by the
logothete of the *dromos*. This may well follow the Byzantine principle that
the competent court is that of the defendant; but it is the first time that the
state formally acknowledges that people resident on its soil are answerable
to an alien court, even though the other party is a Byzantine subject. This
is an alienation of jurisdiction; the foreigner acquires not special privileges
before the judicial system, which he more or less already had, but rights
that take him outside the jurisdiction of Byzantine courts. About the only
thing that survives from the Byzantine system under this charter is the
reaffirmation that justice must be swift, as legislated by Manuel I. For the
rest, if between 992 and 1198 the system of justice served as a means—not
a very successful one—of integrating the foreign, western merchants into
the Byzantine system, with the chrysobull of 1198 this effort collapsed, and
the Byzantine state relinquished any such claims and any such efforts. Even
in criminal cases (except for homicide) this chrysobull states that, if the
Greek plaintiff is not noble (si vero Grecus fuerit ydiota quidem, et non ex
senatus consulto aut de clarioribus hominibus curie Imperii mei consis-
tens), the case will be judged by the Venetian legate. Only if the Greek
plaintiff is a noble will the case be judged before the imperial court, sitting
at Blachernae.[35]

The chrysobull of 1198 has been too closely related to the case of the
Jews mentioned above, primarily because of the fact that the terminology
regarding the oaths taken by the various parties is similar.[36] But in fact the

---

[35] Zepos, *Jus* I, 477 ff. These judicial matters were very important as far as the
Venetian demands were concerned.

[36] Ibid., 478; Patlagean, "Contribution Juridique," 145–47.

two situations had very little in common. In the case of the Jews, whatever local arrangements might have been in place, the state reaffirmed its integrationist policy; with the foreign merchants, it gave it up.

These attitudes are at the basis of the extraterritorial concessions that mark the Palaiologan period, and which have been discussed by a number of scholars, although not necessarily in the light in which we are looking at them here.[37] Without going into any of the details, there are two points I wish to stress. First, our question can no longer be whether the western merchants were subject to Byzantine jurisdiction, but rather, whether the Byzantines (and foreigners who were neither Genoese nor Venetians) were always subject to Byzantine courts or whether they sometimes had to appear before those of the foreign merchant-colonists. Secondly, the answer is clear, and is the result of a fairly rapid development. If in 1261 Michael VIII retained his jurisdiction over such cases, within less than forty years this was becoming modified, and by 1317 the right of Byzantine Greeks to be judged exclusively by Byzantine officials was in dispute; by 1341, the Greeks of Pera had come under the jurisdiction of Genoese courts. But this is simply the substitution of political and therefore judicial authority. The case of judicial relations between Venetians and Byzantines is less extreme, since the Byzantine state did retain jurisdiction over its subjects to some extent. Here too, however, the rights of the state came in dispute, partly because of the intricacies of mixed cases: the Venetians complained that when the court was Greek (if the defendant was Greek), they understood little of what went on, while a Greek who brought action before the *bailo* against a Venetian and lost could appeal to a Byzantine court. Time and again, Byzantine emperors would complain, from one negotiation to another, that they had lost control over their own subjects because of the fiscal and judicial privileges of the Venetians.[38]

My contention is that the Byzantine state was interested in important matters—those that make a state run: the army, the collection of taxes and revenues, and a lawful state, i.e., a state all of whose inhabitants would be subject to the same basic body of law, whatever that might be at any given

---

[37] See, in the last instance, M. Balard, "L'organisation des colonies étrangères dans l'empire byzantin (XIIᵉ-XVᵉ siècle)," in *Hommes et richesses dans l'Empire byzantin, II: VIIIᵉ-XVᵉ siècle,* ed. V. Kravari, J. Lefort, and C. Morrisson (Paris, 1991), 267 ff; cf. A. Laiou, *Constantinople and the Latins: The Foreign Policy of Andronicus II, 1282-1328* (Cambridge, Mass., 1972), 263 ff; M. Balard, *La Romanie génoise (XIIᵉ-début du XVᵉ siècle),* 2 vols. (Rome-Genoa, 1978), I, 327 ff.

[38] Ch. Maltezou, Ὁ θεσμὸς τοῦ ἐν Κωνσταντινουπόλει Βενετοῦ Βαΐλου (1268-1453) (Athens, 1970), 70-77; Laiou, *Andronicus II,* 277, 308 ff.

moment, and subject to identical types of jurisdictions. Within that frame-work, a great deal of latitude was expected and offered. Evidently, there is a tension here, between an integrating state on the one hand, and on the other, particular groups that want to retain their customs either because these customs are tied to a religion; or because they are of long standing and affect family life, which is the hardest area for the state to penetrate; or because they belong to a different type-set of jurisdictions that the foreign group is used to (as with the foreign merchants). The way out of this tension was insistence on basic principles and accommodation in particulars. It was when the basic principles could no longer be held that this edifice collapsed, at least in the realm of justice. Undoubtedly, it collapsed for some groups, while for others it continued to function. In the case of the foreign merchants, the collapse is evident. In the case of various internal ethnic groups there is no discernible change. As far as the state was concerned, the loss of jurisdiction over an important category—the foreign merchants—was an institutional defeat; and it went hand in hand with the declining authority of the state over its own subjects in terms both of justice and of finance, with the growth of private jurisdictions and financial immunities.

Finance

Let us, now, turn briefly to finance. The question is whether the fiscal system was an equalizing mechanism, that is, whether it functioned inde-pendently of ethnicity and therefore was a mechanism of integration. I think that on the whole it did; the land tax was one and the same whether the peasant had a Greek name or a Slavic name; no special tax provisions were made because of ethnicity, and no statistical analysis has suggested that ethnicity played a role in the calculation of the land tax or the house-hold tax, which were, after all, at the basis of the Byzantine fiscal system. Even in the case of heretics, where the normal legal provisions governing dowries and inheritance were suspended, the suspension of the rules speci-fically excluded heretical peasants, who had to cultivate their lands and had to pay taxes; their tenures were subject to the normal Byzantine rules of inheritance.[39] This general statement is not sufficient, however. It is entirely possible that it is meaningless. That is to say, the fact that people

---

[39] *Bas.* I.1.52 = Novel 144 of Justinian on the Samaritans.

paid taxes according to a rate that had little to do with ethnicity may be of neutral value for our topic, fiscality not functioning either as an integrating mechanism or as a significant indicator of ethnicity.

That, however, does not close the question. There are still certain things to say, since it is quite clear that some groups were under a particular fiscal regime, while others were unexpectedly not. Thus the Jews were, as far as the best students of the subject can see, not subject to a Jewish tax per se, i.e., a tax imposed on communities or individuals because they were Jewish. They might pay taxes to a fiscal institution (a monastery, for example) because they lived in the vicinity, or because they were peasants attached to it, or for whatever reason, but then so did Christians. Indeed, I can only repeat here the concluding statement of Steven Bowman on this perplexing question: "because of the insufficient material at our disposal, more may not be said than that Jews, during the late Byzantine period, appear not to have occupied a unique fiscal position within the empire."[40] That summarizes also the situation for the entire period after the sixth century, i.e., after the last attestation of the *aurum coronarium* in relation to the Jews—despite sporadic appearances of taxes that may have been particular to the Jews.[41]

At the other end of the spectrum we have the privileged groups, for example, the foreign merchants, whose distinguishing trait was, from the beginning, a privileged tax status. In their case there is no question but that the fiscal arrangements created a group: the group of merchants, trading in the empire, who paid no duties and had certain judicial privileges as well. In this case, fiscality acts as a mechanism of separating the western merchants from the Byzantine population, which is what the emperors wanted, since they had no intention of freeing all of their subjects from commercial taxes. The group not only becomes identified by its privileges but becomes enlarged through them, i.e., there are people who wish to belong formally to this group, although they have no inherent right to do so, in order to benefit from the privileges. Whereas this may be seen as a way through which the group retains its cohesion, the point is almost not worth making: for by its very act, the state has created practices which tend to negate the state itself—as indeed they did in the end.

---

[40] S. B. Bowman, *The Jews of Byzantium, 1204-1453* (University, Ala., 1985), 41 ff, 48; Sharf, *Byzantine Jewry,* 191 ff.

[41] Sharf, *Byzantine Jewry,* 189-200.

180

There were, however, other groups with a particular fiscality, and they are of greater interest. These are groups which retained an identity of their own, and had their own leaders and perhaps their own language. They paid to the Byzantine Empire a *pakton,* a tax, as a result of having made peace with the Byzantine state and having acknowledged its overlordship. Such were the Milingoi and Ezeritai in the Peloponnese after they had been subdued in the ninth century; the same is true of the inhabitants of Maina who "seeing that they are perfectly submissive and accept a head man from the military governor, and . . . obey the commands of the military governor, they have paid from very ancient times a tribute of 400 nomismata."[42] The same groups, *grosso modo,* received immunities and privileges at a much later period, under Michael VIII. It is not too much to suggest that they had retained, along with their ethnic identity, a particular fiscal and perhaps administrative régime in the intervening centuries. The Bulgarians of Thrace in the thirteenth and fourteenth centuries, the Gypsies of the Peloponnese in the fourteenth century, and perhaps the Albanians and the Vlachs, according to Hélène Ahrweiler's suggestion, would have had a similar situation, where the ethnic group had its own chief, and thus an administrative structure and perhaps a particular fiscal arrangement.[43] Such arrangements undoubtedly had a specific purpose and a probably unintended result: the purpose was to keep the foreign group friendly and subject to the state; the result was certainly to reinforce the solidarity of the group that was thus singled out.

Justice and fiscality worked in ways that seem different yet converge at a certain point. As far as formal justice was concerned, everyone was subject to the same laws, except for the western merchants after 1198; informally, however, we have seen particular laws and even particular and quite spontaneous types of courts in operation, all with the tolerance of the representatives of the state and the church. With fiscality, the situation differed in that the state itself accepted the particular tax status of groups; but that tax was virtually a tribute, and must be seen as such. Such a tax status did not play an integrationist role—quite the opposite—but the Byzantine state held on to it, partly perhaps because it was proof of the subservience of the people in question, and partly because the state could

---

[42] Constantine Porphyrogenitus, *De administrando imperio,* ed. G. Moravcsik and trans. R. J. H. Jenkins, 2 vols., CFHB 1 (Washington, D.C., 1967), I, chap. 50.

[43] H. Ahrweiler, "Le sébaste, chef des groupes ethniques," in eadem, *Etudes sur les structures administratives et sociales de Byzance* (London, 1971), art. xiv.

not do otherwise. By taking this practical measure, the state did not jeopardize its theoretical sovereignty over these people; but what it did do was to recognize their particularity and thereby foster it.

Thus both justice and fiscality played roles that are not crystal clear. They were, however, in their untidiness, which much of the time was deliberate, highly effective. After all, we have few rebellions because of systems of justice (except perhaps in Chios under the Genoese in 1348), and rather few rebellions of ethnic groups because of fiscality.[44] The system of accommodation worked quite well while there was a strong state to support it; but when the state began to give up the very essence of its strength—to outsiders, to peoples from various ethnic groups and to the Byzantine aristocracy—a new and different order of things was created.

[44] As an exception, we may mention the rebellion of the relatively newly incorporated Bulgarian lands in the 1030s, when their taxes were commuted from kind (a privilege granted them by Basil II) to cash (as was normal in the rest of the empire).

IV

BYZANTIUM AND THE CRUSADES IN THE TWELFTH CENTURY: WHY WAS THE FOURTH CRUSADE LATE IN COMING?

Relations between the Byzantine Empire and Western Europe in the twelfth century were close, variegated, and took place on many fronts and in many configurations. Never since the sixth century were Eastern and Western Europe closer than in this period. All three Komnenian emperors, but especially Alexios I and Manuel I, had complex diplomatic arrangements with European powers, both in Western Europe itself and, especially starting with the reign of John Komnenos, with the Latin states established in the East, namely, Antioch and the Kingdom of Jerusalem.[1] They had interests in Western Europe, which brought Manuel to an ill-fated campaign in Italy. There were close cultural connections and marriage alliances. There were continuing efforts to heal the schism between the churches, and even ideas, held by John II and Manuel I Komnenos, to revive Byzantine imperial authority in the West.[2] There were developing commercial ties with Venice, Genoa, and Pisa, although that was a mixed blessing.

Why, then, the provocative title of this paper, which seems to suggest that the Fourth Crusade was inevitable and poses the question, why was it late in coming? I do not believe, in fact, that the Fourth Crusade was inevitable. But neither was it a surprising event with no significant precedents. Every one of the major crusades that preceded it was attended by plans to conquer the Byzantine Empire. The plans were never made at the outset; rather, they were afterthoughts. Some were more threatening than others. Their tenor, the reasons why they were not put into effect, and the nature of the Byzantine response form the topic of this paper.

Let us establish the parameters of the inquiry. It is obvious that the passage of large and unruly armies through the territory of any state, especially a preindustrial one, created practical problems that could and did assume a threatening aspect: primarily, problems of provisioning and currency exchange.[3] These led to hostilities, indeed even to exasperated calls for the capture of Constantinople. They are what I call "opportunistic" hostilities and calls for conquest. We acknowledge their presence and will note their significance at the end. As for real plans for the conquest of the Byzantine Empire, we can say that there was not a linear or cumulative progress that would make each successive plan more dangerous than the last. On the contrary, the first such effort was by far the most threatening in real terms, and it also colored the Byzantine response to later crusades.

---

1. For Manuel's reign see MAGDALINO, P., *The Empire of Manuel I Komnenos, 1143-1180*, Cambridge, 1993.

2. LAIOU, A. E., Οἱ δύο ἐξουσίες: ἡ διαμάχη μεταξὺ Παπῶν καὶ Αὐτοκρατόρων καὶ οἱ θεωρίες τῶν Βυζαντινῶν, *Thesaurismata* 15, 1978, pp. 106-119.

3. I have treated the issues in LAIOU, A. E., Byzantine Trade with Christians and Muslims and the Crusades, in LAIOU, A. E., and MOTTAHEDEH, R. P., eds., *The Crusades from the Perspective of Byzantium and the Muslim World*, Washington, D. C., 2001, pp. 157-196.

The Third Wave of the First Crusade

The First Crusade had been preached in part as an effort to bring help to the Byzantines, at war against the Seljuk Turks in Asia Minor. The last stage of the crusade, however, consisted of an attack on the Byzantine Empire by Bohemond of Taranto.[4] It was planned from early 1105 through 1107, and carried out from October 1107 to September 1108. This first planned "diversion" of the crusade was, to my mind, the most dangerous for the Byzantine Empire. These were still the early days of the crusading movement, when enthusiasm was at its highest. Bohemond commanded extraordinary fame and prestige in the West. He was a handsome, compelling, even seductive man, and a superb tactician.[5] When he left Antioch, in the autumn of 1104, he had with him Daimbert of Pisa, formerly patriarch of Jerusalem, who had his own problems to bring to the pope but who also, according to one source at least, went with Bohemond to lend him support.[6] Besides, Bohemond had acquired papal blessing. A papal legate, Bruno of Segni, who had preached the crusade after the Council of Clermont, and who was a great believer in the use of violence and war to protect the rights of the church even against Christians, was with him during his recruiting trip to Italy and France.[7] Pope Paschal II had already given signs of using crusading rhetoric and ideas in warfare between Christians in Western Europe. Paschal certainly approved of the expedition, although it has been argued that at first he thought the goal was Jerusalem.[8] He gave Bohemond the *vexillum Sancti Petri*, the banner of St. Peter, which signaled that one was fighting a war with papal approval.[9] In a replay of Robert Guiscard's attack, Bohemond had with him a pretender to the Byzantine throne, whom he used as a recruiting device.[10] Furthermore, in a stunning diplomatic coup, he had married Constance, daughter of Louis VI, king of France, and could thus count on French support. The wedding was celebrated with great pomp at Chartres, and the occasion gave Bohemond a pulpit from which to preach the crusade.[11] His triumphal tour of deep crusading country in France must have brought him many eager recruits. Estimates of the

---

4. The basic works are still YEWDALE, R. B., *Bohemond I, Prince of Antioch*, Princeton, N. J., 1924, and ROWE, J. G., Paschal II, Bohemund of Antioch and the Byzantine Empire, *Bulletin of the John Rylands Library* 49, 1966-1967, pp. 165-203. KINDLIMANN, S., *Die Eroberung von Konstantinopel als politische Forderung des Westens im Hochmittelalter*, Zurich, 1969, remains useful because of the source material it assembles, although it no longer holds as an overall interpretation.

5. See, for example, SUGER, *Vie de Louis VI le Gros*, ed. and trans. WAQUET, H., Paris, 1929, p. 44, who mentions Bohemond's renown: "illustris Antiochenus vir Boamundus; virum inter orientales egregium et famosum."

6. BARTOLPH DE NANGIS, *Gesta Francorum expugnantium Ierusalem*, RHC, *Occ*, III, chap. 65, p. 538 (hereafter BARTOLPH DE NANGIS). This author may have received his information from Bohemond's veterans, according to ROWE, Paschal II.

7. For Bruno of Segni's description as "milites Christi" of the soldiers of Pope Leo IX against the Normans of southern Italy in 1053, see HOUSLEY, N., Crusades against Christians: Their Origins and Early Development, c. 1000-1216, in EDBURY, P. W., ed., *Crusade and Settlement*, Cardiff, 1985, p. 18.

8. HOUSLEY, Crusades, pp. 20-21. It has been disputed that the pope actually approved of a crusade against Byzantium in 1106; the argument is that he accepted it after it had become a fait accompli in 1108: ROWE, Paschal II. But the sources do not suggest that Bohemond concealed his plans even in the early stages.

9. For the meaning of the banner, see ERDMANN, C., *The Origin of the Idea of Crusade*, Princeton, N. J., 1977, pp. 182-200. The activities of Bohemond in Italy, until the time he left for France, are fully and economically described by BARTOLPH DE NANGIS, p. 538.

10. Mentioned only by ORDERICUS VITALIS, *The Ecclesiastical History of Orderic Vitalis*, ed. and trans. CHIBNALL, M., Oxford, Bk. XI.12, vol. VI, 1978, pp. 68-70 (hereafter OV).

11. SUGER, *Vie de Louis VI*, pp. 44ff.

size of his army are huge, and suspect: Western sources report 34,000, 45,000, 65,000, 72,000.[12] Even the low estimate must be exaggerated; however, Anna Komnene also speaks, rhetorically no doubt, of an army of tens of thousands.[13] The danger that Bohemond posed to the Byzantine Empire was real, and Emperor Alexios certainly regarded it as such, as his concerted efforts to diffuse it make clear.

That Bohemond's campaign was a crusade, and was considered as such by contemporaries, is beyond dispute.[14] Indeed, the earliest account of Bohemond's expedition, the *Narratio Floriacensis*, presents this campaign as the anti-Byzantine part of the First Crusade, while Orderic Vitalis calls it the third wave of the First Crusade.[15] The Narration begins with the Council of Clermont, discusses the First Crusade, and follows up the mention of the election of Baldwin of Boulogne with the expedition led by William of Aquitaine (1101). At this time, notes the chronicler, Alexios showered the crusaders with presents, but also gave them guides who, either because of ignorance or "fraude imperatoris," were responsible for the defeat of the crusaders. He notes the return home of part of that army. Telescoping events, he says that "eo tempore," Bohemond went to Gaul (in 1106) with the purpose of collecting knights in order to fight against Alexios, who was hindering the way of those who were going to Jerusalem by land or by sea. Thus, in the *Narratio*, Bohemond's expedition is part of the discussion of the crusade, and it is clearly and solely directed against Alexios.

In the sources, the link between Bohemond's campaign and the First Crusade is twofold, although there are variations in the presentation. First, it was argued that Alexios was unjustly attacking Bohemond's possessions in northern Syria. This argumentation accepted unequivocally that the Byzantines had lost all claim to Antioch because they had not brought aid to the crusaders during the siege of the city; therefore Antioch and its surrounding territory belonged by rights to Bohemond, and the emperor was attacking the possessions of a crusader. The second link is to the disastrous crusade of 1101, during which claims were made that Alexios had cooperated with the Turks. Bohemond made heavy weather of this. The argument recurs in Western sources that Alexios was hindering "the passage of the pilgrims (crusaders)," and therefore the crusade itself, which made him, in various registers, an enemy of Christianity. The most virulent statement regarding Alexios's "treachery" in 1101 comes from the pen of Ekkehard of Aura, who participated in that expedition and who wrote his chronicle soon after his return to the West. Ekkehard even accuses Alexios of returning Nicaea to the Seljuks, and says that Bohemond undertook his campaign because Alexios had frequently incited the sultan against the crusaders.[16]

---

12. YEWDALE, *Bohemond I*, p. 118.

13. ANNA KOMNENE, *Alexias,* ed. REIFFERSCHEID, A., Leipzig, 1884, Bk. XII.1, vol. II, pp. 144-145; cf. her not dissimilar account of the army of Robert Guiscard, Bk. IV.1 (hereafter *Alexias*).

14. See YEWDALE, *Bohemond I*, passim; TYERMAN, C. J., Were There Any Crusades in the Twelfth Century? *EHR* 110:437, 1995, pp. 553-577. In the last instance, see RILEY-SMITH, J., *The Crusades, A Short History*, New Haven - London, 1987, pp. 90-91, and IDEM, *The Crusaders 1095-1131*, Cambridge, 1997, pp. 78-79, with a list of participants on pp. 239-242.

15. *Narratio Floriacensis*, RHC, *Occ*, V, pp. 356-361. The text was written around 1110. Cf. OV, Bk. V.19, vol. III, pp. 182-183: "tercia profectio occidentalium in Ierusalem."

16. *Ekkehardi abbatis Uraguiensis Hierosolymita*, RHC, *Occ*, V, chap. 33, pp. 37-38. See also WILLIAM OF TYRE, *Willelmi Archiepiscopi chronicon*, ed. HUYGENS, R. B. C., Turnholt, 1986, Bk. XI.6, vol. I, pp. 503-506. Fulcher of Chartres, although stating that Alexios was hindering passage to the Holy Land, did not, in his discussion of the "secunda peregrinatio," attribute its failure to Alexios's machinations. Nor, for that matter, did ALBERT OF AIX, *Historia Hierosolymitana*, RHC, *Occ*, IV, Paris, 1879, chap. 46, p. 584; but he reported that this was the general feeling "in populo catholico" (hereafter ALBERT OF AIX).

Contemporaries, however, as well as some of the later sources of the twelfth century, saw Bohemond's attack as more than a continuation of the crusade. Those who were not totally tied to Bohemond's plans and his propaganda efforts also saw it as a continuation of the earlier plans of Robert Guiscard and Bohemond to conquer the Byzantine Empire, thus as going back to the campaign of 1081.[17] Anna Komnene presents the events of 1105-1108 as part of a continuum that began with Robert Guiscard's campaign. The First Crusade is a part of this continuum, for she argues that Bohemond only pretended to be interested in Jerusalem, while in fact his purpose was the capture of Constantinople. Seamless, too, is the connection with the crusade of 1101, and with Bohemond's response to the efforts of Alexios to stop the expedition of the Normans into Cilicia, and especially to recover Laodicea (summer 1104), which had been taken by Tancred in early 1103. This, according to her, provided the proximate cause of Bohemond's journey to Italy to find allies against Alexios.[18] One might suppose that this is simply Anna's idée fixe, but one would be wrong. Western chroniclers and other writers make all of these connections, the weakest one being Bohemond's designs upon Constantinople in 1097. The tenor of her remarks regarding the expedition of 1106-1108 places it in the context of the crusade, for she says that the pope was persuaded by Bohemond as to the justice of his cause, gave his assent to the campaign, and for that reason Bohemond was able to recruit a large force of volunteers, who, given the pope's position, could not resist.[19]

Guibert de Nogent clearly connects the events of 1105-1108 with the campaigns of 1081, treating them all as part of the edifying story of Bohemond's rise from humble beginnings to the status of son-in-law of the king of France and claimant to Alexios's empire.[20] Orderic Vitalis makes the connection explicitly when, through a twist in the narration, he presents Robert Guiscard's expedition as a proto-crusade, left unfinished, to be completed by Bohemond whom Robert, in his dying speech, compares to Roland: "Nobilis atheleta Buamunde, militia Thessalo Achilli seu francigenae Rollando equiparande, uiuisne an detineris pernicie?"[21]

---

17. Geoffrey Malaterra also makes a reference to the campaign of 1081 when he speaks of Bohemond's taking the cross in 1096: Pontieri, E., ed., *De rebus gestis Rogerii... auctore Gaufredo Malaterra*, RIS V.1, Bologna, 1927, 102. The fame of Robert Guiscard is faithfully cultivated by pro-Norman chroniclers. Thus, for example, Tudebodus imitatus et continuatus tells the story of Tancred visiting a hermit near the Mount of Olives (in 1099). The hermit inquires as to Tancred's identity, and upon hearing that Tancred is Robert Guiscard's nephew, he says: "Vere de sanguine magno illius ducis es; quem velut fulmen tota Grecia tremuit, quem, dum bellaret, Alexius imperator fugit; cujus imperio tota Bulgaria usque Bardal paruit." RHC, *Occ*, III, 217. "Bardal" is the River Axios.

18. *Alexias*, Bk. X.5, vol. II, pp. 76, 79; the campaign of 1101 is presented as a continuation of the earlier campaigns: Bk. XI.8ff, vol. II, pp. 355ff. There is a connection in the narrative between the capture of Laodicea, the Pisan and Genoese attacks against Byzantine possessions, and Bohemond's final effort to recapture the Byzantine Empire: Bk. XI.9, XI.10, XII. *Alexias*, Bk. XII.4 thematically connects the campaign of 1097 to that of 1105-1108 by mentioning the swarms of locusts in 1097 and a comet as well as other omens in 1108.

19. *Alexias*, Bk. XI.8.

20. Guibert de Nogent, RHC, *Occ*, IV, pp. 151-152. Suger, when discussing Bohemond's return to the West, draws the connection implicitly, for immediately after saying that Bohemond went to France, he recounts Bohemond's capture of Antioch and then goes back to Robert Guiscard, to say that he and Bohemond had won a victory against two emperors on the same day (Alexios I and Henry IV). His narrative, nevertheless, presents the campaign of 1105-1108 clearly and solely as a crusade to Jerusalem: *Vie de Louis le Gros*, p. xi (written ca. 1144).

21. OV, Bk. VII.7, vol. IV, 1973, p. 36.

THE BYZANTINE DEFENSE: THE BENEFITS OF PUBLIC RELATIONS

Alexios I took the threat very seriously, as well he might. Apparently, not all Byzantines were certain that he would emerge victorious. The Life of St. Cyril Phileotes reports that the saint, praying for the emperor as he did every evening, had a reassuring vision. He saw the emperor sitting in glory in a church-shaped tent; on the left side a terrible sea storm raged, destroying many small ships. A huge black dog with bloodshot eyes stood looking at the emperor, but a soldier of resplendent aspect chained the animal and threw it at the feet of the emperor, thus foretelling victory.[22] More mundane acts undertaken by the emperor were at least as important for the final outcome. He countered the threat by diplomatic and military means as well as by an extensive and ultimately successful propaganda effort.

For diplomacy and military matters, he could count on his earlier experience with Robert Guiscard. Bohemond would have to cross the Adriatic. Therefore Alexios opened negotiations not only with Venice, whose support at this point could be counted upon, but also with Genoa and Pisa, which had been active both in the Holy Land and in the coastal areas of Antioch, were allied with Bohemond, and had already attacked Byzantine possessions.[23] Bohemond's letter to Pope Paschal II leaves open the possibility that Alexios also pressed his case in the papal court, although it seems that this was done through Western knights, and so I will treat it under the rubric of propaganda. It must not be forgotten, however, that a few years after the failure of Bohemond's campaign Alexios began negotiations with Paschal II on the union of the churches.

The military aspects of the campaign have been described by other scholars, and there is no reason to discuss them in detail here. A few general statements will suffice. Alexios had had three years to prepare – a much longer lead time than most army commanders are blessed with – and he had used the time well. He spent months, between September 1105 and February/March 1106 in Thessalonike, organizing the defense of his Western provinces. He raised troops, and his fleet patrolled the Adriatic, cutting off Bohemond's communications. The Byzantine army secured the passes, so that Bohemond was contained in Epiros, an infertile and inhospitable area. Alexios for the most part avoided the pitched battles at which Bohemond excelled.[24] The crusaders suffered military defeat, which in the end is what counts. But a significant part of the Byzantine victory must be credited to Alexios's propaganda war. After all, the response in Western Europe did not continue during the long year of the campaign in Epiros; and all sources agree that there were people in Bohemond's army who argued loudly for an end to this inglorious campaign.

Alexios's war of propaganda was carried out for the most part through Westerners whom he had cultivated over the years and some of whom he co-opted precisely around the time of Bohemond's preparations. The emperor had a standard policy of offering Westerners, even after hostile engagements, great gifts and the chance to serve him. This he had already done with Robert Guiscard's followers after the latter's death in 1085.[25]

22. SARGOLOGOS, E., La vie de St. Cyrille le Philéote, moine byzantin (+1110), Brussels, 1964, chap. 36, p. 154.

23. Alexias, Bk. XI.10, XI.11, XII.1, XIV.3; MÜLLER, J., Documenti sulle relazioni delle città toscane coll'oriente cristiano e coi Turchi fino all'anno MDXXXI, Documenti degli archivi toscani, Florence, 1879, reprinted Rome, 1966, no. xxxiv, pp. 44 and 53; DÖLGER, F., Regesten der Kaiserur-kunden des oströmischen Reiches, Munich - Berlin, 1925, no. 1104 and cf. nos. 1254, 1255.

24. On the campaign, see YEWDALE, Bohemond I, pp. 116-120.

25. OV, Bk. XVII.7, vol. IV, p. 38 (written in 1130-1133); cf. Alexias, Bk. VI.1.4, vol. I, p. 187.

22

At the time of the First Crusade, as the crusaders returned home after the capture of Jerusalem, Alexios once again invited them to stay and serve him; he gave them great gifts and honors, but also showered with gifts some of those who left, namely, the counts of Normandy and Flanders.[26] Raymond of St. Gilles remained close to Alexios all his life. And who can forget Stephen of Blois, who wrote to his wife glowing letters from Nicaea, basking in the warmth of Alexios's sumptuous gifts, and his flattering words and appreciation of Stephen's valor (more than he had at home, it seems)?[27]

Better attested is the public relations value of another policy of Alexios, namely, the ransoming or liberation of knights held captive by the Turks. In 1100 a French knight, Arpin of Bourges, imprisoned in Cairo, sent messengers to Alexios through Byzantine merchants. Alexios was able to arrange for his release and showered him with presents. When Arpin returned to France, he spoke at length to Pope Paschal about how to order his life; on the pope's advice, he became a monk at Cluny.[28] It is not stated that he told positive stories of Alexios, but it is most likely that he did, even to the pope, given the favorable way in which the incident is reported by the chroniclers, who must have learned of it by word of mouth. Much more conscious efforts were undertaken in the midst of Bohemond's preparations for his crusade. Anna Komnene reports the ransoming of three hundred Frankish knights, held prisoner in Cairo. This event must be dated around 1106, or a little earlier, because she connects it chronologically to Bohemond's journey to France and his extensive war of anti-Byzantine propaganda. Bohemond, according to Anna, called Alexios a "pagan and an enemy of Christians," a "pagan who aids the pagans wholeheartedly" (τοῖς παγάνοις ὅλῃ γνώμῃ ἐπαρήγοντα).[29] Anna uses the word παγάνος, meaning a non-Christian, extremely rarely, and always in connection with Bohemond.[30] In Western texts of the period of the First Crusade, *paganus* normally refers to the Turks; I think it must be assumed that Anna's use of the word reflects Western usage. Anna does not say that Alexios ransomed the three hundred knights in order to counter Bohemond's "malicious tales."[31] One, however, may be allowed the suspicion that this was his intent; for the historian immediately thereafter says that these knights, who had been enemies of the emperor, and had, indeed, broken their oaths to him, now became very well disposed toward him. On his part, Alexios gave them great presents and told them that those who wished could enter his service, and those who preferred to go home could do so freely. When they and he heard about Bohemond's calumnies, Alexios gave them more presents, sent them home, where in any case they wanted to return, and charged them with gainsaying Bohemond. This they did happily, according to Anna. They

26. OV, Bk. X.12, vol. V, pp. 274-276.

27. HAGENMEYER, H., *Epistulae et chartae ad historiam primi belli sacri spectantes*, Innsbruck, 1901, reprinted Hildesheim - New York, 1973, pp. 138-139, ca. 24 March 1097.

28. OV, Bk. X.23, vol. V, 1975, pp. 350-352. Odo Arpin, viscount of Bourges, was a relative by marriage of Stephen of Blois and had taken the cross with him in 1100: OV, Bk. X.20, vol. V, p. 324; cf. GUIBERT DE NOGENT, RHC, *Occ*, IV, pp. 244-245; ALBERT OF AIX, RHC, *Occ*, IV, pp. 544-555.

29. *Alexias*, Bk. XII.1-2, vol. II, pp. 144-145.

30. Cf. *Alexias*, Bk. XII.1.2, 5, 8.5; XIII.12.2, XIII.12.11.

31. In fact, he did not ransom them, because the sultan in Cairo did not accept the money sent by Alexios, and freed them as an act of courtesy to the emperor: *Alexias*, vol. II, p. 144. An unlikely source, the Miracles of St. Léonard of Noblat, composed ca. 1106, reports that Alexios bribed Danishmend to release Richard of the Principate, even though he knew Richard to be an enemy of his state. Richard was then showered with gifts before being sent home. The source attributes the action to the persuasion of St. Léonard; since the emperor had presumably never heard of this saint, one wonders what lies behind the tale. Perhaps this is one more incident of Alexios liberating a Westerner, in the hope of good publicity in Western Europe: *AASS, Nov. III*, pp. 160ff.

spread the word "in every land and city," calling Bohemond a fraud (ἀπατεώνα), an interesting term which we find echoed in some Western sources, and bearing witness to Alexios's probity from their own experience. Albert of Aix reports that the Egyptian caliph freed Conrad, the *stabularius* of the German emperor, after Alexios's intercession, made at the request of the German emperor.[32] He says that the "rex Babyloniae" released Conrad to Alexios "ob causam dilectionis et mutuae retributionis," which is exactly the tenor of Anna Komnene's description of the freeing of the three hundred captives. Presumably, Conrad was part of that group, since otherwise one is hard put to explain the similarities in the reports of the two historians. It is further said that Alexios sent Conrad back to his suzerain with many presents, including gold, silver, precious stones, and pearls. As a matter of fact, Conrad was unable to return to Germany because of the civil wars, and stayed in Italy where doubtless he became part of Alexios's propaganda machine in the West. Indeed, Albert of Aix sandwiches his report of this episode in the discussion of Bohemond's Illyrian campaign.

Alexios's propaganda campaign was successful. A letter addressed by Bohemond to Pope Paschal either in 1106 or, most probably, in 1108 mentions specifically that certain people "tam longe quam prope," seduced by Alexios's gifts of gold and silver, had taken his part and accused Bohemond to the pope for attacking Alexios unjustly.[33] The pro-Byzantine propaganda must have been very powerful, for Bohemond makes his response to it the center of his letter to the pope: it is to counter these statements that he asks the pope to convoke a church council, to act as a judge between Bohemond and Alexios, or else to remove Greek heresies from the church; this would promote the *iter Ierosolimitanum*, as would Paschal's taking the cross himself. He then proceeds to justify his attack by dwelling upon Alexios's usurpation of the throne, his perseverance in schismatic practices, the injuries he had visited upon the crusaders.[34] Most importantly, the proximate cause for the composition of this letter by Bohemond seems to be that someone had proposed that his army be disbanded, a proposal that he rejects: "Nunc autem, quoniam Dei exercitus ammonicione beati Petri congregatur, nullatenus dimittere potui."[35] This point, taken together with the mention of people who had been bribed, suggests very strongly that the chroniclers who say that Bohemond's own knights urged him to make peace with Alexios are correct. The strongest argument in support of J. G. Rowe's belief that the letter was written in Durazzo in 1108, and not in 1106, is, I believe, Bohemond's concern with the effects of Alexios's propaganda.

32. *Alexias*, Bk. XII.1, vol. II, p. 146. Cf. ALBERT OF AIX, RHC, *Occ*, IV, X.45: "Hic vero, agnita Boemundi fraudulentia" (at the time of the treaty of Devol). Cf. ibid., X.39, pp. 649-650.

33. ROWE, Paschal II, pp. 193ff; HOLTZMANN, W., Bohemund von Antiochien und Alexios I, *Neues Archiv* 50, 1935, pp. 270-282, especially pp. 280-281. ROWE dates the letter to 1108. I think this later dating is correct, for 1106 would have been too early for Alexios's propaganda efforts to have borne fruit. From which perspective is Bohemond construing *prope* and *longe*? Writing from Durazzo or thereabouts, he may be thinking of people in his own army (*prope*) and in Europe or Italy; if the center is Rome, where these people presumably made their representations, *prope* may be the papal curia or Italy, and *longe* either Western Europe or, even, Alexios's court, from which Westerners may have been sending missives to the pope.

34. The heretical beliefs and practices are mentioned briefly as items on a list. They consist of the question of the procession of the Holy Ghost, baptism, practices affecting communion (presumably the azymes), the marriage of the clergy. To my knowledge, this is the first "crusading" text to list the differences, followed later by ODO OF DEUIL, who mentions the eucharist and the procession of the Holy Ghost: *De profectione Ludovici VII in Orientem*, ed. and trans. BERRY, V., New York, 1948, p. 56.

35. HOLTZMANN, Bohemund, p. 280.

24

As a result of Alexios's propaganda, and his blandishments to Bohemond's army, a number of soldiers abandoned the Norman cause and pressured Bohemond to make peace.[36] Their decision was surely helped by Alexios's promise of clemency, perhaps communicated to them by other Westerners in his army.[37] A number of Western sources speak of treachery on the part of Bohemond's brother Guy and other important lieutenants of his, who made secret agreements with Alexios.[38] Ralph Yewdale has disputed this testimony, saying that no Eastern sources mention it. But Anna Komnene does report a variant, namely, that Alexios made sure that accusations of Guy's treason reached Bohemond, a duplicitous act on the part of the emperor, to sow disorder and suspicion among Bohemond's followers; she also claims that a man named Hugh, in Bohemond's army, insisted on making peace.[39] What is more, the *Narratio Floriacensis* corroborates the story of Guy's treachery, reportedly admitted in his deathbed confession, although the report is inscribed in a more general effort of the author to claim that Bohemond was invincible.[40] I see no reason to doubt that Alexios bought the loyalty of some of Bohemond's high officials.

BOHEMOND'S OVERREACH

Perhaps because of Alexios's diplomacy and propaganda efforts, Bohemond got a bad press in this enterprise, for some Western chronicles give lip service to his campaign, while others are openly critical. Guibert de Nogent, one of the more thoughtful chroniclers, who was not unduly favorable to Eastern Christians, who indeed was extremely negative toward Alexios I, a tyrant most foul ("sordidissimus tyrannus"), makes a passing reference to Bohemond's campaign, in the context of the fortunes of the house of Tancred de Hauteville, which rose from insignificance to prominence.[41] Albert of Aix, writing in the 1130s, adduces absolutely no justification for Bohemond's attack against the Byzantine Empire. He gives a matter-of-fact description of the campaign, with never a hint of Alexios's perfidy or heresy or anything else that might explain the Norman attack. Given Bohemond's propaganda, recorded by other chronicles, this is tantamount to tacit criticism. Others were more favorable to the campaign. Fulcher of Chartres buys into the idea that Alexios was opposed to the Westerners and thwarted the voyage of the "pilgrims" to Jerusalem, "vel fraude clandestina vel violentia manifesta."[42] Bartolph de Nangis and

36. ALBERT OF AIX, X.45. Cf. OV, Bk. XI.24, vol. VI, p. 102.
37. According to ALBERT OF AIX, X.42, Alexios's army that fought against Bohemond in 1107-1108 at Durazzo included, along with the Turcopoles, Cumans, and Petchenegs, "Galli qui conventione solidum Imperatori militabant," which, if taken at face value, means Frenchmen who held money fiefs from him, that is, mercenaries.
38. *Secunda pars Historiae Hierosolymitanae*, RHC, *Occ*, III.568; ALBERT OF AIX, X.44; OV, Bk. XI.24-25.
39. *Alexias*, Bk. XIII.4, XIII.9.
40. RHC, *Occ*, V, p. 362.
41. RHC, *Occ*, IV, p. 133.
42. RHC, *Occ*, III, Bk. II, chap. 38. The editor of the English translation thinks that Fulcher, Bartolph de Nangis, and an anonymous chronicler were all trying to write their account (part of it, in Fulcher's case) in time for them to circulate in Western Europe and create enthusiasm for Bohemond's crusade: *A History of the Expedition to Jerusalem, 1095-1127, Fulcher of Chartres*, trans. RYAN, F. R., ed. FINK, H. S., New York, 1969, p. 21. William of Malmesbury says that Bohemond attacked Alexios "praetendens belli causam peregrinorum injuriam, qua ille perinfamis erat": *Willelmi Malmesbiriensis monachi De gestis regum Anglorum libri quinque*, ed. STUBBS, W., reprinted Wiesbaden, 1964, Bk. IV.387, vol. II, p. 454.

later chronicles, such as the *Gesta Tancredi*, or *Tudebodus imitatus et continuatus*, also rehearse Alexios's perfidious ways and state that he was even worse than the Saracens.[43] But the barometer here must be Orderic Vitalis.

Orderic Vitalis's Ecclesiastical History, written between 1114 and 1141,[44] is an excellent guide to informed Western opinion about the Normans, the crusades, and the Byzantine Empire. His sources were many and varied, and he had firsthand knowledge of Bohemond's activities and recruiting efforts in France. His attitude toward the Byzantine Empire and Emperor Alexios I is mixed and inconsistent, reflecting the inconsistencies of both reality and his sources. His narrative serves as a valuable corrective to the idea that there was an unbroken line of anti-Byzantine sentiment in the West during and after the First Crusade, as well as to the opposite and less prevalent view, that anti-Byzantine sentiments were accidental and of no account or significance.[45]

Perhaps the most surprising and telling element in Orderic Vitalis's account is the contradictory portrait of Alexios I. To put it briefly, the author is surprisingly positive toward Alexios; but where he uses the sources for the first wave of the First Crusade (Baldric of Dol) or, much more so, for the "second wave," the crusade of 1100-1101 (Ekkehard of Aura), he repeats negative reports. To start with the negative judgments, Orderic mentions the "unjust" treatment of the crusaders by Alexios in Nicaea.[46] When discussing the crusade of 1100-1101, he recalls that the crusaders spoke of Alexios as *infidus*, but justifies the hostility of the Byzantines by ascribing it to the *malefacta* of the participants in the first wave.[47] He also reports the story of Alexios having sent money to the crusaders in order to reach an estimate of their number and relay it to the Turks; but, on the other hand, he is not convinced that Raymond of Toulouse acted treacherously in 1101 when he led the crusaders along the wrong road.[48] Although Orderic says that the crusaders would have done well to attack Constantinople in 1097 as Bohemond had urged, he does not linger on the "treacheries" of the Greeks during the First Crusade.[49]

For the rest, the portrait of Alexios is positive. In Books III and IV, written ca. 1123-1125, and recounting the history of the Normans in southern Italy and the influx of Anglo-Saxons to the Byzantine Empire after the Norman conquest of England, Alexios, the "Emperor of Constantinople," is depicted as a man of great wisdom and nobility; he treated the Anglo-Saxon refugees well, and they and their heirs served his holy empire faithfully ever since.[50] What are Orderic's sources? Might one suggest that word of mouth had filtered back from these same heirs of the refugees?

43. RHC, *Occ*, III, pp. 568, 712-713, 228ff.

44. OV, vol. I, pp. 37, 48, 60.

45. This last attitude underlies the arguments of MAYR-HARTING, H., Odo of Deuil, the Second Crusade and the Monastery of St. Denis, in MEYER, M. A., *The Culture of Christendom. Essays in Medieval History in Commemoration of Denis L. T. Bethell*, London - Rio Grande, 1993, pp. 225-241.

46. OV, Bk. IX.8, vol. V, p. 59.

47. OV, Bk. X.20, vol. V, p. 327.

48. OV, Bk. X.20, vol. V, 323ff.

49. See Bk. IX. Both ORDERIC VITALIS (Bk. IX.6, vol. V, 1975, pp. 47-49) and WILLIAM OF TYRE (II.10) claim that Bohemond had urged an attack on Constantinople in 1097. Other chroniclers say that, on the contrary, Bohemond dissuaded others, especially Godfrey of Bouillon, from attacking Constantinople. See, for instance, BALDRIC OF DOL, RHC, *Occ*, IV, 22: "Christi milites sumus," Bohemond said, and added that they should not attack other Christians.

50. OV, Bk. IV, vol. II, pp. 202-204: "erat idem multum sapiens et mirae dapsilitatis... Hac itaque de causa Saxones Angli Ioniam expetientur, et ipsi ac haeredes eorum sacro imperio fideliter famulati sunt, et cum magno honore inter Traces Cesari et senatui populoque kari usque nunc persisterunt."

IV

An even more flattering portrait of Alexios is drawn in Book VII, written ca. 1130-1133, which once again recounts Robert Guiscard's exploits, and particularly his wars against the Byzantines. Orderic mentions the deposition of Michael VII by Votaneiates and of the latter by Alexios; he does not, as Bohemond did in 1106-1107, pretend that it was Alexios who had deposed Michael VII. Alexios is described as wise, upright, brave, generous, well loved, merciful to the poor, a brave and illustrious warrior, and, surprisingly, a most diligent servant of divine law.[51] He escaped from his many enemies, which, to Orderic, demonstrates that "none can overthrow or destroy a man defended and cherished by God."[52] This is an interesting statement, especially since it is immediately followed by an account of Robert's unsuccessful expedition in Greece, which is presented as a proto-crusade.

This brings us to the treatment of Bohemond's expedition of 1106-1107. As usual, Orderic's discussion is spread out over various parts of his narrative.[53] After having presented the preparations of the campaign, he says that the expedition failed because of the treachery of Bohemond's brother Guy and Robert de Montfort, who were seduced by Alexios's bribes. Bohemond was persuaded to make peace and returned to Apulia in shame, while many of his companions went to Constantinople and then to Jerusalem.[54]

Although Orderic Vitalis admired Bohemond's courage and bravery, and his report presents a lively picture of Bohemond's triumphant tour of France, his judgment on the crusade is very negative. Twice in his narrative he accuses Bohemond and his followers of overweening ambition and greed, which led them to attack the possessions of others unjustly. The Byzantine Empire is called the *sanctum imperium*. Bohemond's defeat was the judgment of God, who lent favorable ears to the prayers of just men who cried out to him in Greece. These sentiments, expressed most eloquently, are placed in the mouth of Bohemond's companions, who were urging him to make peace.[55]

It then makes sense that the author should ascribe to Fulk of Anjou, king of Jerusalem, a powerful statement that Antioch belonged to the Byzantines by virtue of the oaths taken by the crusaders in 1097, and that therefore Raymond of Antioch should do homage to John Komnenos and hold the city from him: "Ought we to deny the truth and oppose what is right?" And again: "Go and tell your lord from me that he should make peace with the

---

51. OV, Bk. VII.5, vol. IV (1973), p. 14: "erat enim multum sapiens et misericors pauperibus, bellator fortis et magnanimus, affabilis militibus munerumque dator largissimus, diuinaeque legis cultor deuotissimus." It is noteworthy that Orderic Vitalis, in the same context, calls Greece a warlike country from days of old (p. 17), although in his dying speech Robert Guiscard describes the inhabitants of Constantinople as "an effeminate race given up to luxury and wantonness": Bk. VII.7, vol. IV, pp. 33ff.

52. OV, Bk. VII, vol. IV, p. 16: "quem Deus defensat et refouet nemo deicere vel adnichilare preualet."

53. OV, Bk. XI.12, vol. VI, pp. 69ff; Bk. V.19, vol. III, pp. 182-183; Bk. VIII.20, vol. IV, pp. 264-265.

54. OV, Bk. XI.24-25, vol. VI, pp. 102ff. The last part is taken from RHC, *Occ*, III, *Secunda pars historiae Hierosolymitanae*, p. 568. *Tudebodus imitatus et continuatus*, *Historia Peregrinorum*, ibid., p. 228, embroiders upon this by making Alexios adopt Bohemond.

55. OV, Bk. XI.24, vol. VI, pp. 102-104: "Ad tantos ausus nec hereditarium ius nos illexit, nec prophetarum aliquis a Deo destinatus coelesti nos oraculo exciuit, sed cupiditas in alterius dicione dominandi ardua te incipere persuasit, et nos nichilominus appetitus lucrandi ac intolerabilem sarcinam laborum et discriminum sustinendam pertraxit. Verum quia Deus non irridetur, nec supplantat iudicium, nec subuertit quod iustum est preces iustorum qui contra nos ad eum in Graecia clamant benigniter exaudiuit." Cf. V.19, vol. III, pp. 182-183. Note that Orderic Vitalis also describes Alexios in highly positive terms in his discussion of Robert Guiscard's expedition. Students of this author might ponder the possibility that we have here a veiled criticism of the First Crusade itself.

Emperor, and at my bidding receive the city from him to whom it justly belongs and so hold it rightfully. For the Emperor is a Christian who has far-reaching power; if he is respected by the Franks he can, should he so wish, help them greatly."[56] Thus, says Orderic Vitalis, peace was made, and the war which had dragged on *damnose* for forty years, that is, since the appropriation of Antioch by Bohemond in 1098, was brought to an end. This happened in 1137. Book XIII of Orderic Vitalis's narrative was written around the year 1141.[57] A few years later, during the Second Crusade, even Odo of Deuil reports that some of the nobles in Louis VII's army responded as follows to the advice of the bishop of Langres to take Constantinople because Emperor John II Komnenos had attacked Antioch in 1142-1143: "the fact that he attacked Antioch was evil, but he could have had justifiable reasons which we do not know."[58]

The narrative of Orderic Vitalis provides one more reason why Bohemond's campaign failed: what seems to be a considerable number of Europeans still believed in that Christian fraternity which, according to Fulcher of Chartres, had been stressed by Pope Urban II in his Clermont appeal. They did not feel comfortable attacking Constantinople; even the pope clearly had second thoughts, as Bohemond's letter to him abundantly shows.

The Results of Bohemond's Campaign

Thus the first concerted attack on the Byzantine Empire, undertaken as part of the First Crusade but clearly at odds with some powerful ideas governing it, failed. The failure was due to a large extent to the combination of Byzantine diplomacy and military action and the activities of an excellent public relations team that argued Alexios's case to the pope and others. Furthermore, the idea that one should not fight a Christian emperor still had currency, which is important to note.

This crusade left a heavy legacy behind it. It caused the Byzantines to look upon subsequent crusades with fear and suspicion, and this had deleterious results in the long run. Bohemond's campaign also gave additional impetus to the diplomatic bulwarks the Byzantines built against potential future threats, which they saw as coming primarily from the Normans both in Italy and in the principality of Antioch. Alexios had improvised, especially in his propaganda warfare. John II and Manuel I depended less on a network of support from individuals and much more on diplomacy. They built systems of alliances against the Normans, to be sure, but by extension against threats from opportunistic crusaders as well. Good relations with the papacy were important in this context. But the mainstay of Komnenian policy in the West was the alliance with the holy Roman emperors and with Venice, aimed primarily against the Normans. This development placed the Byzantine Empire firmly in the context of European politics: Byzantium was, now, one state among others, making and breaking alliances, and increasingly involved in the ever more complex European world. As a consequence, much of the special mystique the empire might have had was eventually eroded. It is thus not surprising that successive crusaders – those, at least, who traveled through Byzantine possessions – should occasionally have thought of attacking the Byzantine Empire; after all, crusading wars

---

56. OV, Bk. XIII.34, vol. VI, pp. 506, 508: "Christianus enim est imperator magnaeque potentiae, et a Francis honoratus si vult admodum valet illos adiuvare."

57. OV, Bk. XIII.34, vol. VI, pp. 503ff; vol. VI, p. xix. Orderic was somewhat premature in declaring the end of hostilities, which continued for some time.

58. "Quod autem impugnavit Antiochiam malum fuit, potuit tamen causas habere iustitiae quas nescimus": Odo of Deuil, p. 70.

against Christians in Western Europe were well known in the twelfth century. In this light, what is surprising is how long it took for a crusade to attack Constantinople.

THE SECOND CRUSADE: FEARS, SUSPICIONS, REALITIES

The Second Crusade engaged large armies that traveled east through the Byzantine Empire. Realistically, the greatest danger for the Byzantine Empire lay in the fact that Roger II of Sicily, bent on his own expansionist plans in North Africa and the East, launched against the western possessions of the Byzantine Empire an attack that coincided with the passage of the crusading armies. The attack began in the autumn of 1147; the army of the German emperor Conrad III entered Byzantine territory in late July 1147, arrived outside Constantinople on 10 September, and crossed into Asia Minor in late September 1147. Louis VII's army reached the Byzantine frontier at the end of August and Constantinople on 4 October, crossing into Asia Minor ca. 20 October. It is certain that if the crusading armies, or one of them, and Roger had acted in common, attacking by land and by sea, Constantinople would have been in danger. However, given the political relations between the major players in the West, there was no possibility that either Conrad III or Louis VII would cooperate with Roger against Constantinople at this point. The two enterprises remained separate.[59] Was the Byzantine Empire in danger from the crusading armies? This question poses interesting problems of source evaluation and interpretation, for, depending on which combination of sources one accepts, two very different pictures emerge. Nevertheless, under proper examination the situation becomes clear.

THE AMBIGUITY OF THE SOURCES

Let us first look at the "worst-case scenario" that emerges from some of the sources. The Byzantine sources are unambiguous: Manuel feared an attack on the city by the crusaders, in the event, by the German army that was the first to enter Byzantine territory. Interestingly, it is the German forces and the German emperor rather than Louis VII who loom large in the Byzantine sources. Part of the explanation may be that one of the major authors, John Kinnamos, was writing his history between 1180 and 1182, and that Louis VII was the father-in-law of the then reigning emperor, Alexios II.[60] This would still leave unexplained the position of other Byzantine texts, such as those of Niketas Choniates and Manganeios Prodromos. Nor can it account for the fact that Muslim sources also speak primarily of Conrad III, virtually ignoring Louis VII.[61] The answer surely lies in the fact that Conrad III, as holy Roman emperor, was regarded by both Muslim and Byzantine historians as ipso facto leader of the expedition.[62]

---

59. On the Second Crusade, see BERRY, V. G., The Second Crusade, in *A History of the Crusades*, ed. SETTON, K. M., vol. I, Philadelphia, 1955, pp. 463-512; RUNCIMAN, S., *A History of the Crusades*, II, Cambridge, 1957, pp. 247-288. Odo of Deuil does suggest that Roger, or others acting on his behalf, tried to persuade Louis VII to collaborate in an attack against Byzantium: *De profectione Ludovici VII in Orientem*, pp. 11, 15, 59, 83. On this, cf. MATTHEW, D., *The Norman Kingdom of Sicily*, Cambridge, 1992, p. 57.

60. BRAND, C. M., trans., *Deeds of John and Manuel Comnenus by John Kinnamos*, New York, 1976, pp. 4-5.

61. See the knowledgeable Ibn al-Athir, in GABRIELI, F., *Storici arabi delle crociate*, Turin, 1957, pp. 58-60; cf. Ibn al-Qalanisi, ibid., pp. 54-58.

62. Cf., in a similar vein, MAGDALINO, *Manuel I*, pp. 47-49.

The most trustworthy account of Byzantine perceptions of the German "threat" is that of Manganeios Prodromos, who was writing very close to the event, sometime in the late fall of 1147, and therefore without the hindsight of John Kinnamos or Niketas Choniates. He states that Manuel had strengthened the fortifications of the city in order to withstand a possible attack. He insists that Conrad wanted to conquer Constantinople and install a Latin patriarch.[63] Writing much later, Kinnamos and Choniates reflect exactly the same ideas. Thus, if one were to depend on the Byzantine sources alone, one would think that the German emperor was planning an attack and, consequently, that the Second Crusade presented a real danger to the Byzantine Empire.

An uncritical reading of Odo of Deuil's account might well reinforce the second but not the first part of this conclusion: although the French chronicler says nothing about a German plan of attack, he does mention repeated thoughts of an attack on Constantinople by the French army. It is mostly the bishop of Langres who is credited with this hostile attitude; but if this was in fact true in 1147, and is not due to hindsight, it is noteworthy that even the aggressive bishop seems to have realized that attacking Constantinople by land alone was no easy enterprise. That is why he recalled with regret that the crusaders had not allied themselves with Roger II, which would have made such an enterprise feasible. The Byzantine sources, on the other hand, say absolutely nothing about any danger coming from the French army. There were, indeed, problems involving provisioning and currency exchange, as both Choniates and Odo of Deuil reveal, and serious ones at that.[64] But the Byzantines seem not to have feared an attack from the French.

The worst-case scenario can be elicited from a one-sided reading of the Byzantine sources in conjunction with an equally one-sided reading of Odo of Deuil: both Conrad III (according to the Byzantine sources) and important figures in the French army (according to Odo of Deuil) seriously contemplated an attack on the Byzantine Empire in the course of the passage through the Balkans. The reading, however, that would support this scenario would have to be partial indeed. For one thing, the Byzantine sources say nothing about a projected French attack, and Odo of Deuil is equally discreet about the possibility of a German attack. Then there are the German chronicles, which must surely enter the discussion.

No hint of a projected German attack, or, indeed, of profound hostility, finds its way into the pages of the major Western chroniclers of the German crusade. Helmold of Bosau does not discuss the (real) occasional hostilities between Byzantines and Germans in the Balkans; only when he speaks of Asia Minor does he mention the *dolus* of the Byzantine guide, who led the crusaders to the Turkish border through a great desert.[65] The *Annales Herbipolenses* do state, about the participants of the crusade, that "[some people] driven by want and suffering from hardship at home, were ready to fight not only against the enemies of the cross of Christ but also against Christian friends, if there seemed a chance of relieving their poverty."[66] If this is more than the rhetoric of an avowed critic of the Second Crusade, it is a vague reference to improper motivation. Otto of Freising is the most important German source for the Second Crusade. His narrative certainly gives no support to the idea that Conrad contemplated an attack. The major incident he mentions,

63. JEFFREYS, E., and JEFFREYS, M. J., The "Wild Beast from the West": Immediate Literary Reactions in Byzantium to the Second Crusade, in LAIOU and MOTTAHEDEH, *The Crusades* (as above, note 3), pp. 101-116; JEFFREYS, E., and JEFFREYS, M. J., *Manganeios Prodromos Poems 20 and 24*, Oxford - Sydney, 1997, poem 24.215-219.
64. See LAIOU, Byzantine Trade, pp. 164ff.
65. *Helmoldi Cronica Slavorum*, MGH, *ScriptRerGerm*, 3d ed., Hannover, 1937, p. 117.
66. *Annales Herbipolenses*, MGH, *SS*, XVI, Hannover, 1859, Leipzig, 1925, p. 3.

other than the difficulty of passage through Bulgaria, is a great flood from which Frederick of Swabia emerged unscathed.[67] For the rest, there is no word of opprobrium against the Byzantines, no mention of trouble. Constantinople is the *urbs regia* in this connection, as it is throughout his narrative.[68] When discussing earlier contacts between John II and Manuel I on the one hand, and Conrad III on the other, Otto does indeed refer several times to diplomatic skirmishes and unpleasantness stemming from the use of imperial titles.[69] These disputes on the relative role of the Old and the New Rome and their rulers are echoed by Manganeios Prodromos. But they were hardly causes of war.

Hostilities did indeed take place between the German army and the Byzantines in Bulgaria and Thrace. The German army was unruly, there were problems with provisioning, the Byzantine armies may have been overzealous. At the court, in Constantinople, Manganeios Prodromos described the Germans as beasts. But the German attacks were opportunistic, as even Kinnamos seems to understand, for in the more or less fictitious exchange of letters between Conrad and Manuel, he has Conrad disclaiming responsibility for the attacks launched by his troops, on the excuse that such action is not unknown on the part of armies marching through foreign territory.[70] In brief, the German sources do not speak of any general hostility before, during, or after the expedition in the Balkans.

There is, therefore, a "best-case scenario." According to the major German sources, read in conjunction with Odo of Deuil, there was no German threat. According to the Byzantine sources, there was no French threat. All of this seems confusing, but history is not so inexact a science, and it is possible to establish both the parameters of reality and those of perceptions.

THE CONTRADICTION RESOLVED

Fortunately, we have truly contemporary sources which provide the answer to the question of the crusaders' intent. Both Conrad III and Louis VII sent letters to their regents during the campaign. In his letters to Wibald, Conrad calls Manuel his brother ("frater noster Grecorum imperator"), insists on the fact that he had been honorably received in Constantinople, and says that Manuel "showed us such honor as we never heard that he had given to our predecessor."[71] Louis VII's letters to Suger, written in the course of the crusade, breathe no word of any plans to take Constantinople. To the contrary, Louis speaks of his arrival and brief stay in Constantinople in glowing terms: "scripsimus vobis,

67. PERTZ, G. H., ed., *Ottonis episcopi Frisingensis opera, tomus II. Gesta Friderici Imperatoris auctoribus Ottone et Ragewino*, Hannover, 1867, Bk I.45, pp. 65ff (hereafter OTTO OF FREISING).

68. Otto of Freising explains that Constantinople was known as the *urbs regia*, or New Rome, after Constantine had transferred the seat of empire there: *The Two Cities*, trans. MIEROW, C. C., New York, 1928, Bk. IV.5.

69. OTTO OF FREISING, I.23, I.24.

70. *Ioannes Cinnamus*, ed. NIEBUHR, B. G., Bonn, 1836, II.15 and 16 (hereafter KINNAMOS). CHALANDON, F., *Jean II Comnène (1118-1143) et Manuel I Comnène (1143-1180)*, Paris, 1912, p. 279, says that the letters were forged; the events they mention, however, did take place.

71. MGH, *Diplomata*, IX, Vienna, 1969, no. 194 (end of July 1147); no. 195 (end of February 1148: "tantum illic nobis honoris exhibens, quantum nulliumquam predecessori nostro exhibitum esse audivimus." This letter refers to Conrad's campaign in Asia Minor, his illness, and the fact that Manuel and his wife, Bertha/Irene, Conrad's sister-in-law, nursed him back to health; cf. letter no. 229, 16/20 April 1150. Kinnamos too mentions that Conrad was a relative of Manuel's: p. 85. Otto of Freising, in the context of Conrad's return to Constantinople from Jerusalem, speaks of Conrad's sailing to meet "fratrem et amicum suum Manuel, regiae urbis principem": OTTO OF FREISING, I.59.

universa de nobis laeta et prospera vobis annunciantes."[72] The emperor had received them gladly and honorably.[73] Louis accuses Manuel of acting fraudulently and of permitting the Turks to attack the French army; but this accusation comes at the end of the account of the long and difficult passage through Asia Minor and refers to events in that area, not in the Balkans.[74] Furthermore, the actions of the two kings speak louder than words, for they both crossed over to Asia Minor as soon as they could. In brief, there is no credible evidence that either Conrad or Louis contemplated the conquest of Constantinople in the course of the Balkan campaign.[75] Hostilities there were, certainly, but they were opportunistic in nature.

Why, then, do the Byzantine sources, including strictly contemporary ones, dwell on Western plans for the conquest of the empire? It is beyond question that Manuel did indeed fear such plans. The very strength of the Western armies provoked fear of attack against Constantinople as the Byzantines labored under the memories of the long First Crusade. Kinnamos's description of the gathering of the forces of the Second Crusade, countless armies, "the whole Western array," closely parallels, although in abbreviated form, Anna Komnene's unforgettable description of the great commotion of 1097, itself influenced by Bohemond's subsequent crusade.[76] Kinnamos puts the number of German crusaders at more than 900,000 "barbarians," while Choniates claims that Manuel's officials, overwhelmed by the number of crusaders, abandoned the effort to count them in order to arrange for their crossing the Bosphoros.[77]

Historical memory accounts for the fears of the Byzantines. The memory of the First Crusade had taught Manuel that crusader armies could be dangerous. He therefore took measures to counteract any possible attack. He made agreements with both Conrad and Louis, so that he would provide safe passage and provisions, and they would promise not to attack his state. He exacted an oath of fealty from the nobles in Louis's army. He concluded a twelve-year truce with the Turks, to free his eastern forces.[78] It is possible to argue that Manuel's response to the passage of the crusading armies, especially that of the Germans, was exaggerated. Thus he may have taken the dangerous measure, reported by Choniates, of urging the Turks to attack the German army once it had crossed into Asia Minor.[79] He increased considerably his army in the Balkans, thus unfortunately leaving

72. *RHGF*, XV, p. 488, 4-26 October 1147. For the date, see *Suger, Œuvres*, II, Paris, 2001, letter 17.

73. *RHGF*, XV, pp. 495-496, written from Asia Minor after 19 March 1148.

74. Ibid.

75. Unfortunately, some modern scholarship, especially that produced by Byzantinists, continues to fly in the face of evidence with regard to the Second Crusade, perpetuating the idea that an attack against Byzantium was contemplated and planned. See, for a recent example, LILIE, R.-J., *Byzantium and the Crusader States 1096-1204*, Oxford, 1993, pp. 145ff. He uses the two extreme accounts, of Kinnamos and Odo of Deuil, thus positing both a German and a French plan of attack.

76. KINNAMOS, p. 67; cf. *Alexias*, vol. II, pp. 73-76, and *Nicetae Choniatae Historia*, ed. VAN DIETEN, J.-L., Berlin - New York, 1975, pp. 60-61 (hereafter CHONIATES), who calls the Germans "νέφος πολεμίων" and says that Manuel feared they were wolves in sheep's clothing.

77. KINNAMOS, p. 69; CHONIATES, pp. 65-66. Helmold also says that Manuel marveled at the great number of German crusaders.

78. DÖLGER, *Regesten*, Munich, 1925, no. 1352, 1147 (before May?).

79. CHONIATES, p. 67; DÖLGER, *Regesten*, no. 1366, with a question as to the authenticity of the information. GERHOH OF REICHERSBERG, *Opera hactenus inedita*, ed. SCHEIBELBERGER, F., vol. I, Lluz, 1875, chap. 68, who gives quite a lengthy account of the crusade, simply implies that Manuel used Conrad's army in Asia Minor for his own purposes, and had them guided through difficult enemy territory. CHALANDON, *Jean II*, pp. 286-287, says that the action imputed to Manuel is possible, and that according to Arab chroniclers the emperor and the crusaders had made common cause.

western Greece open to Roger's attack. He repaired the fortifications of Constantinople and arranged for its defense. And he had the support of the Venetian allies in the war against Roger, which was real and not a mere threat.[80]

However, the real defense in the case of the Second Crusade was quite different, and it was twofold. On the one hand, there was successful diplomacy and favorable international conditions. Under the first rubric, we must place that linchpin of Byzantine diplomacy since the time of Alexios I: the alliance with the Holy Roman Empire. John II fostered an alliance with Conrad III and also arranged Manuel's marriage to Bertha/Irene. The main purpose of the alliance was the opposition of both emperors to the plans of the kings of Sicily. The alliance was strengthened, during the course of the crusade but after Conrad's illness and return to Constantinople (so, in the winter-early spring of 1147/1148), by the marriage of Conrad's nephew Henry Jasomirgott to Manuel's niece Theodora.[81] The favorable international context was the hostility of the papacy toward Roger II, which, at that specific moment, precluded the possibility of a crusade that would include the Normans.

The second factor is elusive and subject to change according to circumstances. It is the fact that, as far as one can tell, assistance to the Kingdom of Jerusalem and its principalities was the first, main, and, it seems, only priority of both the German and French kings. Within that context, though not as its necessary corollary, one notes the existence, still, of the idea of Christian brotherhood. Even Manganeios Prodromos admitted that, after all, the Westerners, Azymites though they were, were, nevertheless, Christians, whose blood was not to be shed.[82] And to the reported calls of the bishop of Langres to attack the Byzantine Empire, French nobles apparently responded that slaughtering Christians was not a job for crusaders, who were going to the Holy Land to gain salvation.[83] In this context one must also mention an astonishing piece of prose in Choniates' account. He attributes to Conrad III a speech made to his army when they were in desperate straits in Asia Minor. The speech is an *excitatorium*, meant to encourage the troops and send them enthusiastically into battle. The astonishing thing about it is the crusading spirit it exudes, which, if one were to change the flowering Greek prose into Latin, could easily have come from a Western source; indeed, the same feelings, *mutatis mutandis*, are attributed by Odo of Deuil to French nobles. Choniates' Conrad reminds his troops that they had left their country, their wealth and honor, to fight against the enemies of Christ, in whose blood they were called to wash by Davidic psalms, and win eternal salvation. As Christ was superior to the prophet Mohammed, he said, so were the crusaders superior to the Turks; and the River Maeandros would part its waters to let his army pass.[84] "As we are a sacred host and a God-chosen army, let us not ignobly love our lives more than a Christ-loving and everlastingly remembered death. If Christ died for us, how much more justified are we to die for him?... We shall fight with confidence in Christ and in the full knowledge that we shall crush the enemy; the victory will not be difficult, for none will be able to sustain our onslaught, but rather they shall all give way before our first charge. Should we

---

80. Note that Choniates mentions in the same breath the preparations to counter any hostile action on the part of the crusaders and Manuel's announcement to the senate of Roger's campaign: pp. 61-62.

81. For the date, see MAGDALINO, *Manuel I*, p. 52 n. 93.

82. Manganeios Prodromos, JEFFRIES, The "Wild Beast," p. 109 (Poem 20.96).

83. ODO OF DEUIL, p. 70.

84. CHONIATES, pp. 68-70. The narrative is somewhat confused, but it is certain, in my view, that Choniates refers to Conrad rather than to Louis VII (*contra* HARRIS, J., *Byzantium and the Crusades*, London - New York, 2003, p. 138.

fall in battle, God forbid, to die for Christ is a fair winding sheet."[85] Certainly, ideology can be turned on its head at a moment's notice.[86] Nevertheless, the passage suggests at the very least that Choniates was fully aware of and accepted the religious motives of the Second Crusade.

THE FRUITS OF DAMASCUS

Things changed after the disastrous campaign in Syria and the ignominious defeat at Damascus. The shock in Western Europe at the shameful failure of a crusade blessed by the pope, preached by Bernard of Clairvaux, and led by two apocalyptic kings was profound. Various explanations were given, engaging natural, human, and supernatural agents.[87] In some few but important cases, the treachery of the Byzantines was invoked. Louis VII himself had made that suggestion in 1148. In his letter to Suger, written from Antioch, he restated what he had already written in 1147, namely, that he had been honorably received by Manuel. But he also reported that the passage through Asia Minor was made dangerous because of the perfidy of the emperor who had allowed the Turks to attack the French army.[88] It is the first mention of Byzantine involvement in the tribulations of the French army, and it was made by a king who already had been humiliated in Asia Minor and was having a difficult time in Antioch as well. Later, the same accusation was made at some considerable length and with eloquence by Odo of Deuil, who concluded that "the flowers of France withered before they could bear fruit in Damascus."[89]

Odo of Deuil's account of the Second Crusade is both an invective against the Byzantines and an *excitatorium* for a crusade against them. It is a witness for the modalities of negative Western presentations of Byzantium and for the longevity of negative commonplaces. It is not a good witness for the argument that there was imminent threat of attack on Constantinople by the French army during the Second Crusade. Preeminently, it is a source for the plans for a new crusade that would be directed in the first instance against the Byzantine Empire. Such an idea was broached in 1149-1150.[90] The plans remain hazy, to be sure; but they clearly involved Roger of Sicily, perhaps acting in alliance with Louis VII, Peter the Venerable, Bernard of Clairvaux, the bishop of Langres, and possibly Suger. Peter the Venerable and Bernard of Clairvaux tried to make peace between

---

85. Translation by MAGOULIAS, H. J., *O City of Byzantium, Annals of Niketas Choniates*, Detroit, 1984, p. 40.

86. Scholars have noted the quick turnaround of Manganeios Prodromos's position on the Germans, in his panegyric for the marriage of Theodora to Henry Jasomirgott, where the glory and honor of the bridegroom is praised: JEFFRIES, The "Wild Beast," pp. 114-115.

87. This has been fully discussed by CONSTABLE, G., The Second Crusade as Seen by Contemporaries, *Traditio* 9, 1953, pp. 213-279.

88. *Suger, Œuvres*, II, no. 27; *RHGF*, XV, pp. 495-496. William of Tyre, strangely enough, does not dwell on the evildoings of the Greeks against Louis's army (Bk. XVI.24ff), although he buys completely into the story of Manuel's responsibility for the Turkish attacks against the Germans (Bk. XVI.19-23). I do not know where William of Tyre received his information regarding this: it is possible that the stories were put forward by Louis VII and his people.

89. ODO OF DEUIL, p. 119: "marcescunt flores Franciae antequam fructum faciant in Damascus."

90. Much has been written about these plans. See CONSTABLE, G., The Crusading Project of 1150, in KEDAR, B., RILEY-SMITH, J., and HIESTAND, R., eds., *Montjoie: Studies in Crusade History in Honour of Hans Eberhard Mayer*, Aldershot, 1997, pp. 67-75; REUTER,T., The Non-Crusade of 1149-1150, in PHILLIPS, J., and HOCH, M., *The Second Crusade: Scope and Consequences*, Manchester, 2001, pp. 151ff; KINDLIMANN, *Die Eroberung*, pp. 177ff.

Conrad III and Roger, so as to make an anti-Byzantine crusade possible. The letter of Peter the Venerable to Roger, written ca. 1150, speaks of "pene totius Gallie et Germaniae miserabili fraude exctinctum florem," echoing Odo of Deuil, and urges Roger: "Exsurge igitur bone princeps... exsurge in adiutorium populo dei, ... ulciscere tot opprobria, tot iniurias, tot mortes."[91] If those plans had ever come to pass, they would have posed a deadly danger: even without the help of Conrad III, an enterprise that united, under the banner of crusade, a French land army and the Sicilian fleet would have been formidable indeed. The fact that a crusade to the Holy Land, involving much the same cast of characters, was discussed separately but at approximately the same time seems to me not to obviate the threat to the Byzantine Empire but rather to heighten it: doubtless, the two campaigns would have merged.

The plans were dangerous, too, because they brought together some of the most important personalities of the time, all of whom were bound together by long-standing ties. The Norman king was a relative of Louis VII. Langres, in Burgundy, was one of the very first cities the young Louis had visited upon assuming the throne, because he had the loyalty of the count of Burgundy.[92] Burgundy was crusading territory. Suger was a friend of the bishop of Langres, and there were close ties between Peter the Venerable and Bernard of Clairvaux. As for Odo of Deuil, he had been the chaplain of Louis VII on the expedition; he was an important man, with important connections, who became abbot of St. Denis in 1151. His narration regarding the expedition of Louis VII to the Holy Land has now been dated to early 1150.[93] If it was written in the context of the negotiations of 1149-1150, all of the instances in which the bishop of Langres is said to have urged an attack on Constantinople must be evaluated in light of these subsequent negotiations: had we heeded the bishop of Langres and Roger II, Odo was writing, we would not have failed in Damascus; but we did not heed them, and another crusade must avenge the ills done to that army.

The plans failed for two reasons, one outside Byzantine control and the other very much within it. The first was the war-weariness of French nobles and the precipitous decline in the popularity of Bernard of Clairvaux as a preacher of crusades. The second reason was, once again, Manuel's successful diplomacy. In 1148, in Thessalonike, he had confirmed his alliance with Conrad III, probably an agreement that Conrad would attack the king of Sicily.[94] In April 1150, Conrad wrote to Bertha/Irene, his niece and adopted daughter, that Roger along with Louis VII "and the whole nation of the Franks" ("omnis Francorum populus cum ipso rege suo") was preparing to attack Manuel, and that he, in turn, was preparing a campaign against Roger.[95] The papacy was still at odds with Roger, and Conrad's expedition against the king of Sicily was also supposed to help Eugenius III, in return for which Conrad was to be crowned in Rome.[96]

---

91. Constable, G., *The Letters of Peter the Venerable*, Cambridge, Mass., 1967, p. 162.

92. Fragment of Suger's History of Louis VII, in *Suger, Œuvres*, Paris, 1996, vol. I, p. 165.

93. Mayr-Harting, Odo of Deuil, pp. 225-241. I find the arguments for this new dating persuasive.

94. Kinnamos, p. 86; Magdalino, *Manuel I*, pp. 52-53.

95. Phillips, J., The Failure of the 1150 Crusade and the Development of Ties with Byzantium, in Phillips, J., *Defenders of the Holy Land*, Oxford, 1996, pp. 100-131, at p. 114: MGH, *Diplomata*, IX, 1969, no. 229, p. 406.

96. "Cum etiam iurata expeditione in proximo imperii coronam acceptans esset": Otto of Freising, I.63, p. 97.

The German alliance held firm during the early years of Frederick I's reign, despite some problems. The defensive Byzantine strategy against threats from Westerners, whether crusaders or Normans, became aggressive. Manuel completed the establishment of his suzerainty over Antioch and strengthened his ties with the Kingdom of Jerusalem on the one hand; and, on the other, he launched an ill-fated campaign into Italy, in 1154-1156.[97] He and Frederick were still allied against William of Sicily, but only up to a point: according to Otto of Freising, although Frederick hated William, still he had no desire to have foreigners on the lands at the frontiers of his state, which had been usurped by Roger.[98] Eventually, however, diplomatic possibilities and alignments changed. The important stages are the failure of Manuel's Italian campaign; the reconciliation of Frederick I with the papacy and the Lombard cities in 1177; the marriage of his heir, Henry, to Constance of Sicily in 1184, which gave him the claims of the Normans; the death of Amalric I of Jerusalem in 1174; and Manuel's defeat at Myriokephalon in 1176, which for Frederick meant the affirmation of his own authority as sole Roman emperor. Manuel's expulsion of the Venetians from the Byzantine Empire in 1171 was probably the most important nail in that coffin, for the Venetian alliance had been indispensable in 1147 as in 1105. Ominously, the Venetians concluded a twenty-year treaty with the Normans in 1175, an event that reversed a hundred years of relations between the Byzantine Empire, Venice, and the Normans. As a result, Venice sent no help when William II invaded the Byzantine Empire in 1185.[99]

FREDERICK BARBAROSSA PROVOKED

In these changed circumstances, it is no wonder that the preaching of the Third Crusade and the impending campaign of Frederick Barbarossa filled the Byzantines with fear. The major Byzantine and Western sources on this crusade are, for once, in almost perfect agreement regarding the most important events: the purpose of Frederick Barbarossa, the developing hostilities on the ground and the cause thereof, the reaction of the Byzantine government, and the eventual decision of the Western emperor to solve the Greek problem by having a crusade organized against the empire. Since no major problems of interpretation arise, my treatment of the Third Crusade will be brief.[100]

Ansbert and Niketas Choniates both essentially agree that Isaac II was from the beginning suspicious of the crusaders, and was persuaded by some of his advisors that Frederick's true purpose was not to recover Jerusalem but to conquer Constantinople. Ansbert adds the information that Isaac harbored similar suspicions of the king of France; if so, the fact that Philip Augustus went east by sea made any such suspicions moot.[101] Both accounts also agree that the first meeting between Frederick and the Byzantine ambassadors in Nuremberg in November 1188 was a perfect diplomatic failure since, according to Choniates, the ambassadors projected to Frederick the idea that Isaac was ill-disposed toward the German army,[102] while according to Ansbert they relayed to Frederick the imperial message that if he did not assuage Isaac's suspicions, he would be

---

97. MAGDALINO, *Manuel I*, pp. 58ff; PHILLIPS, The Failure, pp. 118ff.

98. OTTO OF FREISING, II.30, pp. 156-157.

99. BRAND, C., *Byzantium Confronts the West, 1180-1204*, Cambridge, Mass., 1968, pp. 195ff.

100. On this crusade, see JOHNSON, E. N., The Crusades of Frederick Barbarossa and Henry VI, in *A History of the Crusades*, ed. SETTON, K. M., vol. II, Philadelphia, 1962, pp. 87-122.

101. CHONIATES, p. 404; ANSBERT in CHROUST, A., ed., *Quellen zur Geschichte des Kreuzzuges Kaiser Friedrichs I.*, Berlin, 1928, p. 15 (hereafter ANSBERT).

102. CHONIATES, p. 402.

denied entry into Byzantine territory.[103] Furthermore, both at some point connect the problems Frederick encountered when he did enter Byzantine lands with the fact that Isaac had a treaty with Saladin, by which, as a matter of fact, he had actually promised to delay and oppose the German army.[104] Within a few weeks of hearing of this agreement, Frederick Barbarossa decided that the crusade could not proceed without first taking Constantinople.

In the best of circumstances, the passage of the German army through the Byzantine Empire would have posed objective problems and might have been expected to lead to situations similar to those that attended the Second Crusade. Frederick's army was huge.[105] Furthermore, as it turned out, it took Frederick Barbarossa nine months to cross the Byzantine possessions in the Balkans; most of this time was spent in southern Bulgaria and Thrace, where he was waiting for the Byzantines to provide passage to Asia Minor.[106] Despite Isaac's promises to give safe passage, provisions, and good terms for currency exchange, and even if he had meant to follow these agreements to the letter, which is not certain, the area could not possibly provide provisions for such a crowd over such a long time and emerge unscathed. In fact, the combination of lack of proper provisioning, bad terms of currency exchange, and Isaac's appalling diplomacy led to widespread looting and destruction, especially in Thrace. Entire cities were deserted by their inhabitants, and the countryside became desolated.[107] The practical matters of provisioning and exchange loom large in the treaty of Adrianople, concluded in February 1090.[108]

So, in the best of circumstances, low-grade hostilities were to be expected; but these were far from the best of circumstances. The Byzantine emperor, Patriarch Dositheos, and the imperial officials were criminally provocative.[109] Isaac II played the most stupid diplomatic games with the old emperor, the victor of the Italian wars and so many others. He also took the unprecedented step of imprisoning Frederick's ambassadors, a breach of diplomatic protocol that was remembered by Henry VI even after the death of Barbarossa.[110]

103. ANSBERT, p. 15.

104. BRAND, *Byzantium Confronts the West*, p. 177.

105. According to Arnold of Lübeck, there were 100,000 foot and 50,000 horse: *Arnoldi Chronica slavorum*, MGH, SS, Hannover, 1868, pp. 130-131. The *Gesta Federici imperatoris in expeditione sacra*, ed. HOLDER-EGGER, O., in *Gesta Federici I imperatoris in Lombardia...*, MGH, ScriptRerGerm, Hannover, 1892, p. 80, gives an estimate of 100,000. BRAND, *Byzantium Confronts the West*, p. 178, gives 15,000 people, of whom 3,000 were knights. FRANCE, J., *Victory in the East: A Military History of the First Crusade*, Cambridge, 1994, p. 136, estimates 100,000 men, of whom 20,000 were mounted troops.

106. LAIOU, Byzantine Trade, p. 162.

107. CHONIATES, pp. 402-404; ANSBERT, pp. 33-34, 37, 38 (Philippoupolis is abandoned), 43ff, 53, 59-60, 63: he writes of the terrible looting carried out by the German contingents, and especially by the Bohemians; cf. *Historia Peregrinorum*, in CHROUST, *Quellen*, pp. 143, 149 (hereafter *HP*; this was written after 1215, not by a participant, but possibly with a participant as a source; ANSBERT too is a source: see pp. lxxxii, lxxxviii); *Epistola de morte Friderici imperatoris*, in CHROUST, *Quellen*, pp. 345-346 (written by a high cleric, participant, probably to the bishop of Würzburg, before 21 June 1190: see the introduction to ANSBERT, p. xcvi).

108. ANSBERT, pp. 64-66; HAMPE, K., Ein ungedruckter Bericht über den Vertrag von Adrianopel zwischen Friedrich I. und Isaak Angelos vom Febr. 1190, *Neues Archiv der Gesellschaft für deutsche Geschichtskunde* 23, 1898, pp. 399-400; LAIOU, Byzantine Trade, pp. 167, 175.

109. On Dositheos, see ANSBERT, pp. 43, 49; *HP*, pp. 142-143.

110. ANSBERT, p. 38; *Epistola*, p. 173; BRAND, *Byzantium Confronts the West*, pp. 188 ff. Cf. Arnold of Lübeck, pp. 132-133, who claims that Frederick had forbidden all looting until he learned of the captivity of his ambassadors. Then he permitted it, and his army collected much gold, silver, precious garments, and arms.

Not only did Isaac revive the title controversy, but in November 1189 he sent Frederick the charming message that he would die before spring.[111] Given the fact that Barbarossa had a large army, and that the Byzantines had been defeated in every battle, this attitude is very hard to comprehend. One may understand that the Byzantines feared an attack even before the crusade had started out, if only because the terrible Norman sack of Thessalonike in 1185 was very recent history indeed. But the way in which they treated the German emperor was almost guaranteed to turn those fears into reality. The more so since, in an act that defies all understanding, Isaac had refused Barbarossa passage into Asia Minor.[112]

Matters reached an impasse as the German army was mired in Thrace, with the winter coming and no way to cross over to Asia Minor. It was in these circumstances that Frederick Barbarossa conceived of a crusade against Constantinople. The main source for this is "Ansbert," who quotes a letter sent by Frederick to his son Henry VI, asking him to prepare a fleet with ships from Venice, Genoa, Pisa, Ancona, and other maritime cities. They were to come to Constantinople in March 1190 and attack it by sea while Frederick himself attacked by land. That the enterprise was meant to be a crusade is indicated by Frederick's exhortation to his son to write to the pope to send preachers "to all the provinces" to rouse the "people of God" against the enemies of the cross and most specifically against the Greeks, whom the patriarch had exhorted to kill crusaders.[113] Had such a crusade taken place it would have been exceedingly dangerous, and Constantinople might well have fallen. The Fourth Crusade would have occurred fourteen years before it did. Around Christmas 1189, reports the *Historia Peregrinorum*, the city of Constantinople lived in terror, expecting the imminent capture of the city and the extermination of its inhabitants.[114]

However, the expedition never took place, although Ansbert reports that Pisan ambassadors did come to Frederick in March 1190, offering him ships with which to besiege the capital.[115] But in February 1190 the Byzantines and Frederick concluded the treaty of Adrianople, and by late March the German troops had been ferried across to Asia Minor. The "crusade" Frederick had suggested to his son did not take place at this point.

Why did it not? Primarily because Frederick Barbarossa was really not interested in capturing Constantinople. He was provoked into contemplating an attack on it, but what he really wanted to do was to go to Jerusalem. Ansbert makes the point strongly, and Barbarossa's actions confirm it.[116] He made several efforts to persuade Isaac to arrange passage even after he had written his letter to Henry.[117] He did not take advantage of the offers of the Serbs and the Bulgarians to attack the Byzantine Empire.[118] And as soon as passage was offered him, he moved on.[119] These are not the actions of a man driven to conquer Constantinople. The account of Niketas Choniates clinches the issue. He clearly

---

111. CHONIATES, p. 410.
112. ANSBERT, p. 39: August 1189.
113. ANSBERT, p. 43.
114. *HP*, p. 148.
115. ANSBERT, p. 67.
116. See, for example, p. 40: Frederick could have occupied "totam Macedoniam, nisi causa crucifixi, quam susceperat tractandam, eum retraxisset."
117. ANSBERT, p. 57 (Christmas 1189), pp. 59-60 (late January).
118. ANSBERT, p. 58. Cf. p. 68, where Ansbert argues that had Frederick wanted to, he had the means to take Constantinople, with the help of the maritime cities of Italy and 60,000 Serbian and "Vlach" auxiliaries.
119. *HP*, p. 152.

places the blame for the hostilities on Isaac. When he reports on the friendly reception of the crusaders in Laodicea, he has Frederick say, in his address to the citizens, that if all the Greeks had been like them, they would have profited from the money the crusaders would have spent in the marketplaces, and no Christian blood would have been shed.[120] The portrait Niketas draws of Frederick Barbarossa after the latter's death is the most sympathetic portrait of a ruler in his entire work.

And he was drowned, a man worthy of being well remembered for a long time, and of being justly envied for his death by the wise, not only because he was of noble birth and a descendant of many nations out of three of his ancestors; but also because, being inflamed with the love of Christ, more so than any of the contemporary Christian emperors anywhere, he abandoned his country, and the royal sumptuousness and comfort, and the prospects of a proud life and an old age spent at home among his dear ones, choosing rather to suffer along with the Christians of Palestine for the sake of the name of Christ and for the honor of the life-giving sepulcher... Not even the little water and bread, which, moreover, had to be bought and at times was given him with malevolence, changed his plans... Much was the man's zeal like that of the apostles, and his purpose was loved by God.[121]

The Third Crusade, then, it is fair to say, originally posed no more than the usual manageable threat occasioned by large armies passing through the Byzantine Empire. A crusading plan against Constantinople did develop, but was never carried out. The Byzantine response to the growing threat was minimal to nonexistent. In the end, the crusade was averted not by Byzantine diplomacy or other actions, but because Isaac II finally saw that he was better served by letting the crusaders go on their way to Palestine, and also, and much more importantly, because Frederick Barbarossa did genuinely want to crown his reign with the reconquest of Jerusalem and not with the conquest of Constantinople.[122]

CONCLUSIONS

I have drawn a distinction between hostilities on the ground on the one hand and, on the other, plans to conquer Constantinople, which in all cases developed subsequently to and as a consequence of the primary expedition. The hostilities on the ground, which I have called opportunistic, were occasioned by practical problems in the first instance. On the other side of the coin, the suspicion with which the Byzantines viewed the crusades played a role, in varying degrees, insofar as the requests for safe passage and provisioning were used to bind the crusaders to the Byzantine state, a desire that, in turn, aroused the suspicions of and created problems with the leaders of the crusades. The fears of the Byzantines were primarily founded on the fact that they saw the crusades as intimately connected with the ambitions of the Normans: in this sense, Robert Guiscard's campaign of 1081 had been a seminal event, for it colored Byzantine attitudes toward the crusaders. Bohemond's crusade sealed the connection, and William II's attack on Thessalonike in 1185 reinforced it, while the coronation of Henry VI as king of Sicily on 24 December

120. CHONIATES, p. 412.
121. CHONIATES, pp. 416-417.
122. This is hardly an original conclusion: cf. BRAND, *Byzantium Confronts the West*, pp. 176ff.

1194 seemed to clinch the link.[123] Fear fed upon suspicion, and sometimes the Byzantines took unjustified and occasionally hysterical measures, notably in the course of the Third Crusade.

Hostilities due to circumstance had important long-term effects. Historical memory in the West surely included memories of fighting against Byzantine armies. Among the crusading families of Western Europe there must have been some who remembered good relations with Byzantium and others who remembered hardship, trouble, and hostility. The attack on Constantinople in 1204 was probably made more palatable by the long history of hostilities on the ground – and even of abortive crusading plans. After all, Villehardouin presents the events of 1203-1204 almost as a series of opportunistic events.

Opportunistic attacks aside, every Western plan to launch an anti-Byzantine crusade was justified by the argument that the Byzantines were hindering the progress of the crusade in the Holy Land, and that therefore no such enterprise could be successful until and unless Constantinople was conquered. By the same token, it must be noted that until mid-century, the elaboration of plans to attack Constantinople came in the wake of crusading failure: the dismal failure of the crusades of 1101 and 1147-1149. In both cases, the Byzantines became the scapegoat, and the capture of Constantinople was seen as a palliative for and a corrective to failure. Scholars have not sufficiently stressed another important fact: in the first two crusades it was the passage not through the Balkans but through Asia Minor that created most of the problems of the crusaders and occasioned most of their complaints, leading to the conclusion that "Constantinopolis delenda est." This was the case in the first stage of the First Crusade, as well as in its second stage (the crusade of 1101), and it was the case also in the Second Crusade. But Asia Minor was the area least tightly controlled by the Byzantine state and army.[124] At the time of the Third Crusade, on the other hand, the breaking point came not in Asia Minor but at the end of nine months in the Balkans.

The role of the Normans was paramount in the development of plans for crusades against the Byzantine Empire and in the formation of the Byzantine response. Surely Bohemond's role needs no further elaboration. At the time of the Second Crusade, it was Roger II who may have proposed to Louis VII a joint attack from the outset; certainly he was involved in, or perhaps elicited, the ill-conceived and ill-fated plans of 1149-1150. As for Henry VI's threats to the Byzantine Empire, they included, according to Niketas Choniates, the demand for the "return" of the lands taken by William II in 1185, on the astonishing grounds that the Byzantines had been guilty of treachery in the decisive battle in which William was defeated.[125]

The Byzantine response to the threat, real and perceived, of a Western crusade also followed certain patterns. Alexios I's extraordinary war of propaganda against Bohemond's crusade was not, as far as we know, duplicated in later crusades. Perhaps it was unnecessary, for his successors did follow another of his policies, to wit, the formation of alliances with Western powers in order to counter the Western threat. It was the failure of the basic policies of alliance with the Holy Roman Empire and Venice that posed a threat during the Third Crusade and, of course, in the Fourth Crusade.

123. CHONIATES, pp. 475-476; BRAND, *Byzantium Confronts the West*, pp. 188ff.

124. The situation had gotten completely out of hand by the time of the Third Crusade: see *Gesta Federici imperatoris*, pp. 85-95, and *Chronicon Magni presbiteri*, MGH, *SS*, XVII, Hannover, 1861, Leipzig, 1925, pp. 513-514.

125. CHONIATES, pp. 476-478. The battle had taken place on 7 November 1185: BRAND, *Byzantium Confronts the West*, p. 171.

All of this forms the background to the Fourth Crusade. Since the very first crusading expedition, the conquest of Constantinople in the name of the defense of the Holy Land had been envisaged, in the circumstances outlined here. There were people in Western Europe, primarily, but not only, the Normans, who had no compunction about attacking the great Christian state. The plans, however, were secondary to the crusade, and were not put into effect except by Bohemond. In the case of the Second Crusade, they were hardly serious. In all cases, they were counterbalanced by other considerations.

This brings me back to my original question: why was the Fourth Crusade so late in coming? First, because Bohemond failed; second, because of successful Byzantine diplomacy, which became a large but delicate edifice in the deft hands of Manuel I, and a disaster in the hands of his successors. There were also external causes. The long hostility between the papacy and the Normans and the Holy Roman Empire and the papacy allowed the Byzantines room to maneuver. Finally, one must stress that throughout the period, and even in 1204, there was a large number of Western Europeans who considered an attack on Byzantium to be a perversion of the crusading movement. The crusades, after all, had a purpose: the recovery of or aid to the Holy Land. In the end, it was the desire of Conrad III, Louis VII, and, above all, Frederick Barbarossa to proceed to the Holy Land that silenced the voices preaching an attack on Constantinople, until each crusade was severely threatened or until it had ended in failure. That is why the Fourth Crusade was so long delayed, but by 1203 most of the safeguards I have discussed were no longer in place.

V

On Just War in Byzantium

The Byzantine Empire was, for long periods of its history, a state in war, or at least a state in which war played an important role, sometimes even a fundamental one. Scholars have given considerable attention to various aspects of the impact of military needs and activities on the state and society, from the point of view of both political history and administrative and social history. The composition of the army, the recruitment of soldiers, and the all-important fiscal questions regarding the mode of payment of soldiers and army officials have all been the object of detailed and profound study. The ideology of war in Byzantium has received less attention. The inquiry into this topic has tended to focus on the question of the existence or nonexistence of the concept of "holy war" in Byzantium. While this interest is understandable, given the fact that two other medieval societies, close neighbors of Byzantium, had rather clear concepts of holy war, whether *jihad* or crusade, it is also somewhat unfortunate, on at least two counts. First, the terms of the discussion have not always been clear, nor have scholars always respected the peculiarities of holy war, for example, that, among other things, it must be promulgated by a religious authority, which is also the sole authority capable of granting remission of sins or declaring the warriors martyrs; as a result, sober assessments of the question have alternated with extravagant claims for a Byzantine "crusade."[1] Second, this discussion is limited in time, centering on the tenth century with occasional forays into the past, as far back as Herakleios; but if the undoubted religious coloring of tenth-century warfare has given scholars visions of holy war, surely no such contention can be made for subsequent periods.[2] And yet the Byzantines continued to wage war; did they have an ideology to justify it?

Most societies need to find justification for warfare, as an ancient author recognized in a somewhat cynical passage.[3] The quest for arguments that would distinguish just from unjust wars has engaged scholars and politicians of the Western tradition from the time of classical Greece to our own day.[4] A summary of the Greek and Roman argumentation may be found in Frederick H. Russell's *The Just War in the Middle Ages* (Cambridge, 1975). For the medieval period, Russell stresses the difference between holy war and just war, the latter being a secular affair whose characteristics are that the authority competent to declare it is a public authority, that it is waged for motives such as defense of territory, or persons or rights, and that, unlike holy war, it limits "violence by codes of right conduct."[5] The Western Middle Ages saw the elaboration of theories of just war, of holy war, and of the crusade, which is a form of just war of the church. These form the basis of the modern Catholic theory of just war, which incorporates formal, elaborate, and complex criteria.[6]

The Byzantines did not produce formal, detailed statements regarding just war. Thus the principles and indeed the existence of such a concept must be sought in and distilled from a number of sources. In this paper, I have a modest aim, which is to address the question primarily on the basis of one text, the *Alexiad* of Anna Komnene. Since the reason for this choice is not self-evident, a few words of justification are necessary. Princess Anna Komnene has a biography which, *prima facie*, would suggest that one might profitably search her work for ideas of just war. She came from a martial family: her father, Alexios I, and his brother, the sebastocrator Isaac, had been famous soldiers before Alexios ascended the throne as the representative of a strong military aristocracy. Her brother, Emperor John II, was a man who spent a great deal of his time on campaign. On his deathbed, he boasted: "The East and the West have seen me in battle; I have fought the foreign peoples on both continents; only for a short while have I remained in the palace; almost my entire life has been spent in a tent."[7] Her nephew, Manuel I, was an equally renowned soldier, who combined military and knightly valor. Yet she disliked both her brother and her nephew, while her historical work, which she began writing in 1138, is an unabashed panegyric of her father. One could suppose that she might be moved to justify Alexios' many wars, and perhaps differentiate them from those of his successors. Second, Anna Komnene was an uncommonly well-educated woman and a patron of letters. She was, even more uncommonly, interested in philosophy, very much including Aristotle.[8] Did any of Aristotle's thoughts on government, war, and peace filter through to her own work? Furthermore, her father's reign had witnessed dramatic events, some of which she had seen, while others she knew from the accounts of eyewitnesses and from official documents. Among these events, the First Crusade is particularly pertinent for our topic. Her father had been drawn into hostilities with Christians and, what is more, Christians who said they were engaged in holy war for the liberation of the Holy Land. The crusade was a new phenomenon in Western Europe as well; one would expect that the presence of these warriors for the faith, and their clash with the Byzantines, might raise questions about what constitutes a just and meritorious war.[9]

Anna Komnene, in her Preface to the *Alexiad*, shows the reader that she knows how history should be written, and that she values objectivity which, she promises, will guide her narrative. What she wrote, however, is in some ways an epic. It looks like an epic partly because most of her history, as indeed much of her father's reign, is concerned with wars. The opponents are clearly drawn: the Byzantine Empire is pitted against the rest of the world, and her father against a succession of enemies. Her view of international affairs has the simplicity of the worldview of empires. The Byzantine Empire is the center, figuratively and geographically; the rest of the world is measured against it and is judged according to the dangers or opportunities it presents to the Empire. In her most expansive moments, she produces the most traditional possible theory of what the limits of the Byzantine Empire were or should be: "There was a time when the frontiers of Roman power were the two pillars at the limits of east and west—the so-called pillars of Hercules in the west, and those of Dionysos, not far from the Indian border, in the east. As far as its extent was concerned, it is impossible to say how great was the power of the Roman Empire: it included Egypt, Meroë, all the land of the Troglodytes, the countries near the Torrid Zone; on the other side, the famous Thule, and all the peoples who live in the region of the North, over whom is the polar star."[10] That is the old Roman Empire at its most extensive. In more sober moments, she considered the legitimate boundaries to be those that existed before the battle of Mantzikert and the Turkish invasions of the late eleventh century.[11] These were also boundaries of strategy: they were the frontiers her father wanted to restore.

The state as conceived by our historian was more than notionally vast; it was also, by unquestioned right in her eyes, the ruler of the world: "all men look upon [the Empire of the Romans] with envy. Being *by nature* the master of other nations, it is the object of enmity on the part of its slaves."[12] Once more, this is a notional mastery; she does not show the Empire engaged in a struggle to subdue the rest of the world. On the contrary, it was a state under attack. Enemies surrounded it on all sides, and they were all attacking it, simultaneously or in waves, during the reign of her father: the "Franks" (a generic name) and the Venetians from the West, the Turks from the East, the barbarian Scythians (Petchenegs and Cumans) from the North.[13] It was God, she says, who allowed such tribulations to fall upon His people, or else it was the incompetence of previous rulers. But it was also God, or fate, that had placed on the throne a man like her father, almost a martyr, almost equal to the apostles, a Christlike figure, to defend and enlarge the state by deeds which not even Demosthenes nor all of the ancient philosophers could adequately describe.[14] She never openly poses the question whether his wars were justified; but her entire narrative makes it clear that she thought they were. On what basis were they justified? I think we can answer this question by looking at her description of the circumstances in which Alexios went to war.

(a) *Self-defense.* First of all, Alexios' wars were defensive—always in Anna's view. When discussing Bohemond's attack on the Byzantine Empire, in 1105, she says, "as for the barbarians, wherever they were, he [Alexios] gave them no pretext for war and did not use compulsion on them; nevertheless, if they did cause trouble, he checked them."[15] This passage is indicative of a more general attitude of hers which suggests that the Byzantines always fought in order to defend themselves, and did not initiate wars. That is very much in evidence in Anna's treatment of Alexios' relations with the leaders of the First Crusade. It is established from the very beginning that the Crusaders had aggressive intentions toward the Byzantine Empire. While Peter the Hermit is acknowledged to have wanted simply to go on pilgrimage to the Holy Sepulcher, "the other counts (and in particular Bohemond) cherished their old grudge against Alexius and sought a good opportunity to avenge the glorious victory which the Emperor had won at Larissa. They were all of one mind and in order to fulfill their dream of taking Constantinople they adopted a common policy."[16] Once this has been established, all of Alexios' actions toward the Crusaders are seen to have been undertaken in self-defense. Even so, Anna repeats every so often the fact that the Crusaders were the aggressors, as, for example, when Alexios refuses to attack them even after repeated provocations outside the walls of Constantinople. He asks them to desist, both because this was Good Thursday and because he did not want to have bloodshed between Christians. In the end, as the Westerners become more menacing, he is forced to attack them, but even so he gives orders that they are to be frightened rather than killed.[17] Similarly, Bohemond's eventual attack against the Byzantine Empire so clearly put the emperor in a defensive position that Anna does not even have to justify this war at great length. It suffices for her to establish Bohemond's unrelieved hostility and the threat he posed to the state: Bohemond wanted to "throw into tumult the Roman world which you rule," and threatened that "with many a murder I will make your cities and your provinces run with blood, until I set up my spear in Byzantium itself."[18]

(b) *The recovery of territory.* If Alexios' wars were undertaken in defense of the state, that state was, it will be remembered, larger than the actual frontiers of the Empire at any time during his reign. In Asia Minor, the Byzantines claimed by right those lands which had been conquered by the Turks after 1071. What in the theory of just war is called the recovery of lost goods (*rebus repetitis*) looms large in the *Alexiad*.[19] It is the basis for Alexios' insistence that the Crusaders swear to restore to him all the lands they took from the Turks that had previously been Byzantine.[20] The oath was greatly resented by the Crusaders, and of course it was broken in the act. But for Anna and her contemporaries, it was evident that the Empire had the right, and the emperor had virtually the obligation, to recover the lost lands. Thus, when Bohemond did not respond to Alexios' demand that he hand over Laodicea and Antioch, Alexios realized that "the frontiers of the Roman Empire must be firmly held," and sent troops to Cilicia to take it as well as to prepare for an assault on Antioch, then held by the Crusaders.[21] These frontiers, of course, were not the actual ones, but rather the frontiers the Byzantines had had in the past. The point is made with perfect clarity in an encounter of Alexios I with the Turkish sultan Malik Shah. The sultan is told that unless he yields to Byzantine authority, stops his attacks against Christians, and withdraws to the lands "where you used to dwell before Romanos Diogenes became emperor," unless he refrains from "crossing the frontiers of the Empire," Alexios will "exterminate your race."[22] The message is clear: the lost territories belong to the Byzantine Empire, and the sultan must return them or face war—and after fair warning, at that.

This position was given legal force in the agreement made at Devol between Alexios I and Bohemond in 1107. An important term of the agreement was that Bohemond and his men would turn over to the Byzantine emperor any land which "either now or in the past was subject to your authority," or "any land once upon a time paying tribute to this Empire."[23] In the same passage, the past boundaries of the Byzantine Empire are said to have extended from the Adriatic to the whole East and along the length of Great Asia. It must be remembered that at the time of the treaty of Devol the Byzantines were speaking from a position of strength and could make large claims. The text of that treaty is the most expansionist in the *Alexiad*. Nevertheless, even at that moment, the actual, as opposed to the theoretical, claims of the Byzantines were not boundless but remained more or less firmly fixed to the eleventh-century frontiers.

Given this position, the wars in Asia Minor are justified. Thus, when Anna mentions that, after the treaty of Devol, Alexios had sent large armies to fight with the Westerners against the Turks, she says that her father did this for two reasons. First, he was concerned for the Westerners, since they were Christians, and he did not want them to be killed at the hands of the Turks. Second, he wanted to ensure that they would return to him the cities of the Turks and thus extend the frontiers of the Roman Empire.

(c) *Breach of agreement*. War is also undertaken if the other side breaks treaties. In such a case, we can consider the war to be defensive, since it follows a hostile act on the part of the opponent. It is also the result of a breach of contract, and a very important contract since in this period, and throughout the twelfth century, treaties or truces or, generally, agreements with other states or peoples were sealed and confirmed by oaths. Bohemond, when he attacked the Empire, is accused by Alexios of having broken his promises and oaths; the failure of his enterprise is the proof of his guilt.[24] When, after Bohemond's death, his nephew Tancred decides to take possession of Antioch in his own right, even though by treaty the ownership of the city belonged to Alexios, Anna produces a wealth of argumentation to justify Alexios' decision to prepare for war against Tancred. The first, and recurring, argument is that the "Franks" had broken the treaties and forsworn their oaths. For that reason, "he could not tolerate the situation, and he had to make strong reprisal (ἀντιδρᾶσαι) and to punish them for such inhumanity." He found the behavior of the Franks heartrending and the insult intolerable. The Greek word for insult is ὕβρις, which is also the term used to render the Latin *injuria*, that is, an injury which may be avenged by war. Tancred was charged with injustice and with breaking his oaths. Nevertheless, Alexios first sent ambassadors to him to persuade him to change his course, and it was only after Tancred's refusal that the emperor contemplated war.[25] It is evident that here we have a conflation of causes which would justify hostile action against Tancred: his breach of the treaties and the oaths, his holding on to lands which according to Alexios belonged to the Byzantine Empire, his injustice, the injury done to the Byzantine state. All of these are, as we shall see below, causes of just war both in the Roman and in the Western medieval traditions.

The case against Tancred is made so carefully partly, no doubt, because Alexios sought help among the leaders of the other Crusader states, and thus had to prepare a full justification. In other cases, the breach of agreement is presented without much discussion. Thus, at one point during the long-drawn-out Petcheneg wars of the first part of Alexios' reign, the emperor offered them a peace treaty, which they accepted. Then the Cumans sent ambassadors to the emperor, asking his permission to attack the Petchenegs. Alexios refused, "because a treaty had already been concluded." The Petchenegs, however, since they no longer feared the Cumans, broke the treaty, for "all barbarians are usually fickle and characteristically unable to keep their pledges."[26] War, therefore, broke out anew.

(d) *Averting a greater evil.* While Anna Komnene does not explicitly justify any particular war on the grounds that it prevents a greater evil, this idea appears in an action connected with warfare. At the time of his war with Robert Guiscard, Alexios had melted down vessels and objects belonging to the church, thus provoking a major crisis. In justifying his action, Anna has the emperor say that the Empire was in mortal danger from the Turks, the Petchenegs, and the Normans, and there was no money to defend it. He continues: "if the whole country is being taken prisoner, if its cities and Constantinople itself are already in danger of becoming captives, if then we, in such a moment of peril, laid our hands on a few objects . . . and used them to secure our freedom, surely we leave no reasonable excuse to our detractors for charging us."[27] The argument here is that danger from the enemy necessitates war; the needs of war, and the greater evil of the destruction of the state and the captivity of its inhabitants, justify an act which is otherwise prohibited by the canons.

(e) *The pursuit of peace.* Aristotle had said that "no one desires to be at war for the sake of being at war, nor deliberately takes steps to cause a war."[28] He had further said that war may be necessary, but peace is noble, and preferable.[29] Anna Komnene's description of her father and his policies seems almost an illustration of these principles. Alexios is a man of peace: by nature peaceful, he became most warlike when he was forced into it by the actions of others.[30] She insists on this, and insists also on his efforts either to preserve the peace or to restore it as soon as possible after hostilities. He was a mild and philanthropic man, who knew, as any good general should, that there were many ways to achieve what he wanted and what was good for the state. Against internal enemies (the Bogomils), he used both words to persuade and the sword to coerce.[31] Against external enemies, he wanted to achieve victory. But, Anna says, a good general can use many means to that end: finesse, treaties, trickery.[32] In her discussion of Alexios' last campaigns against the Turks, she waxes enthusiastic on this theme. Yes, courage is admirable, but it must be informed by reasoning. The good general is one who achieves his objective; and the best objective is victory without danger. This can be achieved by battle or by stratagems; as long as the results are the same, the means are equally good.[33] Sometimes, indeed, peace is sought because the power of the enemy seems too great.[34] But Anna has a general view about peace that transcends the expediencies of the moment. It is presented at its lengthiest in a passage about Bohemond's attack on the Empire, where she laments the many troubles which befell the emperor from internal and external enemies. And yet the emperor was gentle and philanthropic, showering many benefices on his subjects, while to the barbarians he gave no pretext for war, although of course he fought them when they attacked. The mark of a good general, she says, is to prefer peace to war, and this is how Alexios behaved: "he cultivated peace to an unusual degree; its presence was always and by every means cherished and its absence worried him, so that he often spent sleepless nights wondering how it might return." Special pleading all of this may be, but there is one phrase which is interesting: "peace is the purpose of all wars (εἰρήνη μὲν γὰρ τέλος ἐστὶ πολέμου παντός)."[35] This is a quotation from Aristotle, and whereas the particular passage which Anna is quoting is not connected with just war, the connection is made in another passage where the same principle is enunciated: "war must be for the sake of peace."[36] St. Augustine also saw war as an instrument of peace: "Peace is the desired end of war. For every man, even in the act of waging war, is in quest of peace, but no one is in quest of war when he makes peace."[37] By insisting, and at some length, on her father's love of peace, and by showing quite frequently that he resorted to war because peace was not possible, therefore as a last resort, Anna gives a blanket justification of all of Alexios' wars.

This resolves a certain contradiction which is evident in her account. Her father is presented as a man of peace, but he is also pictured as a man of great courage, whose first instinct was for war, but whose reason dictated peace.[38] Anna was a great admirer of courage, valor, martial virtues, and a good seat on a horse. She admired great warriors, whether they were Byzantines or her father's most dangerous enemies, such as Bohemond and Robert Guiscard.[39] Alexios himself is presented as a great soldier, learned in the arts of war.[40] In a particularly striking passage, we find him leading the army against the Turks, "riding on like a great tower or a pillar of fire, or like a divine and celestial apparition."[41] Valor was, we know, an important imperial virtue in the eleventh and twelfth centuries.[42] In Anna Komnene, admiration for it is qualified by the insistence that Alexios, the great soldier, was a man of peace. Undoubtedly this is to some extent a concealed criticism of his successors, particularly of his even more martial son, John II Komnenos. The criticism is occasionally made overtly: in discussing a peace treaty which Alexios had negotiated with the Turks, Anna says that the Emperor's purpose was that the treaty should last for a long time, and indeed there was peace and prosperity for the rest of his reign, "but with him all the benefits disappeared and his efforts came to nothing through the stupidity of those who inherited his throne."[43] Her insistence on Alexios as a man of peace who nevertheless is forced to make war may also be something of a literary ploy, pointing up the tragic element in her father's reign. Finally, however, there is no contradiction; and her description of her father conforms with a good Aristotelian concept that peace is more desirable than war, but war may be necessary and courage is a great virtue in its pursuit.[44]

Does all of the above suggest that we have here a coherent idea of just war? I think that it does, although it must be stressed that nowhere in the *Alexiad* is there a systematic statement about just war. Anna was, after all, neither a lawyer, nor a canonist, nor a philosopher, but a historian, concerned less with establishing criteria for the just war than with showing her father in a good light. Ideas which conform to ancient and medieval theories of just war are subsumed in her description of the reasons for Alexios' wars. Let us return to her various justifications of her father's wars, and examine them from this viewpoint.

(a) *Self-defense.* This is an age-old idea, basic to most Western theories of just war. In an ancient Greek list of arguments for making war, it appears as the need to punish the wrongdoers if there has been injustice in the past and to fight in defense of oneself or one's kinsmen and allies.[45] Self-defense is also a Roman concept, incorporated in the Justinianic Code and eventually in the *Basilics*. There is a legal right to repel force with force, and that certainly applies to war.[46] There is also a strong idea that force and injury or insult (*injuria*) are both to be repelled, and there is an interesting convergence of vocabulary in the *Basilics* and in the *Alexiad*. In *Basilics* 2.1.3, it is stated that τὸ ἀπωθεῖσθαι τὴν ἐπιφερομένην βίαν καὶ ὕβριν is a right governed by the *jus gentium*.[47] In the *Alexiad*, the emperor opposes the ὕβρις committed by Tancred.[48] The subtleties embodied in the concept of self-defense are not elaborated upon in the *Alexiad*; but then it seems that they were not elaborated by the Western medieval civil lawyers either.[49] Self-defense is an important element in the just war theory of Western canonists.

(b) *The recovery of things lost.* This is a basic Roman tenet justifying war. The things lost can be either territory or less tangible possessions. The concept was further elaborated in medieval canon law by Gratian and his successors.[50] In Byzantium, the recovery of things lost appears with some force in the *Epanagoge* (or *Eisagoge*), the law code promulgated by Basil I, Leo VI, and Alexander: "the purpose of the emperor is to safeguard and maintain through his virtue the things which exist; to acquire through vigilance the things lost; and to recover, through his wisdom and through just victories, the things absent."[51] Hélène Ahrweiler has pointed out that we are here in the presence of a concept of the just war which justifies the policies of recovery of territories and even of the expansionism of the late ninth and tenth centuries.[52] She also points out, however, that in the Komnenian period imperial ideology was more defensive, consisting of the recovery of territories and prestige.[53] It is certainly the defensive recovery of things lost that we find in the pages of the *Alexiad*.[54]

(c) *Breach of agreement.* This seems to be an element in the Roman concept of just war.[55] I have the impression that the most important contribution of the Byzantines to the question regarding the grounds for a just war is connected with the breach of contract, that is, of a treaty. The pages of the historians Kinnamos and Choniates are replete with references to breach of treaty by others as a just cause of war. The development of this idea is an interesting one, and I plan to discuss it in another study. For the moment, it is sufficient to mention one particularly striking example. Manuel I Komnenos harangues the Czech king, trying to keep him from allying himself with the Hungarians. In the speech, reported by Kinnamos, he explicitly compares the breach of a treaty (by the Hungarians) to the breach of contract in civil law, and presents it as a cause of just war for the Byzantines: "One who deals with a private individual and, should it happen thus, scorns his agreement does not go unpunished by the law; shall the Hungarians, who have acted against their treaties with such an emperor, remain inviolable? Far from it. Then does the emperor wage war justly?"[56]

(d) *Averting a greater evil.* This idea appears as a part of Aristotle's discussion of the proper use of power and the proper aim of the state. He says that the object of preparing for war is not "in order that men may enslave those who do not deserve slavery, but in order that first they may themselves avoid being enslaved to others." He then lists two other reasons, namely, so that men may seek suzerainty for the sake of the subject peoples but not for world domination, and so that men may hold despotic power over those who deserve to be slaves. The last two points are not relevant to our discussion, since they do not arise for twelfth-century Byzantium.[57] The first, however, is relevant.

(e) *The pursuit of peace.* As we have already noted, the idea that a just war must be waged so that peace may be achieved is an Aristotelian idea, adopted by St. Augustine. The medieval canonists set great store by the proposition that peace is the desirable condition, and that a just war is an instrumentality of peace.[58]

We may thus conclude that Anna's descriptions of the causes of her father's wars incorporate the most important just war criteria of ancient and medieval societies. The objection might be raised that the concordance is forced, because I began by grouping Anna's descriptions in categories which are known categories of just war. It is true that the categorization is my own; but it is equally true that the argumentation and the descriptions are Anna's. If any doubts remain on that score, one should perhaps look again at her discussion of the justification of hostilities against Tancred: he was, by her account, guilty of breach of contract, insult, ingratitude toward those who helped him in war, injustice, and holding on to the lawful possessions of the Byzantine Empire.[59] The ultimate sources of her ideas of just war can be traced to Aristotle and to the Roman concepts which infused the Byzantine legal system. It seems to me, in fact, that her debt to Aristotle is quite considerable, not only with regard to just war, but more generally in her concept of good government. Thus, for example, her statement that "the art of ruling [is] a science, a kind of supreme philosophy," and her description of Alexios as "the master of the science of government" owe a good deal to Aristotle.[60] This should not be surprising, for we do know that Anna was an avid student of Aristotle. Not only had she studied his works, but she organized a project for the production of commentaries on Aristotle, the first for a long time. Among the scholars she supported was Michael of Ephesos, whose commentaries on the *Politics* and the *Rhetoric* were written before 1138, that is, before the composition of the *Alexiad.* There had also been a commentary on the *Nicomachean Ethics,* written during her lifetime. In fact, so driven was she in her demand for work on Aristotle that we find in her funeral oration the interesting statement that Michael of Ephesos attributed his blindness to it, because "he spent sleepless nights over commentaries on Aristotle at her command, whence came the damage done to his eyes by candles through desiccation."[61]

Aristotle and Roman law are, of course, secular influences. What role did Christianity play in Anna's concept of justified warfare? Certainly, statements to the effect that Alexios did not want to fight against Christians and that he was concerned that Christians not be killed by the Turks are the statements of a Christian; but they play no role in the justification of war. Neither does the pious statement that her father was a most saintly man, equal to the apostles, whose fondest hope was to convert all the Muslims and the Petchenegs to Christianity, since that comes at the end of a passage discussing Alexios' good treatment of Turkish deserters, and is not connected with his waging war.[62] Christianity did have an influence, however. I see it in Anna's insistence on Alexios' desire for peace. True, that has impeccable ancient antecedents, as we have seen. Nevertheless, medieval Christian societies faced the problem of reconciling Christian ideas of peace and meekness with the Greek and Roman ideas of war, as well as with political realities. If in Western Europe the reconciliation took place through the development of the concepts of holy war and the just war of the church, in Byzantium there was no such development; the reconciliation in Byzantine society seems to have been at least partly based on the elaboration of the idea that the Empire and the emperor sought peace but were forced into war.

This idea did not, of course, begin with Anna, nor did it develop in the twelfth century. It is much older, and it is present in important texts. A sixth-century text is pertinent, presenting as it does views with only a superficial similarity to those of Anna Komnene. Corippus, in his panegyric of Justin II, speaks specifically of the desire for peace, which, however, does not mean fear of war. On the contrary, says the poet, those who subject themselves to the Empire will live in peace; those who are proud "will perish by war." One must note here the somewhat offhand reference to peace as the desired condition and the aggressive superiority which considers justifiable a war undertaken against those who will not subject themselves to the Empire.[63] Quite different is the attitude of Emperor Leo VI, in the opening statement of the Prooimion to his *Taktika*. This text, which had wide circulation in Byzantium, has a direct relevance to the inquiry about just war in Byzantium, and I would, therefore, like to summarize some of its points.[64] The emperor begins by stating that what makes him rejoice is not power and authority, but rather the peace and prosperity of his subjects and the correction or redressal (ἐπανόρθωσις) of their affairs. This is a good, old, traditional statement, and one made also by Anna Komnene about her father: the emperor looks not after his own well-being but after the common good.[65] The most important factor affecting the well-being of his subjects, continues Leo VI, is the science of strategy. Then there is a long passage, whose vocabulary is heavily indebted to Christian teaching, and which states that all men should have embraced peace and love for one another, since they are created in the image of God and are endowed with reason. However, the Devil has caused men to wage war, contrary to their nature. And, in a telling passage, he continues that it is therefore essential to defend oneself against the enemy, and eradicate the evil, so that peace will be observed by all.[66] The vocabulary is Christian; the idea that man is by nature peace-loving is perhaps also Christian; the idea that one wages a defensive war, and that the purpose of all war is peace is an older, secular idea, here presented in its medieval form. The new, medieval aspect is significant, for it stresses the importance of peace. It is, undoubtedly, the difficulty in reconciling Christian teaching with endemic warfare that led both the Byzantines and the Western Europeans to definitions or descriptions of just war, even though Western thought on the subject was much more systematic than that of the Byzantines, and quite different in content.

Thus, in his *Taktika*, Leo VI states that above all it is important that the cause of a war be just.[67] After all that has been said above, we recognize this statement as a traditional one; not only does Aristotle say that when one is exhorting people to go to war one should make sure to bring forth the right arguments, but Onasander, a writer of the first century A.D., uses a phraseology that is very close to Leo's: "It is most important that the cause of a war must be wisely constituted, and that it be evident to all that the war is being waged justly."[68] And what is a just war for Leo VI? It is a defensive war, since one must only fight against those who invaded his lands.

For the emperor stresses that peace must be preserved with regard both to his own subjects and to the barbarians, and if alien nations are content to stay within their own boundaries, they are not to be disturbed. Fighting against peaceful alien nations would be unjust. A just war is a war fought against those who began the injustice by initiating hostilities and launching an invasion; then will the Byzantines have God on their side. Finally, the emperor reiterates, for the benefit of the general to whom this is addressed, the paramount desire for peace and the paramount necessity to wage war only for just cause.[69]

A few comments are in order. Leo VI's text is medieval and Christian in language and style. It also diverges from ancient Greek and Roman concepts of war in one very important way: it does not advocate war against those who, "although designed by nature to be subjugated, . . . refuse to submit to it"; that is, it does not suggest either that there are those who are by definition meant to rule over others, or that war should be employed to impose good government on those who do not have it.[70] The only just war presented here is a defensive war. Hence it follows that it is also a limited war, with limited objectives. Now these are characteristics of a secular theory of the just war; the main contribution of Christianity, but it is an important one, is the insistence on peace. The difference from Western Europe could not be greater. While medieval Western Europe operated on the basis of Augustine's open-ended idea that a just war is one that avenges injustices, Leo VI had one and only one injustice in mind: the invasion of his territory.[71] One must note particularly Leo's statement that peaceful alien nations are to be left in peace, as an illustration of the fact that for him war, at least in terms of ideology, had limited and secular aims.

It is now possible to see Anna Komnene in a better perspective. Her ideas about what constitutes just causes for war, and therefore a just war, are not hers alone. Most of them can be found in earlier Byzantine texts, as well as in other Byzantine writers of the twelfth century. That is so because the concepts are rooted in Roman ideas of the state and war, and ultimately in ancient Greek ideas as well. At the same time, Byzantine concepts of just war differ from ancient ones, and are far from static. The very preoccupation with justifying warfare is more medieval than ancient, even though the elements of the description or definition of just war go back to Antiquity.[72] The difference is already evident in Leo VI's *Taktika*. Here we see a medieval Christian definition of just war which is not that of Western Europe. His premises are avowedly Christian, but the substance of his statements is secular: he is advocating not a holy war but a just war, even though he imputes an important role to God and the Devil in the conduct of human affairs, and even though the concept of peace is given a special, Christian weight. In the twelfth century, on the other hand, the role of breach of contract as a just cause of war assumes greater significance, at least in my view. As for Anna Komnene, she is more concerned than most Byzantine historians to show that the wars she describes were justified. Historical circumstances forced her to think about such matters. Her particular contribution lies in the fact that, because of her education and her interest in Aristotle, she presents her ideas in a secular vocabulary with a strong Aristotelian flavor, and in a fairly coherent form. The concept of just war, as it emerges from her pages, is a war fought in self-defense, for the recovery of lost territories, occasioned sometimes by a breach of treaty, and undertaken as a last resort, in the pursuit of peace. It is also a limited war, not aiming at the extermination, physical or moral, of the opponent. Therefore, war is only one of the possible means of achieving the objectives of the recovery of lost territory and the establishment of peace. At the same time that she was composing her History, in Western Europe St. Bernard of Clairvaux was advocating unlimited war against the pagan Slavs, in the context of the Second Crusade. He promised Crusader privileges, that is, the remission of sins, to all those who armed themselves "for the total destruction or, at least, the conversion of these peoples," and forbade any treaty with the Slavs "until, with the help of God, either this people or its religion shall be exterminated."[73] Anna Komnene would have been appalled, both by the substance of such a statement and by the fact that it was enunciated by an ecclesiastic.

In Western medieval Europe, one question was of paramount importance for the development of theories of just wars. That is the question of competent authority: a just war could only be declared by a competent authority, but where was the locus of this authority? In Roman law, the competent authority was the Roman people, and eventually the emperor. But in Western Europe, when these questions became a matter of debate, that is, in the twelfth century, the canonists and Romanists were faced with a real situation, in which there already existed groups which had long waged wars that they considered just: the feudal aristocracy and the church. The most important factor, both in terms of the development of ideology and, perhaps, in historical terms, was the role of the church: was the church an authority competent to declare and/or wage a just war? The answer of the canonists, after some equivocation and perhaps with lingering uneasiness, was nevertheless a firm yes; it could not have been otherwise after the developments in the church and in the papacy during the eleventh century.[74] Thus holy war, which can only be proclaimed by the church, and just war overlapped to some extent.

In my view, the basic difference between Byzantium and Western Europe as far as this issue is concerned is that, for historical reasons, there never was a question in Byzantium as to who was the authority competent to wage war. That was, it is perfectly clear, the emperor.[75] While the canonists of Western Europe were debating that burning issue, the twelfth-century Byzantine canonists wrote only two sentences pertinent to it. Significantly, this statement is inserted in the commentary on a canon regarding factions and conspiracy, and it restates the principle of Roman and then Byzantine law, that an individual who wages war despite imperial orders is punished, even if he is victorious.[76] No one dreamed of asking whether the church had the authority to declare or wage war.

Similarly, while in Western Europe the theories of the just war of the church and the theory of the crusade were being elaborated, that is, in the course of the twelfth and thirteenth centuries, in Byzantium the canonists dealt with the problem once, and in a way that was the exact opposite of the Western concepts. The occasion was given by canon 3 of St. Basil, which absolves of the charge of murder the soldiers who kill in war, fighting for pious ends; nevertheless, the soldier is supposed to abstain from communion for three years. The canonists expend most of their ingenuity in trying to justify the fact that the soldier is absolved of the sin of murder, and they do so on the basis that this is averting a greater evil: for if the barbarians were allowed to prevail, there would be neither piety nor temperance. Zonaras and Balsamon go as far as to say that the punishment prescribed by St. Basil was a good idea, but one which cannot be implemented, because if it were, soldiers would never be able to take communion. Both canonists then discuss, more as a curiosity than anything else, a request made by Emperor Nikephoros Phocas to Patriarch Polyeuktos and the synod, that soldiers who fell in war should be counted among the martyrs. The patriarch had refused the request, on the basis of this canon, and both our canonists agree with the decision.[77] Is it any wonder that Anna Komnene was profoundly shocked at the idea (and the reality) of Western priests bearing arms and engaging in battle, or that she should describe the Westerners, not at all in a complimentary fashion, as no less enamored of war than of religion?[78]

The question of who has the right to declare a just war is a question of political authority. The Byzantines took their state seriously, and for good reason. The church never sought and never received the competence to wage war. Hence the secular aspect of the Byzantines' thoughts regarding just war, including the thoughts of Anna Komnene. Certainly she presented her father as a pious man, both in war and in peace. Certainly she has him and the entire Byzantine army praying all night and receiving communion before engaging in battle against Robert Guiscard.[79] She, and her father, were certain he was a Christian ruler waging a just war; they would both have been stunned if anyone had suggested that he ever waged a holy war, such as the one that sent the Crusaders east.

NOTES

1. For sober assessments see, for example, V. Laurent, "L'idée de guerre sainte et la tradition byzantine," *Revue historique du sud-est Européen* 23 (1946): 71–98; the commentary of G. Dagron in G. Dagron and H. Mihăescu, *Le traité sur la guérilla (De velitatione) de l'empereur Nicéphore Phocas (963–969)* (Paris, 1986); for the eleventh and twelfth centuries, P. Lemerle, "Byzance et la croisade," *X Congresso Internazionale di Scienze*

Storiche, Relazioni, vol. 3 (Florence, 1955) (= idem, *Le monde de Byzance: Histoire et institutions* [London, 1978], no. VIII), 595–620, esp. 617–20. French historians of an earlier generation saw in the tenth-century wars between the Byzantines and the Muslims a crusade *avant le mot*. See, for example, G. Schlumberger, *L'épopée byzantine à la fin du dixième siècle, Jean Tzimiscès* (Paris, 1896), 238. A. Kolia-Dermitzaki, " Ἡ ἰδέα τοῦ «Ἱεροῦ Πολέμου» στὸ Βυζάντιο κατά τόν 10⁰ αἰώνα: Ἡ μαρτυρία τῶν Τακτικῶν καὶ τῶν δημηγοριῶν," *Κωνσταντίνος Ζ΄ ὁ Πορφυρογέννητος καί ἡ ἐποχή του* (Athens, 1989), 39–55, is an enthusiastic proponent of the idea that the Byzantines had a full-blown concept of holy war, and even of crusade.

2. There is, however, an exception, namely, a thirteenth-century text of Patriarch Michael Autoreianos, granting remission of sins to those who died in war. The editor of the act notes that this was due to Western influence: N. Oikonomidès, "Cinq actes inédits du patriarche Michel Autoreianos," in Oikonomidès, *Documents et études sur les institutions de Byzance (VIIe–XVe s.)* (London, 1976), no. XV, 115–21, 131–35.

3. [Aristotle], *Rhetorica ad Alexandrum*, Loeb edition (Cambridge, Mass., 1937), 298 ff.

4. See, for example, Michael Walzer, *Just and Unjust Wars: A Moral Argument with Historical Illustrations*, 2d ed. (New York, 1992). To the many contemporary justifications which he adduces, one may add the quite extraordinary effort undertaken shortly before and during the Persian Gulf war to show that even the formal criteria for just war had been met.

5. Russell, *Just War*, 2.

6. See *The Challenge of Peace: God's Promise and Our Response*, a *Pastoral Letter on War and Peace by the National Conference of Catholic Bishops*, May 3, 1983, 36–48.

7. Niketas Choniates, *Historia*, ed. Van Dieten (Berlin, 1975),42–43.

8. Robert Browning, "An Unpublished Funeral Oration on Anna Comnena," in R. Sorabji, ed., *Aristotle Transformed* (London, 1990), 393–406. Cf. Georgina Buckler, *Anna Comnena* (Oxford, 1928), 203–4 and passim. See also above, pp. 133–34.

9. On the *Alexiad* as a source for the Crusade, see Lemerle, "Byzance et la croisade," 596 ff.

10. *Annae Comnenae Porphyrogenitae Alexias*, ed. A. Reifferscheid, vol. 1 (Leipzig, 1984), 214. The translation is that of E. R. A. Sewter, slightly emended: *The Alexiad of Anna Comnena*, (Harmondsworth, 1969), 205–6.

11. *Alexias* II, 285.

12. *Alexias* II, 251. The translation is my own. On the idea of a natural division of peoples into those who are masters and slaves by nature, see Aristotle, *Politics* I, ii.18, and I, i.2–3; cf. above, p. 134.

13. *Alexias* II, 250ff.

14. *Alexias* II, 18, 251–52.

15. *Alexias* II, 156; Sewter, 381.

16. *Alexias* II, 86; the translation is Sewter's, p. 319, with slight changes.

17. *Alexias* II, 87–89.

18. *Alexias* II, 142; Sewter, 368.

19. Russell, *Just War*, 5.

20. *Alexias* II, 91; cf. Sewter, 323: "(Godfrey of Bouillon) swore an oath as he was directed that whatever cities, countries or forts he might in future subdue, which had in the first place belonged to the Roman Empire, he would hand over to the officer appointed by the emperor for this very purpose."

21. *Alexias* II, 130 ff; Sewter, 358–59.

22. *Alexias* II, 285; Sewter, 488.

23. *Alexias* II, 211–13; Sewter, 426.

24. *Alexias* II, 201–2.

25. *Alexias* II, 228–29; Sewter, 438–39.

26. *Alexias* I, 244; Sewter, 230. In another instance, Anna Komnene says that Robert Guiscard and Pope Gregory VII had sworn to support each other, but their oaths were empty words; "and having hastily sworn oaths to one another, they were as quick to break them, the barbarians": *Alexias* I, 47. It is a commonplace in twelfth-century historiography, particularly in John Kinnamos, that barbarians do not keep their oaths or their treaties, while the Byzantines do. The fickleness of barbarians is also an ancient stereotype. Professor Benjamin Isaac has brought to my attention a number of pertinent passages, among which see Livy XXI.4.9, Herodian II.7.8–9, Aurelian 31 in *Scriptores Historiae Augustae*.

27. *Alexias* I, 191; Sewter, 186.

28. *Nicomachean Ethics,* Loeb edition (London and Cambridge, Mass., 1939), X.vii.6.

29. *Politics,* Loeb edition (London and Cambridge, Mass., 1977), VII.xiii.8–9.

30. *Alexias* II, 157: καὶ ἦν ὁ αὐτὸς κατὰ φύσιν μὲν εἰρηνικός, ἀναγκαζόντων δὲ τῶν πραγμάτων πολεμικώτατος.

31. *Alexias* II, 255, 259–60. Cf. II, 186, with a reference to Aristotle.

32. *Alexias* II, 186.

33. *Alexias* II, 271–72. Cf., in the same vein, Kinnamos (Bonn ed.), 168–69.

34. As in the case of a temporary truce with the Petchenegs: *Alexias* I, 245.

35. *Alexias* II, 156–57; Sewter, 380–81.

36. Anna's quotation (II, 156) is from *Politics* VII.xiii.17. It is not listed among the nine allusions from Aristotle mentioned by Buckler, *Anna Comnena,* 203. The second quotation is from *Politics* VII.xiii.8.

37. *The City of God against the Pagans,* Loeb edition, vol. 6 (Cambridge, Mass., and London, 1959), 165 (XIX.12).

38. *Alexias* II, 186.

39. On Robert Guiscard, see *Alexias* I, 36, 155, 201–2; on Bohemond, 206–8; cf. I, 32, on an unnamed Westerner in Alexios' guard: "he was a brave soldier and full of martial valor"; and I, 67 on Gregory Pakourianos: "he was short in stature, but a good soldier."

40. *Alexias* I, 58–59, 155, 160–62, II, 273–75.

41. *Alexias* II, 281; Sewter, 484.

42. Alexander Kazhdan, "The Aristocracy and the Imperial Ideal," in M. Angold, ed., *The Byzantine Aristocracy, IX to XIII Centuries* (Oxford, 1984), 45–52.

43. *Alexias* II, 238; Sewter, 448.

44. To the references in note 36 above, add *Rhetoric* I, ix.3–8.

45. [Aristotle], *Rhetorica ad Alexandrum* II (Loeb edition), p. 300. Punishing those who have been wrongdoers: ἀμύνασθαι τοὺς ἀδικήσαντας. Anna Komnene lists among the reasons for her father's wish to start hostilities against Tancred his desire τῆς τοιαύτης ἀπανθρωπίας αὐτοὺς ἀμύνασθαι: is this an allusion to or a memory of the passage quoted here? For the ancient and Western medieval definitions of the just war I am heavily indebted to Russell's *Just War.*

46. *Digest* 9.2.45.4: "vim vi defendere omnes leges omniaque iura permittunt" = *Basilics* 60.3.45: βία γὰρ τὴν βίαν ἐκδικεῖν ὁ νόμος ἐπιτρέπει, and cf. *Bas.* 50.3.7: ἔξεστι βία τὴν βίαν ἐξωθεῖν καὶ ὅπλα ὅπλοις (= *Digest* 9.2.7). Cf. Russell, *Just War*, 41.

47. Cf. *Digest* 1.1.3: "ut vim atque injuriam propulsemus."

48. *Alexias* II, 228, and cf. above, p.133.

49. Russell, *Just War*, 44. On the defense of the *patria* as the primary just cause of war among medieval theologians, see ibid., 299–300. For the canonists, see ibid., 61ff.

50. Ibid., 5, 60ff.

51. *Jus Graeco-Romanum*, ed. I. and P. Zepos, vol. 2, *Epanagoge* II.1.2.

52. H. Ahrweiler, *L'idéologie politique de l'empire byzantin* (Paris, 1975), 42–43. She translates ἀνάληψις (here translated as "to acquire") as "to recover," and ἀνάκτησις (here: "to recover") as "to acquire." A variant reading of the Greek text gives ἐπίκτησις instead of ἀνάκτησις. That would, indeed, mean "to acquire," and would make better sense.

53. Ibid., 67–74.

54. The argument is also made with clarity by Kinnamos (Bonn ed.), 30.

55. Russell, *Just War*, 4–5.

56. Kinnamos, 222–23: ἄρα δίκαια βασιλεὺς πολεμεῖ; The translation is taken from Charles M. Brand, *Deeds of John and Manuel Comnenus by John Cinnamus* (New York, 1976), 168. Cf. Kinnamos, 224–25, 235, 30; Brand, 170, 177, 34.

57. *Politics* VII, xiii.13–15. See, however, the striking passage quoted above, p. 130 (*Alexias* II, 251); my point is that Anna Komnene, while she does speak of the Byzantines as "being by nature the masters of other nations," does not hold this as a cardinal idea in her discussion of war.

58. See, for example, Russell, *Just War*, 60ff.

59. See above, pp. 133–34, and *Alexias* II, 227–29.

60. *Alexias* I, 103–4; Sewter, 112; cf. Aristotle, *Politics* I.1.1–3; IV.1.

61. Browning's article, "An Unpublished Funeral Oration," is a seminal contribution to the study of Anna Komnene and twelfth-century Aristotelianism. The quotation is from p. 406; the "unpublished" oration has been published (after the article had first appeared) in J. Darrouzès, *Georges et Démétrios Tornikès, lettres et discours* (Paris, 1970).

62. *Alexias* I, 222.

63. Averil Cameron, *In laudem Iustini Augusti minoris Libri* V (London, 1976), III.329–31: "nos more parentum / pacem diligimus, numquam fera bella timemus. / pax est subiectis, pereunt per bella superbi." Cf. III.334–40: "bellum non ingerit ultro, / suscipit inlatum. vel si servire negabunt / ingratae gentes, primum tamen admonet hostes/ more gubernandi. . . . quisquis amat pacem, tutus sub pace manebit. / at qui bella volunt, bellorum clade peribunt." I owe this reference to Professor Isaac.

64. I am grateful to Fr. George Dennis, who directed me to the text, and who also made available to me his translation of various passages.

65. *Alexias* II, 238.

66. R. Vári, *Leonis Imperatoris Tactica* (Budapest, 1917), 3–5.

67. Ibid., *Constitutio* II.44: Πρὸ πάντων δὲ ἐπὶ πολέμους ὁπλιζόμενος, ἀποσκόπει δικαίαν εἶναι τὴν ἀρχὴν τοῦ τοιούτου πολέμου.

68. E. Korzenszky and R. Vári, *Onasandri Strategicus* (Budapest, 1935), 10: Τὰς δὲ ἀρχὰς τοῦ πολέμου μάλιστά φημι χρῆναι φρονίμως συνίστασθαι καὶ μετὰ τοῦ δικαίου πᾶσι φανερὸν γίγνεσθαι πολεμοῦντα.

69. Vári, II.45–46. Onasander, too, advises a defensive war, undertaken after peace overtures have failed.

70. The quotation is from *Politics* I.iii.8; cf. Russell, *Just War*, 3–4.

71. On St. Augustine, see Russell, *Just War*, 16ff.

72. Professor Isaac has pointed out to me that neither the Greeks nor the Romans of the period of the Republic felt deeply that war needed a moral justification or even the justification of self-defense, and that the same was true for the period of the Roman Empire and for Byzantium through the sixth century. Cf. Isaac, *The Limits of Empire: The Roman Army in the East* (Oxford, 1990), 20 ff., 372 ff., and the nuanced treatment by William V. Harris, *War and Imperialism in Republican Rome, 327–70 B.C.* (Oxford, 1979), chap. 5, esp. pp. 163–75. I might, perhaps, add that, as we have seen, normative statements do indeed present ideas of just war; practice, of course, was quite another matter. I am grateful to Professor Isaac for reading this paper, and making thoughtful criticisms and comments. Some of his comments I have been able to incorporate here. The more general question he raised, namely, when the change occurred between the late Antique concepts of war and the concepts which existed in the twelfth century, needs a systematic study of the idea of just war in Byzantium from the sixth century onward. Such a study would be most desirable.

73. "Ad delendas penitus, aut certe convertendas nationes illas" and "donec, auxiliante Deo, aut ritus ipse, aut natio deleatur." *S. Bernardi opera*, vol. 7, *Epistolae*, ed. J. Leclercq and H. Rochais (Rome, 1977), no. 457, p. 433.

74. For the question of the locus of authority, and the answers of the canonists, see Russell, *Just War*, 38, 46 ff., 68 ff., 72 ff., 122–23, and passim. On the eleventh-century developments, see the important work of C. Erdmann, *The Origin of the Idea of Crusade* (Princeton, 1977).

75. The statement may be capable of modification. In the late Byzantine period, especially after the middle of the fourteenth century, at a time of decentralization, people other than the emperor did wage war. Whether it was thought that they had the authority to do so is a question that must be investigated.

76. Balsamon's commentary to canon 34 of the Council in Trullo: G. Rhalles and M. Potles, Σύνταγμα τῶν θείων καὶ ἱερῶν κανόνων, vol. II (Athens, 1852), 382. The reference is to *Basilics* 60.36.3 (= *Digest* 48.4.3).

77. Rhalles and Potles, *Syntagma* 4:131–34. On this, cf. *Ioannis Scylitzae Synopsis Historiarum*, ed. Ioannes Thurn (Berlin and New York, 1973), 274–75. Skylitzes, writing in the late eleventh century, also approves of the action of the patriarch and the synod. On all this, see H.-G. Beck, *Nomos, Kanon und Staatsraison in Byzanz*, Österreichische Akademie der Wissenschaften, Philosophisch-Historische Klasse, Sitzungsberichte, vol. 384 (Vienna, 1981), 20 ff.

78. *Alexias* II, 84: οὕτως ἐστὶ τὸ βάρβαρον τοῦτο γένος οὐχ ἧττον ἱερατικὸν ἢ φιλοπόλεμον. Cf. Darrouzès, "Les documents byzantins du XIIe siècle sur la primauté romaine," *Revue des études byzantines* 23 (1965): 56–57, on a similar attitude on the part of Theodore Smyrnaios.

79. *Alexias* I, 144.

The Just War of Eastern Christians and the Holy War of the Crusaders

On 27 November 1095, Pope Urban II, after having held a Church council in the small French town of Clermont, went outside the town walls and there gave what must be considered one of the most effective speeches in human history. He appealed to the fighting men of Western Europe to stop warring against each other, and instead to turn their arms from fratricidal war to war with a holy purpose: the liberation of the Eastern, that is, the Byzantine, church and of Jerusalem itself from the Seljuk Turks. Their reward was to be a remission of penance, a promise quickly re-interpreted as a remission of sin. The act of fighting a war with avowedly religious purpose against enemies of the Christian faith would bring eternal salvation. This speech launched the First Crusade, and therefore the entire crusading movement, a movement which has captivated the imagination of historians as well as popular writers from that time onwards. From the start, a basic functional element of the crusade, whether it was directed toward the Muslims or, eventually, against the pagan Slavs, the heretics or others, was that this was a holy war for the true faith, declared by the Church as the sole competent authority, whose fighters were rewarded with spiritual rewards.

Urban II's appeal was cast in terms of the brotherhood of Christians Eastern and Western, and of the help that the West should bring to the Byzantines who were the victims of the rapid expansion of the Seljuk Turks. The report of Foucher of Chartres will serve as an example: 'You must hurry to help your brothers living in the Orient, who need your aid for which they have already cried out many times. For the Turks, a race of Persians, have invaded their lands even to the Mediterranean to that point, that is, which is called the Arm of St George, are occupying more and more the land of the Christians within the boundaries of the Romania ... and have killed and captured them, have overthrown churches, and have laid waste God's kingdom. If you permit this for very long, God's faithful ones will be still further subjected.'[1] These are statements of support to the Christians of Byzantine Asia Minor, and are imbued by the spirit of fraternity between Christians in East and West. It was their brother Christians whom the Pope asked the Western knights to help against the Muslims. It was also from brother Christians that Alexios I, the Byzantine Emperor, had sought aid against the advancing Turks.[2] And yet, in a little more than a hundred years, the Christian brethren of the East had become heretical enemies, and the Byzantine Empire was destroyed by the crusaders. Why did this development occur? The question, often asked in the past, still requires answers.

As the armies of the First Crusade set out for the Holy Land, they passed through the Byzantine Empire – the largest Christian state of its day, until a few years earlier and again in the near future the most powerful, a land of virtually legendary wealth, and, according to some scholars, pre-eminently the land to whose aid Urban II had called the knights of Western Europe. The crusades resulted in massive, if periodic, contact between Byzantines and Western Europeans. The armies that went through Byzantine territories on their way to the Holy Land, that is, those of the First and Second Crusades and that of Frederick Barbarossa in the Third Crusade, took anything from two to six months to traverse the Balkans, although Frederick Barbarossa stayed in southern Bulgaria and Thrace for nine long months. Relatively brief as the contact was, it was intense. It was also attended with acute problems of a practical nature.[3] The presence of 60 000–100 000 people, many of them soldiers, on the soil of a pre-industrial state could not but tax the resources of the area. Provisioning was very difficult. Prices soared. Inevitably, the crusader armies plundered Byzantine territories, and thus the problem was compounded. Connected intimately with the problem of provisioning was that of currency exchange. The crusaders complained, not unjustly, that they lost considerably in the exchange. All of this proved to some of them that the Byzantine Emperor was duplicitous, making promises which he had no intention of keeping.[4] Thus, practical problems formed a solid foundation to the image of the Greek as untrustworthy, an image which has its origins in the Roman period, and which was broadcast in Western Europe during the period of the crusades and to a large extent because of them. Soon enough, untrustworthiness became elevated to treachery – and things became much more difficult and far more dangerous.

Surely, however, practical problems alone could have been overcome, indeed *were* overcome time and again, albeit leaving a bitter aftertaste in the historiography, and perhaps traces in the collective memory of crusading families. The excessive weight that practical problems acquire in Western sources must, I think, be ascribed to a fundamental problem which lies at the heart of the relations between crusaders and Byzantines.

The fundamental problem was ideological. The crusaders considered themselves to be the army of God, carrying out the highest duty of a Christian, fighting for the Christian religion. They were the *pugnatores Dei*, the *milites Christi* fighting under Jesus Christ.[5] They expected and almost demanded that other Christians share this view and give them every assistance, with enthusiasm. But the Byzantines did not see them primarily as soldiers of Christ, a term which in any case in Byzantium designated a monk or an ascetic.[6] They considered the crusading armies from a practical, political and statist viewpoint. At best, they saw an army to be used to recover some Byzantine territories lost to the Turks, certainly a potentially dangerous army to be ferried to Asia Minor as soon as possible, and at worst, a grave threat, which could easily divert its activities toward the Empire itself and its capital, Constantinople, and that long before this threat was realised with the Fourth Crusade, in 1204. To a very considerable extent the fear and suspicion went back to Bohemond's crusade against the Byzantine Empire, the third stage of the First Crusade. But at the heart of the matter lies the fact that the crusaders and the Byzantines had two very different conceptions of Christian warfare.

During the eleventh century, Western Europe elaborated older ideas regarding war and gave them the specific form of holy war, that heady brew of warfare and religion. The crusade was launched as a holy war, 'the struggle of good men against wicked men', as St Augustine had put it long before. It was a war for the faith, with spiritual benefits for the warriors, the spiritual and salvationist aspects becoming stronger in the course of the twelfth century. This holy war, on behalf of the Christian religion, was one which was proclaimed by the Church. But the Christian brethren whom the warriors of Western Europe were asked to help in the first instance failed miserably to embrace and even quite to understand the principles of holy war. Indeed, they were the only post-Old Testament people in the Mediterranean and in Europe never to develop the basic principles of holy war ideology. This came to be a fundamental difference between them and the Western Europeans, and one which formed the ideological foundations of the growing mistrust between brothers. There was, I argue, a conflict of ideologies, indeed of cultures. The Byzantines understood very well the concept of Christian brotherhood and Christian community, but not very well at all the novel idea of a Christian holy war.[7]

The fact that the Byzantines neither developed nor embraced the concepts of holy war is in some ways remarkable. They had fought both defensive and aggressive wars against the Muslims for centuries – first the Arabs, then, in the eleventh century, the Seljuk Turks. In some respects, Byzantine society was profoundly religious; its armies certainly prayed before battle and often marched with religious symbols at their head, as they had done since the days of Constantine the Great, the first Christian emperor, and his war against non-Christian Roman armies. There were times in the long history of the Byzantine Empire when its leaders would have been quite comfortable with some of the rhetoric employed by Westerners at the time of the crusades. In the days of the great wars against the Persians in the seventh century, against the Arabs in the tenth, Byzantine rhetoricians and exhortation manuals used statements comparable to those attributed to Urban II. 'On whom,' he had asked the Frankish knights 'is the labor of avenging the wrongs [wrought by the Turks in the Byzantine territories of the East] and of recovering this territory incumbent if not upon you? You, upon whom above other nations God has conferred remarkable glory in arms, great courage, bodily activity, and strength to humble the hairy scalp of those who resist you'.[8] A tenth-century circular letter from the Byzantine Emperor Constantine VII to the army commanders of the East, which was meant as a harangue before an important battle against the Arabs, had proclaimed, 'You shall avenge and defend not only the Christian people, but Christ himself against those who have harmed him.'[9] Baldric of Dol's Urban says: 'Under

Jesus Christ our Leader may you struggle for your Jerusalem, in Christian battle-line, most invincible line, even more successfully than did the sons of Jacob of old'.[10] And Constantine VII: 'He, oh men, He will be your aid, He who alone is mighty in battle, whose glittering sword is whetted and whose arrows are drunk with the blood of those who resist him, who breaks bows and reduces fortified cities to dust, He who humbles the eyes of the proud while to those who have hope in Him He teaches their arms to fight; He places a brazen bow in their hands; He gives them the shield of His salvation [that is, He protects them so they will not be killed].'[11] The examples could be multiplied. There are thus some clear rhetorical parallels between the exhorting decree (*exhortans decretum*) of the Pope in 1095 and the exhorting circular of a Byzantine emperor issued almost a hundred and fifty years earlier.

Yet the rhetoric should not be allowed to obscure the fundamentals of the perception of Christian warfare in Byzantium and Western Europe. Even at the time of the epic struggles against Persians or Arabs, in which some historians have seen a Byzantine crusade, mistakenly in my view, at the very most we find elements of holy war, not the full-blown ideology.[12] The Byzantines were talking about the recovery of their own territories from the infidel invaders, so that behind the emotional religious symbolism there lurked the old Roman concept of just war: the recovery of things lost, the defence of the territory and the subjects of the state. In the case of the Western call for the crusade, the emotional appeal was on behalf of Christians far away; the redressing of injustice is conceivable only if the lands of the East are established as lands which belong by rights to the Christians – an idea that was, indeed, propounded by the Pope at Clermont. Most importantly, in the crusade it is the Church that proclaims the injustice, the brotherhood of Christians, the duty to redress injustice. The basis for the justification of the war that is being declared, the community which is being asked to do the redressing, and the authority which declares the war, are all religious. In Byzantium, the basis for the justification of war is to a large extent secular; the community addressed consists of the subjects and soldiers of the Byzantine state, and the person who proclaims all this is at all times the Emperor, a secular, not an ecclesiastical, authority.

The Byzantine concept of war was not holy war. It was, pre-eminently, that of just war. In the tenth century, as in the eleventh or the twelfth, the concept of just war is rather more indebted to Aristotelian and Roman ideas regarding war than to religious ones. War, according to those Byzantines who wrote about it, and one was a tenth-century emperor, is a measure of last resort, to be undertaken when all else has failed. The war has to be just, and has to be seen to be just. All must strive for the state of peace. Each people, including the 'barbarians', is entitled to inhabit its own territory, and as long as it remains within its own frontiers, it is to be left in peace. The infidels, the Muslims, are subsumed in the larger category of barbarians. War is justified only when the barbarians breach the peace and invade the Empire. At that point, war becomes necessary; it is a just war, and its purpose is the restoration of peace – a good Aristotelian concept. At that point, too, one seeks God's help, tells the soldiers that the fight is for God, 'for our kin and the rest of our Christian brethren', and against the enemies of God.[13] Thus a just war is a defensive war, and by extension, its objectives are limited: they are not the eradication of the enemy.

In texts of the twelfth century, the reasons clearly emerge for which a just war may be waged: for self-defence, for the recovery of territory, for averting a greater evil such as the destruction of the state and its inhabitants; war is also just when the enemy has broken treaties or solemn oaths. This is a secular concept of war.[14] Its most important aspect is that the authority competent to declare war is and always remains a secular one, namely the state. The Church in the Byzantine Empire never declared war, never became engaged in war and rarely issued warlike statements.

The Byzantines and Western Europeans were, to some degree, heirs to the same religious traditions regarding war against peoples of a different religion. They shared both the Old and the New Testament: both the image of the avenging God of Hosts and that of Christ the Prince of Peace. Both cultures could draw on texts such as Deuteronomy 20:16–17 'In the cities of these peoples that the Lord your God gives you for an inheritance, you shall leave nothing alive that breathes, but you shall utterly destroy them ... as the Lord commanded you', but also on texts such as Matthew 26:52: 'Put up again thy sword into its place; for all that take the sword shall perish with the sword.' Both religious communities received mixed messages from the fathers of the early Church. There had been some in the west (Tertullian, Lactantius) who condemned war in powerful terms. The most influential teaching, however, had been that of St Augustine, who had seen war both as a consequence of sin and as a remedy for it: war was a way of punishing sin and sinners, and it was a labour of love, for it prevents the sinner from sinning further. The notion of redressing injustice, a moral idea and thus quite open-ended, is important in St Augustine's thought. In the Eastern Church too, there had been some fourth-century Church Fathers like St Athanasios of Alexandria who had considered the killing of the enemy in war as lawful and praiseworthy.[15] However, the most influential figure in the Eastern tradition was St Basil of Caesarea, who punished the soldiers who killed in war with a three-year abstention from communion: 'Our fathers have not included the murders committed in time of war in the category of murder, pardoning, I think, those who defend prudence and piety. But it seems to me that it is proper to advise them to abstain from communion for three years, for their hands are unclean.'[16] The Byzantines also had retained from the Roman past the idea that wars have to be just, and the idea that a defensive war, and a war for recovery of things lost, was a just war; this was incorporated in their legal system, as was the maxim that only the public authority, namely, the Emperor, may declare war. They also had the corpus of Aristotelian writings, which gave a secular definition of just war.

Common roots, different developments – that is the story of the development of theories of war, as also of the concept of Christian brotherhood. East and West had a mixed heritage in terms of religious approaches; it was social and political conditions that allowed the concept of holy war to develop and spread in Western

Europe. And it was political and social conditions that led to the development in Byzantium of the concept of just war. For the Byzantine Empire was the one state in medieval Europe and the eastern Mediterranean which retained, both in tradition and in reality a strong centralised state that, while very closely connected with the Christian religion, had also a line of descent straight from the Roman Empire. It was therefore normal for them to have had a statist view of war, even against infidels.

Jonathan Riley-Smith has argued that at the time of the First Crusade, members of the fighting elite of Western Europe transferred to Christ the fealty they owed to their overlord.[17] In the matter of warfare, there was no question among Byzantines that the Emperor and the state commanded their loyalty. This was a point of crucial difference at the time. Thus the reaction of Byzantines and Westerners to important events of the crusade was stunningly different. The Byzantine historian whose work covers the First Crusade, Anna Komnene, barely mentions the capture of Jerusalem, that Jerusalem which had so rapidly become the focus and aim of the First Crusade and whose capture, attended by visions and prophecies and ending in the wholesale slaughter of its Muslim and Jewish inhabitants, had brought the crusaders to transports of exultation. 'This day,' wrote Raymond d'Aguilers, 'marks the justification of all Christianity, the humiliation of paganism, and the renewal of our faith.'[18] Anna Komnene's description of the capture of the city is brief, to the point, and with no whiff of exultation in the victory of the Christians: 'The walls were encircled and repeatedly attacked, and after a siege of one lunar month [Jerusalem] fell. Many Saracens and Hebrews in the city were massacred.'[19]

How profound the difference in attitude was with regard to war in general, and more specifically with regard to war against the infidel, in this case the Muslims, can best be seen not in rhetorical statements whose purpose is to incite men to fight, but, rather, in cultural expressions of these attitudes. One litmus test is the treatment of soldiers fighting in war and dying in the course of it. Holy war is a justifying war – the warrior for the faith finds salvation through the very act of war. In Western Europe, the eleventh century saw the evolution of the idea that one who dies fighting for the ideals of the Christian faith deserves the crown of martyrdom. At Clermont, Pope Urban had linked that idea specifically to the war against the Muslims: 'We now hold out to you wars which contain the glorious reward of martyrdom, which will retain praise now and forever.'[20] The first martyrs begin to appear in the sources in 1097.[21]

At the other end of Europe there was, in the late tenth century, a great general and then emperor who had given the most powerful impetus to the Byzantine reconquest of territories lost to the Arabs. Nikephoros II (963–969) is undoubtedly the epitome of the pious warrior fighting for the Christian people. A profoundly religious man, when he became Emperor he called a Church council and asked the prelates to declare that his soldiers who had fallen in war against the Arabs be proclaimed martyrs for the faith. There was much debate, but in the end the prelates refused, on the basis of the teachings of St Basil.[22] Nikephoros Phokas' innovative effort to proclaim his soldiers martyrs was remembered well into the twelfth century. At that point, after a hundred years of being exposed to crusading ideas, and after more than a hundred years of wars against the Seljuks, some canonists argued for an attenuation of the canon of St Basil, saying that it was praiseworthy to fight in defence of piety and prudence. But they did insist that martyrdom is excluded for soldiers dying in battle.[23] In the early thirteenth century, Byzantine theologians still argued against the concept of the remission of the sins of crusaders dying in war.[24] Both before the onset of the crusading movement, and well into the period when it was a cardinal event in the eastern Mediterranean, the crown of martyrdom eluded Byzantine soldiers who fought against the enemy, even if the enemy was an infidel. Thus the 'revolution' of Nikephoros II failed, while that of Urban II had a long life.

The difference in the perception of war, and specifically war against Muslims, can be seen eloquently in the literature of the period. From the time of the First Crusade, a little earlier or a little later, dates the oldest extant version of the great French epic the *Song of Roland*, which, of course, is based on older songs and poems. The *Song of Roland* has long been recognised as a poem which encapsulates the elements of holy war that make up the ideology of the crusades. In the East, the *Song of Digenis* ('The Twyborn') seems to have taken its extant form a few decades later. In both poems, the action takes place in a liminal environment – on the borderlands between Christians and Muslims: on the Spanish march in one case, in eastern Asia Minor in the other. The *Song of Digenis* consists of two parts, of which the second, the story of the Twyborn warrior himself, is really a romance, involving tales of love and adultery, fights against lions, semi-regular soldiers, Arabs and Amazons. He spends a good amount of time engaging in adulterous pursuits and then repenting of them, and dies at a very young age; his funeral is attended by the great rulers of the East, both Christian and Muslim.[25] This is hardly epic stuff. The first part, however, the 'Song of the Emir', the father of Digenis, retains resonances of the Arab–Byzantine wars of the tenth century. It may thus be considered comparable, for our purposes, to the *Song of Roland*, which has the wars of Charlemagne at its core.

The way in which a society perceives and describes its enemy reflects its values. In both poems, Muslim Arabs are the foe. In the *Song of Roland*, the Saracens and Charlemagne's army are depicted in very similar terms. But there is one all-embracing and all-important difference: religion. The verse 'The pagan cause is wrong, the Christian right' encapsulates the morality of the poem. Because they are Muslims, the enemies are always evil, unjust, false and unrighteous. The struggle between Christians and Muslims is a struggle between good and evil. This is most clearly the case at the end of the poem, where Roland, a man surrounded by light, is pitted against the Arab Chernuble:

> the ruler of that land
> men call the Hills of Darkness ...
> In that land, they say,

> the sun shines not, nor rain nor gentle dew
> fall from the heavens, and not a grain of corn
> may ripen. No rock is there that isn't solid black;
> some say it is the devil's habitation.[26]

One of the Saracen leaders is a man named Abisme:

> A Paynim black as molten pitch
> no wickeder than *he* in all the swarm;
> spotted with many sins, believing not
> in God the son of Mary; loving more
> treason and murder of his fellow men
> than good Galician gold ...[27]

His shield had been given him by a demon, in contrast to Roland, whose sword (Durandel) had been given to Charlemagne by an angel. Abisme, the personification of evil, is met in the field by the archbishop Turpin, who with a single blow rends him in half. The symbolism is stark. Muslims have two choices: conversion or death. This was, in fact, the choice given by the crusaders to Muslims and Jews as well as to the pagans of northern Europe at various times in the period of the crusades.

The contrast with the 'song of the Emir' is sharp. The very description of the Emir who, objectively, is the equivalent of Abisme, is indicative:

> Was an Emir of breed, exceeding rich,
> of wisdom seized and bravery to the top,
> not black as Aethiops are, but fair and lovely,
> already bloomed with comely curly beard.
> He had a well-grown and rather matted brow;
> his quick and pleasant gaze and full of love
> shone like a rose from out his countenance.[28]

The early part of the poem presents a scene of destruction: a field of war, strewn with the limbs of lovely girls who had not given in to the illicit desires of the victorious Arabs. But when the brothers of the girl who would eventually become the emir's wife meet him, they greet him thus:

> Emir, servant of God, and prince of Syria,
> ...
> [may you]be found worthy to adore the Prophet's tomb;
> so may you hear the consecrated prayer.[29]

The entire story revolves around the Emir's love for the girl, a Byzantine Christian, for whose sake he abandons Islam and converts to Christianity. The almost metaphysical battle between good and evil is absent from this poem. Instead, we find popular motifs such as the brothers of the Christian Byzantine girl running to her rescue, or the motif of the mother who first scolds the Emir for abandoning his heritage and then follows him out of motherly love. The Emir's conversion comes not at swordpoint, but rather through the arrows of Eros: it is the act of reconciliation, which is sealed with the birth of a son: ' To them a child is born, indeed most fair, / who from his very birth was named Basil, / called also Twyborn as from his parents, / a pagan father and a Roman mother.'[30]

A society that can reduce to a love story the centuries-long struggle between Muslims and Christians on the borderlands of Asia Minor, in Syria and the borders of Iraq, is hard put to understand the crusades. The Pope had asked the crusaders to help their fellow Christians against the Muslims. But when the crusaders met with the Byzantines, there was a meeting of two worlds which, although they had a great deal in common, also had much that set them apart: differences which surprised them both. I suggest that the differences were most unwelcome precisely because the Westerners expected to meet fellow Christians, Christian brethren who would share their views of the enemy. The Byzantines, with a centralised state and a good foreign service, held no such views: at the time of the first crusade, they wanted help from the West, but in the shape of a small, professional army under their own control. And they did recall most vividly throughout the twelfth century that it was Christian Normans, members of the First Crusade, who had tried to conquer the Empire.

Thus the Byzantines had very little truck with holy war and, since the state and not the Church was the authority competent to declare war, this is not surprising. In practical terms, this has certain corollaries. It is true that any war has its horrors, and the wars waged by the Byzantines were certainly not exempt from horrors.[31] On the other hand, it is inherent in the theory of just war that the objectives are limited, and that there are rules governing the treatment of civilians and captives – and the purpose is always the re-establishment of peace. Holy war as elaborated in Western Europe had unlimited objectives and an almost unlimited scope: which is why its victims included not only the Muslims against whom it was first preached, but also the Jews, heretics, pagans, political enemies of the Papacy and, eventually, the Byzantine Christians. The unlimited objective is the domination of the Christians over the infidels or the pagans, and the extinction, physical or moral, of the enemy. This is what permitted the massacre of the inhabitants of Jerusalem in 1099, the atrocities of the Albigensian Crusade, the virtual extermination of some pagan populations along the Baltic. When St Bernard of Clairvaux preached the crusade to the German nobles, he promised remission of sins to those who went to war against the pagan Slavs 'for the total destruction or, at least the conversion (moral destruction) of all these peoples'; he forbade peace treaties with the Slavs 'until, with the help of God, this people, or its religion, should be exterminated'.[32]

What explains the differences between Eastern and Western Christians on the subject of Christian warfare? At the socio-political level, these differences stem from attitudes towards war in general, themselves the result of specificities in the makeup of the state, the ruling class and the warrior class. In Western Europe, of course, the aristocracy was a fighting class, the fighting class *par excellence*. So much was this still the case in the eleventh century that scholars in recent years have based their interpretation of the stunning appeal of the call to the First Crusade on the spiritual needs and martial attitudes of this fighting elite, who had imbued the crusading movement with their warrior ethos.[33] When the Byzantines were exposed to certain egregious forms of this ethos, they sometimes saw it as the strange ravings of stranger people.[34] Anna Komnene reports the vain boastings of a crusader in the army of Godfrey of Bouillon to the Emperor Alexios I: 'I am a pure Frank and of noble birth. At a cross-roads in the country where I was born is an ancient shrine; to this anyone who wishes to engage in single combat goes, prepared to fight; there he prays to God for help and there he stays awaiting the man who will dare to answer his challenge. At that crossroads I myself have spent time, waiting and longing for the man who would fight – but there was never one who dared.'[35] What to the Byzantines seemed a simple boast of an imprudent man, was still, in Western Europe, the way to acquire lands and vassals; the elite still acquired wealth mostly, though not exclusively, through war.

In Byzantium, however, individuals had not traditionally achieved wealth, power and social position through warfare as much as through administrative office, given, withheld or recalled by the Emperor. The accuracy of this general statement certainly would vary with locality and chronology – for there is no question that in the period of Byzantine expansion along the eastern frontier, that is, in the ninth and especially in the tenth century, great private fortunes were formed in the newly conquered lands, which in turn gave the great aristocratic families a strong territorial and economic base. But even in these cases, the early accumulation of fortune had come because of administrative office, and in the tenth century the salaries drawn by the high military officials were probably higher than the revenues from their lands. In other words, the system of rewards was very different indeed in Eastern and Western Christendom. To illustrate the point, one may look at the tenth-century Byzantine text to which reference has already been made, and which has been thought to encapsulate the 'aspect of true "crusades"' that the same scholars consider Byzantine military enterprises to have acquired after the eighth century.[36] This harangue, addressed to military officials in the East before an important battle against the Emir of Aleppo Saif ad-Daulah (952–3), speaks of the soldiers' faith in Christ, contrasts the help that can be given by Christ to that offered by Muhammad to his faithful, and calls 'the fight on behalf of Christians' to be the greatest ambition – none of which, in my opinion, is sufficient to qualify the sentiments behind the text or the enunciations in the text as pertaining to 'holy war', much less to a 'crusade'. There is also an oath involved in this text. Not an oath to fight for the Christian God, or the salvation of Christianity, but an oath to the Emperor, by the generals, who promise that they will send him truthful reports regarding the conduct of individuals in battle, so that the Emperor may reward them. The rewards are not, and indeed cannot be, spiritual: the Emperor cannot offer, as the Pope is said to have done, spiritual salvation.[37] The Emperor's promises are of quite a different order:

the generals of small themes (a theme is an administrative unit) will get large themes, and other donations and rewards, and so hierarchically up and down the list of officers.[38] The rewards, as I have indicated, were anything but negligible – they made a difference between glory and wealth on the one hand, and obscurity on the other. What is clearly considered optimum here is not individual bravery resulting in individual acquisition of wealth, but controlled bravery in the service of the state resulting in rewards derived from the state. This would, of course, apply equally to all wars, whether between Christians and Muslims or other non-believers, or among Christians, or even to civil wars – a rather cold climate for profoundly held concepts of 'holy war' to take root and bear fruit.

And then there was the civil service. In its heyday, the Byzantine Empire was a well-administered state, with a command economy. From the point of view of the state, fiscal policies and their results were of paramount importance, and safeguarding the tax-producing assets (specifically, in this period, agriculture) was a stated purpose of the Emperors. From the point of view of the subjects, fiscality was so important that the tax-payer was one of the best-known figures in the countryside; so important also, that justice was often equated to fiscal justice; and significant enough in terms of the rural economy that it influenced, to a varying but considerable degree, its monetisation. It could not have escaped the eyes of the bureaucracy that the seasons for fighting were the same as for agricultural pursuits; nor could the fact have escaped their eagle eye that although successful war could result in windfalls for the Treasury and territory to increase the tax base, wars were not always successful; campaigns were expensive even in terms of cash alone; campaigns on Byzantine soil had destructive effects which could range from the loss of one year's harvest to the destruction of productive capacity. The glory in gore that we find in Western troubadour songs[39] or in chronicles of the crusades are not reproducible in the Byzantine Empire. In war, the Byzantines were capable of great cruelty and destruction of the enemy's resources: the slaughter of men and beasts were tactics advocated by the *Taktika*.[40] But they did not glory in destruction – they were too well aware of its cost. Much more in the Byzantine tradition is a thirteenth-century exhortation to 'avoid human slaughter and the dreadful bloodshed that are the fruits of war'.[41]

Peace, that ever-present cry in Byzantium, which we find in all sorts of very different sources, from manuals on military tactics to the liturgy,[42] made perfect bureaucratic sense, and it was a rare Emperor who bucked it and engaged in unprovoked and pure wars of expansion. To the bureaucratic ethos, and it was a powerful ingredient of state policy, defensive wars, especially to restore peace in territories under attack, were a clear necessity; we do not really know what they thought of unprovoked wars of expansion, except that, in ideological terms, these were accommodated under the general rubric – a Roman idea – of the restoration of things lost, even if they had been lost for a very long time. The point, of course, is that the pious sentiment that the 'aim of war is the restoration of peace', of good Aristotelian pedigree, and found in the *Taktika* of Leo the Wise, is much more than a pious sentiment; it often governed imperial policy, and it made good financial and therefore bureaucratic sense. Again, not a very fertile soil for the fervours of crusades or holy wars.

We have, then, two views of Christian warfare, which developed through a different mix of elements that had very similar origins, a difference which in turn was due to the social and political conditions in East and West respectively. The imperatives of holy war on the one hand and just war on the other clashed and went on clashing during the period when they had to confront each other, that is, during the period of the crusades. The misunderstandings between Western Europe and Byzantium, between the Orthodox and the Latin Churches that occurred during this period owe a great deal to the different concepts of war and the courses of action each vision dictated. In the end, this ideological difference had a victim of some consequence: this was the cause of Christian brotherhood, in whose name Urban II preached the First Crusade, and which began to erode as soon as the crusaders set foot on Byzantine soil. Ultimately, the victim of such differences and misunderstandings was the Byzantine Empire itself, conquered by Westerners in the course of the Fourth Crusade, when the concept of holy war had expanded to include the Byzantines. The Byzantines watched in horror as their churches were defiled, ancient statues melted down, their state dismembered in the name of the God of Peace. And it is no accident that the one time that an Orthodox Patriarch promised eternal salvation and remission of sins to those who died in war was a few years after the fall of Constantinople to the crusaders. The promise was most probably aimed at the Byzantine soldiers who died fighting the Westerners for the salvation of their country: 'Having received the great gift of the grace Jesus Christ our Lord, we give you, who fight on behalf of the Lord's people, forgiveness for the sins committed during your lifetime, if it should happen that you die in defence of your country and the common salvation and rescue of the people.'[43] It is one of the ironies of history that when one of the two great medieval Christian cultures turned towards holy war, it was to defend itself against the successors of those who had, a hundred-odd years earlier, set out to defend it against a perceived common enemy. Different concepts of the war against Muslims in the end divided Christendom more than they harmed Islam.

Notes

1   *RHC Occ.*, III, 323–4. The translation is adapted from that in Peters, E. (1971), *The First Crusade*, Philadelphia, 52–3.
2   Charanis, P. (1949), 'Byzantium, the West and the Origin of the First Crusade', *Byzantion*, 19, 17–36.
3   For a full discussion of the problems of provisioning and exchange, see Laiou, A. E., 'Byzantine Trade with Christians and Muslims and the Crusade', in A. E. Laiou and R. P. Mottahedeh (eds) (2001), *The Crusades from the Perspective of Byzantium and the Muslim World*, Washington, DC, 157–79.

42

4   Odo of Deuil (1948), V. G. Berry (ed. and trans.) *De profectione Ludovici VII in orientem*, New York, 40–41, 66.

5   Foucher of Chartres, *RHC Occ.*, III, 324; Baldric of Dol, *RHC Occ.*, IV, 14.

6   Dennis, G. T., 'Defenders of the Christian People: Holy War in Byzantium,' in Laiou and Mottahedeh (eds), *The Crusades from the Perspective of Byzantium and the Muslim World*, 36ff.

7   For an incisive argument making similar points specifically in the time of the crusades, see Dagron, G. (1997), 'Byzance entre le djihad et la croisade: quelques remarques', *Le concile de Clermont de 1095 et l'appel à la croisade. Actes du colloque international de Clermont Ferrand, 1995*, École française de Rome, 325–37.

8   Robert the Monk, *RHC Occ.*, III, 728; translation in Peters, *The First Crusade*, 27.

9   Ahrweiler, H. Un discours inédit de Constantin Porphyrogénète,' in *Travaux et Mémoires du centre de recherche d'histoire et civilisation de Byzance*, 2, 1967, 393–404.

10 Baldric of Dol, *RHC Occ.*, IV, 15; translation from Peters, *The First Crusade*, 32.

11 Ahrweiler, 'Un discours inédit', 398; Ps. 23 (24), 8; Deut. 32:41–2; Is. 25:2, Ps. 17 (18): 31, 35–6 in the King James version. See also Pertusi, A., 'Una acolouthia militare inedita del X secolo,' *Aevum*, 22, 1948, 145–68, esp. ll. 22ff, and Kolia-Dermitzaki, A. (1991), *O Vyzantinos ieros polemos: I provoli tou thriskeutikou polemou sto Vyzantio*, Athens.

12 I disagree with Kolia-Dermitzaki, *O Vyzantinos ieros polemos*, who claims that the Byzantines engaged in holy war in the seventh and the tenth centuries. I think that she is misled by rhetoric, and fails to examine the structural and functional elements of holy war.

13 Vari, R. (1917), *Leonis Imperatoris Tactica*, Budapest, II, 44–6.

14 The argument is made in Laiou, A. E., 'On Just War in Byzantium' in (1993), *To Hellenikon: Studies in Honor of Speros Vryonis Jr.*, I, New Rochelle, NY, 153–77.

15 Migne, *Patrologia Graeca*, 26, col. 1175.

16 Canon 13 of St Basil: Ralles, G. and Potles, M. (1854), *Syntagma ton theion kai hieron kanonon*, 4, Athens, 131.

17 Riley-Smith, J. (1980), 'Crusading as an act of love', *History*, 65, 1980, 177–92, esp. 178 80.

18 Raymond of Aguilers, *Historia Francorum qui ceperunt Iherusalem*, *RHC Occ.*, III, 300; Peters, *The First Crusade*, 260.

19 Reifferscheid, A. (ed.) (1884), *Annae Comnenae porphyrogenitae Alexias*, Leipzig, II, XI.6, 123; trans. in Sewter, E. R. A. (1985), *The Alexiad of Anna Comnena*, 352.

20 Baldric of Dol, *ROC Occ.*, IV, 138: *Nunc vobis bella proponimus quae in se habent gloriosum martyrii munus, quibus restat praesentis et eternae laudis titulus.*

21 Flori, J., 'Mort et martyre des guerriers', in *Cahiers de civilisation médiévale* 34, 1991, 120–39.

22 Thurn, Io. (ed.) (1973), *Ioannis Skylitzae Synopsis Historiarum*, Berlin/New York, 274–5.

23 Ralles and Potles, *Syntagma ton theion kai hieron kanonon*, 4, 133.

24 Constantine Stilbes in Darrouzès, J. (1983), 'Le mémoire de Constantin Stilbès contre les Latins,' *REB*, 21, 77; written soon after 1204.

25 The newest edition and translation of the poem is by Jeffreys, E. (1998), *Digenis Akritis: The Grottaferrata and Escorial Versions*, Cambridge. Here, I use the older, poetic translation by Mavrogordato, John (1956), *Digenes Akrites*, Oxford.

26 I have used the most literary translation: Luquiens, F. B. (1952), *The Song of Roland*,

New York, 35. For this quotation, I have also made partial use of Harrison, R. (1970), *The Song of Roland*, New York, 1970, No. 78, 82.

27 Luquiens, *The Song of Roland*, 52.

28 Mavrogordato, *Digenes Akrites*, 5, verses 30–37.

29 Ibid., p. 9, verses 100–105.

30 Mavrogordato, *Digenes Akrites*, p. 69, verses 1028–31. Both Mavrogordato and Jeffreys translate *ethnikos* as 'pagan'. However, by the twelfth century the word meant 'foreigner', which makes more intelligent the juxtaposition with 'Roman'. Thus the verse should be rendered 'a foreign father and a Roman mother'.

31 See below, note 40.

32 Brundage, J. A. (1962) *The Crusades: A Documentary Survey*, Milwaukee, WI, 184–5.

33 Riley-Smith, J. (1987), *The Crusades*, New Haven, CT, xxviii.

34 This statement should be somewhat softened. Some Byzantines were sympathetic to the crusaders' avowed purpose of liberating Jerusalem or bringing aid to it. In the late twelfth century, Niketas Choniates, the most important historian of the period, reports a speech by Conrad III to the German contingent of the second crusade that is reminiscent of crusading rhetoric: Bekker, E. (ed.) (1835), *Nicetae Choniatae Historia*, Bonn, 91–4.

35 Alexias, II, 94–5 (X.10); trans., *The Alexiad*, 326.

36 Ahrweiler, H. (1975), *L'idéologie politique de l'Empire byzantin*, Paris, 35, and Kolia-Dermitzaki, *O Vyzantinos ieros polemos*, 242 ff.

37 Baldric of Dol, *RHC Occ. IV*, 15: '*Tali imperatori militare debetis, cui omnis non deest potentia, cui quae rependat nulla desunt stipendia. Via brevis est, labor permodicus est, qui tamen immarcescibilem vobis rependet coronam.*'

38 Ahrweiler, 'Un discours inédit', 399.

39 See Bertrand de Born: 'When battle is joined, let all men of good lineage think of naught but the breaking of heads and arms, for it is better to die than to be vanquished and live. I tell you, I find no such favour in food, or in wine, or in sleep, as in hearing the shout, 'On, on!' from both sides … in seeing men great and small go down in the grass beyond the fosses; in seeing at last the dead, with pennoned stumps of lances till in their sides', quoted in Miller, T. S. and Nesbitt, J. (1995), *Peace and War in Byzantium: Essays in Honor of George T. Dennis, S.J.*, Washington, DC, 7.

40 There are cases in the historical record where Arab prisoners were tortured horrribly: in 874–5: Skylitzes, 153–4, Bekker, E. (ed.) (1838), *Theophanes Continuatus*, Bonn, 300–301. It is true that these were pirates who had engaged in very destructive raids, and the purpose was to punish them by acts similar to their own and deter them from more attacks. Similarly, the capture of Crete was attended by atrocities: Niebuhr, B. G. (ed.) (1828), *Leo Diaconus*, Bonn, 14–15; Attaliota, M. (1853) *Historia* (ed). E. Bekker, Bonn, 227–8. While the atrocity should not be played down, it should also be said that it was not necessarily due to the demonisation of the Muslim other. After all, possibly the worst horror perpetrated by the Byzantines was the blinding of 15 000 Bulgarians by Basil II, and the Bulgarians had been Christianised for one hundred and sixty years.

41 Theognostos, in Munitiz, J. A., SJ, 'War and Peace Reflected in Some Byzantine *Mirrors of Princes*', in Miller and Nesbitt, *Peace and War in Byzantium*, 52, 54.

42 Taft, R. F., SJ, 'War and Peace in the Divine Liturgy', in Miller and Nesbit, *Peace and War in Byzantium*, 17–32.

43 Oikonomides, N. 'Cinq actes inédits du patriarche Michael Autoreianos', *Revue des études byzantines*, 25, 1967, 119, lines 70–75.

VII

The Many Faces of Medieval Colonization

HE THEME OF THIS YEAR'S SYMPOSIUM is of broad interest, engaging the attention of historians outside the field. Indeed, the interaction of cultures and peoples who, in one way or another, find themselves in close contact is a perennial historical problem and an important question in modern historiography. It is the *permutations* of interaction that make such investigations interesting to historians across fields. More specifically, the developments of the sixteenth century are in many ways dependent upon institutions and ideologies that were deeply ingrained in the practices and minds of the colonizers; it is therefore useful to cast a backward glance and examine what the preceding historical experience was, and this necessarily takes us to the Middle Ages. Medievalists consider the developments of the late fifteenth and the sixteenth centuries to be, in many ways, the continuation of earlier trends: for us, they are Phase Two of the expansion of Europe, the first phase having begun in the late eleventh century, when western Europeans, for the first time in centuries, moved outside the old geographical and cultural frontiers. We are, perhaps, more keenly aware of these connections at the moment, precisely because of the anniversary of Columbus' journey. But this is far from a new perception of medievalists, who have occasionally made extravagant statements regarding continuity. One need not agree wholeheartedly with extreme statements to make the observation that the explorers, soldiers, and colonists who sailed to the Americas had behind them a collective experience of several hundreds of years of contact with other peoples, and also of various types of expansion and colonization.

In the early period of the first phase of European expansion there were two main impulses, two main forms of expansionary movement, intersecting at important points and lending support one to the other. One is economic expansion, focused on the Mediterranean and eventually the Baltic, fueled by trade and later facilitated by the development of manufactures and banking institutions. Hesitantly at first, confidently with the passage of time, the merchants of the Italian maritime cities and eventually of southern France and Spain broke out of the confines of western Europe, bringing their merchandise and their small capital to the ports of the eastern Mediterranean, both Christian and Muslim. That expansion first took the form of trading stations: small colonies with a few houses, a church, weighing stations, and a fluctuating population that both carried out trade in local goods and picked up, from central Asia and the Far East, the commodities of long-distance trade: spices and silks. In terms of institutions, that outward expansion was very much based on the medieval concept of privilege. In the corporate culture of the Middle Ages, the concept of universal freedoms or rights was hardly developed. Instead, the functional mode of operation involved special "freedoms," that is, privileges, attached to members of a group, a social class, or a corporation. As far as the Western merchants were concerned, their activities in the countries of the eastern Mediterranean were regulated by special trade privileges. The most obvious and far-reaching were the privileges that the Venetian merchants received from the Byzantine emperors in 992, in 1082, and then throughout the rest of the Middle Ages. Over other foreign merchants, whose activities were restricted, the Venetians had the advantage of being free to trade and reside in a number of the cities and ports of the Byzantine Empire; over the native merchants, they had the advantage of trading without paying duties, which automatically gave them an economic advantage of about 10 percent of the value of the merchandise. In conceptual terms, the trading privileges created within the Byzantine Empire a group of foreigners who not only worked in advantageous circumstances but were also removed from imperial, state authority because they received special exemptions, that is, extraterritorial concessions: primarily, fiscal exemptions and judicial privileges that removed them from the jurisdiction of the courts of the host country. Similar privileges were acquired in other states of the eastern Mediterranean, and eventually were to have adverse structural effects on the native economies. Thus, we have an expansion fueled by trade and carried out primarily by merchants and sailors. From the trading station, a somewhat passive institution dependent on the goodwill of the native rulers, there eventually grew, in some areas, full-blown colonies of exploitation, which necessitated new ways of dealing with the native populations.

The other impulse of early European expansion came from religion, and it was contemporaneous with the first phase of the economic expansion. I am speaking, of course, of the Crusades, that Holy War which was an invention of medieval western Europe and which left a long-lasting ideological and cultural imprint on European societies. The formal institutional innovations of the Crusades are not, perhaps, of interest here. Of much broader importance is the institutionalization of a particular way of looking at the enemy, and of a particular concept of how to deal with those who did not wish to become a part of the Christian commonwealth. There is no doubt that these questions were capable of receiving and did receive different answers. Thus, on the central question of whether infidel or generally non-Christian rulers had the right to exercise jurisdiction, to rule and to hold property rights, important canonists could hold entirely divergent opinions (Brundage 1976: especially 121ff). But legalistic ideas and definitions came only after both practice and a crude ideology had already developed. That crude ideology, very much in evidence in the late eleventh century, can be seen in art, in literature, in papal speeches (at least as reported to us), in the accounts of chroniclers of the First Crusade, and in the actions of crusaders. The notion of the "Other" that was forged at that time was uncompromising: the "Other" was bad, evil, and vile. It soon became evident how expandable this concept was. In a conscious act, the papacy had sought to substitute wars against "the Other" for internal, European, internecine warfare. The "Other" came to be described as vile, almost beyond the pale, and this element of Holy War ideology was so powerful that it began to expand immediately: the Jews of the Rhineland, many of them burned in their synagogues, were the first victims of the First Crusade; in the holy city of Jerusalem, when it was captured, the Muslim population was put to death by crusaders who joyfully reported that "men rode in blood up to their knees and bridle reins. Indeed, it was a just and splendid judgment of God that the place should be filled with the blood of the unbelievers...."[1] More than a generation later, as St. Bernard of Clairvaux was preaching a crusade against the Slavs, who were pagan, he wrote, "either they or their religion must be exterminated," and his words found a willing audience. Certainly this attitude carried over into the thirteenth century, especially in the Baltic areas, where the people who were being confronted were pagans, and technologically and politically weak. The European expansionary movement, to the degree that it was impelled by religion and by ideas of Holy War, had a deep strain of intolerance, and a concept of Virtue versus Vice. This was disputed by the many voices raised against the Crusade who could not reconcile the use of force, so much a part of the western European tradition, with the theoretical imperative that adherence to Christianity should be freely undertaken.[2] On the other hand, there is also a missionary strain, going back to an older tradition, revived after the Crusades had lost their

---

[1] Peters (1971: 214), here citing Raymond d'Aguiliers on the siege and capture of Jerusalem.
[2] Kedar (1984: 159ff). Cf. Constable 1953 and Siberry 1985.

vigor. This tradition looks toward conversion rather than extermination as the way to achieve the final aim, which in both cases is the extension of the Christian commonwealth to include as many peoples as possible (Kedar 1984: 97ff). By the fourteenth century, Crusades and missionary activities were looked upon as two complementary forms of achieving universality for the Christian religion, and a man such as the Majorcan Ramón Lull could propose both solutions, opting for conversion in the first instance but, if that failed, suggesting that the Muslims be told that there would be perpetual warfare, in which they would be torn asunder and slain.[3] In a variation on these attitudes, Pope Innocent IV had stated, in the mid-thirteenth century, that forcible Christianization was not to be undertaken, but that, on the other hand, Christians were justified in waging war against those Muslim rulers who forbade Christian preachers to preach in their lands (Kedar 1984: 159ff). Medievalists have pointed out that his approach was later used to justify the subjugation of the inhabitants of the New World (Kedar 1984: 203).

Medieval *exploration* is connected with the missionary and mercantile tradition rather than the tradition of crusade, although there are undoubted links to the latter as well. One thinks in this connection of well-known names: on the one hand, there is Marco Polo as a representative of the merchant interest in exploration. Exploration by merchants certainly did not start or end with him, but his account has the advantage of having been written down, and of being the only one of its kind to have survived. At least, that is, it is the only surviving *geographic* exploration by a merchant, for there are other types of exploration: I am thinking primarily of the registering of economic diversity—different marketplaces, systems of coinage, weights and measures, prices—which are incorporated in traders' manuals.[4] The data collected in these texts is different from that of geographic exploration, but the mind-set of the writers is the same. On the other hand, there are the writings connected with missionary hopes: those of the Western ambassadors to the Mongols, John of Plano Carpini and especially William of Rubruck, who produced the first great ethnographic account of central Asia and its peoples.[5] These travelers were interested in recording the social structure, the beliefs, and the mores of the heathen Mongols and Tatars with a view toward their eventual conversion or at least alliance with the Christians. The merchants, deeply pious though they undoubtedly were, were more

---

[3] Kedar (1984: 196): "scindens et interficiens": *Liber de Fine,* 1305.

[4] The most well-known of these is the manual of Francesco Balducci Pegolotti, *La Pratica della Mercatura* (1936).

[5] Christopher Dawson (1955) includes accounts by John of Plano Carpini (1245–1247) and William of Rubruck (in the 1250s).

interested in profits than in conversion, and certainly more interested in profits than in warfare for the expansion of Christianity. Without ascribing benevolence to them, which would be quite unrealistic, it is nevertheless clear that, among western Europeans, they were the ones most capable of what we might call tolerance, although *they* would not recognize it as such: the acceptance of other peoples, their customs, and their faith; and the acceptance of war, when necessary, but a much more constant aversion to war, Holy War or crusade, since after a certain point it interfered with the successful pursuit of trade. A case in point is the reaction of merchants to the papal embargo of trade with Egypt, instituted after the fall of Acre, the last Christian outpost in the Holy Land, in 1291. The merchants of Italy and Spain were very much opposed to the embargo, and found different ways of bypassing it, although openly breaking it was dangerous and thus to be avoided. Such an attitude of tolerance is understandable, for it was, after all, the merchants who had to deal with the diversity of weights, measures, coins, products, peoples, and their customs, and deal with them successfully if they were to be good businessmen. For them, as for few other western Europeans in the Middle Ages, diversity was not something to be subjugated to unicity, but something to profit from, as one does in the marketplace, making the best advantage of different prices, long- and short-term loans, and rates of currency exchange. Thus it was that merchants were the main carriers of that other strain in European expansion and colonization, that is, accommodation and openness to other peoples and cultures. It was, for example, neither crusader nor missionary who produced the first dictionary for strange tongues, but the Genoese—those intrepid and single-minded merchants—who, in the mid-fourteenth century, compiled the Codex Cumanicus, a Latin-Persian-Cuman dictionary.

In terms of colonization patterns, there are three different types that I would like to discuss. The first was that adopted by the Italian merchants of the Middle Ages, primarily those of Venice and Genoa. These two commercial cities differed significantly from each other, especially in the organization of their economic and political lives. The Genoese had a weak state and their expansion was due to the actions of individuals or groups organized into private or semi-private companies. In Venice, on the other hand, much of the economic activity, certainly a great deal of the mercantile activity, was organized, directed, or controlled by the state.[6] Although commercial expansion and colonization were thus undertaken under different conditions, they still present a basically similar pattern with many common elements. Philip Curtin has isolated an important

---

[6] On some of these differences, see Lopez (1975: 35–42).

difference between the trading practices of these merchants and those of other western Europeans, who created less organized trade diasporas, that is, small communities in the middle of larger ones, typically withdrawn unto themselves (Curtin 1984: 115–119). On the other hand, Venice and Genoa created, during the course of the thirteenth century, trading-post empires, that is to say, they established military control over important trading posts, mostly used for long-distance trade. It is the kind of pattern that earned Venice the designation "Empire without lands." Sometimes these trading posts were converted into full-blown colonies of exploitation. This is the case with some of the largest and most productive islands of the eastern Mediterranean—Chios, Cyprus, and Crete. Tied to a broader trade system that was dominated by the Italians and extended over the entire Mediterranean, their economies became satellites of the economic interests of the colonizing power. This had an important impact on the economic activities of the native populations as well as on the organization of production: there were also changes in the patterns of cultivation, the introduction of sugar cultivation in Cyprus, for example. In all of these islands there was a certain number of Italian settlers, both landlords and merchants, and this led to interesting phenomena in terms of internal development.

Crete is the island where one may best observe the effects of contact between settlers and native populations in this form of colonization. Officially, the Western settlers formed an upper class that was meant to be isolated from the rest of the population. They were certainly the ruling class, holding a monopoly of political power until at least the middle of the fourteenth century (Jacoby 1976). Official policy enforced segregation by, for example, establishing legal strictures against intermarriage. In the countryside, the peasant population that toiled under a newly introduced feudal regime remained Greek-speaking and Orthodox in religion. But one of the effects of the Venetian conquest of the island was increased urbanization, and in the cities one may observe from very early on a process of assimilation and acculturation of the foreign elite in terms of language and culture.[7] Here intermarriages occurred early and often between members of the commercial group, and also among the artisans and the rest of the urban population. Typically, as might be expected, marriages were between male colonists and native women, so that the female line of a mixed marriage tended to be Greek, but the reverse could also be the case. Bilingualism developed equally early. While the absence of sources does not permit a detailed investigation of the phenomenon until the early part of the fourteenth century, we do know that within two generations

---

[7] For what follows, see Laiou (1992: 29–43). McKee (n.d.) examines such phenomena.

of the conquest there were Westerners who had learned Greek in a formal manner. The fact that some of them were the children of mixed marriages is neither unexpected nor curious; indeed, it is possible that bilingualism developed rather earlier than our sources indicate, and at first within the informal surroundings of the household. Many wet nurses, for example, were Greek. Be that as it may, apart from unambiguous statements by colonists that they had learned Greek, there is also other evidence that suggests a certain "contamination" of Latin (and presumably also of Venetian) by Greek. Inserted in wills composed in Latin or Venetian, we find Greek words, which presumably are there so that everyone could understand them, that is, because they were commonly used by both Greek and Venetian speakers. On the other hand, we also know that there were Greeks who learned Italian, especially as a language of high culture, and that, quite early on, the Greek of the island was influenced by Italian and Venetian. The future, however, lay unequivocally with the linguistic assimilation not of the Greek element but of the Venetian one: although bilingualism continued to exist, by the sixteenth century the dominant language everywhere was Greek, and this was certainly the language of literature.

This phenomenon of assimilation and acculturation of the colonists was still in its first stage two generations after the conquest, but it was already visible. It marked a society that was not only urban but quite highly commercial. Under Venetian rule, production was commercialized in Crete, the island became an important center of trade in the eastern Mediterranean, and the colony flourished as did the native population. From early on, strong economic ties developed between the two elements of the population, and in fact one may often observe multiple aspects of assimilation taking place simultaneously and within the same family group: two families, linked through economic ties, also forge marriage ties, and their children have a share in both cultures and languages. All of this took place primarily in the cities, and undoubtedly was facilitated by the fact that both colonists and the native population were Christian. On the other hand, one should remember that in the eyes of the Catholic Church the natives were schismatic Christians; indeed, the native church lost its hierarchy and was placed in a position of inferiority relative to the Catholic Church. It would have been entirely possible to have had a situation such as obtained in the Latin Kingdom of Jerusalem in which Christians of different denominations—native and colonist—did not have much contact. Here, however, although religious separation remained, especially at the official level, among the urban inhabitants there was a certain religious "bilingualism" as well. The solution adopted in Crete, one of considerable integration and accommodation to the native population, was undoubtedly the result of a combination of factors:

the relatively small number of immigrants, the relative closeness of the two religions, and the strength of the already existing social structures. However, many of the same factors existed in the Latin Kingdom of Jerusalem, where different solutions were ultimately adopted, as we shall see. For my part, I would ascribe a weighty role to the exigencies of a commercial economy that depends upon interchange and collaboration and therefore creates both the objective conditions and the attitudes that are conducive to the eventual assimilation of the colonists. At the same time, the native population proves resilient and capable of absorbing the foreign ruling elite.

Patterns of colonization were different where the colonizers were states, or feudal landlords, or where the church played a greater role and where the colonized peoples were not Christians, that is, were outside the boundaries of Christendom and the protection offered within these boundaries. A second type of colonization is characterized, on the part of the colonizers, by a mixture of economic exploitation and religious intolerance, which posits either conversion or extermination of the native, pagan population; and on the part of the native population, it is characterized by an initial phase of resistance followed by conversion and assimilation or extinction. This is the case of German expansion in the lands of the Baltic, especially the area between the Elbe and the Vistula Rivers, where we find the other extreme of the Cretan situation.[8] In the course of the twelfth century, as a result of the crusading movement, these lands were conquered and colonized by the German nobility, merchants, and peasants. The native Slavic populations were agriculturalists, hunters, and fishermen, with a simple political-military organization and a dualist religion. They had had relations and connections with the Germans for a long time: in the tenth century, they had paid tithes to the German bishops, but had subsequently thrown off their dependence. Saxon missionaries, too, had had a fairly lengthy presence in these territories, sometimes, as in the early twelfth century, supported by a native Christian prince. German expansion was impelled by economic forces, originally taking the form of extraction of tribute and then, in the course of the early twelfth century, a period of demographic growth, acquiring the aspect of land hunger and therefore conquest. Religion functioned as an ideological justification for conquest, and eventually was to dictate the terms of conquest and colonization.

The connection between the effort to acquire more lands and the Christianization of the Slavs is evident in a proclamation of the leading bishops

---

[8] The major source is Helmold of Bosau (1935); for bibliography and interpretation, see Thompson (1928) and Christianssen (1980). See also, now, Bartlett (1993), published after this essay had been written.

of Saxony in 1108: "[The Slavs] are an abominable people, but their land is very rich in flesh, honey, grain, birds, and abounding in all products of the fertility of the earth, when cultivated, so that none can be compared unto it. So they say who know. Wherefore, O Saxons, Franks, Lotharingians, men of Flanders most famous—here you can both save your souls, and if it please you, acquire the best of land to live in" (Thompson 1928: 497). Here, especially in the Wendish territories, there was little accommodation with the native Slavic population, who were supposed either to convert to Christianity or perish. The Second Crusade, preached against the Slavs as much as against the Muslims in the Holy Land, produced an unequivocal and powerful ideological conceptualization, precisely that of conversion or annihilation. The interests and ideology of the crusaders and colonizers were helped by their undoubted technological superiority. It was "the brilliant glitter of their arms" that the native populations most feared. The response of native society began with resistance: "the laws we inherited from our fathers we will not give up; we are content with the religion we have. . . ."[9] War was followed by the rebellion of defeated Slavic leaders, a rebellion against both economic dependence and religious subjugation. As one Slavic leader put it, "You all know what great calamities and what oppression have come upon our people through the violent might which the Duke of Saxony has exerted. He had taken from us the inheritance of our fathers and settled foreigners in all its bounds. . . . No one save me thinks of the gods of our nation or wishes to raise up its ruins. Again pluck up your courage, O men who are the remnants of the Slavic race, and resume your daring spirit."[10] In the end, the combination of superior technology, ideological pressure, and massive population settlement brought about the conversion of the native population and the absorption of those who survived. By the late 1170s, we are told that "all the country of the Slavs was now, through the help of God, all made, as it were, into one colony of Saxons. And cities and villages were built, and the number of ministers of Christ multiplied."[11] The Slavic population had been reduced in number, as some were killed, others were pushed into different areas, and others were sold as slaves. Those who survived were assimilated, and their culture was supplanted by the western European culture that was brought in by the German church. New German principalities appeared in the areas between the Elbe and the Vistula

---

[9] Pomeranians to Otto, bishop of Bamberg, in 1127, in Thompson (1928: 431), here quoting the monk Herbord.

[10] Helmold (1935: 256), here quoting an address of Pribislav to the Slavs.

[11] Thompson (1928: 513), quoting Helmold. For full text, see Helmold (1935: 252–282).

Rivers: Holstein, Mecklenburg, Brandenburg, Pomerania. Similar phenomena occurred in the conquest and colonization of Prussia, most particularly eastern Prussia, which was heavily Germanized in the late thirteenth and fourteenth centuries, with the influx of colonists, the extermination or expulsion of some Prussian tribes, and the assimilation of others. In all of these cases, the pertinent variables included technological and military superiority on the part of the colonizers, heavy immigration, and an uncompromising religious approach (Christianssen 1980: 100–104; Johnson 1975: 545–585). On the part of the native population, there is a sequence of resistance, rebellion, conversion, and eventual assimilation. In the end, the conquerors supplanted native society.

A third pattern of medieval colonization is exemplified by the Latin Kingdom of Jerusalem, which was established in the late eleventh century and lasted until 1291. Here, too, a foreign—military and later also commercial—group settled as conquerors, amid a local population that included Jews, Muslims, and native Christians of different sects. The first western European approach was that of extermination of at least part of the native population, that is, the Muslims. This approach was short-lived indeed, having been put into practice only at the moment of the conquest of Jerusalem, when the Muslim population of the city was massacred. But Jerusalem, as the locus of Christian and especially crusader fanaticism, was a special case; and the moment was a special one too, since the First Crusade had been nourished by descriptions of the Muslims as, variously, inhuman, semi-human, and an apocalyptic enemy. As the European settlements developed, extermination of the enemy was not an option that was tried. Nor was there massive immigration of western Europeans into the conquered lands of Syria and Palestine. Indeed, the relative paucity of European settlers was one of the defining characteristics of this state and society. What was established here was an exploitative regime, with significant separation between the rulers and the ruled: the rulers kept their culture and language and institutions and, what is most important, a monopoly on political power. Contact with the native rural population, whether Muslim or Christian, was primarily of a fiscal nature: the colonists were not even resident landlords. The native village communities, at the same time, retained their structure, with their own native courts and judges, and their own head men who were responsible for security and for the collection of taxes. Nor did the systems of cultivation or settlement of the local population change. There was greater contact between natives and colonists in the towns, but this had very little impact on the native population. So there were two separate and unequal societies, with undoubted points of contact which, however, were not of an essential nature. True, the colonists acquired some Eastern habits in food and housing; their military architecture profited a great deal from the expertise of native masons; and in ideological terms, they became, as a group, more tolerant of different cultures than were their counterparts in western Europe. But they retained their language, their high culture, and, above all, their separateness in terms of administration and politics, creating a superstructure to which the native population had no access. The two societies met in peace at the level of economics, and in hostility at the level of warfare, but there was no true assimilation on either side. As far as the native population is concerned, it is interesting that, in this crusading state, there was not even a concerted effort to convert the Muslims or the native Christians, who were heretics in the eyes of the Western conquerors.[12] The impact of the colonizers on native society was important primarily to the extent that native agriculture was forced to focus on particular cash crops, for which there was a market in Europe.[13] But this was less the result of the colonization of Syria and Palestine and more the result of the creation of a Mediterranean system of exchange, driven by the needs of Italian commerce.

The type of colonial state and society introduced by western Europeans in the Latin Kingdom of Jerusalem was particularly fragile. Its continued existence depended upon the tolerance of the native population which, in turn, was directly and negatively correlated with the degree of unity and strength of the surrounding Muslim populations.[14] When the Muslims became united under charismatic leaders, the Latin Kingdom of Jerusalem collapsed. What were the factors that led to the adoption of this fragile system? For one thing, there were the mechanics of conquest: this took place very rapidly, and its very rapidity meant that it neither depended on the native population nor was it attended with even partial, piecemeal, assimilation. Secondly, the absence of massive settlement was surely an important factor, and had the obvious effect that the conquerors remained a small minority. This could have led them to choose assimilation with the native population. However, that theoretical choice— which, historically, was adopted by, for example, the Franks in the area which today is France, or the Normans in England—was made impossible by the constituent ideology of the Latin Kingdom of Jerusalem. This state owed its

[12] This interpretation adopts and derives from the views most eloquently set forth by Joshua Prawer (1975). There are other views, which stress the aspects of assimilation of the conquerors. For an example, see LaMonte (1940–41).

[13] On this, see Ashtor (1983: 24, 173ff; 1976: 240ff). On the topic, see also Kedar (1992). Ashtor has also discussed the negative impact of European trade on the manufactures of the Near and Middle East.

[14] For an intriguing study of the organization of the Latin Kingdom of Jerusalem, its internal contradictions, and the international exigencies, see Ben-Ami (1969).

very creation to religion, and its continued existence was dependent upon waves of crusades from Europe. Therefore, a rapid assimilation with the native population was impossible, even though part of that population was Christian (albeit heretical) and thus had many points of similarity with the conquerors. A long-term process of assimilation was rendered impossible by a third major factor: unlike the situation in the Slavic lands of the Baltic, the colonizers had no technological superiority over the native population, indeed quite the contrary was true. That, coupled with the hostility that was cultivated by the colonizers, and with the effect of the conquest upon the large Muslim populations outside the kingdom, who were galvanized into action, brought about the end of the kingdom before long-term factors could come into effect. Thus the westerners could not supplant or eradicate native society, and could not, because of circumstances and their own ideology, make the historical choice of assimilation.

What is the relevance of all this to the topic at hand? A number of connections, superficial or profound, have been made with great eloquence by other scholars. I will not dwell on facile and well-known connections. It is a still impressive but by now unsurprising fact that Columbus sailed with a well-annotated copy of Marco Polo, and found the earthly Paradise at the mouth of the Orinoco River. Years ago, Eileen Power remarked that this is the most important miracle of Marco Polo: alive, in the thirteenth century, he discovered China; dead, in the fifteenth century, he discovered America (Power 1926: 124–158). It is also not necessary to insist on the cliché that Prince Henry the Navigator, who is above all responsible for creating the preconditions for Portuguese expansion, went in search of spices, infidels to convert, and Prester John to discover. At a more complex level, scholars have traced the transfer of techniques and personnel from the Mediterranean to the Atlantic states, especially Spain and Portugal, in the fifteenth century (Heers 1961; Fernández-Armesto 1987: 96–148, 203–222). They have insisted, and rightly so, on the versatility of the Genoese, who reoriented their trading activities, when the need arose, from luxury items to bulk commodities, and built up a trade complex that depended heavily on the Atlantic-bordering states; they immigrated into the Iberian Peninsula, and behaved as merchants had done in the past: settled down, became bilingual, married with the local population, even became officeholders (Fernández-Armesto 1987: 113). They brought with them techniques acquired in the Mediterranean for trading and settlement companies, banks, contracts, and they revitalized the economy of the Iberian Peninsula. The same scholars have also pointed to the transfer of the production of certain commodities from the eastern Mediterranean to the Madeiras and the

Canaries, and then eventually to the Americas: this is most obviously the case with sugar cultivation, which had been flourishing in Cyprus with slave labor, and was then introduced by the Genoese into Sicily, Portugal, the Madeiras, the Canaries, the Cape Verde islands, until it was brought to Haiti. All of these lines of filiation have been established, and there is no reason for me to dwell on them.

Historians, too, have made the connection between the crusading movement and the discovery and settlement of the Americas: thus Friedrich Heer suggests that "the discovery of America was ... itself a unique latter-day product of the European crusading movement, whose fervour was so quick to die down, but was kindled again and again with consequences no one could have foreseen" (Heer 1962: 122).

Given all of these connections, by now well established, what strikes me when I contemplate the medieval legacy of the late fifteenth century are certain broad traits. Primarily, I suppose, thinking about this topic brought home to me the great diversity of the medieval experience of expansion and colonization. Western European thought and practice run the gamut of possibilities from separation to assimilation. The conversion and extinction of populations with which they came into contact were contemplated, discussed, and sometimes put into practice. *Whether* they were put into practice depended considerably on the numerical and political strength of the native peoples in question. Both of these sets of attitudes are also part of a particular way of approaching the "Other": the "Other" has to change, to give up his distinguishing traits in order to be allowed to survive. Much of western European expansion and settlement is premised on this profound intolerance, which was formalized and institutionalized in the Middle Ages, mostly in connection with the crusading movement. The idea of perpetual crusade as a way of unifying the world under western European domination is one of the largest legacies of medieval western Europe, all the more dangerous because it was promoted and espoused by the carriers of ideology—the church—and by a number of medieval kings. Yet it was the same society that produced divergent views, capable of different ramifications. It was the same society that said that infidel rulers have no right to hold land legitimately (so the canonist Hostiensis), and that produced individuals who argued that they could, and that therefore the Christians could not dispossess them (so the Pope Innocent IV). The debate was far from irrelevant to the debates that followed the Spanish expansion into America (Elliott 1964: 45–50). It was also the same society that produced varying patterns of colonization: from the unsuccessful, untenable closed system of the Latin Kingdom of Jerusalem, to the porous system of the mercantile colonies, where contact between European merchants and native populations was constant, and where the native societies (in a number of cases, but by no means in all) adapted to the new conditions by participating in them, although never fully. It seems to me that in terms of the contact of western Europeans and other peoples in the Middle Ages, we have a variety of responses to European intrusion: from a basically unchanged fabric of native societies (the Latin Kingdom of Jerusalem), to economic adaptation, to a certain degree of cultural integration, to, finally, annihilation. And it also seems to me that symbiosis was easier in the merchant colonies, and that by the same token the adaptations of native society were more considerable, even if restricted to particular kinds of activity.

The question then arises, whether one can isolate more precisely the constituent factors of each of these different colonial experiences. Let me say at the outset that I do not believe it possible to set up a predictive model, that is, one that would establish categories capable of predicting what would happen in other situations. Predictability and inevitability are rendered impossible by the fact that each situation is the result of the interplay of many factors on both sides; the permutations allow for similarities between historical experiences, but hardly for model building. That having been said, it is, nevertheless, possible and useful to identify the factors that eventually determine colonial attitudes and native response; overall, there is a dialectic relationship between the colonizers and the native populations, in which each factor may have a different effect, depending on the other factors operating at the same time. On the colonists' side of the relationship, ideology seems to play an overwhelmingly important role in creating a predisposition toward assimilation, annihilation, or separation. Yet the translation of ideological position into action is itself determined by other factors, so that the same aggressive Christianity acted differently upon the pagan populations of the Baltic and the Muslim populations of Syria and Palestine. Economic factors play an important role, different according to whether the colonizer participates in an extractive system (agriculture, mining) or in a system of exchange. The numerical strength of the colonizers is undoubtedly important but, once again, its effects vary: the small number of colonists in the Latin Kingdom of Jerusalem created a closed, exclusionist, defensive system, while the small number of Venetian colonists in Crete were eventually assimilated. Finally, the conditions of conquest—the rapidity of conquest, the patterns of settlement that followed it—can help determine the outcome. As far as the native populations are concerned, their part in the relationship is conditioned by a variety and combination of factors. Numerical strength is important, but perhaps more important is the degree of social complexity. A complex society in Crete was able easily to assimilate the colonizers, whereas the more simple social structures of some of the Baltic populations gave in to the technological and institutional superiority of the German crusaders. Active resistance, a form of reaction by the native population, also in turn becomes a factor influencing the colonial experience, since it plays a dynamic role in the relationship between colonizers and native populations. There is, finally, an external component which is also important: the connection of the colonists and/or the native populations with outside populations, cultures, institutions, or states. The crusaders' links with western Europe on the one hand, and, on the other, the fact that Muslim leaders outside the Latin Kingdom of Jerusalem saw themselves as the protectors of the Muslims of the kingdom and of the Muslim holy places, were of primary importance in determining the fate of that state and society. Similarly, but with different effect, the native population of Crete kept up its resistance for about a hundred and fifty years, partly because there was an Orthodox Christian state—the Byzantine Empire—to which Crete had once belonged and which from time to time gave the population a shadowy support. The various factors I have identified here were important, or even crucial, in shaping colonial experiences; but the exercise of identification is valuable primarily because it shows the complexity and variety of historical situations, rather than because it permits neat categorizations.

These many experiences, and that varied ideological baggage, were all bequeathed by the medieval phase of expansion to the late fifteenth century. What aspects of it were dominant in the attitudes and practices of the colonizers of the Americas I do not know, nor is it the focus of this symposium as I understand it.

I was, however, interested to see in a number of papers that diversity of attitude is recognized as having played an important role in the colonizing experience (for example, Burkhart, this volume). Certain questions which were in my mind before the symposium remain open, although partial answers have been supplied by the papers at the conference. First, one wonders to what aspect of the Spaniards' varied ideological baggage the response of native societies was directed, and whether Guaman Poma de Ayala's appeal to the social and political constructs of the colonists (discussed by MacCormack, this volume) is the same type of response as the compilation of *títulos,* and the ceremonies of the Nahuas (discussed by Wood and Burkhart). Secondly, it is quite clear that in the colonial period native societies in the Americas were resilient and kept basic structures and ideas alive, though couched in a new vocabulary. The intriguing question in my mind is about the extent to which the attitude of the colonists was also influenced by this response, and therefore about the depth of the dialectic relationship. The response, or, more accurately, the responses, of the Spaniards to Nahua Christianization is a case in which such a dialogue between attitudes and responses is evident; I wonder how widespread such phenomena were. Thirdly, I was interested in finding out whether the patterns of change in the native traditions and in the structural contexts within which indigenous traditions and new elements came to be integrated into uniquely colonial systems have structural similarities in the patterns of response of colonized societies in the Middle Ages. I cannot say that I have found an answer to this question, or indeed that I am much further along in the quest for an answer. That is only to be expected, since a real answer would have to take into account the varieties of the New World experience as well as those of the Old World, and therefore is too daunting a task, perhaps more interesting in the pursuit than in the achievement.

BIBLIOGRAPHY

ASHTOR, ELIYAHU

    1976   *A Social and Economic History of the Near East in the Middle Ages.* Collins, London.

    1983   *Levant Trade in the Later Middle Ages.* Princeton University Press, Princeton, N.J.

BARTLETT, ROBERT

    1993   *The Making of Europe: Conquest, Colonization and Cultural Change, 950–1350.* Princeton University Press, Princeton, N.J.

BEN-AMI, AHARON

    1969   *Social Change in a Hostile Environment: The Crusaders' Kingdom of Jerusalem.* Princeton University Press, Princeton, N.J.

BRUNDAGE, JAMES A.

    1976   Holy War and the Medieval Lawyers. In *The Holy War* (Thomas Murphy, ed.): 99–140. Ohio State University Press, Columbus.

CHRISTIANSSEN, ERIC

    1980   *The Northern Crusades: The Baltic and the Catholic Frontiers, 1100–1525.* University of Minnesota Press, Minneapolis.

CONSTABLE, GILES

    1953   The Second Crusade as Seen by Contemporaries. *Traditio* 9: 213–279.

CURTIN, PHILIP D.

    1984   *Cross-Cultural Trade in World History.* Cambridge University Press, Cambridge.

DAWSON, CHRISTOPHER

    1955   *The Mongol Mission: Narratives and Letters of the Franciscan Missionaries in Mongolia and China in the Thirteenth and Fourteenth Centuries.* Sheed and Ward, New York.

    1980   *Mission to Asia* (reprint of Dawson 1955). Medieval Academy of America, Toronto.

ELLIOTT, JOHN H.

    1964   *The Old World and the New, 1492–1650.* Cambridge University Press, Cambridge.

FERNÁNDEZ-ARMESTO, FELIPE

    1987   *Before Columbus: Exploration and Colonisation from the Mediterranean to the Atlantic, 1229–1492.* Macmillan Education, Basingstoke, England.

HEER, FRIEDRICH

    1962   *The Medieval World: Europe, 1100–1350.* World Publishing Co., Cleveland and New York.

HEERS, JACQUES

    1961   *Gênes au XVe siècle: Activité économique et problèmes sociaux.* S.E.V.P.E.N., Paris.

HELMOLD OF BOSAU

    1935   *The Chronicle of the Slavs* (Francis Tschan, trans.). Columbia University Press, New York.

30

JACOBY, DAVID
1976   Les états latins en Romanie: Phénomènes sociaux et économiques (1204–1350 environ). In *XVe Congrès international d'études byzantines, Rapports*. Athens.

JOHNSON, EDGAR N.
1975   The German Crusade on the Baltic. In *A History of the Crusades*, vol. 3 (Kenneth Setton, ed.): 545–585. University of Wisconsin Press, Madison.

KEDAR, BENJAMIN Z.
1984   *Crusade and Mission*. Princeton University Press, Princeton, N.J.
1992   The Crusading Kingdom of Jerusalem—The First European Colonial Society? A Symposium. In *The Horns of Hattin* (B. Z. Kedar, ed.): 341–366. Variorum, London and Jerusalem.

LAIOU, ANGELIKI E.
1992   Venetians and Byzantines: Investigations of Forms of Contact in the Fourteenth Century. *Thesaurismata* 22: 29–43.

LAMONTE, JOHN L.
1940–41   The Significance of the Crusaders' States in Medieval History. *Byzantion* 15: 300–315.

LOPEZ, ROBERTO S.
1975   Venise et Gênes: deux styles, une réussite. In idem, *Su e giù per la storia di Genova*: 35–42. Università di Genova, Genova.

MCKEE, SALLY
n.d.   Uncommon Dominion: The Latins and Greeks of Venetian Crete in the Fourteenth Century. Ph.D. dissertation, University of Toronto, 1992.

PEGOLOTTI, FRANCESCO BALDUCCI
1936   *La Practica della Mercatura* (Allan Evans, ed.). Medieval Academy of America, Cambridge, Mass.

PETERS, EDWARD
1971   *The First Crusade*. University of Pennsylvania Press, Philadelphia.

POWER, EILEEN
1926   The Opening of the Land Routes to Cathay. In *Travel and Travellers of the Middle Ages* (Arthur Newton, ed.): 124–158. A. A. Knopf, New York.

PRAWER, JOSHUA
1975   *Histoire du royaume latin de Jérusalem*. 2 vols. CNRS, Paris.

SIBERRY, ELIZABETH
1985   *Criticism of Crusading, 1095–1274*. Clarendon Press, Oxford.

THOMPSON, JAMES WESTFALL
1928   *Feudal Germany*. University of Chicago Press, Chicago.

VIII

Byzantine Trade with Christians and Muslims and the Crusades

In May 1192, at a time when the Third Crusade was still in progress, the Byzantine emperor Isaac II sent one of his virtually annual embassies to Saladin, seeking, among other things, an offensive and defensive alliance directed, inevitably, against Western Europeans. In late summer or early autumn of the same year, a Venetian ship carrying the Byzantine ambassadors, Saladin's envoys and gifts to Isaac, and goods and merchandise belonging to Isaac, his brother and future emperor Alexios, an imperial official, and "Greek and Syrian merchants," set sail from Egypt toward Constantinople. Near Rhodes, it was attacked by Pisan and Genoese ships led by the Genoese corsair Guglielmo Grasso. The goods were seized, and the ambassadors and the merchants were killed, or so Isaac said in his letter of complaint to Genoa.[1] Nor were the sums involved negligible. Isaac claimed that the merchandise was valued at 96,000 hyperpyra and 566 nomismata,[2] of which 39,000 hyperpyra and 193 nomismata belonged to merchants of Constantinople.

This affair initiated a series of diplomatic and not-so-diplomatic negotiations that lasted until September 1195. Almost immediately after the attack, in November 1192, Isaac wrote to the Commune of Genoa describing what had happened and seeking satisfaction (ἱκάνωσις) for the property lost. Otherwise, he said, the Genoese merchants in

---

I should like to thank my research assistant, Charles Dibble, for his help.

[1] The main information about this incident is contained in G. Bertolotto, *Nuova serie di documenti sulle relazioni di Genova coll'Impero bizantino,* Atti della Società Ligure di storia patria 28.2 (Genoa, 1898), doc. XII, pp. 448–53 (= F. Miklosich and J. Müller, *Acta et diplomata graeca medii aevi sacra et profana,* 6 vols. [Vienna, 1860–90], 3:37–40), and doc. XIII, pp. 454–64, and J. Müller, *Documenti sulle relazioni delle città Toscane coll'oriente cristiano e coi Turchi fino all'anno MDXXXI,* Documenti degli archivi toscani (Florence, 1879; repr. Rome, 1966), nos. XXXVIII (pp. 61–64) and XLI (pp. 66–67). Brief discussions of the affair in C. M. Brand, "The Byzantines and Saladin," *Speculum* 37 (1962): 173–78, and W. Heyd, *Histoire du commerce du Levant au Moyen Age,* 2d ed., 2 vols. (Leipzig, 1936; repr. Amsterdam, 1967), 1:233–35. On piracy, cf. H. Ahrweiler, *Byzance et la mer* (Paris, 1966), passim, esp. 288–92, and M. Balard, *La Romanie génoise,* vol. 1 (Rome, 1978), 35.

[2] χιλιάδας ὑπερπύρων ἐννενήκοντα ἕξ, νομίσματα ὅμοια πεντακόσια ἑξήκοντα ἕξ. The two different terms may refer to two different coins: the gold hyperpyron and the electrum "nomisma." The small number of the electrum coins would reflect their limited usefulness for international trade. I owe this observation to C. Morrisson. But see also M. F. Hendy, *Coinage and Money in the Byzantine Empire, 1081–1204,* DOS 12 (Washington, D.C., 1969), 35–37.

Constantinople must sell their goods and deposit the money as a guarantee of the eventual restitution to be made by the Commune.[3] Similar letters, with a similar content, must have been sent to Pisa: although the early phases of negotiations with Pisa elude us, the surviving documentation makes reference to previous embassies. Very soon thereafter, indeed in the same month of November 1192,[4] Isaac did seize the property of Genoese and, undoubtedly, Pisan merchants. The name of a Genoese merchant, Enrico Novitella, who had sailed into Constantinople in November, is specifically mentioned.

In a *sigillion* given to the city of Genoa in October 1193, Isaac explained why he had taken this extraordinary measure. Once again, he recalled Grasso's attack, which had taken place, he reminded the Genoese, shortly after the conclusion of a treaty with Genoa.[5] He was most emphatic on the damages suffered by his merchants, many of whom, he said, were from Constantinople itself, and among the most important merchants in the City (καὶ τὰ πρῶτα τῶν ἐν αὐτῇ πραγματευτῶν φερομένους). He, Isaac, could not take this lightly, especially since the merchants (or, one assumes, the heirs or creditors of those who were killed) vociferously demanded justice, revenge, and reparation. They had asked to be allowed to get satisfaction from the property of Genoese merchants in Constantinople; the Genoese in question had not responded to the emperor's request that they make reparations, which upset their Byzantine counterparts even more. Isaac held the city of Genoa responsible, even though it had tried to claim that the corsairs were outlaws—expelled from the city—and that therefore the Commune bore no responsibility for their actions. In the second instance, Isaac held responsible the Genoese merchants active in Constantinople. Under heavy pressure from the people,[6] and fearing a riot,[7] but not wanting to take extreme measures such as rescinding the privileges of the Genoese, he had seized a portion of the money and goods of some Genoese merchants and given them to Byzantine "guarantors" (ἐγγυητάς) to hold in deposit (παρακαταθήκη). The sum so deposited was 20,000 hyperpyra, just over half what the Byzantine merchants claimed to have lost; it is legitimate to suppose that the goods of Pisan merchants, which we also know to have been seized,[8] made up the other half. This property was meant to be returned if the Genoese (and Pisan) Commune made reparations. If not, it would be given outright to the Byzantine merchants in reparation (ἱκάνωσις).

Between November 1192 and October 1193, the Genoese (and the Pisans, one assumes) had sent envoys, promising to pursue the corsairs and deliver them into Isaac's hands, and asking that the Commune not be made to suffer for the actions of individuals. Isaac chose to believe that the Commune would make restitution, or else that the prom-

[3] Bertolotto, *Nuova serie,* doc. xii.

[4] For the date, see Bertolotto, *Nuova serie,* p. 457.

[5] For the treaty (April 1192), see F. Dölger, *Regesten der Kaiserurkunden des oströmischen Reiches,* vol. 1.2 (Munich, 1925), no. 1610; Miklosich and Müller, 3:25–37; Bertolotto, *Nuova serie,* pp. 413–33.

[6] The text uses the word *demos;* must one assume general popular discontent, or the discontent of merchants?

[7] On riots on the part of "the men of the marketplace" during the reign of Alexios III, cf. Niketas Choniates, *Historia,* ed. J. L. van Dieten (Berlin-New York, 1975), 523–26.

[8] Müller, *Documenti,* no. xli, p. 67.

ise itself was sufficient. In any event, although the Genoese did not send the money seized by the corsairs,[9] the Byzantines returned the 20,000 hyperpyra held in deposit. The man who returned it, and who perhaps had held it in deposit, was John Oxeobapho-poulos.[10] The transaction was effected with all the Byzantine legal forms: the Genoese, for example, gave formal assurance that they had, indeed, received the money (ἀναργυ-ρίαν προβαλέσθαι οὐκ ἔχομεν). The Genoese Commune agreed not to raise any further claims for damages suffered by its merchants whose goods had been confiscated, not to refer to the matter again, nor to seek revenge. And in return, the emperor issued his *sigillion,* closing the matter, and renewing Genoese privileges.

That the accused neatly turned into accusers is only one of the interesting aspects of the story. Clearly, we are at a crossroads in the development of the law of reprisals, and the principle prevailed that reprisals should not be sought of innocent parties; but in the process, the Byzantine merchants did not receive restitution. It is, I think, unlikely that in closing the matter in this way Isaac II was swayed by arguments regarding the respective responsibilities of individuals and collectivities. For the dispute with Pisa dragged on until 1195. It was, eventually, resolved in a way parallel to the settlement with Genoa, but only because Pisan ships kept harassing the environs of Constantinople, attacking Byzantine ships, seizing goods, and killing people.[11] One wonders whether in the Genoese case as well there was not an element of military or political persuasion.

The origins of the events of 1192–95 were embedded in political affairs: the last effort on the part of Isaac II to ally himself with Saladin against the Crusaders. It has been argued that the corsair attack was also in some degree political, the corsairs being in part bent on creating trouble for Saladin, the great enemy of the Crusader states.[12] The conclusion of the affair was also, it would seem, political, for the capture and murder of the ambassadors ended the close relationship between Isaac and Saladin. That having proved unproductive or even counterproductive, Isaac now made a full turn toward Genoa, Pisa, the pope, and the Normans[13]—which may serve as another explanation of the ease with which Pisan and Genoese goods were returned. Despite the political aspects, however, the role of the merchants is central to the story, and the importance of Constantinopolitan merchants is especially noteworthy. They appear as a large, influential, rich, and dangerous group, and it is no accident that Isaac began by demanding restitution for everyone's goods (including his own, his brother's, and his official's), then very quickly limited his demands to reparations for the goods of the merchants, even though in the end he got nothing.

Modern scholars have given this story scant attention. Yet it cannot be equaled as a

---

[9] Heyd, *Commerce,* 1:234, says that restitution of the money was, in fact, made, but the documentation nowhere suggests that; he may have misunderstood the text in Bertolotto, *Nuova serie,* p. 457. Brand, "The Byzantines and Saladin," 178, follows Heyd.

[10] Cf. below, 177.

[11] Müller, *Documenti,* no. XLI.

[12] Heyd, *Commerce,* 1:233. Heyd presents this as a hypothesis, suggesting that Isaac's alliance with Saladin and the presence of Egyptian ambassadors aboard this ship made it doubly interesting to the Genoese pirates.

[13] Brand, "The Byzantines and Saladin," 178: "Saladin was disillusioned with Isaac's military capabilities, while Isaac finally realized that Saladin was too distant to protect him from the Latins."

snapshot of conditions in the eastern Mediterranean in the late twelfth century, for it illustrates a number of important developments. For one thing, it makes evident the close connections between the Crusades and the increasingly strong presence of Italian merchants in the eastern Mediterranean. It brings to the fore the Byzantine bankers and merchants, here engaged in international money transactions. It allows us more than a glance into the developing law of the sea regarding issues of paramount importance to merchants, here the question of reparations and reprisals. And it hints at the nature of political and commercial connections between the Byzantine Empire and the Muslims during the time of the Crusades. These topics will be discussed in what follows.

For the Byzantine Empire, the question of the economic influence—if any—of the Crusades is almost inextricably connected with the question of the influence of the Italian merchants on the Byzantine economy, which both predates the crusading movement and becomes closely tied to it, certainly by the time of the Fourth Crusade. Indeed, the presence of Italian merchants on Byzantine soil eventually became dominant, reducing the degrees of freedom of the native merchants, although possibly increasing their opportunities. This is a topic of significance, touching primarily the economy of exchange, and it has been treated by a number of scholars.[14] I will not offer a reconsideration of the question; I simply note the double presence of Italian merchants and Crusaders in many geographic areas, constant but in small numbers in the case of the first; somewhat more sporadic but sometimes in huge numbers in the case of the Crusaders.

The "Crusades" were a frequent phenomenon of the twelfth and thirteenth centuries. We are accustomed to taking account of the major crusades, the ones with numbers, but crusading expeditions of one kind or another took place often, and certainly the Christians and Muslims of the area were aware of the fact. The First Crusade, insofar as the Byzantine Empire was concerned, did not end in 1099. It extended from 1096 until 1108 and the Treaty of Devol, which marked the end of Bohemond's quasi-crusade. And the 1120s were punctuated by crusading expeditions undertaken by Pisans and Genoese by sea, while in 1122 a Venetian Crusader fleet on its way to Palestine attacked Corfu in retaliation for the attempt of John II Komnenos to reduce Venice's commercial privileges; it pillaged Byzantine lands on the way to and from Palestine and extracted the confirmation and expansion of Venetian commercial privileges in the Byzantine Empire.[15] Thus large armies and small and large fleets often traversed Byzantine lands and waters, presenting the Byzantines with the new problem of dealing, in economic ways too, with theoretical friends in large numbers.

The other general point that should be remembered is the existence of Crusader states

---

[14] See, most recently, D. Jacoby, "Italian Privileges and Trade in Byzantium before the Fourth Crusade: A Reconsideration," *Anuario de estudios medievales* 24 (1994): 349–68; A. Laiou, "Byzantium and the Commercial Revolution," in G. Arnaldi and G. Cavallo, eds., *Europa medievale e mondo bizantino: Contatti effetivi e possibilità di studi comparati*, Istituto Storico Italiano per il Medio Evo, Nuovi Studi Storici 40 (Rome, 1997), 239–53; M. F. Hendy, "Byzantium, 1081–1204: 'The Economy Revisited,' Twenty Years On," in idem, *The Economy, Fiscal Administration, and Coinage of Byzantium* (Northampton, 1989), no. III.

[15] J. Riley-Smith, "The Venetian Crusade of 1122–1124," in G. Airaldi and B. Kedar, eds., *I comuni italiani nel regno crociato di Gerusalemme*, Jerusalem, 24–28 May 1984, Collana Storica di Fonti e Studi 48 (Genoa, 1986), 337–50.

after 1099, which meant that there were three sets of Christians in the eastern Mediterranean: Byzantines, Crusader states, and Italian merchants (not to mention the native Christians of the East, who will not enter this discussion); the interconnections between them will be seen to have been of importance.

That having been said, I should like to pose a few questions that are somewhat different from the questions scholars have been asking. The focus, to the extent possible, and bearing in mind the sometimes inextricable interconnections between Crusaders and merchants, will be on the effects of the Crusades themselves, and of the Crusader states, on Byzantine commercial relations. What new and specific problems and challenges did the Crusaders and the existence of the Crusader states pose to the Byzantine Empire? Did they influence the mechanisms and methods of trade? Did they help bring about any structural changes? Or were they irrelevant, and do the only questions continue to be those associated with the Italian presence and eventual dominance over the commerce of these areas?

I will concentrate here not on the overall canvas (the bird's-eye view), but rather on the worm's-eye view to start with, and then on the point of view of the flying-fish— the middle distance, the structural and institutional developments that took place in Byzantine trade with Christians and Muslims especially during the twelfth century, but also in the later period—connected with conditions in which the Crusades played a role. I will take for granted the *very* large changes after 1204, insofar as Byzantine trade with Western Christians is concerned.

I. The Byzantine Economy and the Crusades

This is a time when armies and navies passed through the territories of a still relatively intact and prosperous Byzantine Empire. The discussion of the First Crusade will include the expedition of 1100–1101 and end in 1108.[16] There were two major relevant problems: that of provisioning the armies as they crossed Byzantine lands and the related problem of currency exchange.

A. Provisioning

Major challenges were posed by the large size of the crusading armies. According to the most recent estimates, the Peasant Crusade had around 20,000 participants; the main armies at Nicaea counted approximately 50,000 to 60,000 members including noncombatants. Many had already died on the way to Constantinople. The Crusade of 1101, for which there are huge contemporary estimates, must have been larger.[17] No figures are

---

[16] J. France, *Victory in the East: A Military History of the First Crusade* (Cambridge–New York, 1994), 142, and J. Flori, "Un problème de méthodologie: La valeur des nombres chez les chroniqueurs du Moyen Age: A propos des effectifs de la première Croisade," *Moyen Age* 99 (1995): 399–422. J. Heers, *Libérer Jérusalem: La première Croisade (1095–1107)* (Paris, 1995), does not give estimates. On the Crusade of 1100–1101, see J. L. Cate, "The Crusade of 1101," in K. M. Setton, ed., *History of the Crusades*, vol. 1, *The First Hundred Years*, ed. M. W. Baldwin (Madison, Wisc., 1969), 343–67.

[17] Cate, "The Crusade of 1101," 351.

given for the French and German armies of the Second Crusade, but combined they must have been as large as those of the First Crusade. For the army of Frederick I Barbarossa, we have the figure of 100,000, which includes 20,000 mounted troops.[18] In terms of the problems of provisioning, we might compare these figures with the most recent and persuasive estimates of the size of the Komnenian army on campaign, which is approximately 15,000 to 20,000 men, thus much smaller than the Crusaders' armies.[19] One must also take into account the length of time the Crusaders spent on Byzantine soil; thinking only of the Balkans, I have estimated an average of two to two and a half months for most of the armies of the First Crusade, except for those of Raymond of Toulouse and Bohemond, which took five and a half to six months. The passage of most of the armies, including the Peasant Crusade, was swift: the comparison to locusts, found in both Anna Komnene and Orderic Vitalis,[20] seems apposite. The armies of the Second Crusade took two and a half to three months. But that of Frederick Barbarossa spent almost nine months on Byzantine soil, mostly in southern Bulgaria and Thrace, heavily taxing the resources of the area. As these numbers suggest, the problems of provisioning were ubiquitous; as for questions of exchange, those arose on the ground, and, during the Second and Third Crusades, formed a part of the negotiations for safe passage.

As is well known, the First Crusade was too amorphous and disorganized for formal arrangements to have been made beforehand to assure provisioning, although by 1101 agreements were indeed concluded as the Lombard army was about to enter Bulgaria.[21] Provisions do not seem to have been brought as far as the Byzantine Empire, although one of the chroniclers mentions that the Crusaders carried some provisions with them;[22] these undoubtedly were exhausted before the Crusaders left Western Europe. The Crusaders also brought money and marks of silver with them, presumably to be used to buy provisions.[23]

The problem of provisioning was recurrent during the passage of the armies of the First Crusade and of the subsequent two. The army of Raymond of St. Gilles, passing through Dalmatia, could get neither safe-conduct nor *commercium* until it reached Skoutari, where, in January 1097, Raymond made a pact with the local ruler (Vodin), giving him much money so that the army would be allowed to buy provisions, although Vodin's promises seem to have remained a dead letter.[24] The Crusaders were certainly expected, by the Byzantine authorities, to buy their food: Alexios I, as soon as he heard of the Crusade, had sent generals to Durazzo and Avlona to ensure that there would be *panegyreis* (the Latin term is usually *mercatum* or *necessarium negotium*)[25] in all the lands along the

---

[18] France, *Victory in the East*, 136.

[19] J.-C. Cheynet, "Les effectifs de l'armée byzantine aux Xe–XIe siècle," *CahCM* 38 (1995): 319–35, at 331–32.

[20] *Alexiade* 10.5.7, ed. B. Leib (with P. Gautier), 4 vols. (Paris, 1939–76), 2:208; Orderic Vitalis, *The Ecclesiastical History*, ed. and trans. M. Chibnall, 6 vols. (Oxford, 1969–80), 5.30.

[21] Albert of Aix, *Historia Hierosolymitana*, RHC, HOcc 4 (Paris, 1879), 559; Orderic Vitalis, 5:327.

[22] *Roberti Monachi Historia Iherosolimitana*, RHC, HOcc 3 (Paris, 1866), 744, on Bohemond.

[23] See below, 168–69.

[24] J. Hugh and L. Hill, eds., *Le "Liber" de Raymond d'Aguilers* (Paris, 1969), 37–38; Guillaume de Tyr, *Chronique*, ed. R. Huygens, CC continuatio mediaevalis 63–63A (Turnhout, 1986), 2.17 (1:182 ff).

[25] E.g., Orderic Vitalis, 5:31, 33, 43, 49, 69.

way.[26] Some Crusaders, especially the excitable Tancred,[27] thought it too bad that they should have to buy food—and they took different courses of action.[28] The emperor, perhaps in response, seems to have made the availability of provisions contingent on the Crusaders' oath of fealty or friendship, as also happened during the Second and Third Crusades.[29] The Byzantine authorities seem to have been confident that they *could* provide adequate markets, so much so that Niketas Choniates thought that Manuel Komnenos' failure to supply adequate markets to the participants of the Second Crusade was deliberate.

Byzantine armies on campaign normally brought some of their provisions with them, or bought them along the way, as long as they were on friendly territory.[30] But the Crusader armies, especially those of the Second and Third Crusades, which crossed into the Balkans all together, were much larger than a Byzantine army on campaign. In fact, the passage of the crusading armies taxed the productive resources of the area and most particularly the mechanisms of distribution. It is surprising that the system did not significantly break down before the time of Frederick Barbarossa.

The provisioning of the armies of the First Crusade (including that of 1101) on Byzantine territory was carried out in three ways. First, the Crusaders bought food, and a recurrent complaint is that there was no food to be bought or, as in Kastoria, that the inhabitants did not wish to sell, being suspicious of the Crusaders' motives.[31] In the Balkans, in Asia Minor, and also in the Holy Land, much of the provisioning of the crusading army depended on the *purchase* of food (and fodder for the horses), as William of Tyre makes most clearly evident. Indeed, the fact that various crusading chronicles quote prices, mostly at times of famine, proves that food was bought.[32] The second way they found food was from imperial donations—either at times of joint victory or at times of considerable hardship. Alexios I perhaps fed some of the army of Peter the Hermit in Constantinople and promised Hugh of Vermandois not only an adequate market (*copiosum mercatum*) but also alms for the poor.[33] Before the capture of Nicaea,

---

[26] *Alexiade* 10.5.9 (ed. Leib, 2:209). According to Anna, when Alexios heard of the crusade, he told his officials to πανηγύρεις τε δαψιλεῖς ἐξ ἁπασῶν τῶν χωρῶν κατὰ τὴν ὁδὸν ἐξάγειν. Later, Alexios heard about the arrival of more Crusaders, and again he sent word to τὰ ζωαρκῆ τούτοις ἐρχομένοις ἐπιχορηγεῖν ἐπ' αὐτῷ τούτῳ τεταγμένοις, ὡς μὴ λαβεῖν αὐτοὺς τὸ παράπαν ἐσχηκέναι. *Alexiade* 10.10.3 (ed. Leib, 2:228). Orderic Vitalis says that during the passage of the crusaders of Walter Sans-Avoir, the *doux* and the officials of Philippopolis allowed them to enter the city "et mercatum concesserunt," which they had not done before: *Ecclesiastical History*, 5.31 (this information is found nowhere else, according to the editor's note).

[27] R. Hill, ed., *Gesta Francorum et aliorum Hierosolimitanorum* (London, 1962), 10.

[28] See below, 164.

[29] E.g., Robert the Monk, 744, 748, 749. Also William of Tyre, 2.6, 2.12, 2.14 (1:168–69, 175–77, 178–79).

[30] R. Vári, *Leonis imperatoris Tactica,* 2 vols. (Budapest, 1917–22), 1:225.

[31] Robert the Monk, 745: Bohemond tries to get "forum rerum venalium"; cf. Hill, *Gesta Francorum* 8: "quesivimus mercatum." Cf. Orderic Vitalis, 5.45, 49.

[32] Among the prices, see *Alexiade* 11.4.3 (ed. Leib, 3:20): in Antioch, ἡ κεφαλὴ τοῦ βοὸς ἐπὶ τρισὶ χρυσίνοις στατῆρσι ἀπεμπολεῖτο. On the fact that food was normally purchased as opposed to donated or acquired by raids, see William of Tyre, 1:142, 143, 148, 164–65, 173, 176, 178, 184.

[33] "[I]mperator iusserat dari mercatum, sicuti erat in civitate": Hill, *Gesta Francorum* 2; but he uses *mercatum* also to mean a market; cf. Robert the Monk, 732: "mercatum eis habere concedebat, quod etiam in civitate erat." Orderic Vitalis, 5.43; cf. p. 327 on *ingentia dona* to the leaders of the Crusade of 1101 and p. 335 on ship-

Alexios allowed a ship to bring provisions for purchase; but after the fall of that city, he gave to the poor of the army alms, which Stephen of Blois defines as distributions of food.[34] The third way in which the Crusaders found food was plunder. Relatively limited during the First Crusade, at least on Byzantine territory, despite the depredations of Tancred and Bohemond and those of the Lombard participants in the Crusade of 1101,[35] it became a way of life when the Crusaders entered Turkish territory. Spoils of war, not quite plunder, were also available, as also were large donations by the rulers of various Muslim towns once the Crusaders had entered Syria and Palestine.

As for the Second and Third Crusades, the matter of provisioning was paramount in the eyes of the Crusader leaders, and in the eyes of the Byzantine emperors it had become, along with safe conduct, the most powerful negotiating tool. In his letter to the pope regarding the crusade of Louis VII, Manuel I Komnenos promised safe passage and markets (and suitable exchange: "forum idoneum, concambium competens"), in exchange for an oath of security for his realm.[36] He then sent orders everywhere to have provisions brought to the roads through which the Crusaders would pass.[37] The German army too was promised "hospitality" (ὑποδοχῆς τε ἀπολαύοντας εἰς τὸ εἰκὸς καὶ φιλοφροσύνης τῆς ἄλλης) in exchange for an oath of friendship.[38] The governor of Nish, Michael Branas, was ordered to provide "necessities" (προὐνοεῖτο ἤδη τῶν ἀναγ-καίων αὐτοῖς, οὕτω προστεταγμένον αὐτῷ),[39] and similarly in Sofia. In Sofia, at least, it is certain that its governor made sure that Louis VII had the right to buy provisions.[40] Manuel forced the French to reconfirm their oaths in exchange for market privileges several times: most importantly in Constantinople, where he exacted the oath of homage in return for a promise of guides, fair exchange, and markets everywhere,[41] and, later, in Attaleia.[42] When arrangements broke down, either by design on the part of the Byzantines or by chance, or because there was not enough food to feed the Crusaders (as in Attaleia), the Crusaders plundered.[43]

The arrangements with Frederick Barbarossa, as reported by Niketas Choniates, Ansbert and other sources, were almost a point-by-point copy of those made earlier with Conrad and Louis VII—which means that the imperial bureaucracy had learned more

---

loads of tetartera given by Alexios to the Crusaders in 1101 to persuade them to cross into Asia Minor. Ekkehard of Aura (*Hierosolymita*, ed. H. Hagenmeyer [Tübingen, 1877], 233–34), also says that in 1100 (1101?) Alexios promised to provide markets and give alms to the poor.

[34] Robert the Monk, 778; First letter of Stephen of Blois to his wife, RHC, HOcc 3:886. According to Stephen, Alexios distributed food to the poor even before the fall of Nicaea, daily. After the capture of the city, "omnia vero victualia peditibus distribuantur."

[35] Albert of Aix, 559–60. Cf. the attack on Adrianople in 1101: Ekkehard of Aura, 234–35.

[36] Νέος Ἑλλ. 11 (1914): 111–12; Odo of Deuil, *De profectione Ludovici VII in orientem*, ed. V. G. Berry (New York, 1948; repr. 1965), 29.

[37] Choniates, ed. van Dieten, 61 ff.

[38] *Ioannis Cinnami Epitome rerum ab Ioanne et Alexio Comnenis gestarum*, ed. A. Meineke (Bonn, 1836), 2.2, p. 68.

[39] Kinnamos (Bonn ed.), 2.13; p. 70.

[40] Odo of Deuil, 45.

[41] Odo of Deuil, 77–83.

[42] Odo of Deuil, 129.

[43] Odo of Deuil, 41, 97; Kinnamos (Bonn ed.), 2.15 ff, pp. 75 ff.

or less what to do, unless it simply means that Choniates is repeating himself. The second eventuality, however, is unlikely, since he had firsthand knowledge of the later arrangements, and the statements of Odo of Deuil (and Ansbert) and Choniates corroborate each other at several points.[44] Once again the quid pro quo was safety for imperial lands in return for markets, although, as is well known, the problem deteriorated into a conflict over imperial titles. Once again the emperor appealed to the provincial governors to "transfer goods from the various regions to where the king would pass."[45] In the case of the Third Crusade, promises of safe-conduct and *optimi fori* were made in Nuremberg in November 1186, and repeated in Nish and Branitsevo. The question of *iustum concambium* arose in October 1189.[46] But arrangements broke down very soon indeed, and the German army—100,000 of them—found its food by plunder, which must have been very painful for the population. Permission to plunder was solemnized by the Treaty of Adrianople in February 1190. According to Choniates, at the time of the Third Crusade, the Turks of Konya also promised safe-passage and provisions, but broke their promises.[47]

How was this food marketed, and who sold it? In all cases, the emperors gave the original orders, which mandated two courses of action: that markets should be provided to the armies and that provisions should be collected by the governors of the regions.[48] William of Tyre, perhaps not entirely trustworthy on this point, adds that Alexios' edict regarding the army of Bohemond envisaged the death penalty for anyone who disregarded his orders to "iusto precio et equo pondere ducis exercitui quelibet mercimonia venderentur." His narrative often reiterates that Alexios not only gave the Crusaders the right to buy and sell, but also ordered that the sale be carried out with correct weights and measures and at a just price.[49] During the Crusade of 1100–1101, permission was given the Crusaders to buy and sell ("emendi et vendendi") in Rosa (the Rusa of the First Crusade: Xanthe or Komotini), Panidos, Rodosto, Didymoteichon, "castello . . . de Natura," Selymbria, Adrianople, Philippopolis;[50] some of these towns, like Panidos and Rodosto, were major grain markets.

What content we should give to these statements is another story. In some cases, for example, Alexios' gratis provisioning of the poor at Nicaea, it is probable that imperial stores were implicated. When it is a matter of markets, *panegyreis, mercatum, fora*, we have to imagine one-time markets, for the most part situated in towns along the way, which

---

[44] See, for example, the story about the inhabitants of cities carrying out their transactions with the Crusaders by means of ropes thrown down from the walls: Odo of Deuil, 40; Choniates, ed. van Dieten, 66. A further and amazing corroboration: According to both Odo of Deuil (76, 82) and Ansbert (*Historia de expeditione Friderici*, ed. A. Chroust, MGH, *ScriptRerGerm*, n.s., 5 [Berlin, 1928], 65), Manuel and Isaac II respectively agreed that if the army was not able to buy provisions, it had the right to plunder, though not to occupy the territory in question—or, in the case of Frederick I, not to give it to the Turks. This underlines the problems posed by provisioning at politically difficult times: Roger of Sicily was attacking Greece at the time of the Second Crusade.

[45] Choniates, ed. van Dieten, 402.

[46] Ansbert, 15–16, 29, 33, 48.

[47] Ansbert, 25, 26, 37, 39, 44, 59, 66, 71, 73. On the Turks, see Choniates, ed. van Dieten, 412; Ansbert, 69.

[48] Cf. Choniates, ed. van Dieten, 402–3, for the Third Crusade.

[49] William of Tyre, 2.12 (1:176); cf. 1.18.54 (1:142), 1.19.12 (1:143); 2.14.15 (1:179).

[50] Albert of Aix, 559.

in any case would have known the institution of the periodic market or fair. The imperial orders would have been to agree to sell to the Crusaders, a somewhat frightening proposition considering the vast numbers of people going through. Imperial officials would do their best to persuade the inhabitants to sell commodities: this was the role given to the *pansebastos* Eustathios Philokales, who was to accompany the army of Frederick I as far as Philadelphia, for exactly that purpose.[51] What the Crusaders "sold" would have been jewels, silver plate, their arms and horses in times of dire need, and money.[52]

There was, undoubtedly, a combination of factors that created a market. Despite the fact that the emperor issued orders regarding provisioning, generally speaking the markets were not, I think, state controlled, but were, rather, composed of producers (both landlords and peasants) and merchants.[53] In other words, as far as we can see, food was not requisitioned by the Byzantine state, nor were imperial or military stores opened. Occasional references allow us a glimpse at the various groups of people who sold food to the Crusaders. Fulcher of Chartres mentions "citizens" of Constantinople, who, by order of the emperor, brought food to sell outside the walls of the city.[54] These were, presumably, merchants. In Attaleia, during the Second Crusade, the food supply depended entirely on maritime trade, for the surrounding territory was in Turkish hands. The grain must have been brought in by merchants.[55]

Direct sale by producers may be deduced from other texts. William of Tyre ascribes the absence of markets at Nish, during the First Crusade, partly to the actions of the Byzantine governor and partly to the fact that the peasants had fled.[56] As the army crossed Macedonia, its escort told the "inhabitants of the land" to bring provisions, the Crusaders not being allowed to enter the cities.[57] These "inhabitants" could be either merchants or direct producers. When Bohemond reached Nicaea, he ordered "maximum mercatum conduci per mare, et pariter utrinque veniebant, ille per terram et ille per mare, et fuit maxima ubertas in tota Christi militia."[58] Since 50,000 to 60,000 people had to be fed, the sellers can hardly have been peasants: they must have been either merchants or landlords.

Food seems to have been concentrated mostly in cities and towns; the process would have been something like the one that brought to Halmyros, along a west-east axis, Greeks with grain to sell, as reported by Edrisi, writing at approximately the time of the Second Crusade.[59]

Prices seem to have been formed on the ground, although the Crusaders clearly expected state control of both prices and weights and measures. An indication of this, at a

---

[51] Ansbert, 65.

[52] Cf. below, 167–68, and Odo of Deuil, 75.

[53] See Kinnamos (Bonn ed.), 2.13, pp. 70–71: the Germans apply unjust force "on those offering them food for sale in the market," in the plains that come after Dacia, i.e., in Bulgaria: τοῖς τε κατ᾽ ἐμπορίαν τὰ ὤνια σφίσιν ἀποδιδοῦσι χεῖρα ἐπέβαλον ἄδικον.

[54] Fulcher of Chartres, *Historia Hierosolymitana (1095–1127)*, ed. H. Hagenmayer (Heidelberg, 1913), 331.

[55] Odo of Deuil, 129; William of Tyre, 16.26 (2:753).

[56] William of Tyre, 1.19.26–36 (1:143) (army of Walter Sans-Avoir).

[57] *Gesta Francorum* 10.

[58] *Gesta Francorum* 14.

[59] P. A. Jaubert, *La géographie d'Edrisi*, 2 vols. (Paris, 1840), 2:291, 196.

later period to be sure, is offered by the reports of the final accord between Isaac II and Frederick I (the Treaty of Adrianople, February 1190)—namely, that the emperor was obliged to ensure that there would be "good" (i.e., fair) markets (*bona mercata*), selling at a just price (*iusto pretio*), which here seems to be understood as the price that the emperor would have had to pay if he were buying the food.[60] An anonymous letter says that the sale should be at half the price the Crusaders were paying until then.[61] So one job of the imperial officials would have been to guarantee fair prices and stop speculative sales at famine prices. Such, at least, seems to have been the case in 1190, and William of Tyre's narrative suggests that it was also the case during the First Crusade; but this historian's insistence on "just prices" may well be anachronistic. Indeed, the great fluctuation in food prices because of scarcity, or because the armies were so large, suggests that fair prices, even if promised, were not delivered.[62] Choniates wrote scathingly about the inhabitants of cities who did not provide adequate markets and seized the opportunity to sell at extravagant prices. They closed their gates, he says, and threw down ropes, to collect the money of the Crusaders and then send down whatever victuals they saw fit—while the worst of them simply took the money and gave nothing in return. They used unjust weights and measures and even tampered with the quality of the food.[63] Finally, during the Third Crusade also, the inhabitants of some cities, such as Philippopolis, refused to sell to the Crusaders.[64] All this shows the limits of imperial control of the situation.

There was an interplay, then, of free-market forces and imperial orders; this was free exchange in which the state was expected to intervene and did intervene to a limited extent. There was some pressure toward increased state control, but it was not very successful.

Freedom for foreigners to buy and sell within the frontiers of the empire was a specific privilege. It was originally granted to the Venetians and was then extended to Crusaders; there are, therefore, formal connections between commercial institutions and the provisioning of the crusading armies. Also, the distribution mechanisms must have been influenced by the problems of provisioning. However, the acute and episodic nature of arrangements for the provisioning of the armies in all probability did not have long-lasting effects on the Byzantine economy. Rather, these arrangements are inscribed in the larger framework of developing commercial mechanisms.

It may be otherwise with questions regarding currency exchange. It must first be stressed that provisioning and currency exchange were closely connected. Even when

---

[60] The reference is undoubtedly to the ἐξώνησις, the obligatory sale to the state of various products, at fixed prices, on which see N. Oikonomidès, *Fiscalité et exemption fiscale à Byzance (IXe–XIe siècle)* (Athens, 1996), 97–99.

[61] Ansbert, 65–66; K. Hampe, "Ein ungedruckter Bericht über den Vertrag von Adrianopel zwischen Friedrich I. und Isaak Angelos vom Febr. 1190," *Neues Archiv der Gesellschaft für deutsche Geschichtskunde* 23 (1898): 400. The editor of the letter thinks that this was impossible and simply the stuff of rumor.

[62] Cf. Robert the Monk, 749: the price of bread falls. See also Odo of Deuil, 135, who complains of extremely high prices exacted by the Greeks in Attaleia. Cf. idem, p. 97, on the high price of food outside Nicaea, where the sellers demanded cuirasses and swords in payment.

[63] Choniates, ed. van Dieten, 66–67; Odo of Deuil, 41.

[64] Choniates, ed. van Dieten, 403.

sources such as William of Tyre refer to the buying and "selling" by the members of the First Crusade, they may actually be referring to the "sale" of coins, that is, to exchange transactions. It should also be noted that Crusader sources normally quote prices in Western coins, which again raises the problem of currency transactions.

B. Currency Exchange

During the First Crusade, through 1101, not a word is spoken about the problem of currency exchange. The Crusaders brought with them a multiplicity of coins (Raymond of Aguilers mentions seven types, but we know there were many more)—all billon deniers of different intrinsic values (some quite good silver)—and marks of silver. The idea floated by M. Matzke, that perhaps they took a limited and deliberately chosen type of coin does not seem plausible.[65] Some of the great barons, like Godfrey of Bouillon, brought with them considerable quantities of marks of silver. How did the Crusaders fend for themselves, once they had reached the frontiers of the Byzantine Empire?

While the sources of the First Crusade remain mute on the problem of currency exchange, it must have been posed brutally by reality. The problem of "markets" and high prices, omnipresent in the sources, undoubtedly but tacitly includes that of exchange—not only a fair exchange, but, to start with, exchange itself. Who, in the towns along the way, would have been willing to change the Western deniers against Byzantine coins, and at what equivalence? If there was no exchange, how many people would have been willing to accept this unlikely money in payment and, again, at what value? Ingots of silver may have been easier for the locals to accept. While marks of silver were too valuable for small-scale transactions, smaller ingots (not attested in our sources, but possible) may have been used. In this case, one must assume that the Byzantine money changer or merchant would have had the opportunity to give an exchange rate lower than the intrinsic value of the ingot.

The exiguous number of coins datable to the First Crusade that has been found in the Balkans,[66] Asia Minor, and Syria-Palestine could be interpreted in a number of ways: as evidence that the Crusaders did not so much purchase their food as live off the land, which contradicts the rest of the evidence, at least for the Balkans or, more plausibly, as

---

[65] M. Matzke, "Die sieben Kreuzfahrermünzen und das Papsttum," *SM* 44 (1994): 13–19, mentioned in D. M. Metcalf, *Coinage of the Crusades and the Latin East in the Ashmolean Museum, Oxford,* 2d ed. (London, 1995), 13–14. As Metcalf says, this proposition depends on the accuracy and completeness of Raymond of Aguilers' list of coins, which is doubtful. Godfrey of Bouillon got from the bishop of Liège 1,300 or 1,500 marks of silver: *History of the Crusades,* 1.267. At Antioch, Tancred asked for and was promised 400 marks of silver for guarding a castle: *Gesta Francorum* 43. The list of coins appears in Raymond of Aguilers, ed. Hill, 111–12.

[66] The only significant find in terms of numbers is a hoard of 83 coins in Constantinople possibly associated with the First Crusade: Metcalf, *Coinage of the Crusades,* 6. A. M. Stahl ("The Circulation of European Coinage in the Crusader States," in V. Goss, ed., *The Meeting of Two Worlds: Cultural Exchange between East and West during the Period of the Crusades,* Studies in Medieval Culture 21 [Kalamazoo, Mich., 1986], 85–102, at 86) mentions the hoard of 1,600 coins found in 1884 in Zombor, Croatia, as belonging to the First Crusade, but the hoard has been dated to the Second Crusade. Another 3,000 coins found in Hungary may be datable to the Second Crusade. A very large hoard of 7,700 coins and ingots (with, unfortunately, an unknown find-spot) has been associated with a member of Frederick Barbarossa's army during the Third Crusade: see Metcalf, *Coinage of the Crusades,* 7–10.

an indication that the Crusaders' coins were routinely and quickly melted down by the Byzantines, perhaps to be reminted; if so, there must have been some sort of government service that bought the coins from the citizens.[67] Similarly, the fact that coins were minted very soon after the conquest of Syria and Palestine suggests that Western coins were not originally well received in the East.[68] After 1140, the Crusader states began to mint silver pennies. Before and after, there was a heavy flow of silver to the East.[69]

Once the members of the First Crusade reached Constantinople, their money supply began to become replenished through imperial gifts of cash, and the problem of exchange was eased to some extent, though only partially. Large gifts of gold and silver on the part of Alexios to the Crusader leaders put Byzantine money into circulation: Fulcher of Chartres reports that after the Crusader leaders had taken the oath of fealty, Alexios gave them "de numismatibus suis," clearly coined gold and perhaps silver.[70] Anna Komnene speaks of huge gifts to Bohemond, including gold and silver coins.[71] There were also gifts of smaller coins. After the fall of Nicaea, the emperor distributed to the leaders gold, silver ("de auro suo et argento"),[72] as well as other precious things, both from the spoils and from his treasury. The rank and file—the foot soldiers—received distributions "de sumis suis aeneis quos vocant tartarones."[73] The tetarteron in question here is Alexios' tetarteron, made first of lead, then of billon, then of copper.[74] Small-scale transactions, at a time when markets were pretty well established outside Nicaea, were made possible with these coins. In 1101 Alexios distributed boatloads of tetartera, according to Orderic Vitalis.[75]

When the Crusaders began to be victorious over the Muslims, gold came their way; some undoubtedly was minted gold, as we know for the case when the governors of the towns of Syria and Palestine offered the Crusaders tribute—or gifts with which they bought immunity—not to mention the ghoulish recovery of bezants from the inside of the corpses of slain Turks.[76] It is telling that the leaders, when they were in Syria and Palestine, still had substantial sums of money, in marks of silver, even after the long trip.[77]

Only two rates of exchange are mentioned in the sources of the First Crusade, and

---

[67] Metcalf, *Coinage of the Crusades*, 3–11, gives a list of the coins that belong to the first three crusades.

[68] The princes of Antioch and the counts of Edessa seem to have struck almost immediately copper coins imitating the Byzantine follis of the late 11th century. See Metcalf, *Coinage of the Crusades*, 22–23, 31 ff.

[69] Stahl estimates a total of ca. 1 million kg of silver = 1,000 tons throughout the crusading period: "Circulation of European Coinage," 97.

[70] According to William of Tyre, after his accord with Godfrey of Bouillon, Alexios sent him every week, between Epiphany and Ascension, as many gold coins ("auree monete") as two strong men could carry, and 10 *modioi* of copper coins ("de ereis vero denariis X modii"), to be distributed among his nobles and the plain soldiers: William of Tyre, 2.12 (1:176 ff).

[71] *Alexiade* 10.11.5 (ed. Leib, 2:233).

[72] Fulcher of Chartres, 333–34. Is the "silver" coin the electrum trachy?

[73] Fulcher of Chartres, 333–34; Stephen of Blois boasted to his wife that he doubled his worth in gold and silver: RHC, HOcc 3:886.

[74] M. F. Hendy, *Studies in the Byzantine Monetary Economy c. 300–1450* (Cambridge, 1985), 515.

[75] Orderic Vitalis, 5.334, says that the tetartera were as current as bezants in transactions in Thrace and Bithynia.

[76] E.g., Raymond d'Aguilers, ed. Hill, 111: 15,000 aureos from the governor of Tripoli; *Gesta Francorum* 80.

[77] See, e.g., *Gesta Francorum* 97; Raymond d'Aguilers, ed. Hill, 111–12.

they are not for small coins, but rather for gold hyperpyra or dinars exchanged for silver (billon) deniers. One is the rate of 8 hyperpyra for 120 soldi (1 soldo, a unit of account = 12 deniers), outside Antioch, at a time of famine: "vendebant [the Syrians and Armenians] onus unius asini octo purpuratis, qui appreciabantur centum viginti solidis denariorum," that is, 1 hyperpyron for 15 soldi, or 1 hyperpyron for 180 deniers.[78] This is high in terms of the approximate intrinsic value of the coins in question.[79] It represents a rate of exchange for poor Western coins in times of famine. The other rate of exchange is not with the hyperpyron but rather with the gold coin of Tripoli: "Valebat quippe unus aureus eo tempore octo vel novem solidos monetae nostri exercitus," says Raymond of Aguilers, and continues with the famous list of seven coins that he considered to be the army's money (or at least the money of the army of Raymond of St. Gilles).[80] Of these coins, the denier of Le Puy is said by Raymond of Aguilers to have been worth only half the value of the others.[81] One wonders whether the difference in fineness was as obvious to the locals as it was to Raymond of Aguilers and is to modern numismatists. In any case, if the gold coin in question was the normal dinar, the Crusaders got approximately double what they had received outside Antioch. The rate of exchange with the dinar seems normal, and therefore the Byzantine one was very detrimental to the Crusaders. Gold and silver were apparently exchanged on the basis of intrinsic value. Outside Antioch, the exchange was between hyperpyra and billon deniers, and was heavily influenced by the Crusaders' need.

More interesting phenomena start with the Second Crusade. The Second and Third Crusades were different from the First in the matter of exchange as in other matters. All the kings who planned to go through the Byzantine Empire asked not only for markets but for fair exchange; and undoubtedly Manuel I was as interested as they were in some kind of regularization of the currency exchange, without which the problem of provisioning was bound to become exacerbated. Also, the participants of these better-organized expeditions seem to have carried considerable amounts of money with them.

It is also with the Second Crusade that Western sources begin to show an evident concern with problems of currency exchange, and there are strident complaints from the pen of Odo of Deuil.[82] The complaints, and the situation to which they refer, repay close examination.

The members of the French army had brought both silver deniers (presumably the denier Parisis, which I will take as the basis for calculations) and marks of silver (it is not clear which mark is meant). The money, as far as we can tell from the complaints, was not accepted as means of payment in the local markets. The insistence of Louis VII on *concambium competens* also suggests that coins were exchanged, as does Choniates' state-

---

[78] *Gesta Francorum* 33. I am very grateful to Philip Grierson and Cécile Morrisson for their valuable help with this section. According to Michael Hendy, the "purpuratus" is the nomisma trachy, 20.5 carats fine, introduced by Alexios I: Hendy, *Coinage and Money*, 34–35. Throughout this section, the reader should consult the table and Cécile Morrisson's appendix.

[79] See the appendix below.

[80] Raymond of Aguilers, ed. Hill, 111–12.

[81] Metcalf, *Coinage of the Crusades*, 13.

[82] Odo of Deuil, 40, 66.

TABLE 1
EXCHANGE RATES

Early 1098
    1 hyperpyron = 15 soldi = 180 deniers[1]

Second Crusade
  In the Balkans
    1 stamenon = 5 deniers[2]
    [1 hyperpyron = 240 deniers]

    144 stamena = 1 mark of silver[3]
    [3 hyperpyra = 1 mark of silver][4]
    [Official value of the billon trachy in 1136: 1/48 hyperpyron][4]

  In Constantinople
    1 stamenon = less than 2 deniers
    396 stamena = 1 mark of silver[5]

Third Crusade (Treaty of Adrianople, 1190)
    5.5 hyperpyra = 1 mark of (pure?) silver[6]
    3 hyperpyra = 1 mark of (impure?) silver[7]
    120 stamena = 1 hyperpyron[8]

---

[1] *Gesta Francorum* 33.

[2] Odo de Deuil, 41.

[3] Ibid.

[4] For the official value, see Dmitrievskii, *Opisanie,* 689 (as in note 86). The equivalences 1 hyperpyron = 240 deniers and 3 hyperpyra = 1 mark of silver are not mentioned in the sources for 1147–1148. They are theoretical and derive from the official value of the billon trachy.

[5] Odo de Deuil, 89–90.

[6] Ansbert, 66.

[7] Hampe, "Ungedruckter Bericht," 400.

[8] Ansbert, 66.

ment—unless it is rhetorical—that people cheated the participants of the Second Crusade of their gold and silver.[83] On what basis did the exchange take place?

We note, first, that Odo of Deuil quotes the exchange rates as between the denier and the mark of silver and the "stamenon," that is, the petty Byzantine coin, not the gold hyperpyron. The stamenon, a corruption of the rare Byzantine term *histamenon,* is the billon trachy ("aspron trachy"), a billon coin, mostly copper, with, at that time, 6.3

---

[83] Choniates, ed. van Dieten, 66. See also P. Grierson, "A German Crusaders' Hoard of 1147 from Side (Turkey)," in *LAGOM: Festschrift für Peter Berghaus* (Munster, 1981), 195–203. The West had no gold coinage yet; Choniates may be referring to either unminted gold or Byzantine gold coins acquired by exchange. C. Morrisson and Marc Bompaire suggest that by "concambium competens" Louis VII may have meant that the French coins should be exchanged on the basis of their intrinsic value plus a corresponding premium. According to M. Bompaire, such a practice is attested in French documents of the late 12th century for coins circulating outside the territory where they were legal tender and where they had a nominal value higher than their real value. Cf. M. Castaing-Sicard, *Monnaies féodales et circulation en Languedoc, XIIe au XIIIe siècle* (Toulouse, 1961). I am grateful to M. Bompaire for this information and for the reference.

percent silver.[84] The Crusaders refer to it as a copper coin, as, to all intents and purposes, it was. Thus they suffered a first, psychological, shock, at the exchange of silver for copper.

Within the Byzantine Empire, the billon trachy functioned as a virtual token or quasi-token coin.[85] Its equivalence to the hyperpyron was legislated, and, in 1136, it was worth 1/48 of an hyperpyron, that is to say, one gold coin was worth 48 billon trachea or stamena.[86] The intrinsic value of the billon trachy (based on its silver content) would have been much lower. It was, then, against this token coin that the denier and the mark were exchanged.

The question arises whether the exchange was based on the intrinsic value of the coins or not. M. Hendy has suggested that the Crusaders would have expected an exchange based on the intrinsic value of each denomination, while the Byzantines would have insisted on the official (partly token) value of the billon trachy.[87] This is a highly plausible hypothesis and may well help interpret some of the complaints of the Western sources; but by itself it does not suffice to explain the actual exchange rates.

Odo of Deuil mentions three exchange rates, two in the provinces and one in Constantinople. The rates in the Balkans and in Asia Minor were very close to each other, and very different from that in Constantinople.

According to Odo of Deuil, when the Crusaders first entered the Byzantine Empire, they bought 1 stamenon for 5 deniers, "et pro duodecim solidis [earum] marcam triste dabamus vel potius perdebamus," that is, they bought 144 billon trachea for one mark of silver.[88] In Asia Minor, three days' march away from Constantinople, the exchange rate was almost exactly the same.[89]

This exchange rate was very unfavorable to the Crusaders, whether the exchange was

---

[84] Hendy, *Coinage and Money*, 21, 31. The billon aspron trachy, with a "pronounced silvery surface" (on which see M. F. Hendy and J. A. Charles, "The Production Techniques, Silver Content, and Circulation History of the Twelfth-Century Byzantine Trachy," in Hendy, *The Economy*, no. xii), would not have been mistaken for a silver coin.

[85] Copper money was almost always a token coin in Byzantium. The billon coin is called by C. Morrisson "'fausse monnaie' ou monnaie fiduciaire au sens large": "La monnaie fiduciaire à Byzance, ou 'vraie monnaie,' 'monnaie fiduciaire' et 'fausse monnaie' à Byzance," *Bulletin de la Société française de Numismatique* 34 (1979): 615–16.

[86] The rate is given in the typikon of the monastery of Pantokrator in Constantinople: A. Dmitrievskii, *Opisanie liturgičeskih rukopisei, hranyaščihsya v bibliotekah pravoslavnogo Vostoka*, vol. 1 (Kiev, 1895), 689. See the Table, above.

[87] Hendy, *Coinage and Money*, 21. Cf. above, note 82.

[88] Odo of Deuil, 41. The part about the exchange rate of the mark has been misunderstood by Chalandon, *Les Comnènes*, 2 vols. (Paris, 1900–1912), vol. 2, *Jean II Comnène (1118–1143) et Manuel I Comnène (1143–1180)*, 298–99 n. 2, and, following him, by the most recent editor of Odo of Deuil. The correct interpretation was suggested to me by Philip Grierson and hinges on the fact that the "duodecim solidi" means 12 units of 12 stamena, i.e., 144 stamena. There is a further uncertainty concerning the mark, which had different weights in different parts of Europe. I assume that, unless the sources explicitly state otherwise, when they mention marks they refer to pure silver weighing one mark. On the circulation of unminted silver, traveling in bars of ingots of a standard fineness and "frequently of a standard weight," see P. Spufford, *Money and Its Uses in Mediaeval Europe* (Cambridge, 1988), 209–24. I owe this reference to C. Morrisson. On the ingots in the "Barbarossa hoard," see below, note 100.

[89] Odo of Deuil, 66: they bought one stamenon for 5 or 6 deniers and paid one mark of silver for 144 deniers.

based on the nominal value of the billon trachy or on the intrinsic value of the coins.[90] If, indeed, the equivalence in the Byzantine Empire was 1 hyperpyron = 48 billon trachea, the Crusaders paid 240 deniers for 1 hyperpyron (and 1 mark of silver for 3 hyperpyra), much more than in the First Crusade or in the negotiated settlement of 1190.[91] This shows that, if the calculations are made on the basis of the hyperpyron, the Crusaders would have lost even more money than would be expected by an exchange on the *nominal* value of the billon trachy.

They lost considerable money also if the exchange was in terms of the intrinsic value of the coins. It is very difficult to figure the intrinsic value of such coins, but an exercise might be interesting. The denier Parisis at the time of Philip Augustus weighed approximately 1 gram, and contained 36–37 percent silver, thus having about 0.4 g silver. The billon trachy weighed around 4.30 g and its fineness was 6.3 percent silver, therefore its silver content was about 0.27 g.[92] The difference was visible to the naked eye. The silver content of the billon trachy was less than that of the denier Parisis both absolutely and relatively, and any exchange rate that quoted the billon trachy in multiples of the denier Parisis was bound to be excessive.

A fair exchange, in the eyes of the Crusaders, was what they got in Constantinople, after an agreement with the emperor: 1 stamenon for less than 2 deniers,[93] and 396 stamena for 1 mark of silver.[94] If we translate that into hyperpyra, and assume a nominal value of 1/48 hyperpyron for the stamenon, the Crusaders would have bought 8.25 hyperpyra for 1 mark of silver in Constantinople, a rate much more favorable to the mark than at the time of Frederick Barbarossa. The implied gold-silver ratio would be 1:7.86, very weak for Byzantium.

Certain observations are in order. The exchange rate between the stamenon and the denier, as that between the stamenon and the mark of silver, is consistent, *grosso modo*, with an exchange based on the *nominal* value of the stamenon, which normally was overvalued by something like 2.5 times its intrinsic value.[95] If the Crusaders then bought hyperpyra with their stamena, the gold-silver ratio would have been 1:8. It is, however, much more likely that the conversion of stamena to hyperpyra was either impossible or extremely limited, since both the fiduciary nature of the stamenon and the cheap rate that would result for the hyperpyron argue against it.

The difference in exchange rates between Constantinople and the provinces is striking indeed. In part, it reflects the real problems of exchanging money in the provinces. The presence of large Crusader armies would mean a sharp rise in demand and a shortage of Byzantine coins, thus making them expensive. Add to this the cost of metallic exchange to the money changer. The result was high rates and a psychological shock to the Crusaders, who exchanged silver for what looked to them like copper.

In Constantinople, Manuel seems to have insisted on the nominal value of the sta-

---

[90] See the Table, above.
[91] The difficulty with the mark, mentioned in note 88, must be kept in mind. For 1190, see below, 175.
[92] See the appendix below.
[93] Odo of Deuil, 66; cf. Chalandon, *Jean II Comnène*, 298–99 n. 2.
[94] "[E]arum triginta tres solidos propter marcam," i.e., 33 units of 12 stamena for one mark of silver.
[95] Cf. the appendix below.

menon, a deal that the Crusaders also considered to be fair. He may also, however, at the same time, have devalued the stamenon given to the Crusaders, as Choniates charges, taking with one hand what he had given with the other. Hendy discounts the possibility that Manuel had minted debased billon trachea specifically for the Crusaders, as charged by Choniates: ἀργύριον ἀδόκιμον εἰς νόμισμα κόπτεται καὶ τοῦτο προβάλλεται τοῖς ἐκ τοῦ τῶν Ἰταλῶν στρατεύματος ἀποδόσθαι τι θέλουσι.[96] Numismatic evidence, it seems, indicates that the debasement of the billon trachy (the stamenon) took place much later, and, it would appear, very fast. Yet it is not impossible that Manuel may have done exactly what Choniates accuses him of, that is, minted a debased billon trachy (with more copper) precisely to defraud the Crusaders and for use in Constantinople.

One other point is worth noting. None of the sources for the Second Crusade mentions an exchange rate for the hyperpyron, although we are told that in Constantinople the Crusaders did, in fact, exchange silver, both minted and unminted, for gold.[97] This suggests that the negotiated rates involved only the petty Byzantine coin and did not extend to gold-silver exchanges. In this case, the rate of exchange for gold and silver would have been negotiated on the ground, leaving open the possibility that the Crusaders overpaid for Byzantine gold, according to their need.

This hypothesis finds some corroboration in a wonderful story, related by Odo of Deuil, which also shows how the exchange took place. In Constantinople the Crusaders could exchange money on board the food ships and also "ante palatium vel etiam in tentoribus," that is, the money changers came to them at the site of the camp; or they could change money in the money changer's shops.[98] Once the Crusaders had left the city to cross over to Asia, they were attended by food ships, on which there were also money changers (*cum cambitoribus*). The money changers disembarked and set up their benches, which *fulgent auro*. Here came the Crusaders to exchange money as they needed to. Odo of Deuil speaks of the silver vessels that the money changers had bought from the Crusaders; so they also exchanged unminted metal for coin. A fairly orderly procedure, except for the fact that there were some heroic Crusaders who thought this a good occasion for plunder. A riot ensued, where the money changers lost their money and fled to Constantinople. Eventually Louis VII made restitution, and the money changers returned. But this is a rare picture of how operations took place: the money changers were right at the place where the food was, and the currency exchange went hand in hand with the purchase of necessities.[99]

How such transactions were carried out in the provinces is less clear; in fact, we have no information. One can imagine, however, that part of the business of creating a market included setting up facilities of exchange. Indeed, it is almost necessary to posit this, and it is not at all a far-fetched supposition, since we know that at Byzantine fairs credit transactions also took place; so the money changers were used to being at fairs. Nor

[96] Choniates, ed. van Dieten, 67; cf. Hendy, *Coinage and Money*, 22, 170–71.
[97] Odo of Deuil, 66.
[98] Odo of Deuil, 66.
[99] Odo of Deuil, 75.

would the money changers have been averse to setting up business on the route of the Crusaders: even if Manuel had not debased the coinage (indeed, *especially* if he had not debased the coinage), they stood to gain quite a lot in their transactions with people in need who had money of which to be relieved.

By the time of the Third Crusade, the balance of blackmail had changed, so that Frederick Barbarossa was able to exert great political and military pressure on the Byzantines.[100] The exchange agreements between the German emperor and Isaac II, in 1190, were highly sophisticated. The Treaty of Adrianople quotes both the exchange rate of the mark of silver, in hyperpyra, *and* the equivalence between the hyperpyron and the billon trachy. One mark of (pure) silver would sell at 5.5 hyperpyra, each hyperpyron to be counted as being worth 120 stamena, whether these were old or new stamena.[101] Thus no one could play games by giving different rates for hyperpyra and stamena. According to another Western source, the exchange rate between the mark and the hyperpyron varied according to whether the mark was *non examinata* or *examinata,* that is, non-assayed or assayed, with a control stamp, in other words, impure or pure. In the first place, the exchange rate would be 3 hyperpyra to the mark, in the second, 5 hyperpyra to the mark.[102] The distinction may well have been made on the insistence, not of the Germans, but of Isaac II or, more likely, the money changers of Constantinople, who would otherwise have assumed the risk involved in changing impure silver ingots into gold hyperpyra. The rate offered for the impure mark represented considerable compensation for the risk of the money changers.

The rate of exchange between the hyperpyron and the pure mark of silver seems to be within the normal boundaries of the gold–silver ratio. The growing sophistication of exchange transactions is indicated by the fact that the treaty states the equivalences between the hyperpyron and the billon trachy. The equivalence 120 new (debased) stamena to the hyperpyron implies the overvaluation of the stamenon and thus its fiduciary nature. When the same equivalence is applied to the old stamenon, however, then the fiduciary nature of the coin is undermined, and the emperor abandons part of his seignorage, that is, the state's premium, the buying power that is over and above the intrinsic value of the coin. One may suppose that this latter equivalence was a special arrangement extracted by Frederick I and did not obtain in normal transactions in Constantinople.

Later in the century, in 1199, Pisan notarial records give the rate of 184 stamena to the hyperpyron.[103] This was undoubtedly the market (exchange) value current in Constantinople. There may have been a further devaluation of the billon trachy between

---

[100] Barbarossa's army must have brought quite a lot of money. The "Barbarossa hoard" contains 7,700 coins as well as ingots: Metcalf, *Coinage of the Crusades,* 8–10. The Byzantines, too, had learned that their coins were much sought after: as Frederick Barbarossa attacked the area of the monastery of Bačkovo, in the fall of 1189, its treasurer buried part of the annual budget: M. F. Hendy, "The Gornoslav Hoard, the Emperor Frederick I, and the Monastery of Bachkovo," in idem, *The Economy,* no. xi.

[101] Ansbert, 66; Hendy, *Coinage and Money,* 21–22. Hendy posits a devaluation of the billon trachy, which would have been the reason for this last provision.

[102] Hampe, "Ungedruckter Bericht," 400.

[103] Müller, *Documenti,* no. xlvii, p. 77; Hendy, *Coinage and Money,* 22.

1190 and 1199, although the coins of Alexios III do not show lower silver content than those of Isaac II.[104] But devaluation is not really what makes the difference between the negotiated rates of 1190 and the attested rates of 1199. Rather, the difference is due to a revaluation down of the billon trachy, to reflect a demand that would bring it closer to its intrinsic value, probably as a result of the double pressure of foreign merchants and Crusaders. Thus the highly overvalued equivalences mandated by the state in the 1130s were no longer effective, even though the face value of the stamenon remained lower than the nominal value; that is to say, the overvaluation of the billon trachy continued, but at lower levels than had obtained earlier. A hundred and fifty years later, Pegolotti wrote of the stamenon: "ma a questi stammini non si fa nullo pagamento se none in passagio di Gostantinopoli per lo paese, e per erbe e cose minute."[105]

In their exchange transactions with the Crusaders, the Byzantines seem to have made good money and shown considerable knowledge of monetary matters. The merchants must have played an important role in transactions on the ground, if only because exchange was so closely tied to the purchase of merchandise on the part of the Crusaders. Those merchants who had activities both with the countryside and with Constantinople would have profited very considerably, especially given the unequal exchange rates obtaining in the capital and in the provinces. The merchants would have acted also as money changers.

There are indications of such a development in the exceptional importance assumed by merchants and money changers in late twelfth-century Constantinople. The Treaty of Adrianople provides a first glimpse into this development, but it is a striking one. The treaty was guaranteed not only by the oaths of representatives of the two emperors and the confirmation of the patriarch, but also by the oaths of large numbers of their subjects. In the case of the crusading army, the oath was taken in Adrianople by 15,000 *milites,* in the presence of Byzantine ambassadors.[106] This was given in exchange for an oath taken in Constantinople, in the solemn precincts of Hagia Sophia, by "500 men of the market-place and the court" (ἀπὸ τῶν ἀγοραίων καὶ τῆς βασιλείου αὐλῆς),[107] who swore "that the emperor would keep the treaties inviolate and would give the leaders of the Germans safe passage and provisions."[108] This is an unprecedented event in Byzantine international relations, with obvious constitutional overtones. The oath was undoubtedly demanded by Frederick Barbarossa, as Ansbert's text suggests; and the men who took it, whom another source calls "quingenti de melioribus terrae," were understood to have sworn "quod ipse rex Grecie concanbium bonum et forum rectum et omnium suorum tutelam sine mala fraude ineundo et redeundo postaret."[109] The latter source is a letter, by an unknown author, that reports on the terms of the treaty as he heard them

[104] Hendy explains the drop in the value of the billon trachy between the time of John II and the end of the 12th century by the decline in fineness: *Studies,* 518. However, his own figures show that the rate of decline in fineness is *less* than the rate of decline in value.

[105] Francesco Balducci Pegolotti, *La pratica della mercatura,* ed. A. Evans, Medieval Academy of America Publication 24 (Cambridge, Mass., 1936), 40.

[106] Ansbert, 66.

[107] Ansbert, 66, calls them "quingenti homines meliores civitatis et imperii."

[108] Choniates, ed. van Dieten, 411.

[109] Hampe, "Ungedruckter Bericht," 399.

from "cives noti qui . . . Constantinopoli fuerunt"; the editor of the letter suggests, very plausibly, that the *cives noti* were (Italian) merchants.[110] These Italian merchants, then, understood that their equivalent Byzantines, the very men who would have been engaged in trade and money changing, were made to guarantee the Treaty of Adrianople. Was their oath (along with that of some of Isaac's aristocrats) demanded by the German emperor because he was used to dealing with the "best men" of cities? Or were the "best" businessmen of Constantinople playing a new role in relations with Westerners, merchants, and states?

Here we must recall the near-contemporary affair of the piratical attack of summer 1192 and the subsequent negotiations, with which we began, and Isaac II's efforts to get reparations for the goods of "the first among the merchants of Constantinople," in whom it is legitimate to see a subgroup of the *meliores terrae* of the Treaty of Adrianople.[111] It is pertinent to our discussion that it was these merchants (and money changers too, undoubtedly) who functioned as guarantors (ἐγγυηταί) of the goods of Genoese and Pisan merchants held in deposit. Thus they engaged in money business as well, a phenomenon already mentioned above in connection with the probable role of merchants in money transactions during the Crusades.[112] John Oxeobaphopoulos, who returned the deposit to the Genoese, bears a name that clearly connects him to the marketplace, for it means the "'red' purple dyer"; whether he was a silk manufacturer or a silk merchant, or both, or whether his was a family name, cannot, of course, be determined. Kalomodios, the one great merchant and money changer whose name and profession are explicitly attested, lived in the same period, during the reign of Alexios III. We also know that during Alexios III's reign, cloth merchants and money changers and other tradesmen were able to buy honorific titles: οἱ ἐν τριόδοις καὶ ἀγοραῖς καὶ κολλυβισταὶ καὶ πραταὶ τῶν ὀθονῶν σεβαστοὶ ἐτιμήθησαν.[113]

The important and complex role of the Constantinopolitan merchant and banker is the result of many developments: the extensive commercial activity of the Byzantines in the twelfth century; the development of Byzantine-Italian relations, which, on the institutional front (and I mean legal and economic institutions), was proceeding at a rapid pace and creating new situations; and undoubtedly to some extent it was also due to the active role of the merchants and money changers in the negotiations with Crusaders and in the implementation of agreements. The Treaty of Adrianople did not create this group. But it gave its existence a certain solemnity; and it may have contributed something to this group's apparently significant power in Constantinople, and so to the fact that its interests were very much taken into account in the state relations between the empire, Genoa, and Pisa—and in the discussion of the terms in which both trade and piracy were to be conducted. The expanded role of the merchants and money changers, which recalls the earlier developments of the eleventh century, was cut short by the events of 1204.

Would these developments have been different in degree or in kind without the pas-

---

[110] Ibid., 400 n. 5.
[111] Above, 157–59.
[112] Above, 176.
[113] Choniates, ed. van Dieten, 523–24, 483–84.

VIII

sage of the Crusader armies? One does not wish to engage in counterfactual argumentation. What may be stressed is the fact that relations between Crusaders and Byzantines, especially during the Second and Third Crusades, were arrangements between states. Thus they ratified and confirmed developments that may already have been taking place.

In sum, the Crusades (always speaking of the first three major movements) had a number of influences on the Byzantine terms of trade with Westerners. Sometimes the connection is obvious: thus the first Pisan commercial privileges incorporate a clause that anyone who travels on Pisan ships to Jerusalem "against the pagans" will suffer no impediment in terms of passage, or of *dapanai* (*stipendia* in the Latin text), which is not really the equivalent of *mercatus,* although it does refer to provisions, or in terms of their military equipment.[114] This guarantee of safe-conduct applied only to those Crusaders who would swear an oath to the Pisan ship captain not to harm the Byzantine Empire— hence R.-J. Lilie's correct interpretation that those who did *not* swear not to harm the Byzantine Empire would not be guaranteed safe passage, and thus that there was a partial Byzantine boycott of the transport of Crusaders. These provisions bear considerable substantive similarity to the terms on which Bohemond had been allowed to recruit soldiers from Western Europe to Antioch, terms included in the Treaty of Devol, three years earlier.[115]

The connection between the two events is real at the political level. Since 1099 Alexios had been in conflict with Pisan and Genoese ships sailing to the Holy Land, absolutely parallel to the skirmishes and sometimes overt hostilities that took place with the passage of Crusader armies over land.[116] After Bohemond went west to raise troops for an anti-Byzantine crusade, Alexios tried to include the Pisans (as well as the Genoese and the Venetians) in his system of defense against Bohemond; the Pisans had engaged in hostile piratical action in the wake of the war with Bohemond (in 1111).[117] There is also a diplomatic connection, or a formal, institutional connection, since similar provisions found their way into commercial privileges very early indeed, and in treaties with the Crusaders (and Bohemond), almost from the beginning.

Such connections, however, I have not discussed, preferring instead to concentrate on other issues. Sometimes the crusading arrangements and those with Italian city-states were based on different principles: a combination of statism and free trade in the case of some arrangements with the Crusaders regarding markets and exchange rates, versus the free trade agreements that characterized, to a significant extent, the commercial privileges, and that created a market response to currency exchange rates in Constantinople. Sometimes the two form part of a developing global pattern, as was the case with repara-

---

[114] Müller, *Documenti,* no. xxxiv, pp. 44 and 53. This is the privilege of 1111, inserted into the treaty of 1192. Cf. R.-J. Lilie, *Handel und Politik: Zwischen dem byzantinischen Reich und den italienischen Kommunen Venedig, Pisa und Genua in der Epoche der Komnenen und der Angeloi (1081–1204)* (Amsterdam, 1984), 69 ff.

[115] *Alexiade* 13.12.17 (ed. Leib, 3:133): Bohemond agrees that all who cross the Adriatic with him will swear δουλείαν to the empire, in the person of a man whom Alexios will send to Italy (the equivalent of swearing an oath to the ship captain—in both cases, before departure): εἰ δ᾽ ἀποπηδῶσι τὸν ὅρκον, μὴ ἄλλως ἐᾶσαι διαπερᾶν ὡς τὰ αὐτὰ φρονεῖν ἡμῖν ἀπαναινομένους.

[116] *Alexiade* 11.10, 11 (ed. Leib, 3:42–48); Heyd, *Histoire du commerce,* 1:190–91.

[117] *Alexiade* 12.1.2, 14.3 (ed. Leib, 3:54, 154 ff). The Genoese had also participated in the piratical attacks.

tions and reprisal arrangements. Thus there were new ways of dealing with the Westerners in commercial matters; and this went in tandem with dealings with the Crusaders, one set of arrangements reinforcing the other.

Similarly, the bilateral agreements, confirmed by oaths, which we see most clearly in the Treaty of Adrianople, are a part of an evolving pattern of relationships with Western powers, primarily the crusading sovereigns and the maritime cities of Italy. Here, too, the Crusades are inscribed in a larger pattern of evolution, which includes the first bilateral state agreements (with Venice in 1186–87, with Pisa in the treaty of 1192, and with Genoa in 1155).[118] Scholars have pointed out that the chrysobull issued by Isaac II in February 1187 differs in form from earlier privileges, for it is clearly bilateral, incorporating, on the one hand, the obligations of the Venetians, and on the other hand, and in exchange, the concessions given by the Byzantine emperor.[119] This document preserves the traditional form in one important way: that the Venetians swear by oath to keep their promises, whereas the emperor's word is his chrysobull. The Treaty of Adrianople, on the other hand, is a bilateral convention in this also: that both parties swear an oath through their representatives and an exchange of presents, bilateral in Choniates,[120] unilateral in Ansbert.[121] Of constitutional significance for Byzantium, this conjunction of bilateral arrangements also suggests a pattern of international agreements between states, whether crusading or mercantile, agreements that undoubtedly reinforced each other.

II. "International" Commercial Institutions

In political terms, we can detect in the Byzantine Empire a certain dissolution of native institutions regarding aspects of trade and the exercise of the merchant's profession. These then reappear in more general, Mediterranean, forms. In the course of the twelfth and thirteenth centuries, one may see the elaboration of similar general provisions and institutions throughout the eastern Mediterranean, in the trade relations between Byzantines, other Christians, and Muslims.[122] In some instances, the first stages of

[118] Lilie, *Handel und Politik*, 82.

[119] M. Pozza and G. Ravegnani, eds., *I trattati con Bisanzio, 992–1198*, Pacta veneta (Venice, 1993), p. 80, and doc. 8, pp. 90 ff.

[120] Ed. van Dieten, 411.

[121] Ansbert, 64, 66; Choniates (ed. van Dieten, 411) says the "emperor and the king renewed their oaths"; Frederick's magnates gave the oath, and Isaac gave hostages. He then moves into the discussion of the oath taken in Constantinople.

[122] S. D. Goitein ("Mediterranean Trade in the Eleventh Century: Some Facts and Problems," in *Studies in the Economic History of the Middle East*, ed. M. A. Cook [London, 1970], 51–62) has argued that already in the 11th century, and before the Crusades, the "Mediterranean area gave the impression of a free-trade area." Here I argue that the Crusades and the Crusader states were instrumental in the development and spread of institutions that facilitated Mediterranean trade. Many important topics, for example, the institutional impact of Western trading stations in Egypt on the development of Italian trading colonies in Constantinople, are necessarily left out of this discussion. I also do not discuss the Amalfitan and Venetian trading stations in Constantinople. These predate the crusading period, but neither their existence nor their evolution is critical to the topics elaborated below.

VIII

development took place in the Byzantine Empire; in other cases in the Crusader states; in all cases the Crusader states played a pivotal role in this development.

In general terms, it may be argued that states give up some prerogatives in the general trend toward the free and safe movement of men and merchandise—as was also the case with the freedom from, or the reduction of, the *commercium*. This is a very rich topic, with many aspects to it. I should like to examine one example only: the law of salvage, which is connected with the law of reprisals and seems to be developing together with laws regarding the disposition of the goods of merchants dying in a host country. The first two have to do not only with the normal risks run by merchants who carried out their business at the mercy of the elements, but also with piracy, increasingly a problem in the Mediterranean in the twelfth century and after.[123] I will not deal with the evolving laws on reprisals here.

Salvage

In the case of salvage, one must begin with the Byzantine law, which derived from but became stricter than the Roman (i.e., Justinianic) law of salvage. There are two aspects to the question: who has the right to salvaged goods, and what penalties there are for those who pilfer them. As to the first point, Justinianic law, repeated in the *Basilics*, is quite clear: the goods belong to their owner; there is no time limitation on his rights; and what he can salvage he may keep.[124] The Rhodian Sea Law adds some practical provisions that give a reward to those who help salvage the ship or the goods it carries, presumably in an effort to avoid looting: the people who help salvage a ship or parts of a ship are entitled to 1/5 of its value; if they find goods on land and return them, they get 1/10 of the value; and if they dive to salvage gold or silver or anything else, they are entitled to 1/3 or 1/2, depending on the depth.[125]

As for penalties for those who seize the goods of shipwrecks, while the Rhodian Sea Law does not mention any, in the *Basilics* there were very high financial penalties: within the first year, the pilferers had to restore to the owners the goods at their value in quadruple; after the first year, there was simple restitution.[126] This was the Roman, Justinianic, provision. But the *Procheiros Nomos* stated that after the first year the goods should be restored at double their value.[127] Custom, apparently, was even stricter than the law. A novel of Leo VI mentions the custom that mandated the death penalty for those who hid goods lost in shipwreck, for it was deemed a sin to deprive individuals of their wealth.

---

[123] The connection has been made by H. Ahrweiler, "Course et piraterie dans la Méditerranée orientale aux IVème–XVème siècles (empire byzantin)," in *Course et piraterie: Etudes présentées à la Commission Internationale d'Histoire Maritime à l'occasion de son XVe colloque internationale pendant le XIVe Congrès International des Sciences Historiques, San Francisco, 1975*, 2 vols. (Paris, 1975), 1:10, 16, 17–19. Salvage is connected with jettison, on which see O. R. Constable, "The Problem of Jettison in Medieval Mediterranean Maritime Law," *Journal of Medieval History* 20 (1994): 207–20.

[124] Bas. 53.3.23 = D 41.2.21, §§ 1.22 jo. D 16.3.18; Bas. 53.3.15 = D 14.2.7.

[125] Bas. 53, appendix, pt. 2, nos. 45, 46, 47. The Rhodian Sea Law has many other provisions regarding shipwreck, but they deal with the respective rights of the captain and the merchants aboard the ship. See, e.g., nos. 27, 29, 37, 40.

[126] Bas. 60.20.1 = D 47.9.1; cf. Cod. 4.2.18.

[127] Pr. 39.25 (= *Eisagoge* 40.28), in Zepos, *Jus* 2:218, 361.

The emperor delivered himself of a somewhat rhetorical argument by analogy, to show that the death penalty was too heavy a punishment for a sin that is, after all, a crime of property: it is not just, he argues, to take an immaterial and immortal thing, one's soul, in compensation for material and perishable things.[128] Instead, the emperor restored the Roman penalty of a fine at four times the value of the objects in question, payable to the owner, although he gave no limitation of time, that is, the fine was not reduced after one year had elapsed.

However, it would seem that all of this legislation applied only to Byzantine subjects, not to foreigners. What happened in the case of foreigners in the early and middle Byzantine period is not clear. The question of salvage came up in the Russo-Byzantine treaty of 911, where the Rus and the Byzantines engaged themselves to help each other's ships during a tempest; if there was a shipwreck, and the goods were pilfered or the sailors/merchants were murdered, the penalties for theft and murder would apply.[129] In the twelfth century, it would seem that the goods aboard the ships of foreigners not covered by treaties and wrecked in Byzantine waters were considered to belong to the fisc: indirect evidence to that effect is to be found in the chrysobull for Pisa (1111) and in an incident ca. 1200.[130] The Seljuks and the Latin rulers of Cyprus in the late twelfth and early thirteenth century apparently also considered that such goods belonged to the fisc.

Quite early in Byzantine relations with the Westerners, clauses referring to shipwreck and salvage were incorporated in Imperial privileges. The treaties with Venice did not incorporate any such clauses, presumably because the Venetians, treated as Byzantine subjects, were covered by Byzantine law. Pisa was another matter. The chrysobull of 1111 was the first commercial privilege granted to an Italian power whose friendship was not a given, and with which, indeed, there had already been hostilities at sea. The Pisans requested and received a privilege regarding both piracy and shipwreck.[131] It constitutes a key text in some respects. The emperor promised that if there was shipwreck in Byzantine waters, the Pisans could have without impediment their salvaged goods (the implication is that until then they could not). If some Byzantines helped salvage goods, the Pisans were allowed to keep those too, after making payment "according to the custom of the place, or according to any agreement they may have made." While this was less than what had been agreed with the Rus, since no help was promised, it did lift the impediments on the recovery of shipwrecked goods. The Pisans retained the ownership of salvaged goods and had to pay those who helped recover them. But the emperor did not guarantee the safety of these goods.

This is a highly simplified and attenuated form of the Byzantine law on salvage. We next find legislation on salvage in the privileges granted to Italian merchants in the vari-

---

[128] P. Noailles and A. Dain, *Les Novelles de Léon VI le Sage* (Paris, 1944), novel 64.

[129] I. Sorlin, "Les traités de Byzance avec la Russie au Xe siècle," *Cahiers du monde russe et soviétique* 3 (1961): 334, 357; in 944 the Rus engage themselves not to harm shipwrecked Byzantine ships; those who steal goods will be judged according to Byzantine law: ibid., 4 (1961): 450, 461.

[130] Below, 184.

[131] Müller, *Documenti*, no. xxxiv, p. 44. The clause on piracy says that if a Pisan ship is seized in Byzantine waters and goods are taken by Byzantine subjects, the emperor will examine the matter and do the right thing, at the right time.

ous Crusader states, where they appear in a simple but significantly stronger form. The first mention is in the privilege granted to the Venetians by the king of Jerusalem in 1123, as repayment for their help in the siege of Tyre: "Si vero aliquis Veneticorum naufragium passus fuerit, *nullum de suis rebus patiatur dampnum.*" Significantly, this is followed by the clause "si naufragio mortuus fuerit, suis heredibus aut aliis Veneticis res sue remanentes reddantur," that is, the heirs of the shipwrecked person or other Venetians retained their rights on his property.[132] Exactly the same clause was inserted in the privilege given by Baldwin II, king of Jerusalem (1118–31) to the Venetians; Renault of Châtillon, regent of Antioch, and Bohemond III gave similar privileges in 1153 and 1167, respectively.[133] There was an implicit guarantee given in these treaties, certainly greater than the mere permission to recover their goods that Alexios I Komnenos had given to the Pisans. Although no penalties are mentioned for those who seized goods, the state did promise their safety, a clause almost certain to eventually lead to reprisals.

Some years later, the Byzantines also gave new guarantees to Italian merchants; in substance they are similar to the implicit guarantees given by the Crusader states, but in form they are more developed. In 1169 Manuel I was trying to bring Genoa into an anti-German alliance and was also negotiating a commercial treaty. He stated that in case of shipwreck, if goods were seized by someone, he, the emperor, charged himself with avenging the ill done and restoring the goods to the Genoese: "fiat de his vindicta a majestate mea et restauratio hujusmodi rerum" ("My majesty will give satisfaction and restore these goods").[134] This clause was incorporated in the treaty of 1192, which states: καὶ ἐὰν πλοῖον Γενουϊτικὸν ἀφ᾽ οἱουδήτινος τόπου ἐρχόμενον εἰς Ῥωμανίαν κινδυνεύσῃ καὶ συμβῇ τινὰ τῶν ἐν αὐτῷ πραγμάτων ἀφαιρεθῆναι ὑπό τινων, ἵνα γένηται πρὸς ταῦτα τῆς βασιλείας μου ἐκδίκησις καὶ ἐπανάσωσις τῶν τοιούτων πραγμάτων.[135]

There seems to be a development that would bring the treatment of shipwrecked Italian ships closer to that of Byzantine subjects; in 1169 Manuel, unlike Alexios in 1111, guarantees the return of the merchandise of the Genoese, and if the penalty of the quadruple does not appear, the word *vindicta* in the text suggests punishment. Like the privileges granted earlier by the Crusader states, this is, I believe, partly an effort to preclude

---

[132] The privilege also is the first one to state that if a Venetian dies in Tyre, his property goes to the Venetian authorities: William of Tyre, 12.25 (1:577 ff); cf. G. L. F. Tafel and G. Thomas, *Urkunden zur älteren Handels- und Staatsgeschichte der Republik Venedig,* Fontes rerum Austriacarum, Diplomataria et acta 12–14, 3 vols. (Vienna, 1856–57), 1:79 ff.

[133] Tafel and Thomas, *Urkunden,* 1:92, 134, 148–49. Cf. also the privilege of Renault of Châtillon to Pisa in 1154, with return of goods to heirs: Müller, *Documenti,* no. IV; privilege to Pisa by Bohemond III in 1170, with return of goods to heirs: Müller, *Documenti,* no. XIII; cf. Venice and the Seljuks, Tafel and Thomas, *Urkunden,* 2:484–86 (1254). On the early privileges granted to Italian merchants in crusader Syria and Palestine, cf. M. Balard, "Les républiques maritimes italiennes et le commerce en Syrie-Palestine (XIe–XIIIe siècles)," *Anuario de estudios medievales* 24 (1994): 313–48, and J. Riley-Smith, "Government in Latin Syria and the Commercial Privileges of Foreign Merchants," in *Relations between East and West in the Middle Ages,* ed. D. Baker (Edinburgh, 1973), 109–32.

[134] Bertolotto, *Nuova serie,* 351; Balard, *La Romanie génoise,* 1:28 ff.

[135] Miklosich and Müller, 3:36.

reprisals. But one may also suggest that the Italians, having received a greater guarantee from the Crusader states, returned to Byzantium asking here, too, for better guarantees. In the 1180s, Andronikos I passed a measure of exceptional harshness toward those who pilfered shipwrecks. Choniates, who reports the measure, informs us that from time to time Byzantine emperors passed laws on salvage, although, after the Rhodian Sea Law, the only extant legislation, to my knowledge, is the Macedonian one, including Leo VI's novel. But he also says that the laws were not applied and complains that there was a long-standing custom, found only among the Byzantines, that ships that foundered or were cast ashore were not helped by the inhabitants; rather, the natives seized anything that the sea did not.[136] Andronikos' measure is not transmitted in the form of a novel, but is rather in that of an *entole,* an order addressed to his relatives and the imperial officials.[137]

The emperor begins by saying that he believes his predecessors were incapable of exacting obedience to their laws because they only pretended to wish to put a stop to this evil; if they had really wanted to, they would have punished it with the death penalty. He himself wants to stop practices that harm the commonweal, especially the custom of seizing the cargo of shipwrecks and sometimes even demolishing the ship. The penalty he decrees is harsh: those who do not heed his orders will be hanged from the ship's mast or will be impaled on the coast, so that they will be visible from afar and become a lesson to those who see them. Andronikos holds responsible not only those who physically plunder the ships, but also the imperial officials who govern the area, as well as the landlords whose tenants engage in such activities. Given Andronikos' reputation as a man of his word, Choniates tells us that the officials wrote to those who ruled the provinces in their names, and the landlords to their agents, not to harm the shipwrecks. As a result, nothing was stolen, no ships were destroyed, no anchors taken away, and the people of the coastlands as well as the officials helped the shipwrecked sailors and merchants to recover all their possessions.[138]

Choniates relates this imperial order at some length, using it as the single detailed illustration of his general statement that Andronikos tried to ease the lot of the poorer people, partly by insisting on fair and predictable taxation (no multiplication of dues), and partly by stopping the sale of offices and by appointing officials who would not use their office to enrich themselves. It is thus presented as part of the populist policy of this otherwise hateful (at least to Choniates) emperor. But it is, in fact, much more than that.

It is a stage in the development of a law of the sea, established in a harsh and inelegant way, to be sure, that aims to protect merchants and to minimize claims. Although noth-

---

[136] Choniates, ed. van Dieten, 326: ἔθους . . . ἀλογωτάτου. Interestingly, Hugh I of Lusignan, in his treaty with the sultan of Konya (1216), also mentions that such an unjust custom prevailed in Cyprus (κατὰ τὴν ἐπικρατήσασαν ἄδικον συνήθειαν)—from Byzantine days? See S. Lambros, "Ἡ Ἑλληνικὴ ὡς ἐπίσημος γλῶσσα τῶν Σουλτάνων," Νέος Ἑλλ. 5 (1908): 49. A much later text, from the 1320s, gives details about people who cause shipwrecks in order to steal the goods aboard ship—a simple form of piracy: Theodoulos Monachos, Περὶ βασιλείας, PG 145:481–84; cf. Ahrweiler, "Course et piraterie," 17 ff.

[137] Dölger, *Regesten,* no. 1566, s.a.

[138] Choniates, ed. van Dieten, 326–39; Skoutareiotes in K. Sathas, Μεσαιωνικὴ Βιβλιοθήκη, vol. 7 (Paris, 1894), 350; cf. A. Laiou, "Byzantine Traders and Seafarers," in *The Greeks and the Sea,* ed. S. Vryonis Jr. (New Rochelle, N.Y., 1993), 89–90.

VIII

ing in the text suggests that this was prompted by foreign merchants or was to apply to them, the international implications are clear. Even Choniates' opening statement, that this was "an extremely irrational custom that is practiced only among the Romans" suggests that international concerns were present. Andronikos' measure was made necessary both because of the increased volume of maritime trade and because the increased presence of foreign merchants created a situation where the emperor was responding to pressures for safety in sailing, pressures coming not only from his own subjects but also from foreigners. The measure carries imperial orders one step further: people are to help salvage goods. And it is general enough to be applicable to both Byzantine and foreign shipping, despite Andronikos' well-known hostility to the Latins.

Indeed, a number of incidents in the Black Sea at the turn of the century show both the need for a proper law of salvage and the fact that the powers of the area still considered that, in the absence of treaties to the contrary, salvaged goods belonged to the fisc. One incident implicated merchants both Byzantine and Turkish. Around 1200,[139] Alexios III sent to the Black Sea a certain Constantine Frangopoulos, ostensibly to examine the cargo of a ship sailing from Phasis and shipwrecked near Kerasous—a clear indication that the fisc was claiming goods salvaged from foreign ships.[140] The man, perhaps on imperial orders, perhaps (as Alexios later claimed) not, plundered merchantmen sailing to and from Constantinople, near Samsous, it seems,[141] and killed some of the merchants. The loot—or part of it—came to Alexios who added it to his treasury, oblivious to the complaints of the merchants. But some of them were subjects of the sultan of Konya. Since this happened at a time when a treaty (or the renewal of a treaty)[142] was being discussed, the sultan tied the treaty negotiations with the reparation demands of the merchants. Eventually, the sultan got, along with other things, "50 pounds of silver" as damages for his merchants.[143] The other incident happened in 1223 and involved Russian merchants fleeing Sudak and shipwrecked near Sinope. The Turks claimed the right to keep salvaged goods, "according to a custom with regard to a place where there existed no concessions."[144]

The laws on salvage, which began in the Byzantine Empire, developed significantly in the Crusader states and returned to Byzantium to develop further. They spread all over the eastern Mediterranean in the thirteenth century, in one form or another, depending on the model that was being followed.

The treaties between the sultan of Konya Kaikaus I and Hugh I of Lusignan of Cyprus in 1216 contain clauses on both piracy and salvage, as does the Byzantine-Genoese treaty

[139] Dölger, *Regesten*, no. 1658 (1201); cf. C. Cahen, *La Turquie pré-ottomane*, Varia turcica 7 (Istanbul-Paris, 1988), 64, 122–23.

[140] Similar rights were claimed by Kaikaus in 1216; cf. below, 184–85.

[141] Samsous had fallen to the Turks shortly before 1194: Cahen, *La Turquie pré-ottomane*, 64.

[142] There were earlier treaties with Kaikaus I of Konya, which Alexios broke (perhaps in 1198), again by attacking the properties (merchandise and animals—ὑποζύγια) of Greek and Turkish merchants, subjects of the sultan: Choniates, ed. van Dieten, 493–94.

[143] Choniates, ed. van Dieten, 529: εἰς ἀπόδομα ὧν οἱ ἔμποροι ἀφῃρέθησαν. Dölger, *Regesten*, no. 1658 (the sultan was Rukn al-Din). Reparations for goods seized by the fisc were also given to the Venetians, after the seizure of their goods by Manuel I in 1171—again, a parallel development.

[144] Cahen, *La Turquie pré-ottomane*, 125. The quotation is from Cahen.

of 1192. In both states it seems that salvaged goods of foreigners were seized; the treaties put an end to that, promising the return of the surviving men and their merchandise.[145] Hugh I promised that if pirates attack and pillage a ship and its merchandise and go to Cyprus, the spoils will be returned to the rightful owners, if the king captures the pirates. And in cases of shipwreck, "the surviving men as well as the salvaged goods shall be kept safe and restored, and not seized as per the prevailing unjust custom"; similar provisions, although somewhat differently worded, were included in the sultan's letter to Hugh, which repeats and confirms the terms of the treaty.[146]

A few years later, in 1220, Alaeddin Kaikobad, sultan of Konya, signed a treaty with Jacopo Tiepolo, *podestà* of the Venetians in Constantinople. A lengthy clause addresses the issue of salvage and, in vaguer terms, of piracy (or rather, of Venetian ships being chased by ships of other powers). On the issue of shipwreck, the sultan promises not only that the goods of Venetians would be restored, but also that his subjects would help the Venetians recover them—a clause that appears only in the Russian-Byzantine treaty of 911 and implicitly in Andronikos' measure.[147]

The same privilege was given to the Venetians by the lord of Rhodes, the Caesar Leo Gabalas, in 1234: "et omnes a gente mea habebunt subsidium et favorem."[148] The privilege granted by Theodore I Laskaris to the Venetians (Jacopo Tiepolo again) in 1219 contains two clauses that make reciprocal arrangements for ships and merchants of the two powers, to return their property to the men who survive the shipwreck. The Venetians are given the added privilege, contained already in the Byzantine privilege of 1198, but appearing for the first time in the *Pactum Warmundi* in 1123, that the goods of Venetians who died in the Empire of Nicaea would revert to their heirs.[149] Italian treaties with Egypt, after the middle of the thirteenth century, also incorporate clauses promising safety for men and goods in case of shipwreck.[150]

What all of this indicates is that a law of the sea was developing in the twelfth century and into the thirteenth, which regulated certain important matters and which eventually applied to all merchants active in the area and to the states whose subjects they were.

---

[145] Lambros, "Ἡ Ἑλληνική," 48–50; A. Savvides, *Byzantium in the Near East: Its Relations with the Seljuk Sultanate of Rum in Asia Minor, the Armenians of Cilicia and the Mongols, A.D. c. 1192–1237*, Byzantina keimena kai meletai 17 (Thessaloniki, 1981), 141–42; C. Cahen, "Le commerce anatolien au début du XIIIe siècle," in idem, *Turcobyzantina et Oriens Christianus* (London, 1974), no. XII, 93.

[146] Lambros, "Ἡ Ἑλληνική," 52.

[147] Tafel and Thomas, *Urkunden*, 2:223; the reciprocal privilege to the sultan's men is found on pp. 223–34; it includes a clause that, if the man dies, his property will be given to his heirs, which harks back to the Venetian privileges in the *Pactum Warmundi* and the Byzantine treaty of 1198 (Pozza and Ravegnani, *I trattati*, doc. 11, p. 136). The sultan also promises that any Crusaders found on Venetian ships will not be imprisoned but will be freed. There do not seem to be extant privileges to the Genoese: Cahen, "Le commerce anatolien," 98–99.

[148] Tafel and Thomas, *Urkunden*, 2:321–22; cf. M. Angold, *A Byzantine Government in Exile: Government and Society under the Laskarids of Nicaea, 1204–1261* (London, 1975), 114. Again, no privileges to the Genoese seem to have been issued.

[149] Tafel and Thomas, *Urkunden*, 2:206–7.

[150] See, for example, the treaty with Venice, in 1254, Tafel and Thomas, *Urkunden*, 2:484: "et omnes Veneti sint salui et securi in personis et hauere et toto suo navigio." Cf. the treaty of 1290 with Genoa, and of 1281 with Byzantium (below, 189–91).

Italian merchants, Byzantines, and Turks were all covered by the same protections, at least in the law of salvage. Crusader states, the sultanate of Konya, the Byzantine Empire, and then the Empire of Nicaea, and Egypt, incorporated in their agreements with each other the same or similar arrangements. There are intriguing connecting lines between some of these agreements: for example, the occasional appearance in this connection of the guarantee of the inheritance of merchants dying abroad; the similarities in phraseology between the treaties of Hugh of Cyprus and Kaikaus I on the one hand, and Manuel I's agreements with the Genoese on the other. Most important, not in any intrinsic way, but for our topic, is the similar concern expressed by Andronikos I and Hugh I of Cyprus regarding the "unjust custom" (ἐπικρατήσασαν ἄδικον συνήθειαν) (Hugh I) or the irrational custom (ἔθους ἀλογωτάτου) (Andronikos I) of plundering shipwrecks. Both men opposed this custom, and treaties incorporated clauses that forbade the seizure of goods and sometimes pledged help for their recovery. There was, thus, an effort throughout the eastern Mediterranean to improve the conditions of trade and travel, an effort that almost certainly originated with the concerns of Western merchants and Crusaders, who plied these seas, but that led to measures that became generally adopted. Political considerations connected with the politics of crusading and the Crusader states were important indeed for the adoption and spread of such institutions, but the motive force behind them was commercial. The old Byzantine laws regulating these issues became simplified as their substance was generally adopted. Gone is the distinction between the first year of the seizure of goods and subsequent years; gone also the obligation to return the goods in quadruple for the first year; these elements had disappeared already at the time of Andronikos I, but equally, his extremely severe measures were unique to him. Complex arrangements would have been impossible to implement in this mobile world, hence the simplicity. The simplification is evident as early as the Pisan privilege of 1111, which, along with the *Pactum Warmundi,* is the basic document.

The law of the sea and mercantile law were also constantly evolving, as may be seen from the provisions regarding the goods of men dying outside their own country, whether with a testament or intestate. While this issue cannot be examined here, it may be noted that the process of its development is very similar to that of the law of salvage. The principle of the devolution of property to a man's heirs or his fellow nationals, rather than to the fisc of the country in which he died, a very important principle for merchants, appears first in the privilege granted to the Genoese by Baldwin I of Jerusalem (1105)[151] and the *Pactum Warmundi* in 1123. It then took the form of the return of the goods to Venetian authorities, but by the middle of the twelfth century, in the Crusader states, the right devolved to the heirs.[152] In the Byzantine Empire such certainly was not yet the practice in 1165–66, when the considerable property of the Pisan merchant Signoretto, who was also a *burgensis,* was claimed by the fisc.[153] It appears for the first time in the treaty of 1198 with Venice. There can be no doubt that this principle devel-

---

[151] C. Imperiale di Sant'Angelo, ed., *Codice diplomatico della repubblica di Genova,* 3 vols., Fonti per la storia d'Italia 77, 79, 89 (Rome, 1936–42), 1: no. 15, pp. 20 ff.

[152] See above, note 129.

[153] Müller, *Documenti,* no. x, pp. 11–13.

oped in the Crusader states, traveled to Byzantium some ninety years later, and became generalized in the eastern Mediterranean, including Egypt, in the course of the thirteenth century.

III. Trading with Muslims

Regarding Byzantine trade with the Muslims during the period of the Crusades, the available information is sporadic and can perhaps best be understood in the light of what has already been said regarding the institutional and structural changes in the conditions of trade in the Byzantine Empire and in the eastern Mediterranean generally.[154] Quite as was the case with Western merchants, the ideology of Holy War did not interrupt trade between the Byzantines and the Muslims; the opposite in fact was the case with Western merchants,[155] whose presence and business in Egypt increased in the course of the twelfth and thirteenth centuries, with a short interruption for a few years after 1187. Byzantine trade with Egypt continued in the course of the twelfth century, as we know from the testimony of Benjamin of Tudela,[156] as well as from a few narrative and documentary sources such as the affair regarding the piratical activities of Guglielmo Grasso and his fellow corsairs. However, S. Goitein's statement that the Geniza documents show a shift of importance, suggesting an increased presence of Western merchants relative to the Byzantines, must stand.

Some other observations may also be made. The relations of the Byzantines with Muslim powers had always had a strong political and military component, which overwhelmed private and commercial relations, existent but difficult to discern in the sources. The statement has been made by M. Canard with regard to the tenth century.[157] It remains true in the twelfth century and then again in the second half of the thirteenth and the fourteenth century, for the Byzantines not only had political and ceremonial relations with the Muslim rulers of Egypt, but also considered themselves and were considered by others as having a special role to play in the protection of the Christian populations of the Egyptian state. As a result, virtually all of the commercial contacts that are visible to us from Byzantine or Muslim sources appear in the context of political relations. It is primarily the Geniza documents that show an ongoing commercial activity of the Byzantines in the eleventh and twelfth centuries that is quite independent of official exchanges of embassies.

---

[154] On the topic generally, cf. S. Labib, "Egyptian Commercial Policy in the Middle Ages," in Cook, *Studies in the Economic History of the Middle East* (as above, note 122), 63–77, and idem, *Handelsgeschichte Ägyptens im Spätmittelalter, 1171–1517*, Vierteljahrschrift für Sozial- und Wirtschaftsgeschichte Beihefte 46 (Wiesbaden, 1965).

[155] D. Jacoby, "Les Italiens en Égypte aux XIIe et XIIIe siècles: Du comptoir à la colonie?" in *Coloniser au Moyen Âge*, ed. M. Balard and A. Ducellier (Paris, 1995), 78 ff.

[156] Benjamin bar Jonah of Tudela, *The Itinerary of Benjamin of Tudela*, trans. M. Adler, A. Asher, ed. M. Singer (Malibu, Calif., 1993), 70.

[157] M. Canard, "Deux épisodes des relations diplomatiques arabo-byzantines au Xe siècle," in idem, *Byzance et les musulmans du Proche Orient* (London, 1973), no. XII, p. 51. On trade see, among others, P. von Sivers, "Taxes and Trade in the Arab Thugur, 750–962/133–351," *Journal of the Economic and Social History of the Orient* 25 (1982): 71–99.

An interesting mention of Byzantine merchants in the early twelfth century shows them having quite a prominent position in Alexandria. The information comes from Orderic Vitalis, who notes, in 1102, the presence in Cairo of merchants from Constantinople, *multimodis mercimoniis*. He says that, according to the laws of the people (or of nations—*leges gentium*), they paid the required taxes and stayed there for some time. They were very rich, and during their stay they visited churches, the poor Christians, and the Latin captives who had been brought to Cairo after the fall of Ramleh. They are credited with persuading Alexios I to blackmail the sultan into releasing Arpin of Bourges, under the threat that otherwise he, Alexios, would "have all the Egyptian factors and mercenaries in the whole Empire of Constantinople arrested" ("omnes Babilonicos institores et stipendiarios per totum imperium Constantinopolitanum comprehendi iuberet").[158] According to this account, Byzantine merchants seem to have been visiting Cairo in a routine fashion, staying for certain periods of time; they paid commercial duties, and their movements, at least within the city, were not restricted. Anna Komnene mentions that the emperor heard of the imprisonment of many famous Crusader knights and sent "a certain Vardales" and gave him letters to the sultan along with a great deal of money.[159] The phrase τινὰ Βαρδαλῆν suggests that this was not a prominent courtier and may, indeed, have been a merchant.

In the course of the twelfth century, trade with Egypt seems to have been connected, to some extent, with political relations intimately related to the Crusades: the clearest example is the combined ambassadorial and trade mission to Saladin in 1192, which had the unhappy end that we have mentioned.[160] Its main purpose had been diplomatic, while trade (and gift exchange) played an important but secondary role.

There were also changes in the commercial relations between Byzantines and Muslims during the period in question. The Fourth Crusade reoriented the trade of the Byzantines (the Empire of Nicaea) with the Muslims. Relations with Egypt were interrupted. Very few embassies (I count two) are attested from the Empire of Nicaea to Egypt, and their object was either ceremonial or unknown to us.[161] There are no indications anywhere of continuing trade relations with Egypt; the inward-looking policy of the Nicene emperors and the sumptuary laws passed by John III Vatatzes[162] would suggest that the absence of information is not a matter of chance but reflects the reality of very limited relations. On the other hand, political contacts with the sultanate of Konya were frequent, and, although there is again very limited information about trade relations, one may assume that they existed; their extent is impossible to recover. In the late twelfth century, there had been an active trade between the sultanate of Rum and Constantinople, through the Black Sea.[163] But we have little information regarding Black Sea commerce between 1204 and 1261. We find here Venetians and Turks, with the

---

[158] Orderic Vitalis, 5.351–52. Arpin may have been the prior of Charité-sur-Loire: ibid., p. 350 n. 1. Albert of Aix attributes Arpin's release to a Byzantine knight: RHC, HOcc 4:594.

[159] *Alexiade* 11.7.3 (ed. Leib, 3:33); cf. Dölger, *Regesten*, no. 1216.

[160] Ibn al-Athīr also mentions Greeks, along with "Franks," in Acre in 1187: RHC, HOrient, vol. 1 (Paris, 1872), 689.

[161] Dölger, *Regesten*, nos. 1713a (1226) and 1763a (after 13 Aug. 1238).

[162] Dölger, *Regesten*, no. 1777 (early 1243).

[163] See above, 184, during the reigns of Andronikos I and Alexios III.

Empire of Trebizond fighting to retain some control. Trade with Constantinople would have bypassed the Nicene Empire. The sultans of Rum had developed a very significant trade network including central Anatolia and the ports of the southern coasts and the Black Sea coast, cemented by the capture of Sinope (1214) and Attaleia (1207) and the establishment of a Seljukid protectorate in Sudak in 1225.[164] How much this commercial flourishing involved the Empire of Nicaea is not certain; it has been suggested that commercial relations between Nicaea and Konya increased after the Mongol invasion of Asia Minor in 1243.[165]

What is certain is that at least at one point, at a time of famine in the Seljuk state, there were massive exports of grain, sheep, goats, oxen, and other foodstuffs from Nicaea to the Seljuks; according to Gregoras, all the wealth of the Turks, in gold, silver, precious textiles, and other luxury objects, was drained into the coffers of both the state and private individuals.[166] The export of wheat, forbidden in Byzantium for centuries,[167] seems to have been entirely free in this instance.

With the recovery of Constantinople, there was, once again, a political and to some degree economic reorientation toward Egypt. Of primary importance to the Mamluks, and also important for the nexus of relationships between the Byzantines and the Muslims, was the slave trade, which brought to Egypt slaves for its armies from the Crimea through Constantinople. Almost immediately after the recovery of the capital, Emperor Michael VIII and the Egyptian sultan Baibars exchanged embassies regarding the importation of slaves from the Black Sea.[168] Relations with Egypt went through ups and downs after 1264–65, but in 1281 there was, once again, a treaty between Michael VIII and the new sultan, Qalawun. This was the time when Michael VIII was engaged in full-scale hostilities with Charles of Anjou, and the original plan of the treaty incorporated a clause that would have guaranteed that Michael VIII would have denied free passage to anyone who wanted to go through his state to attack the Egyptians.[169]

The treaty of 1281, which has been published and analyzed by Canard, embodies some elements important to our topic. It should be read in conjunction with the treaty signed in 1290 between Qalawun and the Genoese,[170] and against the background of

---

[164] Cahen, "Le commerce anatolien," 94–95.

[165] Angold, *A Byzantine Government in Exile*, 115–16.

[166] Nikephoros Gregoras, *Byzantina historia*, ed. L. Schopen and I. Bekker, 3 vols. (Bonn, 1829–55), 1:42–43.

[167] Cf. Leo VI's novel 63, Noailles and Dain, pp. 231–33 (but it does not mention grain specifically; it deals with punishment of export of *kekolymena* generally).

[168] George Pachymeres, *Relations historiques*, ed. A. Failler (Paris, 1984), 234; cf. 243, relations with Nogai. Gregoras (Bonn ed.), 1:101–2, makes the explicit connection with the Egyptian need to sail to the northern coast of the Black Sea once a year, to procure slaves. Cf. Dölger, *Regesten*, nos. 1902–4 (Nov. 1261–Nov. 1262); M. Canard, "Le traité de 1281 entre Michel Paléologue et le Sultan Qala'un," *Byzantion* 10 (1935): 669–80.

[169] Canard, "Le traité," 679. Canard thinks that this clause was dropped because Charles of Anjou reached an agreement with Qalawun. It may be noted that Michael VIII, despite a treaty with Baibars in 1261, renewed in 1267, had undertaken the obligation of joining a crusade against Egypt in 1274–76: D. J. Geanakoplos, *Emperor Michael Palaeologus and the West: A Study in Byzantine-Latin Relations* (Cambridge, Mass., 1959), 285–94.

[170] Latin text published by Antoine Isaac Sylvestre de Sacy, *Notices et extraits des manuscrits de la Bibliothèque du Roi* (Paris, 1827), 33–52 (p. 42); 33, 40: reciprocal vs. simple guarantee of shipwrecked goods; p. 38 on the goods of merchants dying abroad. The Arabic text is translated by P. M. Holt, "Qalawun's Treaty with Genoa in 1290," *Der Islam* 57 (1980): 101–8.

other treaties signed between the Egyptians and the maritime cities of Italy in the course of the thirteenth century. Such a reading reveals the following. The treaty of 1281 includes reciprocal clauses guaranteeing the free access of the merchants of both countries to the markets of both countries, against payment of the appropriate dues. Such a clause is usual in all treaties of the period.[171] Other clauses, which had been general in the Mediterranean since the thirteenth century, include the statement that neither state would take reprisals against the merchants of the other for piratical activities undertaken in its territorial waters or by people who claimed to be its subjects; reprisals could only be taken against the individuals guilty of the act of piracy.[172] A clause that is unique to this document has to do with the right of the Byzantines to buy off Christian slaves and the right of freed Christian slaves to sail to the Byzantine Empire. The treaty allows the Egyptians to export Byzantine wheat: an interesting clause because the Palaiologan emperors tried mightily to restrict the export of Byzantine wheat by Western merchants: in the treaty of 1265 with Venice, export was permitted only after its price in Constantinople was under 50 hyperpyra per kentenarion, which rose to 100 hyperpyra in the treaty of 1277, while treaties with the Genoese allowed export only after specific imperial permission.[173] The reciprocal privilege allows Byzantine merchants to buy thoroughbred horses in the Egyptian possessions. The principle of free access to markets and merchandise extends even to the controlled wheat trade.

On the other hand, this treaty lacks the very detailed provisions regarding residence, the payment of duties, exemption from forced purchases, relations with customs officials, relations with the fisc (what happens to the property of foreign merchants dying in the state), and relations between individuals (resolution of private disputes and debts) that appear in the treaties between the Italian maritime states and Egypt or Byzantium. What this suggests is that the commercial relations between Egypt and the Byzantines, which we know existed,[174] were nowhere nearly as extensive as those of the Italian merchants and these two states. Thus the same general principles of trade existed between the Byzantines, the Christian merchants, and the Muslims (and similarly between the Egyptians and Byzantine and Western merchants), but the realities of trade were that Byzantine relations with Egypt were much more heavily political than economic/commercial in nature.

What distinguishes Michael VIII's treaty with Qalawun from most others is the insistence of the Egyptians to have freedom of access to the Black Sea area ("le pays de

[171] Cf., e.g., Tafel and Thomas, *Urkunden*, 3:68 (treaty between Michael VIII and Venice, 1265); cf. ibid., 141–43, 146 (treaty of 1277). Similar though not identical provisions in the Arab text of the treaty between Genoa and Qalawun in 1290: Holt, "Qalawun's Treaty," 106.

[172] Canard, "Le traité," 677–80. There is, however, nothing on shipwreck, which, on the contrary, appears in both Venetian-Byzantine treaties and treaties between the Egyptians and Western maritime cities. See, for example, Tafel and Thomas, *Urkunden*, 3:73, 144 (with Byzantium, 1265, 1277), and 2:338–39, 484–85 (Venetian-Egyptian treaties of 1238 and 1254). Cf. Holt, "Qalawun's Treaty," 102.

[173] A. Laiou, *Constantinople and the Latins: The Foreign Policy of Andronicus II, 1282–1328* (Cambridge, Mass., 1972), 65, 73; eadem, "The Byzantine Economy in the Mediterranean Trade System," in eadem, *Gender, Society and Economic Life in Byzantium* (Hampshire, 1992), no. VII, 213. On the grain trade see also J. Chrysostomides, "Venetian Commercial Privileges under the Palaeologi," *StVen* 12 (1970): 267–356.

[174] See, for example, Bertolotto, *Nuova serie*, 521 (ca. 1290), and Theodore Metochites, *AASS*, Nov. 4: 672.

Sudaq"), for the specific reason of buying slaves, with the proviso that they not be Christian slaves. This was, in fact, the major interest of the Egyptians in the Byzantine Empire and the principal reason why this treaty was concluded. And it was intimately connected with the politics surrounding the crusading movement as it developed after the Fourth Crusade, that is, in this specific case, with the plans of Charles of Anjou and the fate of the last remaining outposts of the kingdom of Acre.

In their formal aspects, that is, in the matter of treaties and official agreements, Byzantine trade relations with Egypt remained connected with political concerns and with the concerns of the Byzantine emperors for the non-Latin Christians of the East. This was so in the late thirteenth century and remained so in 1348/49, in the negotiations of John VI Kantakouzenos with Malik Nasir Hasan, in which the security of Byzantine merchants in Egypt is embedded in discussions regarding the Christians of the Mamluk empire.[175] While the formal relations were embedded in politics, the general conditions and mechanisms were similar to those between Byzantine and Western Christians, following the general lines elaborated in the twelfth century.

After 1291 and the fall of Acre, we know that there were repeated calls in the West for a boycott of trade with Egypt. This did not involve Byzantium; on the contrary, some of the plans for a boycott of Egyptian trade included, as a side effect of the eventual rearrangements in the eastern Mediterranean, the reconquest of Byzantium by the Crusaders.[176] Interestingly, however, there were, in the early fourteenth century, some vague and some not-so-vague mutterings in Byzantium against the continuation of good relations with Egypt: vague in the comments of Theodore Metochites, who, in his Oration to the neo-martyr St. Michael, somewhat sheepishly and defensively explains that the Byzantine emperor was in the habit of sending frequent embassies and friendly messages to the "impious ruler . . . not because of some need," since they were not contiguous neighbors and thus did not have the close contact of contiguous neighbors, but because the emperor always did everything in his power for the protection and well-being of Christians in the Mamluk possessions.[177] In a much more explicit manner, George Pachymeres criticized in no uncertain terms the policy of Michael VIII that "opened the way" to the Egyptians toward the "Scythians," that is, the Cumans of the Black Sea. He

---

[175] *Ioannis Cantacuzeni eximperatoris historiarum libri quattuor,* ed. L. Schopen, 3 vols. (Bonn, 1828–29), 3:90–104; cf. M. Canard, "Une lettre du Sultan Malik Nâsir Hasan à Jean VI Cantacuzène (760/1349)," in idem, *Byzance et les musulmans du Proche Orient* (as above, note 157), no. x, 29–52.

[176] This includes the early plans of Marino Sanudo, ca. 1306–12: A. Laiou, "Marino Sanudo Torsello, Byzantium and the Turks: The Background to the Anti-Turkish League of 1332–1334," *Speculum* 45 (1970): 374–92. On the crusading plans of this period, see S. Schein, *Fideles Crucis: The Papacy, the West, and the Recovery of the Holy Land (1274–1314)* (Oxford, 1991).

[177] *AASS,* Nov. 4: 672–73. Dölger thinks the embassy in question may have been the one dated 1311–13: *Regesten,* no. 2326. This text also provides important information regarding Byzantine trade relations with Egypt. According to Metochites, Alexandria is always full of people—among them, Byzantines—who go there for trade and other reasons (676D). At the time of the martyrdom of St. Michael, there were, in the city, both Byzantine ambassadors and Byzantine merchants (673A, 676E). The ambassadors seem to have sailed on a Byzantine ship, for Michael, a captive in Alexandria, tried to escape on this ship by disguising himself as one of the passengers or crew who were to sail back to Constantinople (673C). This incidental information suggests that even in the early 14th century there were Byzantine ships sailing these seas and that the Italian control of shipping in the eastern Mediterranean was not absolute.

connected that with the Egyptian offensive against the last remaining Crusader possessions in Palestine (1268–91); he lamented the fall of these possessions; and he ended
this narrative with the statement: "This is the profit to Christendom wrought by our
imprudence and our ungoverned impulsive actions and appetites."[178] Pachymeres,
clearly, would much rather have seen a Christian economic and political alliance that
would have kept the Egyptians out: something like the boycott advocated in Western
Europe. Thus, after a very long time, the Byzantines themselves connected the Crusades
and the fate of the Crusader states with the trading policies of the Byzantines and the
Muslims.

To the modern scholar, the connections between the crusading movement and the
Byzantine commercial relations with Christians and Muslims appear much more complex. The complexity is partly the result of the fact that with the Crusades the entire
political scene of the Middle East changed; and with the expansion of Italian merchants
the economics of the area changed as well. These are long-term phenomena, and there
is a broad and long-term connection between political and economic affairs. There are
also short-term and immediate connections between specific crusading efforts and matters affecting commerce, for example the grant of specific charters of privilege. I have
tried to focus on the phenomena that lie between the long term and the short term and
to point out some of the structural and institutional developments that may be considered to have occurred because of the Crusades wholly or, more often, in part. The development of exchange mechanisms and mechanisms of negotiation in Byzantium were
connected both to specific events, the Second and Third Crusades, and to the evolving
presence of Western merchants. The terms of trade with Christians and Muslims, in the
exemplar case of the law of salvage, have been seen to have evolved over the entire
eastern Mediterranean, in response to both political events and economic necessities,
the evolution starting in Byzantium and making the rounds of the Crusader states and
Egypt, becoming reinforced on the way. In the case of Byzantine trade relations with
the Muslims, the Crusades appear to have imposed two successive reorientations—and
political and economic affairs were closely intertwined. In sum, in my view, the Crusades
and the existence of the Crusader states played a much greater role than modern scholars
tend to allow, not only in the general patterns of trade in the eastern Mediterranean but
also in the conditions and mechanisms of trade between the Byzantines and the Muslims,
and especially between the Byzantines and the Western Christians.

[178] Ed. Failler, 241, 243; cf. *Georgii Pachymeris de Michaele et Andronico Palaeologis libri tredecem*, ed. I. Bekker,
2 vols. (Bonn, 1835), 2:87, 456–58. Cf. A. Laiou, "On Political Geography: The Black Sea of Pachymeres,"
in *The Making of Byzantine History*, ed. R. Beaton and C. Roueché (London, 1993), 110–11, 119.

Appendix
by Cécile Morrisson

1. Comparison of the Known Exchange Rates from the First Crusade (comments on pp. 169–70)

The exchange rate deduced from the *Gesta Francorum* (1 hyperpyron = 15 soldi = 180 deniers) is evidently one obtaining in an exceptional context (famine and the presence of a huge army). The intended coins are obviously, on the one hand, the hyperpyron, although the *Gesta* provides, to my knowledge, the only occurrence of the form *purpurati*.[1] The Crusaders may have coined this name by identifying hyperpyra with "imperial" coins, as *purpuratus* had primarily this meaning. On the other hand, which deniers the author of the *Gesta* may have had in mind is not clear. His South Italian origin could have made him allude to the deniers from Pavia, Lucca, Venice, and Rouen,[2] which are attested there by textual and archaeological evidence in the late eleventh century. Or he might simply have alluded to the various French and Italian deniers that the Crusaders brought with them.

Little is known of the silver fineness of these,[3] and we have to be content with mentioning figures for royal French deniers of the late eleventh century. The deniers Parisis

The tentative estimates of coins' real values given here are, it must be stressed, based on average values of weights and metal contents and should not be taken as absolute values but as indications of order of magnitude. The reliability of the figures is even less for Western denominations, namely deniers, than it is for Byzantine coins because of the great variety of issuing authorities, the scattered nature of the data, the virtual absence in the 12th century of surviving monetary specifications, and the small number of available analyses. I am most grateful to Marc Bompaire for advice on Western European numismatics and for communication of his and Maria Guerra's forthcoming article (M. Bompaire and M. Guerra, "Analyse de monnaies françaises du XIe siècle: Le problème du zinc," in *Actes du XIIe Congrès international de numismatique, Berlin, 1997*, ed. B. Kluge). The results obtained for silver fineness are not commented upon there but show great variety in time and space.

[1] The only reference in Du Cange, *Glossarium mediae et infimae Latinitatis* (Paris, 1937–38), is to the *Gesta* and its various versions or compilations. This source and coin name are not mentioned by B. Koutava-Delivoria, "Les *chichata*, les *protocharaga* et la réforme monétaire d'Alexis I Comnène," *RBN* 141 (1995): 13–36.

[2] See L. Travaini, *La monetazione nell'Italia normanna* (Rome, 1995), 362–94, esp. 394; J.-M. Martin, "Le monete d'argento nell'Italia meridionale del secolo XII secondo i documenti di archivio," *Bollettino di numismatica* 6–7 (Jan.–Dec. 1986): 85–96, at 86; F. Dumas and J. Pilet-Lemière, "La monnaie normande, Xe–XIIe siècle. Le point de la recherche en 1987," in *Les Mondes Normands (VIIIe–XIIe s.): Actes du IIe Congrès International d'Archéologie Médiévale, Caen 2–4 octobre 1987*, ed. H. Galinie (Caen, 1989), 125–31.

[3] The denier of Pavia in the early 12th century (ca. 1102) contained some 0.5 g fine silver, according to C. Brambilla quoted by C. Cipolla, "Currency Depreciation in Medieval Europe," *EcHistR* 15 (1963): 413–22, at 24. Such a *poids de fin* is very close to that of the contemporary denier Parisis that I use in the following estimates. One denier of Rouen of the late 11th century with a fineness of some 40–49% contained ca. 0.3–0.7 g (F. Dumas, "Les monnaies normandes (Xe–XIIe s.) avec un répertoire des trouvailles," *RN* 21 [1979]: 84–140, at 103).

of Philip I (1060–1108) were struck at 1/312 or 1/324 to the pound (1.30–1.26 g) and had a fineness of 40 percent.[4] Alexios I's hyperpyra, weighing ca. 4.30 g, are, according to the latest analyses,[5] some 82 percent fine. The comparison of these average intrinsic values, ± 3.74 g fine gold = 90.7–93.6 g fine silver,[6] entails a gold-silver ratio of 1:24 to 1:25, apparently excessive but understandable in the circumstances.

The rate of 1 "aureus" to 8 or 9 soldi (96–108 deniers) appears to be a more "normal" one. In fact, the contemporary Tripoli dinar had, like the other Fatimid dinars, a very high purity (ca. 97%).[7] Reckoning a denier with some 0.5 g silver fine, the comparison becomes: ± 4.07 g fine gold = 48–54 g fine silver, entailing a gold-silver ratio of 1:11.8 or 1:13.2, more usual in an eastern Mediterranean context.[8] Michael Metcalf is therefore right when he comments on this famous statement of Raymond of Aguilers and concludes that "eight or nine shillings does not sound in any way extortionate as an exchange-rate against the Islamic gold dinar."[9]

2. Intrinsic Value of Coins Exchanged during the Second Crusade (comments on pp. 170–75)

The exchange rate in the Balkans of 1 stamenon to 5 deniers, in terms of the intrinsic values involved, implies equating ca. 0.27 g fine silver in the Byzantine stamenon[10] to the 2 or 1.9 g represented by 5 deniers Parisis of the time.[11] The denier's real value was thus grossly underestimated (by about 7 to 8 times). As A. Laiou points out (p. 173), "any exchange rate that quoted the billon trachy in multiples of the denier Parisis was bound to be excessive."

The other equivalence between 1 mark of silver and 3 hyperpyra (144 stamena rated

---

[4] J. Lafaurie, "Numismatique: Des Carolingiens aux Capétiens," *CahCM* 13 (1970): 117–36, at 136. The figures given by Lafaurie imply some 0.5–0.52 g fine silver in a denier.

[5] C. Morrisson, et al., *L'or monnayé*, vol. 1, *Purification et altérations. De Rome à Byzance*, Cahiers Ernest-Babelon 2, CNRS (Paris, 1985), 154 and 232.

[6] Estimating at 87.2% the fine content of a hyperpyron weighing ca. 4.3 g (containing 86.4% Au and 10% Ag reckoned as equivalent to 0.84% Au at a 1:12 gold-silver ratio).

[7] According to reliable specific gravity measurements. See A. S. Ehrenkreutz, "Studies in the Monetary History of the Near East in the Middle Ages—the Standard of Fineness of Some Types of Dinars," *Journal of the Economic and Social History of the Orient* 2 (1959): 128–61, and W. A. Oddy, "The Gold Contents of Fatimid Coins Reconsidered," in *Metallurgy in Numismatics*, vol. 1, ed. D. M. Metcalf and W. A. Oddy (London, 1980), 98–118.

[8] The calculations of the gold-silver ratio and the identification of its nature (ratio for unminted metal, market ratio for coins, etc.) are, as is well known, tricky. See A. M. Watson, "Back to Gold—and Silver," *EcHistR* 20.1 (1967): 1–34, at 33. In what follows I have relied on Watson's results (23–29). Neither the details of his calculations nor their sources could be given in his article.

[9] Metcalf, *Coinage of the Crusades* (above, note 65), 12.

[10] A "billon trachy" of some 4.45–4.30 g with a 6.3% silver content; see Hendy and Charles, above, note 84. The average fineness is that of Manuel's first and second coinages.

[11] Louis VII's (1137–80) deniers were struck at 1/240 or 1/250 to the mark (1.01–0.97 g) and had a fineness of ca. 39.8%, according to Lafaurie, "Numismatique," 136 n. 6.

at 48 to the hyperpyron) implied the following approximate intrinsic values: 234.4 g fine silver[12] $= 10.86$ g fine gold.[13] This entails an excessive gold-silver ratio of 1:26.

The rate in Constantinople of 1 stamenon to less than 2 deniers amounts to equating the Byzantine billon coin containing 0.28–0.26 g fine silver with two Western silver ones containing 0.8–0.76 g silver. It implies overvaluating the stamenon nearly three times (2.8–2.9) and agrees with M. Hendy's conclusion, on a different basis, that "the overvaluation will have been something in the order of 2 1/2 times the bullion value of the trachy."[14]

The other Constantinopolitan exchange rate of 396 stamena for 1 mark of silver leads to roughly the same result: 396×0.27 g $= 106.9$ g, being considered equivalent to the 234.4 g fine silver in a mark, which implies an overvaluation of the stamenon of some 2.1 times.

The more favorable rating of the mark may be attributed to its guaranteed, or easily assayable, fineness and to its mere bulk (important absolute value) compared to retail exchanges dealing with small sums in all sorts of deniers of varying fineness.

3. Intrinsic Value of Coins Exchanged during the Third Crusade and the Exchange Rates (comments on pp. 175–76)

The 1190 treaty probably involved the Cologne mark, which was slightly lighter and contained some 231 g of highly pure silver. The rate of 5.5 hyperpyra for an assayed (examinatum)[15] mark amounts to equating some 19.7 g[16] fine gold to 231 g fine silver and implies a gold-silver ratio of 1:11.8.[17]

The difference between examinata and non examinata (the latter rated 1.8 times less than the former, at 3 hyperpyra) seems at first very high, but must have incorporated an important premium for risk. Moreover, it is known that "all of the surviving German

---

[12] A Troyes mark with a weight of 244.7 g and a fineness of 12d in argent-le-roi (95.8%). If the mark were one of pure or nearly pure silver, the silver weight would be ca. 240 g and the ratio 1:21.87. The order of magnitude is the same.

[13] Manuel's hyperpyron with a weight of 4.3 g and a fineness of ca. 85% (84.2% Au and 12% Ag) would amount to 3.65 g fine (see above, note 5).

[14] M. F. Hendy and J. A. Charles, "The Production Techniques, Silver Content, and Circulation History of the Twelfth-Century Byzantine Trachy," in M. F. Hendy, The Economy, Fiscal Administration, and Coinage of Byzantium (Northampton, 1989), 18.

[15] "Examinatum" is clearly a technical word for assay. In the late 12th century, the mint of Melgueil, for instance, had two gardes: one in charge of the custody of dies and the other in charge of issag, i.e., the punch used to certify the testing of the ingots' fineness.

[16] Isaac II's hyperpyron with a weight of 4.3 g and a fineness of ca. 83.3% (82.2% Au and 14% Ag) would amount to 3.58 g fine (see above, note 5).

[17] Watson, "Back to Gold," 23: "before Europe returned to gold the ratio in most parts of Europe was generally between 9 and 10." See P. Spufford, Money and Its Use in Medieval Europe (Cambridge, 1988), table 2, p. 272.

ingots that have been analyzed have proved to be of various poor qualities of *argentum usuale.*"[18]

The official value of 120 stamena to the hyperpyron equates the ca. 12 g silver contained in the now debased billon coin[19] with ca. 3.58 g fine gold. The implicit gold-silver ratio is three times less than the one derived from the exchange rate of the assayed mark and three times less as well than the one assumed to have prevailed in the eastern Mediterranean. This is a good index of the persisting overvaluation (partly token nature) of the billon denomination.

In 1199 the decreasing value of 184 stamena to the hyperpyron deduced from Pisan documents equates ca. 14.7 g silver with 3.6 g fine gold. The implicit gold-silver ratio is 21 percent higher than the 1190 one and confirms the downward trend of the stamenon overvaluation emphasized above (p. 175).

It should be pointed out that comparisons between the metal contents of the stamenon and the hyperpyron as well as the implicit derived ratios are very unreliable for two reasons: first, the uncertainty of metrological figures, but above all the limits certainly fixed to the exchange of stamena into hyperpyra, as is always the case with token coinages.[20]

---

[18] Spufford, *Money,* 221, quoting A. [von] Loehr, "Probleme der Silberbarren," *NZ* 64 (1931): 101–9, with illustrations. The figures given by von Loehr (p. 106) for ingots of the early 13th century vary between 85.4% and 79.8% fine.

[19] Assuming 120 stamena of 4–3 g with a fineness of 2.5% (0.1 to 0.07 g fine silver), equating a hyperpyron of 3.58 g. Hendy and Charles, "Byzantine Trachy"; T. Bertelè, *Numismatique byzantine* (Wetteren, 1978), 77.

[20] To the observation of Pegolotti mentioned above (176 n. 105) might be added the fact that the Nea Logarike, according to my interpretation at least, only accepted the (electrum) aspron trachy and not the stamenon in payment of taxes (C. Morrisson, *Monnaie et finances à Byzance* [Aldershot, 1994], no. VI, 460–64).

VENICE AS A CENTRE OF TRADE AND OF ARTISTIC PRODUCTION IN THE THIRTEENTH CENTURY

The thirteenth century is a period of great importance for the history of Venice, and particulary for its economic development. In the course of this century Venice established an extensive trade system, which included the eastern Mediterranean and Italy, and extended to the Atlantic and the North Sea. Her merchants functioned as middle-men between the eastern Mediterranean and the west, both in terms of economic exchange and to some extent in art and culture [1].

The thirteenth century also presents considerable interest for the artistic development of Venice. It is marked by the extension of Byzantine influence on Venetian art, and by the penetration of western elements into the Byzantine tradition. Venice, in this period, is a center where both western European and Byzantine currents are present, as can be seen in painting, in miniatures, and even in the work of Venetian goldsmiths. Venice functions to some extent as a trasmitter of the Byzantine style to the West, and to Dalmatia. The various elements which influence Venetian art will result in the creation of a Venetian style as reflected, for example, in the frescoes of San Zan Degolà of the last quarter of the century, and as seen, in the next century, in the work of Paolo Veneziano [2].

The many aspects of the development of Venice as a major commercial center and as a center of artistic production cannot all be treated here. I will, therefore, concentrate on Venetian commercial relations with the Levant, and especially with the Byzantine Empire in an effort to offer an analysis of the prevailing forms of exchange and dominance; secondly, I should like to discuss the development of the minor arts in Venice in connection with the creation of a commercial empire.

The expansion of Venetian merchants in the Levant began in the late eleventh century, and developed in the course of the twelfth. Their first field of enterprise was the Byzantine Empire, with which Venice had long had political, economic and cultural ties. During the twelfth century, as the Venetian economy expanded, and as western European markets were formed that could absorb some eastern products, the presence of Venetian merchants in the Empire became consolidated. By the middle of the century, there were Venetians in Constantinople, Thessalonica, Almyros, Thebes. Corinth, and Sparta, and in fewer numbers in Arta, Corfu, Rodosto, Lemnos, Adramyttion and Smyrna. Some of these cities functioned as centers for the further activities of the Venetians, to the Latin Kingdom of Jerusalem, Antioch, Syria, Damietta, and Alexandria, sometimes by way of Crete [3].

From Constantinople and Alexandria, and, to a lesser extent, from the Latin Kingdom of Jerusalem, the Venetians brought back the luxury products of the eastern trade; pepper, spices, and precious stones. However, just as it is true that for Venetian trade in general these items had no greater importance than the humbler commodities of salt and grain, so it must be pointed out that the Levant trade dealt in bulky and less precious commodities (grain and oil, especially) as well as in spices. During the 12th century there is a slow infiltration of Venetian merchants into the local, internal trade of the Byzantine Empire, a phenomenon whose extent and importance has not been adequately studied. Indicative in this matter is not only the significant number of Venetian traders settled in the cities mentioned here (although the numbers of 10,000, 20,000 or 30,000 Venetians attested in Constantinople in 1171 are surely exaggerated), not only the fact that Venetians of poor and humble extraction could make great fortunes in this internal trade, but also the fact that when the Venetians received a confirmation of their original commercial privileges in 1198, the list of towns in which they were allowed to trade without paying customs duties included provincial cities of the interior, like Janina, Ochrid, Castoria, Zagora, Veroia, whose only importance can have been for the internal trade of the Byzantine Empire [4].

The conquest of the Byzantine Empire in 1204 by the participants of the fourth Crusade was a dramatic event which marked an important stage in the history of Venice. She acquired 3/8 of Constantinople and, theoretically, 3/8 of the dismembered Byzantine Empire. She could now trade in these areas without fear that her commercial privileges might be withdrawn. Her merchants penetrated into the Black Sea, with its vast grain production, the last major area from which the Byzantines had excluded westerners up to that time. The Venetians also had freedom of trade in the Latin Empire, in the Despotate of Epirus and in the Peloponnese, where their presence was pervasive.

Equally important was the acquisition by Venice of several islands of the Aegean, part of Nigroponte, the ports of Modon and Coron, and Crete; these became Venetian colonies, with a special economic significance [5].

Thereafter, Venetian commercial expansion and settlement in the East was rapid, and her economy entered an upward trend which became stronger from the middle of the thirteenth century until the middle of the fourteenth; this is the time of the formation of what has been called an « impero senza terre », a commercial empire unique in the Middle Ages. Her commercial relations with the Italian cities developed, helped by a series of agreements with Padova, Treviso, Ferrara; her uneasy domination over the eastern coast of the Adriatic was established. Her merchants reached India and China, while in the second half of the thirteenth century her economic and commercial activities extended to the western Mediterranean and the Atlantic, to Sicily, the Balearic Islands, Catalonia, the Languedoc, Provence, France, Flanders, and England. To the western European countries Venice re-exported the luxury merchandise of the Far East and of Syria and Alexandria, as well as the products of her own colonial lands (for example, the wine of Crete) and imported mostly cloth, to be sent to the East and to Italian cities. Her role was primarily that of a middleman [6].

Venice's commercial position in the Mediterranean, which was particularly strong in the eastern part, was challenged only by Genoa with which Venice fought two major wars in the course of the thirteenth century, wars whose causes are to be found in the commercial rivalries of the two cities. Her economic activities were safeguarded by a government which took strong protectionist measures, and controlled navigation and trade along the main routes to the Levant and to Flanders [7].

The Venetian predominance in the eastern Mediterranean was so secure that it was only partly affected by the reconquest of Constantinople by the Byzantines in 1261. This was followed by the return of the Genoese in these areas and Venice had to share the Aegean with Genoa. But she retained her colonies in the Aegean and in Constantinople, and her commercial activity increased considerably in the second half of the thirteenth century. This was due in part to the fact that western Europe had developed active markets, capable of absorbing the products of the East and partly to the fact that the Mongol domination of Central Asia and the Far East created conditions favorable to communications and trade.

In the second half of the thirteenth century, Venetian and Genoese merchants were settled in various parts of the eastern Mediterranean: Constantinople was an important port for both, while Tana and Soldaia for Venice, Caffa for Genoa, were the main outles in the Black sea. Both cities had merchant colonies in Cyprus, Cilician Armenia and Acre, until its fall to the Egyptians in 1291. Venice, moreover, preserved her colonies in the Aegean, and an active trade with Alexandria [8].

In the late thirteenth century and after, the eastern Mediterranean exhibits some of the characteristics of an international market, organized and run primarily by the Italian merchants. There is an evident division of labor: the eastern Mediterranean exported to the West food and raw materials, and acted as an entrepôt for the luxury products of the East, while it imported manufactured articles from the West. The Italian merchants were the main intermediares of the exchange. They dominated the information mechanisms and the currency transactions; they had virtually sole access to both the eastern and the western markets; with their ships, they dominated both communications and trade [9]. Venice which, in the late twelfth century, had increased her naval capacity to such an extent that she could place 100 ships at the disposal of her Byzantine allies, sent each year about 30-50 galleys on organized trade ventures, while the so-called free navigation, carried out on larger and slower ships, used in the early fifteenth century about 300 *nave* and 3000 smaller ships [10].

These developments had a profound effect on the economy and society of the eastern Mediterranean, primarily on the Byzantine lands where the presence of Venetian - and Genoese - merchants as pervasive. The

14

local economy of exchange was active, but it was increasingly secondary to the main commercial activities which were the preserve of the Italian merchants. The Byzantine merchants engaged primarily in retail activities, or in the small-scale trade which, carrying to the Italian colonies food-stuffs, wax, and other commodities, fed the larger trade whose ultimate destination was Genoa or Venice. Thus, there was a class of Byzantine merchants, and it was in close contact with the Italians both at the commercial level, and at the level of finance; one has only to look at the accounts of the Venetian banker Giacomo Badoer, in early fifteenth-century Constantinople to find a number of Byzantine bankers with constant transactions with the Italians. But close as the relationships were, they were not those of equals: the dominant role of the Italians is clear [11].

The presence of Venetian and other Italian merchants in this area, then, resulted in the development of an economy of exchange which was active at all levels; but it was also concomitant with a substitution of products and means of exchange and with the creation of new commodities markets. Thus, the Byzantine trader who reached Alexandria in the twelfth century, and appears in the Jewish documents of the Cairo Geniza, is replaced by the Venetian merchant [12]. The Byzantine *hyperpyron* in Venetian possessions becomes a money of account, whose value is determined by that of the Venetian or other western currency. Byzantine cloth manufacturing declines, because of the import of European cloth. And even Byzantine production in the minor arts is to some degree replaced by Venetian products.

One case of substitution, the case of glass manufacturing, is particularly clear. It is well known that before 1204 the Byzantine Empire had a highly developed glass industry, some of whose products may be seen in the Tesoro of San Marco. Apart from Constantinople, the city of Corinth was also a center of glass manufacturing in the 11th-12th centuries. Nicetas Choniates describes the city as a very wealthy one, with two ports, into which sailed ships from Italy and the Levant, and where products from East and West were exchanged [13]. The excavations of the American School of Classical Studies at Athens have shown that Corinth also had an extensive glass industry which produced glassware of very fine quality and in a great variety of patterns [14]. It is very likely that such glass was exported to Venice in the course of the 12th century, although it does not appear in the documents; the lack of documentation is not surprising, since the sources are generally not very informative about the kinds of merchandise carried on Venetian ships. In the last few decades, there have been found, in the areas around Venice and Friuli, glass fragments dating from the 12th through the 14th centuries, which are identifiable as being of the types prevalent in Corinth [15]; and they are similar to glass found in Dalmatia, Apulia, Bosnia, Hungary and elsewhere. A. Gasparetto has suggested that we are dealing here with the transferring of techniques and patterns from Corinth (and, indirectly, from Egypt and Syria) to western Europe and the Balkans through the intermediary of Venice; and that this transfer is primarily due to the activities of merchants carrying the glass of Corinth to Venice and the glass of Venice to western Europe, and less to a possible migration of artisans. This theory is entirely plausible, for Venice had commercial relations with Dalmatia and Hungary from an early period, while her contacts with Germany, France and Flanders became massive in the second half of the 13th century. And her role in such trade was, precisely, that of a middleman, that is, she reexported eastern commodities in exchange for western products, especially cloth [16].

It should be added that Corinth declined both as a center of manufacture and as a city after the 12th century, and that this decline cannot be ascribed to the Norman invasion of 1147. The Normans raided the lower city, and took captive the richest men and the most buxom women, but did not, according to the sources, destroy the glass furnaces or abduct the artisans [17]. I would suggest that the decline is in great part due to the flourishing of the Venetian glass industry in the course of the 13th century. It is, perhaps, indicative of the new course of events that in the early fourteenth century we find a Venetian glassmaker working in Crete and Constantinople [18]. It is even more characteristic that in 1276 a glassmaker from Murano lists two big cases of « mojoli » of two different types, one for local consumption and one for export to the Romania [19]. If this phenomenon is widespread, (and this is suggested by the existence of a «type» of glass specifically for the East) then we have a case of substitution: a native industry in Greece is replaced by imports from the West, in this case Venice. Of course the glass industry is also a branch of the minor arts, and therein lies its interest for our topic.

In Venice's commercial system, the colonies played a particularly important role. They functioned both as strategic points and as centers from which local products were exported. From Modon and Coron Venice received the products of the Peloponnese, primarily silk, purple, dye, wax, and grain [20]. But the merchants also continued to export from here works of art, long after 1204. This may be seen in a maritime loan contract made in Coron, on June 22, 1291. It is a loan for 200 *hyperpyra*, between two Venetians; the exchange rate is stipulated at 20 « turonenses » per *hyperpyron*; but it is not to be repaid in cash, a fact which indicates that the *hyperpyron* was used here as a money of account, as was the case in Crete also. It is to be repaid in kind: 1,500 *libres* of wax will be delivered in Coron by September 8, 1291. Thus, the contract is essentially one of advance sale of merchandise, a far from unusual phenomenon in the Mediterranean of the 13th-14th centuries, and in itself a kind of credit transaction. As security for the loan, Giacomo Trevisan, the borrower, offers 39 « columpnas marmoreas », of which one is «a capite fracta », 4 smaller columns (« palestratas »), 3 « platas planas », that is, unornamented plaques, and one « liium », which I take to be a « lilium », that is, an architectural ornament in the form of, or with fleurs de lys [21]. Clearly, the mortgage is taken from an ancient temple or a church; although it is difficult to see how anything but a large basilica could yield that many columns. In any case, this is not a simple mortgage. At the end of the elapsed time, the marble may be transported to Venice by the lender, but the borrower promises to be responsible for the transport fee, at the rate of 25 *solidi* per *hyperpyron* paid. Once in Venice, Matteo de Medio shall offer these columns for sale either to Marco Ghisi of Nigroponte, or to Marco Polo (who seem to act as Trevisan's representatives), for the sum borrowed and the fare, paid in Venetian currency. If the price of the marbles is higher than the loan, then the money must be deposited with one of the people mentioned above. Thus, we are dealing here with a case in which a Venetian merchant includes the export of spolia as part of his commercial activities.

The most important colony was the island of Crete. It was situated at a key point in the Mediterranean and had a multiple political, strategic, and economic significance. Along with Nigroponte, Modon, and Coron, Crete was one of the main points at which the Venetian fleet would congregate for attack, or to defend Venetian possessions in the Romania against the Genoese, the Byzantines, or the Turks. The island, with its production of grain, oil, wine, wool, and to a lesser extent, cotton, became an important center for the provisioning both of Venice and of the Venetian-held islands of the Aegean [22]. For this reason, Venice settled many of its subjects on the island from 1211 onwards, and held onto it tenaciously until 1669.

In terms of the overall commercial interests of Venice, Crete was a focal point. Documents and notarial records of the last quarter of the thirteenth century show that in this period Crete functioned as an important station in the long-distance trade with Alexandria and Syria. Merchandise from Alexandria (especially pepper and other spices) was collected here, and then exported to Venice. Crete was equally active as a center of exchange with Acre. After its fall, in 1291, ships sailed from Crete to Cyprus, or to lesser Armenia, and back, carrying to these areas some of the local produce (oil and wine) and tin, imported from the West. Along with spices, the ships that sailed to these areas brought back alum from Syria, to be used both in the Italian wool cloth industry and in the Venetian glass manufacturing. At a more local level, there are active exchanges between Crete. Nigroponte, Thessaly, the Peloponnese, and the islands of the Aegean [23].

Crete was also important to Venice for its own production, primarily grain, wine (which was re-exported to Flanders), wool, and eventtually sugar. The rather massive export of Cretan agricultural products to Venice had an effect both on the agricultural economy of the island and on its economy of exchange. Agricultural production was already commercialized in the late thirteenth century. The producers sold their merchandise, in small or larger quantities, to Venetian or other merchants who then exported it to Venice. A very common form of contract for agricultural products was that of advance sale, a kind of credit mechanism which ensured the commercialization of part at least of the harvest, allowed the concentration of crops into the hands of those with greater access to the international market, and resulted in the more rapid circulation of money [24].

The pull exercised by the needs of the Venetian commercial system also resulted in the development of trade within the island. This is primarily, but not exclusively, trade in agricultural products. But also, some cloth is sold, fake jewels, gold, silk, amber buttons, all from Venice, are exchanged within Crete. The large number of colleganza contracts made to trade within Crete, by land or by sea, testify to the existence of this internal trade.

Thus, the incorporation of Crete in the Venetian trade network resulted in the development of an active commercial life in the island, and in a certain urbanization. Trade here, as everywhere, also created the possibility of contact between various peoples and cultures. In Crete there were merchants from Venice, Genoa, Catalonia [25]. There were also the native Greeks, who participated to a large extent in the economic life of the island. They, too, owned shops in Candia, were active in trade and navigation, exchanged commodities with the Venetians, even held official positions in government. In the late thirteenth century, Cretan society was one in which Greeks and Venetians were in close contact, although the position of the Venetians was clearly dominant. It was also a society which was becoming urbanized and commercialized. And in this sense, it is not surprising that Crete, as the research of M. Cattapan has shown, also became a center of profound artistic symbiosis. There were Venetian painters in Crete already in the thirteenth century, and in much larger numbers in the fourteenth century. They worked alongside, and sometimes in cooperation with, the local Greek painters, and do not seem to have monopolized artistic production [26]. They painted in the Byzantine tradition, and their massive presence in Crete probably suggests that they created these works for dissemination throughout the eastern Mediterranean, where Crete was an important focus of Venetian trade in the thirteenth century and later [27].

The case of Crete sheds some light on the conditions that existed in the Eastern Mediterranean in that period. Venice created a network of exchange which quickened the economic life of some areas. She took advantage of existing markets and created new ones, sometimes by substituting western products for the products of local industry, sometimes indirectly, through the effect of the more rapid circulation of goods.

These developments, in turn, stimulated the production of art objects in Venice itself, a production which took place under specific conditions, closely tied to Venice's particular kind of commercial economy. The observations which follow will be limited to the minor arts which, by their nature, are connected with manufacturing and are, therefore, more susceptible to the influence of economic developments than are other kinds of art.

A first observation is, that Venice's most important industries—apart from shipbuilding—were, precisely, involved with the manufacturing of luxury items, and received their impetus from the export trade. Thus, in the statutes of the guild of the painters, particular and numerous provisions were made for those decorated objects (shield covers, saddles, etc.) which were manufactured specifically for the Levant (*de carevane*) [28]. The statutes of the *fiolarii*, the glass-makers, show how closely the development of the industry was connected to that of Venetian trade. Imports of raw materials from the East included alum and masses of broken glass which was melted and reused (there is mention of this in a treaty with Antioch in 1277) [29]. The import of foreign glass objects into Venice was strictly controlled, as was, after 1295, the export of technology. Masters of the art who had left Venice and worked in glass furnaces in other Italian cities (Treviso, Padua, Ferrara, Bologna, Mantua, Ravenna, Ancona, Vicenza) where banned from exercising their profession in Venice because, as the decree of the Major Council stated, their activities caused Venice to lose money, since merchants no longer came to the city to seek glass [30]. The statutes which governed the guild of the *cristellarii* (1284) gave voice to somewhat different concerns. Crystal was considered a precious substance in the Middle Ages, and its production was a luxury industry. The Venetians imported rock crystal from Switzerland, and fashioned it into bowls, reliquaries, crosses, candelabras. Thus, the *cristellarii* manufactured objects which were more expensive and rarer than those of the glass industry; the primary concern, therefore, was to regulate the availability of raw materials (hence the provisions limiting the amount of crystal one might buy, and provisions which tried to prevent the monopolisation of crystal, jasper and emery by particular masters), and to ensure the quality of the final product. It was forbidden to the *cristellarii* to manufacture fake crystal out of glass, and it was forbidden to everyone to buy such fake objects in order to resell them in Venice or *extra terram* [31]. The effort to institute quality control is clear, as is the fact that some, at least, of the production was destined for the export trade. Similar provisions may be found in the statutes of the goldsmiths. They were subject to strict regulations concerning the gold and silver content of their products, as well as of the jewels set in gold; no counterfeit diamonds (made of glass), or painted glass, or even tinted crystal (tinted to look like rubies) or amethysts or balas rubies could be set in gold [32].

The connection of the minor arts with the export trade is clear from other evidence as well. In the case of glass manufacturing, there is mention of a case of glass consigned from Venice to Candia to a Venetian merchant, who then sent it to Rhodes, its final destination [33]. These were probably plain glasses which, in 1279, sold for 7.5 lire per thousand if they were of ordinary size, and 3 lire per thousand if they were small [34]. But there were also more elaborate glasses, as we know from the activities of a man who may be a Greek, named Gregorio da Napoli. He was a « tintor de moiolis », who in 1287 contracted to decorate about 4,000 glasses at 13 grossi (less than 35 soldi) per hundred [35]. There was, in the late thirteenth century, another Greek working in Murano, a Guglielmo Greco, who appears in 1291. On the other hand, there was, in 1338, a *fiolarius* from Murano named Pace, who worked in Crete and Constantinople for a while, and who, on his return, asked that he be permitted to resume work without paying the necessary fine [36]. All of which shows clearly that the Venetians made glass for export. Another product of Venetian glass manufacturing, medallions of glass paste with representations of the Virgin or saints, were sold both to the Levant and to western Europe [37].

Objects made of crystal, and sometimes worked with silver or gold, precious stones, and/or miniatures under crystal were items in a somewhat more exclusive and lucrative export trade. An early proof of this appears in the will of a Venetian merchant, Pietro Vioni, who died in Tabriz after December 10, 1265 [38]. Vioni was from a merchant family; when he died, he was the travelling partner in a number of colleganze which he had contracted with his father, among others; and his father, Vitale, who lived until 1285, also had commercial interests in the Levant. In his will, Vioni mentioned the merchandise he was carrying and made careful provisions about its sale after his death. Some of the merchandise was his own, but most of it he held in colleganza, on the usual conditions which would give him 1/4 of the profits. He had with him cloth from Lombardy, Germany, and Venice, which he ordered to be sold at the current market price. He had already reinvested some of his money in sugar and in small pearls. But he also carried—and his very unexceptional position as a merchant suggests that this was quite usual—several objects made of crystal, and decorated with jasper, silver gilt and pearls. They included a backgammon set (of crystal and jasper), a chess set, a bottle, two candelabras, there cups, one saddle decorated with crystal, jasper, silver, pearls and green silk, and a gown equally splendidly bejeweled. All of these things he carried from Venice, and he made provisions for their sale at a set minimum price, which shows them to have been very costly. It is not stated that they were manufactured in Venice, but this can safely, I think, be posited, since otherwise Vioni would probably have mentioned their provenance. This piece of evidence, unique, as far as I know, for the thirteenth century, establishes the early flourishing of the manufacturing of crystal objects, and the fact that production was tied to trade, even long distance trade. It is not surprising, then, that when, in 1338, a Genoese merchant was asked by the khan of Cathay, Toghan Timur, to request from the Pope certain gifts, he should have addressed himself to Venice for the purchase of some horses and some crystal objects, for a combined value of 1-2000 florins—even if the transaction did not, in the end, take place [39].

In the course of the thirteenth century, Venetian crystal objects became famous, as can be attested by the fact that they were ordered for various churches, and may be found in several parts of Europe. Among them are the two crystal candelabras given to the Church of San Nicolò of Bari by Venice's ally, Charles II of Anjou, in 1296 (« duo magnas candelabras de cristallo munito argento ad opus Venetiarum »), and those of crystal and silver preserved at San Marco [40]. Venetian crystal and goldsmith production replaces to some extent that of northern Europe.

A second observation concerning production in the minor arts is that Venice develops a certain substitutive role. She becomes, to some

extent, a famous center of artistic production such as the Byzantine
Empire had been before 1204; churches and princes order here crowns,
mitres, candelabras, crosses and other devotional objects, as, in the past,
they might acquire them in the Byzantine Empire. However, the substitution is not a simple one. Because Venice had an economy based on
exchange, because she had access to markets in which the Byzantines had
no interest, the process of substitution affected not only the location of
the center of production, but also the type of object produced. Characteristically, some objects are more or less mass produced. Two examples
may be adduced here. One consists of the glass medallions of the Virgin
and various saints, which were mass-produced in Venice in the first half
of the thirteenth century (1204-1261). They are byzantinizing in style,
and emulate Byzantine cameos, but are cheaper, and probably catered to
a much larger and more diversified market (figs. 11,12). Hans Wentzel
has shown that their hagiographic subjects varied according to the area
of export: specifically eastern subjects for the Balkans and the Latin
Empire of Costantinople, and western types for the Italian and European
markets [41]. The second example consists of what may be the most characteristic Venetian production in the minor arts in this period, that is,
objects with miniatures under crystal or quartz. There is a considerable
number of such objects, including crosses, candelabras, diptychs, triptychs
and a mitre. For their production, the *Cristellarii* cooperated with goldsmiths and miniaturists, who painted on parchment miniatures that were
later covered with small plaques of crystal [42].

Chronologically, these objects range from about 1290 to the middle
of the fourteenth century [43]. The major pieces have been studied, since
they offer, among other things, precious information about Venetian
miniatures in this period. Therefore, I shall limit myself to a few
comments on the production, dissemination and importance of these
objects.

First, it should be noted that their geographic dissemination is
rather wide: apart from the Italian cities, they may be found in Coimbra
(Portugal), in Germany, in Hungary, in two monasteries of Mount Athos
(Chilandar and Agiou Pavlou), in Sinai and in Trogir. All of these are
areas in which Venetian commercial presence was strong in the late
thirteenth and early fourteenth centuries, while of course Dalmatia and,
for a time, Hungary, had also close political ties with Venice. From what
we know of the history of some these pieces, they seem to have been
ordered in Venice: thus, the king of Hungary Andrew III, the
« Venetian », whose mother was a Morosini and the sister of the
governor of Zara, ordered a small portable altar, which is the Bern
diptych. It is made of wood, and covered with gold filigree, pearls, gems
and miniatures under crystal. It also has two cameos with the Crucifixion
and the Ascension [44]. The objects found at Mount Athos belong to two
Serbian monasteries, one of which, Chilandar, was rebuilt by King
Stephen Uroš II Milyutin in the late thirteenth century (fig. 13). They
were probably ordered by him for the monasteries as gifts [45]. The cross

of St. Nicolas of Pisa was ordered by a sacristan of that church, ca. 1320 [46]. Venice, in other words, had become a center where prestigious works of art were ordered, just as Byzantium had been in an earlier period. But the production of such objects must have been more extensive than is indicated by the objects which have survived or are mentioned in the sources, since the *cristellarii* apparently made fake crystal for some of them, presumably for those destined for a wider market [47].

The miniature decoration of the objects under discussion is rather conservative, and preserves a great deal of the Byzantine style, although an evolution may be observed. Characteristic of many of the miniatures is the use of pearls to outline the nimbus of sacred personages (fig. 14), a feature which probably is influenced by the use of small pearls to frame Byzantine enamels (fig. 15); the same treatment was given by the Venetians to Christ, the evangelists, and the archangel Michael in the Pala d'Oro of 1345. Characteristic also is the use of precious or semi-precious stones in the setting, copying the Byzantine use of precious stones in icons such as that of St. Michael in Venice. These facts and the brilliant colors of the miniatures suggest that the type of object described here evolved as a cheaper substitute for the expensive Byzantine enamels [48].

In effect, what I suggest happened in Venice was that its merchants acquired a strong economic position within an area which included the Levant and parts of western Europe. In these areas, there were already established artistic traditions and a taste for certain kinds of objets d'art, that is, the possibilities of a market. This stimulated production of such objects in Venice, but also enlarged the existing markets, since the Venetian products were cheaper, and more easily available through the activities of the merchants. We have, therefore, a certain commodification of artistic production. And it is possible that the production of large numbers of Byzantinizing icons in Crete in the fourteenth century and later must also be seen as the result of similar processes.

Finally, it may be observed that in the minor arts Venice functioned as a center in which artistic influences and currents from various areas met and fused. This may be seen particularly in the miniatures under crystal, which exhibit the blend of Byzantine and western styles that is typical of Venetian art of the 13th and early 14th centuries [49]. Many of them are in the formal, byzantinising style (fig. 16) which may also be seen in the Antifonario of the Museo Correr (1311) [50]. But a certain evolution as well as a mixture of styles may be discerned. The miniatures of the diptych and cross of Agiou Pavlou have an iconography that is close to the Byzantine one: the diptych, for example, is the only one of these objects to conform to the cycle af the twelve great feasts of the Orthodox church (fig. 17) [51]. The miniatures of the Bern diptych have been compared by Hahnloser to these of the Epistolary of Padua (1259) (fig. 18), which had extensive influence on miniature production in Venice and Dalmatia, and even on frescoes made in Germany [52]. Both works show a strong Byzantine influence in iconography and the use of color, but this coexists with western traits. Iconographically, as Millet has suggested, the artists of the Bern diptych held fast to eastern models, but they combined this with a more plastic treatment of figures and a freer disposition of the figures in space [53]. The Chilandar diptych, almost contemporany with the portable altar of Bern, exhibits similar characteristics.

On the other hand, some early fourteenth century miniatures-under-crystal, executed for Italian cities, have much stronger western influences. This group includes the Pisa cross of 1320 and the Atri cross, while the clearest example is provided by the two miniatures of the Assisi cross (1337) (fig. 19) [54]. These, made for an Italian city and perhaps executed in the workshop of Marco Veneziano, the brother of Paolo, have been connected with the Bolognese school of miniature painting [55]. Their western style is not to be attributed simply to the later date, for in the same period the Venetians produced highly Byzantinising miniatures, such as these of the Mariegola of the Scuola of San Teodoro (fig. 20) [56]. As in the case of glass paste medallions, the style of these miniatures may have varied according to the taste of the clients—another characteristic of production for the market.

The miniatures under crystal also influenced painting on small wooden panels executed in a miniaturistic technique. But the importance of these miniatures transcends the territory of Venice. They were generally characterised by Byzantine or Byzantinising tendencies and, being popular and easily transported, they carried this style to other areas and other media [57]. Thus, K. Weitzmann has found strong stylistic affinities between the Bern diptych and an iconostasis beam at Mount Sinai, which he attributes to a Venetian painter working in the Levant in the third quarter of the thirteenth century [58]. Of course, given the chronology attributed to the two objects, there is no question of direct influence. Djurić, too, finds that the late-thirteenth and early-fourteenth-century frescoes of some churches of Zara, Brač, and Kotor owe their style to the influences of Venetian miniatures-under-crystal, particularly of the group that included the Chilandar diptych and the Trogir mitre miniatures [59].

Economic and cultural (including artistic) phenomena are both complex and their distinct development is, to some extent, subject to an internal dynamic. The interconnection betwen the two is even more multi-dimensional, as either set of phenomena may be differentially affected by a number of factors. Non-economic factors, religion, aesthetic traditions, politics, may influence artistic development more than do the immediate economic conditions. Nevertheless specifically in the development of the minor arts in Venice in the thirteenth century, the connection with economics is quite strong. Venetian commercial activity created the preconditions for the circulation of art objects in areas where the presence of the Venetian merchant was pervasive. The substitution of the Venetian for the Byzantine dominance in the Byzantine Empire is paralleled by the substitution of Venetian-made objects for Byzantine ones. And the heightened economic activity led to the production of art objects for the market; in other words, artistic production became, to some extent, a part of the commercial system, and its products became commodities for exchange.

This paper is based on research done for a much larger project. I am grateful to the Guggenheim Foundation for a grant which financed a considerable part of this research.

[1] For the economic history of Venice in this period see Luzzato, G., *Storia economica di Venezia dall'XI al XVI secolo*, Venezia, 1961; idem, *Studi di storia economica veneziana*, Padua, 1954; Lane, F. C., *Venice, A Maritime Republic*, Baltimore and London, 1973; Sestan, E., *La politica veneziana nel duecento*, in « Arch. Stor. Ital.» n. 135 (1977), 295-331; Lopez, R. S., *Venezia e le grandi linee dell'espansione commerciale nel secolo XIII*, in *La civiltà veneziana del secolo di Marco Polo*, Firenze, 1955.

[2] See, in general, Demus, O., *Oriente e Occidente nell'arte Veneta del Duecento*, in *La civiltà veneziana del secolo di Marco Polo*, Firenze, 1955, 111-126; Toesca, P., *Il Trecento*, Torino, 1951, 608 ff; Lasareff, V., *Saggi sulla pittura veneziana dei secoli XIII-XIV. La maniera greca e il problema della scuola cretese*, in « Arte Veneta », 1966, 17-31, 43-59; Muraro, M., *Varie fasi di influenza bizantina a Venezia nel trecento*, in « Thesaurismata », 9 (1972), 180-201.

[3] Pertusi, A., *Venezia e Bisanzio nel secolo XI*, in *Venezia del Mille*, Firenze, 1965, 119-160; Thiriet, F., *La Romanie vénitienne au Moyen Age*, anastatic edition, Paris, 1975, 29-62, with earlier bibliography.

[4] Borsari, S., *Il commercio veneziano nell'impero bizantino nel XII secolo*, in « Rivista storica Italiana », LXXVI (1964), 982-1011; idem, *Per la storia del commercio veneziano col mondo bizantino nel XII secolo*, in « Rivista storica italiana », 88 (1976), 104-126.

[5] Thiriet, *op. cit.*, 63 ff; Luzzatto, *Storia*, 35-143; Longnon, J., *L'empire latin de Constantinople et la principauté de Morée*, Paris, 1949, 133 ff; Morozzo della Rocca, R., and Lombardo, A., *Documenti del commercio Veneziano nei secoli X-XIII*, Torino, 1940, nos. 635, 692, 471, 551, 598, 591, 519, 491, 573.

[6] Luzzatto, *Storia*, 35-145; idem, *Il mercante veneziano del tempo di Marco Polo*, in *Nel VII Centenario della nascità di Marco Polo*, Venezia, 1955, 241-254; Cessi, R., *Storia della repubblica di Venezia*, 2nd edition, Milano and Messina, 1968, passim; Renouard, Yves, *Mercati e mercanti veneziani alla fine del duecento*, in *Civiltà veneziana del secolo di Marco Polo*, 85-108.

[7] Lane, F. C., *Venice and History*, Baltimore, 1966, passim.

[8] Heyd, W., *Histoire du commerce du Levant au Moyen Age*, 2 vols., Leipzig, 1923, passim.

[9] Laiou, A., *The Byzantine Economy in the Mediterranean Trade System, 13th-15th centuries*, in « Dumbarton Oaks Papers », 1980, passim.

[10] Luzzatto, *Storia*, 45-47.

[11] Laiou, *op.cit.*, passim.

[12] Goitein, S. D., *A Mediterranean Society*, vol. I, *Economic Foundations*, Berkeley-Los Angeles, 1967, passim.

[13] Nicetas Choniates, *Historia*, ed. Im. Bekker, Bonn, 1835, 99-100.

[14] See Davidson, G. R., *A Medieval Glass Factory at Corinth*, in « American Journal of Archaeology », 44 (1940), 297-327.

[15] See Gasparetto, G., *La verrerie vénitienne et ses relations avec le Levant balkanique au Moyen âge*, in *Verre médiéval aux Balkans (Ve-XVe siècle)*, Institut

24

des études balkaniques, Académie serbe des sciences et des arts, Belgrade, 1975, 143-154, and compare the photographs of glass fragments with the photographs and sketches in Davidson, op.cit.

[16] Cessi, *Storia*, 70 ff; Renouard, *Mercati*, 86-87.

[17] Choniates, 101.

[18] Zecchin, L., *Chronologia vetraria veneziana*, in « Rivista della stazione sperimentale del vetro », 3, n. 1, 214.

[19] Zecchin, 19-22. For Venetian glass especially designed for the Ottoman Empire which, however, had a flourishing industry of its own, (16th century), see Gasparetto, A., *Note sulla vetraria e sull'iconografia vetraria bizantine*.

[20] Borsari, S., *Studi sulle colonie veneziane in Romania nel XIII secolo*, Napoli, 1966, passim. On the type of trading activity present in Coron, see also the documents in Lombardo, A., *Pasquale Longo, notaio in Corone, 1289-1293*, Torino, 1952, especially nos. 92, 109, 12, 26, 63, and Morozzo della Rocca and Lombardo, *Documenti*, no. 756.

[21] Lombardo, *Longo*, no. 55. I take « liium » to be « lilium », meaning fleur de lys: cf. Sella, P., *Glossario Latino-italiano*, Vaticano, 1944, s.v. *lilium*.

[22] On Crete see Borsari, S., *Il dominio Veneziano a Creta nel XIII secolo*, Napoli, 1963. For further bibliography, see Manoussacas, M. I., *L'isola di Creta sotto il dominio veneziano — Problemi e ricerche*, in Pertusi, A., ed., *Venezia e il Levante fino al secolo XV*, Firenze, 1973, I, 473-514.

[23] See Abrate, M., *Creta colonia Veneziana nei secoli XIII-XV*, in « Economia e Storia », IV (1957), 253 ff, for the fourteenth century, and Thiriet, *Romanie vénitienne*, 215-313. On the system of land tenure, see Santschi, E., *La notion de « feudum » en Crète vénitienne (XIIIe-XVe siècles)*, Montreux, 1976. Information on the commerce of Crete may be found in several documents, among which Morozzo della Rocca-Lombardo, no. 564; Morozzo della Rocca, M., *Benvenuto de Brixano, notaio in Candia (1301-1302)*, Venezia, 1950, nos. 131, 134, 139, 307, 352-354, 306, 233, 282; Lombardo, A., *Imbreviature di Pietro Scardon (1271)*, Torino, 1942, nos. 50, 209, 60, 367; Chiaudano, M. and Lombardo, A., *Leonardo Marcello, notaio in Candia, 1278-81*, Venezia, 1960, nos. 172, 239, 241; Carbone, S., *Pietro Pizolo, notaio in Candia, I (1300)*, Venezia, 1978, nos. 594, 473, 77, 129, 138, 321; Tafel, G. L. and Thomas, G. M., *Urkunden zur älteren Handels-und Staatsgeschichte der Republik Venedig*, III, Wien 1857; anastatic edition, 1964, pp. 159-280.

[24] On the export of Cretam agricultural products, see among others, Sp. Theotokes, *Apophaseis Meizonos Symbouliou Venetias*, Athens, 1933, pp. 76, 87-88. Thiriet, F., *Délibérations des assemblées vénitiennes concernant la Romanie*, I, Paris, 1966, nos. CLXVII, CLIII; Lombardo, *Sacrdon*, no. 65; Morozzo della Rocca, *Brixano*, no. 201; Thiriet, *Romanie*, 232-233, 326 ff. On a different interpretation of the mechanism of advance sale, cf. Abrate, *Creta*, 263-4, 267.

[25] Cf. Carbone, *Pizolo*, I, nos. 73, 80, 81, 196, 138, 443, 639; Theotokes, *Apophaseis*, p. 12.

[26] Cattapan, M., *Nuovi documenti riguardanti pittori cretesi dal 1300 al 1500*, in « Pepragmena tou B. Diethnous Kretologikou Synedriou », III (1968), 29-46; idem, *Nuovi elenchi e documenti dei pittori in Creta dal 1300 al 1500*, in *Candia*, « Thesaurismata », 10 (1973), 238-282.

[27] The bibliography on the art of Crete is extensive. Among the latest works. which incorporate earlier bibliography, see Muraro, M., *L'isola di Creta e l'arte bizantina a Venezia*, in *Scritti di storia dell'arte in onore di U. Procacci*, I, Milano, 1977, 69-72; Chatzidakis, M., *Essai sur l'Ecole dite « Italogreque » précédé d'une note sur les rapports de l'art vénitien avec l'art crétois jusqu' à 1500*, in Pertusi, A., ed., *Venezia e il Levante fino al secolo XV*, II, Firenze, 1974, 69-124; Chatzi dakis, *La peinture des « Madonneri » ou véneto-crétoise et sa destination*, in Beck, H.-G., Manoussakas, M., Pertusi, A., eds., *Venezia centro di mediazione tra oriente e occidente (sec. XV-XVI)*, Firenze, 1977; Bettini. S., *Ascendenze e significato della pittura veneto-cretese*, ibid.

[28] Monticolo, G., *I capitolari delle arti veneziane sottoposte alla Giustizia Vecchia*, in *Fonti per la storia d'Italia*, 4 vols., Roma, 1896-1914, vol. II, 360 ff. and III, 671; cf. Cecchetti, B., *Nomi di pittori e lapicidi antichi*, in « Archivio Veneto », IV, 225.

[29] Gasparetto, A., *Il vetro di Murano*, Venezia, 1950, 38; Monticolo, *Capitolari*, vol. II, p. 95.

[30] Monticolo, *Capitolari*, « Capitolare de fiolariis » articles XXVI, LXXXII, LVI; Cessi, R., *Deliberazioni del Maggior Consiglio di Venezia*, vol. III, Bologna, 1934, 381; Gasparetto, *Vetro*, 52ff.

[31] Monticolo, *Capitolari*, « Capitolare de cristellariis », vol. IV, articles VIII, XXXV, III, XIII, XLI, XL; Lipinsky, A., *Oro, argento gemmi e smalti*, Firenze, 1975, p. 295 ff.

[32] Cecchetti, B., *Le industrie in Venezia nel secolo XIII*, in « Archivio Veneto », IV, 1872, 212-257.

[33] Morozzo della Rocca, R., *Lettere di mercanti a Pignol Zucchello (1336-1350)*, Venezia, 1957, no. 15 (26 May, 1345).

[34] Zecchin, *Chronologia*, year 1279.

[35] *Ibid.*, year 1280, and p. 62.

[36] *Ibid.*, pp. 64, 214.

[37] Wentzel, H., *Das Medaillon mit dem Hl. Theodor und die venezianischen Glaspasten im byzantinischen Stil*, in *Festschrift für Erich Meyer*, Hamburg, 1959, 50-67, and *infra*, p. 15.

[38] *Testamento di Pietro Vioni, Veneziano, fatto in Tauris (Persia) MCCLXIV, X Dicembre*, in « Archivio Veneto », 26 (1883), 161-165.

[39] Lopez, *Venezia*, 50-51.

[40] Hahnloser, H. R., ed., *Il Tesoro di San Marco*, II, *Il Tesoro e il Museo*, Firenze, 1971, pp. 133 ff, and plates CXXXII, CXXXIII. Cf. Fiocco, G., *A proposito di occhiali e cristalli*, in « Arte Veneta », 10 (1956), 213-214.

[41] Wentzel, *Medaillon*, passim.

[42] On these objects, see Zocca, E., *Catalogo delle cose d'arte e di antichità d'Italia*; Assisi, Roma, 1936, 144-145; Hahnloser, H. R., *Das Venezianer Kristallkreuz im Bernischen Historischen Museum*, in « Jahrbuch des Bernischen Historischen Museums », 34 (1954), 33-47; Idem, *Scola et artes cristellariorum de Veneciis, 1284-1319; Opus Venetum ad filum*, in « Atti Congr. int. storia dell'arte », Venezia, 1956, 157-165; Maurer, E., and Hahnloser, H. R., *Kunstdenkmäler des Kantons Aargau*, III, 1954; Radojčić, Sv., *Miniature d'origine veneziana nel monastero di Hilandar sul Monte Athos*, in « Atti Congr. int. storia dell'arte », Venezia, 1956, 166; Radojčić, *Etudes sur l'art du XIIIe siècle; le diptyque de Chilandari*, in « Glas de l'académie serbe des sciences », 234, 1959, no. 7, 3-8 (in Serbian); Toesca, P., *Un capolavoro dell'oreficeria veneziana della fine del Duecento*, in « Arte Veneta », 5 (1951), 15-20; Volbach, W. F., *Venetian-Byzantine Works of Art in Rome*, in « The Art Bulletin », 29 (1947), 86-94; Djurić, V. J. *Vizantijske i italo-vizantinijske tsarine u Dalmaciji*, in « Prilozi povijesti umjetnosti u Dalmaciji », 12 (Split, 1960), 123-145; mention of an « urceum de argento de opere venetico ad filum cum diversis imaginibus sub cristallis », in an inventory of the Holy See: Molmenti, P., *La Storia di Venezia nella vita privata*, I, Bergamo, 1927, 322. Partial lists of these objects may be found in Hahnloser, *Venezianer Kristallkreuz*, and in Toesca, P., *Storia dell'arte italiana, Il Medioevo*, II (Torino, 1927), 1148, n. 64. On the existence of a crystal cross with two miniatures at Saint Catherine's at Sinai, see Weizmann, K., *Icon Painting in the Crusader Kingdom*, in « Dumbarton Oaks Papers », 20 (1966), 61.

[43] The diptych and cross of Agiou Pavlou, as well as a small reliquary in the same monastery have been dated to the first half of the 13th century, (Huber, P., *Image et message; Miniatures byzantines de l'Ancien et du Nouveau Testament*, Zürich, 1975, pp. 121-123), but there are no good grounds for this early dating.

[44] Hahnloser, *Venezianer Kristallkreuz*, 36-37.

26

45 Huber, *Image*, 121, 143.

46 Hahnloser, *Venezianer Kristallkreuz*, 37.

47 Zecchin, *Chronologia*, year 1334.

48 Bettini, S., *Opere d'arte importate a Venezia durante le crocate*, in *Venezia, della prima crociata alla conquista di Costantinopoli del 1204*, Venezia, 1965, 160-161.

49 On Venetian miniatures, see Toesca, *Storia*, 1045 ff; idem, *Trecento*, 841 ff; Palluchini, R., *La pittura veneziana del Trecento*, Venezia-Roma, 1964, 9 ff, 81-93.

50 Museo Correr, MS V, no. 131; cf. also the miniatures in Marciana, Zanetti 547 = 1924, Marino Sanudo, *Conditiones Terrae Sanctae*.

51 Huber, *Image*, 125 - 142.

52 Hahnloser, *Scola*, 151 ff; cf. Hänsel, J., *Die Miniaturmalerei einer Paduaner Schule in Duecento* in « Jahrbuch der Oesterreichischen byzantinischen Gesellschaft », 2 (1952), 105-148.

53 Millet, G., *Recherches sur l'iconographie de l'Evangile*, Paris, 1916 (reprinted, 1960), 667-669.

54 Toesca, P., *Quelques miniatures vénitiennes du XIV siècle*, in « Scriptorium », 1 (1946-47), 70-74; Toesca, *Trecento*, 841-842.

55 Walcker Casotti, M., *Miniature e miniatori a Venezia nella prima metà del XIV secolo*, in « Istituto di storia dell'Arte antica e moderna », no. 15 (1962), 1-46.

56 Museo Correr, MS IV no. 21.

57 But see the opposite opinion of Bettini, S., *Elementi favorevoli e contrari all'espansione dell'arte veneziana nel Levante*, in Pertusi, *Venezia e il Levante*, II, 17-18.

58 Weitzmann, *Icon Painting*, 61 ff.

59 Djurić, V., *Influence de l'art vénitien sur la peinture murale en Dalmatie jusqu' à la fin du XVe siècle* in Pertusi, *Venezia e il Levante*, II, 139-162; Pecarski, B., *Venice, Italo-Byzantine and Dalmatian Painting during the Twelfth and Thirteenth Centuries* in « Arte Veneta », 22 (1968), 167-170.

Italy and the Italians in the Political Geography of the Byzantines (14th Century)

I n the fourteenth century, the Byzantines were in close contact with the Italians, in a variety of political, commercial, and cultural contexts. What I should like to examine here is the place of Italy and the Italians in the political geography of the Byzantines: how much did the Byzantines know, and how much did they care about the area, its people, and its politics? Political geography, as I use the term, combines geography, ethnography, and political history; whether the Byzantines used such categories with regard to Italy and the Italians is part of the question.[1] The texts I will use are those of the three major narrative historians of the fourteenth century—George Pachymeres, John Cantacuzenus, and Nikephoros Gregoras—and it therefore should be clear that this is not a general inquiry into the topic but, rather, a historiographical one.

Of the three, Pachymeres is, in my view, by far the most interesting historian, followed by Gregoras. Pachymeres has a certain curiosity about peoples and their mores, especially evident in his discussion of the Cumans and the Mongols, where internal politics and international complexities are presented along with ethnographic observations, at a rather high level of sophistication. His geographic observations on Asia Minor and the Black Sea area are of impressive accuracy, especially when one looks at a Ptolemaic map, with which Pachymeres was undoubtedly acquainted. In comparison, where the Italian peninsula and the Italians are concerned, there is little geographic reference, and no ethnographic observations, except for a few clichés that are traditional in the Byzantine descriptions of westerners in general or Italians in particular: the mercenaries under the command of Michael VIII (the "Italian" foreign contingent) are called "the blond and bellicose race" (τὸ ξανθόν τε καί ἀρμάνιον γένος); to the contrary, the army of William of Achaia at the battle of Pelagonia, also called Italians, are qualified as "stupid, cowardly,

[1] For the general issue, see my "On Political Geography: The Black Sea of Pachymeres," in *The Making of Byzantine History: Studies Dedicated to Donald M. Nicol*, ed. R. Beaton and Ch. Roueché (London, 1993), 94–121. On Genoa, see S. Origone, "Genova vista da Bisanzio," *La Storia dei Genovesi*, IX (1989), 485–505; and eadem, "Genova nel confronto con Bisanzio: Il giudizio degli storici bizantini (secoli XIV–XV)," in her *Bisanzio e Genova* (Genoa, 1992), 251–61. For a study of the Genoese view of Byzantium, see M. Balard, "Il mondo bizantino visto da Genova," in *Europa e Mediterraneo tra medioevo e prima età moderna: l'osservatorio italiano*, ed. S. Gensini (Comune San Miniato, s.a.), 281–95.

and effeminate" (βλαξὶ καὶ τρυφεροῖς οὖσι)² —the former being more of a cliché than the latter. Not surprisingly, Pachymeres often refers to the superciliousness of the "Italians," in a stock phrase known at least since the twelfth century, which Pachymeres favors, perhaps because the Greek is learned: he speaks of the κόροζα of the race (as had twelfth-century authors), whether in reference to the Italians in general or in relation to the Catalans.³ In fact, this cliché, called an "Italian" attribute, is the one most frequently used for westerners in general.

It is not peculiar that there should be an absence of ethnographic observations, for traditionally in Byzantine historiography (and perhaps in medieval historiography generally) ethnographic observations tend to be applied to nomadic peoples or peoples on the move—the "barbarians" par excellence—while settled peoples, especially those known from antiquity, are rarely described, time-honored characterizations being sufficient. Given this fact, our question becomes more focused on the political issue: that is, where do Pachymeres and the other historians place the Italians in their political universe? We come, then, to a second observation. Pachymeres almost never uses the term "Italy."⁴ He sees neither Europe nor Italy as a monolithic unit, even in geographic terms. Instead, he sees the division of the peninsula into various political entities: he refers specifically to the maritime republics of Venice, Genoa, and Pisa, to the marquisate of Montferrat, to the "kingdom of Apulia," i.e., the Angevin kingdom of Naples, and to Sicily.⁵ He knows not only that there are different political entities, but also that there are political antagonisms between them, such as that between Venice and Genoa. Contrasted to this individuation of political entities is the use of the term "Italian" in a very general, indeed generic, way. This disjunction between the use of the term "Italy" and that of the word "Italians" is not repeated by the other fourteenth-century historians.

In Pachymeres' history, the adjective "Italian" is used to describe a number of things: both specifically Italian affairs and people, and, more interestingly, westerners in general. In this second, generic use, it is the equivalent of the term "Latins," more common in other sources but fairly rare in Pachymeres. Thus, counterintuitively for us, the members of the Fourth Crusade and the rulers of the Latin Empire of Constantinople are called "Italians." Baldwin II of Courtenay is called the "emperor of the Italians";⁶ when the city is retaken by the Byzantines, the palace is cleansed of the Italian soot (καπνοῦ καὶ λιγνύος Ἰταλικῆς).⁷ Similarly, the princes and forces of the principality of Achaia are called Italians, at least for the most part; occasionally, the more common term "Latin" is used interchangeably with Italian.⁸ The plans of the houses of Anjou and Valois to recover Constantinople are described as the ambitions of "the Italians."⁹ This generic use extends

²G. Pachymeres, *Relations historiques*, ed. and trans. A. Failler, I (Paris, 1984), 79, 121 (hereafter Failler); see on this, H. Hunger, *Graeculus Perfidus ΙΤΑΛΟΣ ΙΤΑΜΟΣ* (Rome, 1987).
³Failler, 219; G. Pachymeres, *De Michaele et Andronico Palaeologis*, Bonn ed., 2 vols. (1835), II, 237 (hereafter Pachymeres, [Bonn]): the Venetians act with much "Italian arrogance" (Ἰταλικῆς κορύζης καὶ φρυάγματος); cf. II, 70. The Catalans are also said to have behaved with Italian κόρυζα: e.g., II, 572.
⁴For an exception, see Failler, 255: Michael Palaeologus sends embassies πρὸς τοὺς ἐπιδόξους τῆς Ἰταλίας.
⁵On Apulia, see Pachymeres, (Bonn), II, 153, 202; Failler, 127, on Manfred, "king of Apulia."
⁶Failler, 227.
⁷Failler, 219.
⁸Failler, 275, 421.
⁹Pachymeres, (Bonn), II, 70.

to the Catalans, who are variously described as "Catalans," "Almugavars," and "Italians."[10] It cannot be that Pachymeres was unaware of their true provenance, for he seems to have known quite well the political events that brought the house of Aragon and the Spaniards to Sicily, where the Catalan company had fought before coming to the Byzantine Empire; he was simply using the term generically, to designate westerners. In the same way, he calls Roger de Flor both "Latin" and "Italian by race."[11] Pachymeres knew something of Roger de Flor's career—for example, that he had been a Templar in Acre before the fall of the city and then had fought for Frederick III of Sicily; so it is possible that he also knew that Roger's father was a German, but that he considered the term "Italian" appropriate anyway.[12] Most curiously, perhaps, the army of Louis IX, on crusade in Tunis, is called both "Latins" and "Italians," nicely contrasted to the "Hagarenes" and "Ethiopians."[13]

Sometimes the term "Italian" is, indeed, used to designate Italians resident in the Byzantine Empire or ruling parts of the old empire. Thus, when describing Michael VIII's actions after the capture of Constantinople, Pachymeres speaks of how the emperor treated the Latin φυλαί (races, national groups), and immediately afterwards tells us that Michael considered how he would persuade the notables of "the Italian races" (τῶν Ἰταλικῶν γενῶν) to come under his authority.[14] Similarly, Crete is recognized as being under Venetian rule, which is sometimes called "the rule of the Italians" (Ἰταλῶν ἐπικράτεια).[15] In the case of Gregory III Kyprios, patriarch of Constantinople, his opponent John Bekkos called him "a man who had been born and raised among the Italians . . . and wore their clothes and spoke their tongue."[16] Given, however, the generic use of the term, it is not clear that in these instances the historian is using it in a specific (Italian) rather than a general (Western) sense.

Also generic is the use of the term to refer to the kingdom of Acre. It was the "Italians" who lived along the coasts of Syria "from old," and it was from them that the Egyptians conquered the "great cities of the Italians," i.e., Beirut, Sidon, Laodicea, Tripoli and Acre. Gregoras, who follows Pachymeres but also goes beyond him, correctly identifies the inhabitants of the crusader kingdom as descendants of French crusaders; so he understood well the meaning of Pachymeres' "Italians," although he himself did not use the term in this way. Interestingly enough, Pachymeres laments in a genuine voice the loss of the kingdom of Acre, which to some extent he ascribes to the policy of alliance of Michael VIII with the sultan Baybars.[17] He says that of all those areas, the only one that remains is the state of the Armenians, and that the inhabitants of those "cities of the

[10] For examples of the use of the term "Italian" for the Catalans, see Pachymeres, (Bonn), II, 405, 421, 451–52, 608 ff, 632–34, etc.

[11] Pachymeres, (Bonn), II, 393, 521–22.

[12] On Roger de Flor, see A. E. Laiou, *Constantinople and the Latins: The Foreign Policy of Andronicus II, 1282–1328* (Cambridge, Mass., 1972), 131.

[13] Failler, 467.

[14] Failler, 219. Are the "Italians" of Constantinople who welcomed Andronicus II after his two-year stay in Thessalonica only the merchants of Genoa, Pisa, and Venice, or other westerners as well? Pachymeres, (Bonn), II, 195, 291.

[15] Pachymeres, (Bonn), II, 209, 241.

[16] Pachymeres, (Bonn), II, 89; cf. Laiou, *Constantinople*, 35.

[17] Failler, 241, 243; Pachymeres, (Bonn), II, 86–87.

Italians" have been dispersed, except for those who died, either in war or as martyrs, refusing to become renegades. Clearly, he is speaking here of the great Christian community, and it does not matter to him that the inhabitants of the crusader states were not Orthodox but Catholic Christians. This is a striking and counterintuitive sentiment. Here the term "Italians" perhaps designates not only westerners, but also Catholic Christians generally.

This brings me to the other use of the term "Italian," to mean Catholic. Pachymeres has a vocabulary of religious designation that is somewhat unusual, though not unique, being shared, for example, with Akropolites. In it, the Byzantines are Romans, to be sure, but also "Graikoi," to be juxtaposed to "Italians." Thus, on January 5, 1282, at Vespers, a great mass was celebrated in the church of St. Sophia, newly cleansed to mark the end of the Unionist policy. Present on this occasion were both "Greeks [Γραικοί] and Italians." Some people, says Pachymeres, were astounded to see in the Great Church the Italians, holding candles, even though it was of *their* errors that the church had been cleansed only a short time ago.[18] Clearly here "Italians" means Catholics, and Γραικοί means Orthodox; Pachymeres uses the term Γραικός only when he refers to ecclesiastical matters, and at one point he makes it clear that this term was the term used by the papal hierarchy—or the Italians—to designate the "Romans," i.e., the Byzantines; once again, in this passage the Graikoi are opposed to the Italians, i.e., the Orthodox to the Catholic.[19] Elsewhere, the "Italians" are accused of heresy.[20] Sometimes, the term "Latin" is used for "Catholic," thus being interchangeable with "Italian."[21] Surprisingly, too, the word "Roman," which normally means Byzantine, is sometimes used to designate an inhabitant of Rome, or even a Catholic, in a juxtaposition of Γραικός (Orthodox) and Ῥωμαῖος (Catholic).[22] Thus, the generic term "Italian" to mean westerner seems to derive from the equally generic, but differently charged use of the term to mean Catholic Christian. Here, undoubtedly, is the origin of the designation of all westerners, i.e., all adherents to the Church of Rome, as Italians.

The juxtaposition Γραικός—Ἰταλός seems to go back to Akropolites' distinction of Ancient Greeks (Γραικοί) and Romans (Ἰταλοί).[23] Herbert Hunger has already suggested that a minority of Byzantines argued that the Greeks and the Italians had originally been united, and shared much in common.[24] While the anti-Unionist Pachymeres never explicitly adopted this position, his use of terminology reflects such views as a subtext. Besides, Pachymeres sometimes speaks of a community of Christians, either in opposition to the Muslims or in terms of common adherence to the same God, therefore, deploring

[18] Pachymeres, (Bonn), II, 22–23. "Italians" meaning Catholics: cf. II, 47, 109.

[19] Failler, 461. Similarly, Failler, 481: Michael VIII argues that the Graikoi (Orthodox) and the Italians are very close in the great mysteries of the faith, and can commune with each other as easily as exchanging languages. Pachymeres claims that the Catholics considered the Graikoi to be "white Hagarenes": Failler, 471.

[20] Failler, 479, 481, 529–31.

[21] Failler, 625.

[22] For inhabitants of Rome, Failler, 55. Cf. Failler, 495: πρὸς τὴν τῶν Ῥωμαίων ἐκκλησίαν=the Church of Rome; in the ceremony of the union of the two churches, the Gospels are read in Greek and Latin: Γραικικῶς τε ὁμοῦ καὶ Ῥωμαϊκῶς: Failler, 511.

[23] G. Akropolites, *Opera*, ed. A. Heisenberg (Stuttgart, 1928), Κατὰ Λατίνων Β, 64–65.

[24] Hunger, *Graeculus Perfidus ΙΤΑΛΟΣ ΙΤΑΜΟΣ*, 44–45; cf. pp. 21, 33, 34, 37.

wars between Christians.[25] Pious and well-worn statements these undoubtedly were, but they appear to reflect something real as well. Pachymeres' overriding and overwhelming concern is with the fate of Asia Minor. All his other interests are subordinated to that and circumscribed by it. As far as westerners are concerned, one of the recurring themes is that they weakened the Byzantine Empire, both by the conquest of Constantinople and by their subsequent hostility, after 1261; this forced the Byzantines first to make alliances with the Turks, and secondly to divert resources from Asia Minor to the West, a combination of factors that facilitated Turkish expansion.[26] To this extent, then, he holds the westerners responsible for the fall of Asia Minor. But given his preoccupation, it also makes sense that the primary opposition in his mind is that not between Catholics and Orthodox Christians, but between Christians and Muslims. Opposed to church union he may have been, but this other conceptual framework is equally important, and has not been noticed sufficiently.

The term "Italian," then, as used by Pachymeres, only rarely refers specifically to Italians, and then appears to be restricted to the citizens of the maritime cities. Let us now turn to the question of knowledge. What did Pachymeres know about Italy and the Italians, and what did he care to know? His knowledge of the geography of Italy can only be detected through his discussion of political events; it owes something to ancient geography and something to contemporary affairs. Thus, Venice is called both Aquileia (as it was on contemporary Ptolemaic maps) and Venice. The kingdom of Naples is called Apulia; Gregoras calls it Italy. The marquisate of Montferrat is, interestingly enough, placed in Lombardy or considered as part of Lombardy, both by Pachymeres and by Gregoras.[27] "Lombardy" is perhaps used, in a very broad sense, to mean northern Italy, as it was sometimes also used in contemporary Italian sources.[28] But placing Montferrat in Lombardy may be a political as well as a geographic statement: Pachymeres calls the marquis of Montferrat the "archon of Lombardy," and indeed it is a fact that during the rule of Marquis William (d. 1292), Montferrat was an important power within the politics of Lombardy.[29] Still, in terms of geography, I note that Pachymeres accurately describes the route from Constantinople to Tunis (which he calls both Tunis and Carthage): from Avlona, past Pachino at the southeastern part of Sicily (Πάχυνος ἄκρα, as in a Ptolemaic map) and then through the Tyrrhenian Sea.[30]

In terms of political geography, we find that Italian politics interests him only as it touches Byzantium, which occurs in rather specific ways. According to Pachymeres, the Italian political scene is dominated by the personality and politics of Charles of Anjou, and of course he is right. The papacy and the royal house of Aragon are important to the extent that they are connected with Charles of Anjou or with the matrimonial and

[25] This occurs on at least two occasions: Michael VIII is said to have told some friars, soon after 1267, that the pope should not permit war between Christians, since "the Romans, whom they call Graikoi, are of the same Christ and the same church as the Italians" (Failler, 461, 463); Andronicus II is supposed to have sent a similar message to the Catalans: Pachymeres, (Bonn), II, 566.

[26] For example, Failler, 29 ff.

[27] Theodore Palaeologus, going to Montferrat, is said to go to Lombardy: Pachymeres, (Bonn), II, 87–88, 597–602.

[28] See *Enciclopedia italiana*, s.v. Lombardia.

[29] See *Enciclopedia italiana*, s.v. Montferrato; *Cambridge Medieval History*, VII, 23–24.

[30] Failler, 465–67.

defensive plans of the Byzantines. The pivotal event, in his eyes, is the defeat of Manfred of Sicily by Charles of Anjou at the battle of Benevento, in 1266. The great struggles between papacy and empire, Guelphs and Ghibellines in Italy, are telescoped in a statement about the hostility of German emperors toward the papacy, inherited from father to son.[31] About Manfred, Pachymeres says that he had, as a sort of inheritance from his father (Frederick II), hostility toward the church (of Rome), and for that reason it was quite understandable that he should send German forces to fight against the "Italians" who held Constantinople. The occasion for this remark is the coalition between Michael II of Epirus, Manfred, and William II of Achaia against the forces of Nicaea, a coalition which came to an inglorious end at the battle of Pelagonia, in 1259. It is possible that each of these allies had in mind the conquest of Constantinople, which is the specific reference of Pachymeres' remark.[32] Pachymeres knows, too, that it was the papacy that had called Charles of Anjou to Sicily, and he thinks the reason was that the Hohenstaufen wanted to rule Sicily independently of the papacy, which is fairly close to the truth.[33] With Manfred's defeat, we are told, Charles of Anjou, formerly a count, became king of Sicily, a reward he had been promised by the pope; he acquired the ambition of conquering Constantinople, as well as the arrogance with which Pachymeres credits him, built a fleet, and received the support of Clement IV for the conquest of Constantinople.[34] From then on, until Charles' death in 1285, Pachymeres' discussion of Italian politics is dominated by the interplay between Charles of Anjou, Michael VIII, the royal house of Aragon, and successive popes, whose policies he outlines fairly accurately although sketchily. A well-drawn scene has Charles of Anjou fuming at the arrival of Byzantine emissaries to the papal court of Gregory X, rolling at the feet of the pope, and gnawing on his scepter. The pope, however, says Pachymeres, defended the rights of the "Greeks," saying that Constantinople had been theirs before and belonged to them now.[35]

If Italian politics during the reign of Michael VIII is dominated by Charles of Anjou and his plans, during the reign of Andronicus II the focus of interest is on Sicily, because of the connections of its king, Frederick III, with the Catalan mercenaries who were ravaging the empire. Indeed, virtually all mention of Sicily is in connection with the Catalan campaign, with only incidental information about other matters. That information, however, tends to be accurate. Thus, there is mention of the war in Sicily between Frederick III, correctly identified as Frederick II's grandson (through Frederick II's mother Constance, Manfred's daughter), and Charles of Valois, who had come to the aid of the Angevins of Naples. Frederick III, says Pachymeres, opposed the church almost by family tradition. There is then an allusion to the peace of Caltabelotta, the marriage of Charles of Valois to Catherine of Courtenay (Pachymeres calls her, correctly, Baldwin's granddaughter), through whom he acquired claims on Constantinople, and his "corona-

---

[31] Other major Italian affairs, such as the civil troubles in Florence in the early years of the 14th century, are not mentioned.

[32] Failler, 117–18; cf. D. J. Geanakoplos, *Emperor Michael Paleologus and the West, 1258–1282* (Cambridge, Mass., 1959), 47 ff.

[33] Failler, 249.

[34] Failler, 411, 461, 641; N. Gregoras, *Byzantina Historia*, Bonn ed., 3 vols. (1829–55), I, 123 (hereafter Gregoras), for Charles' ambitions.

[35] Failler, 523; M.-H. Laurent, *Le bienheureux Innocent V et son temps*, ST 129 (Vatican City, 1947).

tion" by the pope as "δίχα τέρας, εἴτ᾽ οὖν γῆς, . . . κράτορα."[36] Thus, it appears that Pachymeres was quite well informed about the intricacies of European, or at least Italian, politics and marriage alliances, but he rarely reports them except when they touch directly on Byzantium. He also seems to know something about Western feudal customs, since he reports Berengar d' Entença's oath of hommage to Andronicus II, saving his liege hommage to his king, Frederick III.[37]

Insofar as the internal politics of Italian powers are concerned, Pachymeres knows something about the political structure of Venice and Genoa, namely, about communal government. He uses the word κοινὸν συνέδριον for the Venetian Senate, and συνέδριον for the Genoese councils or commune.[38] He knows that the political structure of the Genoese colonies was patterned on that of Genoa,[39] and that all the Genoese colonies cooperated.[40] He knows, too, that the *abbate del popolo* of Pera was appointed from Genoa, and was, in name and originally in function, the equivalent of the Roman *tribunus plebis*, which he rendered as πραίτωρ τοῦ δήμου.[41] He knows at least the name of Spinola (Opizzino Spinola), one of the two captains of the people of Genoa, whose daughter had married Theodore, son of Adronicus II and marquis of Montferrat.[42] For the rest, he is not concerned with the internal politics of these two states, or, even less so, of Pisa. What he is quite knowledgeable about, and in a rather sophisticated manner, is Genoese commercial policy in the old Byzantine Empire and the Black Sea area. He details the beginnings of Genoese predominance in the Black Sea—based partly on imperial privileges, partly on the fact that they navigated even in winter. He gives an intelligent account of the problems of Alexius III of Trebizond and the Genoese, who wanted relief from the *kommerkion*,[43] but then, he was generally very interested and very well informed about the Black Sea area. He is equally well informed about the Zaccaria monopoly of the alum mines of Phocaea and their effort to entirely corner the market by having Michael VIII forbid the export of Asia Minor alum by their compatriots; nor is he ignorant of the objections of the other Genoese to this imperial policy.[44] Generally speaking, he shows quite a remarkable understanding of the means through which the Italian cities, but especially Genoa, estab-

[36] Pachymeres, (Bonn), II, 394. Cf. Laiou, *Constantinople*, 129 ff.

[37] Pachymeres, (Bonn), II, 499.

[38] Pachymeres, (Bonn), II, 243: Planoudes speaks to the Venetian Senate. Other Byzantine sources of the period call the Venetian Senate βουλή: F. Miklosich and J. Müller, *Acta et Diplomata Graeca Medii Aevi* (Venice, 1865), III, 86 (1277). The Venetian state is rendered, in the treaties, as the περιφανὲς κουμούνιον καὶ ὁλότης Βενετίας or ἐπιφανῆ δούκα καὶ κουμούνιον Βενετίας, a translation of "illustris ducis et communis Veneciarum": see Miklosich and Müller, *Acta*, III, 84, 100, and G. M. Thomas, *Diplomatarium Veneto-Levantinum* (New York, 1966), I, 82, 200 ff. The word "συνέδριον," when applied to Genoa, may refer to the communal government, that is, it may be equivalent to "commune." Cf. *Liber Jurium Reipublicae Genuensis*, ed. H. Ricottius, in *Monumenta Historiae Patriae* (Turin, 1872), I, no. 945 (ambaxatores comunis Janue); col. 1356: dominus Guiglielmus Bucanigra comunis et populi ianuensis capitaneus et consilium magnum.

[39] Pachymeres, (Bonn), II, 495, 624: ἐκ τῶν ἑκασταχοῦ κοινῶν συνεδρίων τοῦ γένους αὐτῶν.

[40] Pachymeres, (Bonn), II, 243, 624.

[41] Pachymeres, (Bonn), II, 624. See also W. Heyd, *Histoire du commerce du Levant au moyen-âge* (Leipzig, 1936), I, 458, who says that the reference is to the first *abbate del popolo* of Pera and notes that Pachymeres has a remarkably clear knowledge of the office.

[42] Pachymeres, (Bonn), II, 598. On the other hand, Pachymeres does not refer to the internal politics of Genoa at the time of Guglielmo Boccanegra, an important period for Byzantium.

[43] Pachymeres, (Bonn), II, 448–50.

[44] Failler, 535 ff. Cf. M. Balard, *La Romanie génoise*, 2 vols. (Rome, 1978), II, 776 ff.

lished their supremacy, even as he regrets the deleterious effects on the Byzantine economy.

Pachymeres' attitude toward the Italians is conditioned by a few important factors. The most fundamental one is the fact that for him, Nicaean born and bred, the heart and kernel of the empire lay in the East. It is the loss of Asia Minor that he laments, and for this he holds the Italians partly responsible. Their conquest of Constantinople in 1204, and the subsequent "thalassocracy" which they established, forced the Byzantines to divert resources for the defense of the littoral and did not allow them to stem the Turkish advance, as they could have done; in order to fight against the Italians, they had to make opportunistic alliances with the Cumans and the Turks.[45] The Italians here, are generally the Catholics, but specifically and historically the Venetians and the Genoese. This comes at the very beginning of his *History*, and sets the tone. The same theme is carried through in the discussion of the plans of the Angevins or of successive popes for the recovery of Constantinople. It carries over, for example, in his frequently raised objections to the destruction of the Byzantine fleet after 1285; the fleet was needed primarily against westerners, and it was no longer there. On the other hand, there is no question that Pachymeres considers that there is a community of Christians, to which both the Catholics and the Orthodox belong, although the former are misguided. To what has been said above on this subject, one may add the remark that references to Italian states, Sicily, the Venetians, and the Genoese have a strangely familiar feel about them—as though these are areas and people with whom one is quite well acquainted. They are, of course, clearly and unambiguously, "other": the immediate world of Pachymeres consists of the East (Asia Minor) and the West (lands west of Constantinople, primarily Epirus). Italy does not at all appear within these geographic parameters. Pachymeres was a realist. At one point he has Michael VIII say that in the old days, before 1204, the frontiers of the empire extended from the Tigris and the Euphrates to Sicily and Apulia, and from Egypt to the arctic regions; we know of course that the rhetoric of the Palaeologan period is the rhetoric of ecumenicism.[46] But Pachymeres, both overtly and in his signifiers, never has such claims. So for him, the Italians, both *qua* Italians and *qua* Catholic, are foreign, but a very familiar foreigner who might have been a brother.

The two other major historians of the fourteenth century, John Cantacuzenus and Nikephoros Gregoras, have a certain amount in common, but also considerable differences.[47] What they share in the first instance is certain blunt, concrete, and unsubtle realities: for one thing, they both had first-hand experience of the great civil war, although for Cantacuzenus the stakes were much higher than for Gregoras, and the experience had quite a different effect on each of them. Also, they lived in a world that they both realized had much shrunk for the Byzantines. There is no reason to dwell on obvious facts here, for example, on the fact that a very considerable part of the old Byzantine Empire was still, or newly, in the hands of westerners—the Peloponnese, Rhodes, the islands of the Aegean and the Ionian Seas, Crete, and Cyprus, not to mention Pera. I

---

[45] Failler, 27, 29.

[46] Failler, 209.

[47] Pachymeres' history stops in 1308; Cantacuzenus covers the years 1320 to 1356, and Gregoras the period 1204 to 1359. For Gregoras' dependence on Pachymeres, see R. Guilland, *Essai sur Nicéphore Grégoras: l'homme et l'oeuvre* (Paris, 1926).

may be allowed to posit as a fact, without having to prove it, that educated Byzantines of the fourteenth century, or indeed any Byzantines of any period, were not *ipso facto* stupid; I will add that much as they may have wished to conceal reality, some aspects of it were hard to conceal even from themselves. Thus, both Gregoras and Cantacuzenus, from different viewpoints to be sure, were perfectly aware that they lived in a world where the actions of outsiders—Serbs, Bulgarians, Turks, and even Italians—could spell life and death. The question here is how specifically they dealt with this reality, in particular with regard to Italy and the Italians.

It is not surprising that both historians, writing in the middle of the fourteenth century, after decades of intensive contact, should be quite familiar with westerners in general and with Italians in particular. The marriages of Palaeologan emperors with Western princesses had played a role complementary to that of the presence of Western merchants. Each of these ladies—Irene of Montferrat, Adelheid (Irene) of Brunswick-Grubenhagen, and Anne of Savoy, especially the latter—had brought with them large retinues, and the Byzantines at the court had become well accustomed to Western, and Italian, mores, Italian dress, and Western forms of entertainment. Both Gregoras and Cantacuzenus mention the jousts and tournaments in which Andronicus III and his compatriots indulged and in which, says Cantacuzenus, he proved himself better than the Savoyards, the French, the Germans, and the Burgundians who were the experts in such things. Gregoras gives definitions and long descriptions of jousts and tournaments, differentiating between the two.[48] Contact with people from these retinues, with ambassadors who almost routinely traveled back and forth from Italy to negotiate church union or political and matrimonial alliances, and with the Franciscans and Dominicans of Constantinople had made Italy and the Italians a very familiar part of the social as well as the political landscape. Cantacuzenus in particular moved in circles that included highly placed Western aristocrats and important people among the Genoese of Pera; he spoke some kind of "Latin" language, presumably an Italian dialect.[49] Some of the individuals who came to the Byzantine Empire with the Western princesses played an important role in subsequent political developments, and Cantacuzenus was in close contact with them too; a case in point is Zampea (Isabeau) and her son Artotos (Odoardo?) from the retinue of Anne of Savoy, whose adventures in Byzantium and Italy would repay a little study.[50] Gregoras, too, had his own contacts with Italians. Given this background, let us see what place Italy and the Italians occupied in their worldview.

First, let us turn to some questions of terminology. Both Gregoras and Cantacuzenus revert to the term "Latin" as a generic designation of westerners, including Italians; the

---

[48] J. Cantacuzenus, *Historiarum*, Bonn ed., 3 vols. (1828–32), I, 204–5 (hereafter Cantacuzenus); Gregoras, I, 481–83.

[49] Cantacuzenus, III, 303. One of his friends, "Ntziuan de Spinia" (Giovanni Spinola), who was "glorious among the Latins," also knew Greek: I, 484. Andronicus III had among his confidants three Genoese of noble family from Pera—Raffo Doria, Raffo de Mari, and Federico Spinola: I, 39. On the activities of the Franciscans, see M. Roncaglia, *Les frères mineurs et l'église grecque orthodoxe au XIIIe siècle (1231–1274)* (Cairo, 1954); D. Geanakoplos, "Bonaventura, the Two Mendicant Orders and the Greeks at the Council of Lyons (1274)," *The Orthodox Church and the West* (Oxford, 1975), 183–211. On the Dominicans see M. H. Congourdeau, "Frère Simon le Constantinopolitain, O.P. (1235?–1325?)," *REB* 45 (1987), 165–81.

[50] Cantacuzenus, I, 205; II, 123, 126, etc. Cf. D. M. Nicol, *The Byzantine Family of Kantakouzenos (Cantacuzenus) ca. 1100–1460* (Washington, D.C., 1968), 47.

term "Italian" has the restricted meaning of an inhabitant of the Italian peninsula or some part thereof. The Western rulers of Constantinople, whom Pachymeres called "Italian," are here called "Latin."[51] The same people, for example the rulers of Euboea, are sometimes called Latins and sometimes designated more specifically as Venetians or Genoese; indeed, the Genoese inhabitants of Pera are often called the "Latins of Galata."[52] Along with the generic descriptions, we have the differentiation of westerners and their lands: France, Burgundy, Savoy, Montferrat, Spain, England, and "Germany" all are specifically mentioned. As far as the Italian peninsula is concerned, there is quite close differentiation, as we shall see. Italy is part of a broader Western world, the most important part for the fourteenth-century Byzantines, and it is as part of that broader world that its role is best understood.

The world of Cantacuzenus and Gregoras has shifted west in a significant way in comparison to Pachymeres. Let us first have a look at the world as they knew it, i.e., the places they mention. Cantacuzenus' world includes the coasts of Asia Minor, the Byzantine possessions of the Balkans, the possessions of the various Western powers in the former Byzantine lands; the areas inhabited or ruled by Albanians, Serbs, and Bulgarians; to the north, there is Caffa and Tana, to which he devotes a certain amount of attention in connection with the War of the Straits that started in September 1350; in the same connection he mentions the Mongols of the Golden Horde.[53] Moving west, we find a proliferation of specificities: there is mention of Germany or Germans, France, Aragon, Burgundy, and Humbert II, dauphin of Viennois.[54] In Italy, he mentions Venice, Genoa, Sardenia, Corsica, Sicily, Montferrat, Savoy, Taranto, Calabria, and Lombardy.[55] Egypt and Syria, which had been integral parts of Pachymeres' world, and, by imitation, also of that of Gregoras, appear once, with Cantacuzenus' embassy to Sultan al-Nasir al-Hasan to seek protection or favors for the Christians, and, primarily it seems, to place Lazaros on the patriarchal throne of Jerusalem.[56] Cantacuzenus' oikoumene can be reconstructed from his description of the areas struck by the great plague of 1347: the lands of the "Scythians" (here, Mongols), the Black Sea, Thrace, Macedonia, Greece, Italy, "all of the islands," Egypt, Libya, Judaea, and Syria, "and [it] virtually (invaded) the entire

[51] Gregoras, I, 17, 81 ff, 85–86; Cantacuzenus, I, 520–21, 173–74.

[52] See, for example, Gregoras, I, 117, 95, and Cantacuzenus, III, 211 ff. The equivalent of Pachymeres' Ἰταλικὴ κόρυζα is Λατινικὴ ὀφρύς. Cf. Gregoras, I, 96, 447; II, 834.

[53] Cantacuzenus, III, 192 ff. On this, see C. P. Kyrris, "John Cantacuzenus, the Genoese, the Venetians and the Catalans (1348–1354)," Byzantina 4 (1972), 331–56; M. Balard, "A propos de la bataille du Bosphore: l'expédition génoise de Paganino Doria à Constantinople (1351–1352)," TM 4 (1970), 431–69.

[54] For the dauphin of Viennois, see Cantacuzenus, III, 13 ff; The form of the name (Δελφίνου Ντεβιάνα, Ἰνιμπέρτῳ Δελφίνῳ Ντεβιάνα) might suggest that Cantacuzenus uses "Dauphin de Viennois" as a name rather than a title; there is also similar usage of "marquis" in the reference to the marquis of Montferrat (III, 12); I think he is perfectly aware of the realities, but uses the title simply as a referent to the person in question, which is why it looks like a name. Interestingly, it is the form used by G. Stella, RISS 17:1088 (147): Ingibertus Delfinus Vienne. On the dauphin, see K. M. Setton, The Papacy and the Levant (1204–1571) (Philadelphia, 1976), I, 205 ff.

[55] Cantacuzenus, II, 508–10; I, 256, 510. The "princess of Taranto" is his usual way of referring to Joanna I of Naples.

[56] Cantacuzenus, III, 90 ff. Included here is a very interesting "letter" of the sultan, written in a sort of demotic Greek similar to that used later in Ottoman documents.

oikoumene in a circle."[57] This is a medieval world: certainly the Hyperborean Scythians belong to the world of antiquity, but the marquis of Montferrat (otherwise described as "Markesis o Loumpardias archon"),[58] the count of Savoy, the dauphin de Viennois, "Frantza," and "Burgunia" place us firmly in the fourteenth century.

Cantacuzenus' world looks large, but in fact it is not. He may know perfectly well that places, states, and peoples, even outside the ones he mentions, exist, but he is not very interested in them; indeed, the areas he is interested in have shrunk since the time of Pachymeres. His focus is upon Constantinople, the southern Balkan states—Serbia and Bulgaria—the Peloponnese, the islands of the Aegean, and the coasts of Asia Minor. The interior of Asia Minor, lost to the Byzantines, is not of interest to him, nor are the Mongols, except as their actions on the coast, especially the coast of the Crimea and the Sea of Azov, touch upon the affairs of the Mediterranean powers, Venice and Genoa, and tangentially upon Byzantium. He neither knows nor cares (or perhaps he knows but does not care) about the internal affairs of the Mongols, as Pachymeres had. Furthermore, his historical work is one long apologia for the great civil war: all of Book Three is dedicated to it, and Book Four, a considerable part of which relates to conflicts with and between westerners (primarily the Venetians and the Genoese), is also concerned with the continuation of the civil war. Nor is this simply a statistical matter—how many words are dedicated to the civil war; it is, rather, a conceptual matter, since his view of the world is highly colored by his own concerns about class, aristocratic privilege, contempt of the plebs, and his need to justify his actions during the civil war.

So it is with Cantacuzenus' approach to Italy and the Italians. The term "Italy" as used by him is a geographic term to designate the entire peninsula. Thus, he talks of the dynasts (the rulers) of Italy to refer to those whom Clement VI approached (in fact or in fiction) for a crusade; he mentions that he feared lest the expedition being prepared by the pope and "those of Italy and the rest of the West" be sent against him.[59] In 1347 he speaks of a great war all over Italy (κατὰ τὴν Ἰταλίαν), whose kings would move one against the other and which put an end to the plans of Clement VI for a crusade. The references to war may have to do with the Cola di Rienzo affair in Rome or with the activities of Giovanni Visconti or with the conflict between the three branches of the house of Savoy.[60] He gives no geographic information about Italy, just as he gives no geographic or anthropological information on any area or people outside his immediate focus of interest. What interests him about Italy can be summarized under three headings: the opinion of important Italians (particularly the Genoese, whether of Pera or of Genoa), as well as of the pope, regarding himself and his role in the civil war; the politics of Italian powers with regard to the Byzantine Empire, which in fact took place primarily in the years of the civil war and its immediate aftermath; and the internal politics of some

[57]Cantacuzenus, III, 49. Cf. similarly Gregoras, III, 797–98, who takes us to the Strait of Gibraltar, and who insists on the fact that the plague struck only the coastal lands.

[58]Cantacuzenus, III, 12.

[59]Cantacuzenus, III, 54, 56. Similarly, another envoy, from Savoy, will return "to Italy": II, 510. Cantacuzenus is either ignorant or careless about the seat of the papacy at this time. He talks about the return of the ambassadors of Clement VI to Italy, although the papacy was, at the time, in Avignon.

[60]Cantacuzenus, III, 62.

Italian states, primarily Genoa, which he understood in ways similar to the way he understood the Byzantine civil war. A fourth point of considerable interest, namely, the see-saw between Byzantines and Genoese with regard to the islands and cities of the northern Aegean, i.e., Chios, Lesbos, Phocaea, is tangential to our topic, and I will not deal with it.

The Italian areas or states that are mentioned by Cantacuzenus are the papacy, as a political and religious power (but there is no mention of the papal states), Venice, Genoa, Sardinia, Milan, Montferrat, Savoy, the kingdom of Naples.[61] One focal point of Cantacuzenus' interest, in my view, lies in his desire to persuade the Italians and other westerners (as well as the reader) that he was more sinned against than sinning in the civil war. He mentions several embassies going back and forth between Pera and himself and between Constantinople and the papacy, all eventually declaring him innocent. The people he was trying to persuade were the Genoese of Pera (and eventually of Italy), Savoy, the Avignonese papacy, and the dauphin of Viennois. The first embassy, in 1345, consisted of a man named Henry, who was a Franciscan from Savoy, and another, unnamed, Franciscan; both of them were sent to Cantacuzenus by the Genoese of Pera to inquire about the causes of the war, or so Cantacuzenus tells us. Cantacuzenus persuades them that he was in the right, and they promise to bring the news to both Italy and Constantinople/Pera.[62] The second embassy was actually sent by the dauphin of Viennois to Anne of Savoy, but reached Constantinople after the end of the civil war, to find Cantacuzenus on the throne. The ambassador, a certain Bartholomew, then wrote letters to both the pope and the dauphin in which he extolled Cantacuzenus in fulsome terms, or so Cantacuzenus reports. A few sentences will give the flavor of these letters. To the pope, he is supposed to have written, "Let the entire people under Roman rule exalt, let the entire world rejoice in the victory of such an Emperor. On the third of February [1347], a day dawned that is holy among all Christians, on which the Lord send His angel to prepare the way before Him, and with His splendid light to send far away the darkness of battle, bringing peace like an olive branch. For this is the King of peace, the second Solomon, whose countenance is desired by the entire creation . . ." To the dauphin, he wrote, "Let the entire faithful people rejoice: let the Christians sing hymns; let the glorious feast days renew themselves in the splendid temples . . ." Cantacuzenus is described as more philanthropic than Augustus, more pious than Theodosius (I), more equitable and good than Scipio, "who subjugated Africa to our Italians." "Now," the ambassador says, "I am hopeful that his reign will bring peace among the Christians and will repel the Ismaelites."[63]

There were, of course, good political reasons for this interest of Cantacuzenus in persuading various Western powers of his probity: Pope Clement VI (1342–52) was one of the popes who had the crusade very much at heart, and the crusade of Smyrna was a recent event, of which Cantacuzenus was very much aware;[64] he was also fearful that,

---

[61] For some reason, the kingdom of Naples has the most variegated designations in the 14th century: Pachymeres calls it "Apulia," Cantacuzenus "Taranto," and Gregoras "Italy."

[62] Cantacuzenus, II, 502 ff.

[63] Cantacuzenus, III, 12 ff (1347).

[64] On the crusade of Smyrna, see Cantacuzenus, II, 422–23, 529, 582–83. Cf. Setton, *Papacy and the Levant,* I, 182 ff.

with the wrong public relations, another crusade might well be directed against him. Furthermore, it appears that the marquis of Montferrat was collecting forces to claim the Byzantine throne, as protector perhaps of John V, his nephew, and he had, it seems, the support of the papacy and of some Italian rulers. Cantacuzenus was to claim that the fact that he persuaded the pope of his own good conduct brought these ambitions to an end. Most of all, Cantacuzenus was sensitive to the charge that he had brought the Turks into Europe, a charge of which he tried strenuously to clear himself. Given the political climate, and the interests of Clement VI, he might well fear that such a charge would make him not only morally culpable but also easy prey to any westerner, Genoese or crusader, who could claim to act in the interest of Christendom.

Beyond these political and practical considerations, however, one is struck by the fact that for Cantacuzenus the papacy as well as the westerners and the Italians, collectively and separately, function as arbiters of the legitimacy of his claims—as a sort of international public opinion to which he appeals and which he tries to sway. This is a very different matter from Pachymeres' view of a community of Christians with common interests. Pachymeres talks of the economic superiority and the political arrogance of the Italians—primarily the Genoese—but not of any control they had over the affairs of the empire. For Cantacuzenus, the civil war ended with the empire in thrall to the westerners, on whose good will and good opinion he felt he depended. This is different, too, from the dependence the empire had developed on the Turks and the Serbs, with whom it made alliances and fought battles. Cantacuzenus does not seem opposed to this dependence on the Italians, which is not an entirely tangible one. Certainly their hostility could have had disastrous effects for him, but he also saw them as one important set of powers who had an interest in the Byzantine Empire because of imperial intermarriages, because of commercial interests, and, finally, because the presence of the Turks in Europe touched both their religious sensibilities and their political life. Historians generally note that the civil war brought the Serbs and the Turks into prominence and made them the arbiters of the fate of the Byzantine Empire: this dependence on the Italians (as well as on the papacy), no less clear, has been less noticed.

The second theme of Cantacuzenus—the policy of various Italian powers with regard to Byzantium—has already been partly treated in the discussion of the Italians as a forum of international opinion. It may be observed in a general way, that whereas Cantacuzenus treats in some detail the politics of the Venetians and the Genoese in various parts of the Byzantine Empire—Pera, Chios, Lesbos, Phocaea, etc.—his treatment of the policies of the Italian states themselves is shallow. He mentions, for example, the Venetian efforts to forge an alliance with him against the Genoese in the course of the War of the Straits, but his frame of reference is simply the Venetian-Genoese rivalry.[65] Genoese policy in the Levant is simply and briefly interpreted as a desire for the mastery of the seas, without the lengthier and quite circumstantial discussion provided by Gregoras.[66] This shallowness remains true of his discussion of Western politics generally. The reader of Cantacuzenus, for example, receives no explanation of the Aragonese alliance with Venice at the time of the War of the Straits, whereas the reader of Gregoras does.

---

[65]Cantacuzenus, III, 185 ff.
[66]Cantacuzenus, III, 68 ff, 185 ff.

This shallowness results in part from Cantacuzenus' lack of interest, and partly from his concept of politics, which seems to center primarily on the actions of individuals, especially members of the aristocracy. I have already mentioned the fact that he is as conscious of rank among the Italians and the westerners in general as he is among the Byzantines. Occasionally, he bestows higher rank to the former, because it suits his purpose in terms of his Byzantine interests. Thus, the duke of Brunswick-Grubenhagen is called ἐπιφανέστατος because his daughter married Andronicus III.[67] Andronicus III's German mercenaries are aristocrats, as are the Genoese ambassadors sent to John VI in 1347 to discuss the question of Chios.[68] Andronicus' three Genoese friends, who were told of his intention to rebel, are called not noble but powerful among the Genoese of Galata; Cantacuzenus' way of giving their names makes it clear that they were, in fact, of noble lineage: "Their names were, from the family of Oria, Raffo d'Oria; from the Spinula, Frerigo Spinula; from that of Demar, Raffo Demar."[69] Indeed, these three families had a very weighty presence in Pera; it has been estimated that of thirty podestàs of Pera, from 1264 to 1348, seventeen belonged to them.[70] His interest in internal Italian politics forms part of the same conceptualization. He knows that there are different forms of government in Italy, and mentions, for example, the count of Savoy, the marquis "of Lombardy" (Montferrat), and the princess of Taranto. Venice, he knows, is governed by the doge and the Senate (δούξ, βουλή).[71] Genoa he calls, quite properly, a "commune" (τὸ κοινόν Γεννούας), and refers to decisions of the Senate and the people of Genoa, or of the doge and the people (δούξ, βουλή, δῆμος), and to ambassadors sent to the doge, the Senate, and the people of Genoa to negotiate the return of Chios to the Byzantines.[72] He also knows something about the mahona of Chios, namely, that it was a group of private individuals, aristocrats who had financed and armed their own fleet and taken the island, even though he does not dispute, as perhaps he should have done, the Genoese government's disclaimer of any responsibility for the affair.[73]

The civil wars in Italy, especially in Genoa, Cantacuzenus knew about, and presented in a way fully consonant with his views of who should rule and how. He mentions the revolution of 1339 in terms redolent of the Byzantine civil war, as he saw it.[74] The people of Genoa, he said, rose against their aristocracy, exiling some, forbidding others to partic-

[67]Cantacuzenus, I, 52.

[68]Cantacuzenus, I, 98; III, 81–82. Some noble Latins are knighted: II, 166.

[69]Cantacuzenus, I, 39. This is also the way such names appear in the Genoese annals: illi de Auria, illi de Spinollis, illi de Flisco, illi de Grimaldis. See T. O. de Negri, Storia di Genova (Florence, 1986), 397. Cf. Origone, Bisanzio e Genova, 252. Cantacuzenus also had a great and old friend, Giovanni Spinola: Cantacuzenus, I, 482. Cf. Gregoras, I, 233, 237, who says that (Opizzino) Spinola, whose daughter married Theodore of Montferrat, was of low rank since westerners will not allow nobles to marry even imperial Byzantine offspring.

[70]Origone, Bisanzio e Genova, 213–14; she also notes that after the middle of the 14th century only eight of these names belong to the Doria and the Spinola.

[71]Cantacuzenus, III, 219 ff: ὅ, τε γὰρ Βενετίας δοὺξ καὶ ἡ βουλὴ τῶν ἰδίων ἀνέθηκαν ἐκείνῳ (N. Pisano) τὴν ἀρχὴν.

[72]Cantacuzenus, I, 489, 492, 486; III, 234 ff. The response also comes in the name of the doge, the commune, and the people of Genoa: III, 81.

[73]Cantacuzenus, III, 81: οἰκείοις ἀναλώμασι. Cf. Balard, La Romanie génoise, 173 ff, on Simone Vignoso and the mahona.

[74]On what follows, see also Stella, RISS, 129 ff.

ipate in the government, "and humiliating them in every way." They chose instead "someone called Simone Boccanegra," from among the people, and made him their ruler (ἄρχων).[75] Then came the Venetian war, declared in 1350. The Genoese saw that the war needed a lot of money, so they recalled the exiled nobles and asked them to help govern. The nobles behaved responsibly and magnanimously, thinking it better to give their help than for the entire commune to be defeated and humiliated. So they berated the people for their poor judgment and ingratitude in "that they behaved shamefully (προπιλακίζουσιν) to the best people, having nothing to accuse them of, except that they were better than they," but did then participate eagerly in the war. The result was the appointment of Pagano Doria, "the most illustrious of the lineage of the Doria," as admiral.[76] Later, Pagano Doria was accused by Boccanegra and the people of having been responsible for the defeat, and replaced. This led to greater defeat at the battle of Alghero (off Sardinia), and to the subjugation of Genoa to Giovanni Visconti of Milan (1353): "thus the Genoese were forced by the war to take ignoble actions against their own liberty, and, abandoning their earlier arrogance, and deposing their archon, Simone Boccanegra, they received as archon (doge) of the city the man appointed by the ruler of Milan."[77]

All of this is simply the plight of the aristocracy as understood and related by Cantacuzenus. It is one more case that proves his point, for in Byzantium too, according to him, the best people had been taken out of government by Alexios Apokaukos and the Zealots; it was for that reason, he tells us elsewhere in his *History*, that the state could find no one with the wherewithal, the spirit, the courage, and the expertise to defend it. He considered himself among those who had been ill-treated yet always worked for the common good; the reported sentiments of the nobles of Genoa are very much what he relates about himself, when, at about the same time, he accused the merchants of Constantinople of not having given him money to build a fleet against the Genoese, but nevertheless forgave them. Genoese politics comes to confirm, once again, Cantacuzenus' position during the civil war.[78] It does so because he twists and manipulates Genoese history and, given his detailed knowledge of it, he alters it consciously. His discussion of the first stages of Boccanegra's accession is, generally speaking, accurate. It is true that in 1339 all nobles were excluded from the Consiglio and the government generally, and that the Guelphs and some of the Ghibellines were exiled or left Genoa temporarily. For the rest, Simone Boccanegra, the merchant who challenged the rule of noble families, is made responsible for all the evils that befell the city, much as Alexios Apokaukos was made responsible for all the evils of the Byzantine civil war. To this purpose, Cantacuzenus extends the first "dogado" of Boccanegra to cover the period 1339 to 1353 continuously. Yet, we know that the Genoese war with Venice had not yet begun (1350) when Boccanegra was forced to abdicate by the very nobles he had admitted back into the Council of Twelve (on 23 December 1344). It was surely not the merchant Boccanegra but the noble Giovanni di

---

[75] Boccanegra was, indeed, named *signore* and *duca*.
[76] Cantacuzenus, III, 197–98. Origone, *Bisanzio e Genova*, quite rightly points out Cantacuzenus' admiration for his foremost enemy in the War of the Straits.
[77] Cantacuzenus, III, 234–35. On the battle of Alghero, see Balard, *La Romanie génoise*, 109–10; and T. N. Bisson, *The Medieval Crown of Aragon* (Oxford, 1991).
[78] Cf. Origone, *Bisanzio e Genova*, 253.

Valente who was responsible for Pagano Doria's replacement by Antonio Grimaldi, another member of the nobility, and also responsible for the surrender of the city to Milan.[79] Both in this abuse of Genoese history and in his own efforts to persuade the Italians that he was in the right, Cantacuzenus makes Italy function as an extension of Byzantium, not necessarily because such was the reality, but because of his own need for justification, and also, because by then Italian and Byzantine affairs were closely intertwined.

Gregoras' concerns being different from those of Cantacuzenus, his approach to Italy and Italian affairs or matters connected with them is also somewhat different. In Gregoras' *History* the civil war of John VI and the regency for John V occupies a central place, but for reasons other than those behind Cantacuzenus' narrative: he was detailing the decline of the Byzantine Empire, in which the civil war was instrumental, and he was, of course, deeply embroiled in the Palamist controversy, to which he devotes a very considerable proportion of his work. At the same time, he is a successor of Pachymeres in a variety of ways. Primary for us is the fact that he has a much broader view of the world than does Cantacuzenus, and also a great deal more curiosity, which makes him take shorter or longer excursions into geography, the description of political affairs and mores, and even ethnographic descriptions.

The affairs of Byzantium take place in a world that is larger, more variegated, and better known to the author than that of Cantacuzenus. It includes the coasts of Asia Minor (though not the interior, which had not been discussed since the time of Pachymeres), Syria, and Palestine, where the fall of the crusader states (the states of the Keltogalatai as he calls them) in 1291 is recorded, following Pachymeres.[80] Egypt is very much present, and its expansion westward into north Africa (Morocco and Libya) in the late thirteenth century is mentioned. The travels of Agathangelos to the Christian lands of the East cause Gregoras to mention Egypt, Phoenicia, Syria, Arabia, Cyprus, Crete, and Euboea.[81] Tana, Caffa, the Crimea, the Sea of Azov, the Mongols of Nogai and the Golden Horde appear several times, as does Trebizond.[82] Rus and Lithuania are mentioned at surprising length for reasons mostly connected with ecclesiastical matters. About the Russians, he says that they border the western ocean and the Hyperborean Scythians, and he is much impressed by the size and the wealth of their land. He knows about the Mongol invasions, and the translation of the see of the metropolitan of Kiev to Vladimir and about the rivalry of Moscow and the Lithuanians.[83] Finally, there is mention of Germany, and he knows something about England and France and the beginnings of the Hundred Years War (1338, though the passage, close chronologically to the crusade of

---

[79] See de Negri, *Storia di Genova*, 455 ff. I find it surprising that some scholars have stated that Cantacuzenus knew about the second dogado of Boccanegra and that he describes accurately the cession of Genoa to Milan: Origone, *Bisanzio e Genova*, 253. It is perfectly clear that Cantacuzenus is talking of a continuous dogado, from 1339 to 1353. I cannot find any mention of Boccanegra's second dogado which, in any case, began in 1356, when Cantacuzenus' *History* ends.

[80] Gregoras, I, 106–7.

[81] Gregoras, III, 11 ff.

[82] See, for example, Gregoras, I, 149 ff; II, 877 ff.

[83] Gregoras, III, 113 ff, 199, 511 ff. Cf. D. Obolensky, *The Byzantine Commonwealth: Eastern Europe, 500–1453* (London, 1971), 261 ff.

Smyrna, may refer to Edward III's 1346 campaign in France).[84] He does, of course, know about Spain; in fact, there is a fair amount about the politics of the house of Aragon. The islands of Sardinia, Corsica, and Sicily he not only mentions, but provides geographic descriptions of, at least for Sardinia and Sicily.[85]

The two ends of the inhabited world, for Gregoras, are the lands inhabited by the Celts and the people who border the (western) ocean on the one hand, and on the other those inhabited by the Indians.[86] Thus, a good part of the "inhabited world" of the ancient and the enlightened medieval world makes an appearance, although sometimes a cameo one, on the pages of Gregoras. This is all quite unexceptional for the fourteenth century, when the knowledge of Ptolemaic geography was completed with rather elegant maps. The terminology, too, is ancient: the Germans (Alamanoi) are called ἑσπέριοι Γαλάται; the French are Keltogalatai; there is also Maurousia (Morocco).[87] The description of various lands derives from ancient knowledge. Thus, for example, in a brief discussion of the First Crusade, Gregoras takes pains to situate his reader in the appropriate place in western Europe: "There are, in Europe, very high mountains, called the Alps, from which a great River called the Rhine flows toward the British Ocean; it has to the south both Gallias" (μεσημβρινωτέρας ποιεῖ τὰς ἄμφω Γαλλίας). And he traces the route of the First Crusade, "from the Rhine down the Danube, a very great river which also springs from the Alps and comes out in the Black Sea, breaking up into five mouths."[88] But there is a curious passage that contradicts all of this and plunges us back into the unreconstructed, i.e., western, Middle Ages. In the middle of one of his orations to Cantacuzenus, in 1351, Gregoras is arguing for φιλαλληλία, love of one another, as a sort of dialectic relationship between two people or sets of people, and also as a general law of nature: "This," he says, "is what gives land a navigable sea and, on the other hand, gives passable land to the sea. That is how the Don, traversing its boundaries, flows out into Greece, and the Danube comes into Egypt, and the Nile communicates with the Sea of Azov."[89] We are, now, in a different world, with a different geographic system from the one I have been describing—a world quite medieval, and with an allegorical significance.

Whatever the reasons may be for this excursion into a different geographic system, it is clear that Gregoras' world exists not only as a geographic unity, but also as a series of political or religious units. Part of it is held together by adherence to the Orthodox religion—from Rus to the Christian communities of Syria, Palestine, and Arabia. The European world and the world around the Mediterranean is sometimes seen to function as a unit, or form an entity. Thus, the Egyptian expansion in the late thirteenth century

---

[84] Gregoras, II, 687 ff.

[85] Gregoras, III, 190–92, for the description of Sardinia.

[86] Gregoras, I, 332. Cf. III, 354, which gives the same diametrical opposition between East and West, between the Ethiopians and the Indians on the one hand and the Celts and the inhabitants of Britain on the other. The connection of Ethiopians and Indians is interesting; presumably this is Ethiopia *sub Aegypto*, and is used to designate eastern parts, not southern parts; the world, then, for him, would end somewhere around the Indus River.

[87] Gregoras, I, 477. See also "Πατριβαλοί" for "Serbians": II, 703.

[88] Gregoras, I, 102–3.

[89] Gregoras, II, 933: Καὶ τοῦτ' ἔστιν ὃ γῆ μὲν πλωτὴν ἐργάζεται θάλασσαν καὶ ταύτην αὖθις ἐκείνη βάσιμον· καὶ Τάναϊς μὲν δι' αὐτό γέ τοι τοῦτο δρόμον ποιούμενος ὑπερόριον ἐπιρρεῖ τῇ Ἑλλάδι, καὶ Ἴστρος ἐπ' Αἴγυπτον ἔρχεται, καὶ Μαιώτιδι Νεῖλος κοινοῦται τὸ ῥεῦμα.

is tied both to the Black Sea area, from which the Egyptians got their slaves, and to Africa and Asia, for with these Cuman slaves, says Gregoras, the Egyptians moved out of their frontiers, and expanded greatly, subjugating the Libyans and the Moroccans in the west, while in the east they took Arabia Felix and that part of Arabia which is defined by the Indian Ocean and, on either side, the Persian and the Arabian Gulf. Then they took Koile Syria and Phoenicia, bordered by the Orontes River.[90] What is detailed here owes something to Pachymeres—for example, the Black Sea connection, the very mention of the destruction of the crusader states—but the concept of a Christendom that is shaken by the Muslim counterattack, which we find in Pachymeres, is absent here; it is, rather, the political expansion of Egypt that is being described. Other parts of the inhabited world function as parts of a system: In the early 1340s, Gregoras finds the whole of Europe and north Africa in turmoil as though, he says, God had ordered that throughout the *oikoumene* both democracies and aristocracies should rebel and engage in civil wars, so that virtually no country was left untouched. First he mentions the Genoese expulsion of Boccanegra (1344), then the civil war in Egypt among the many sons of Sultan Muhammad bin Qalawun, who died in 1340. The inhabitants of Libya and Morocco "who live around the western Atlas mountains" attacked Spain, a correct reference for the year 1340. The English started a great war in France; the eastern Mongols dissolved into civil wars; and various Latins attacked the Turkish naval and piratical forces as well as Smyrna (October 1344).[91]

If this is his world, the Mediterranean lands are at its center, and it is about these that Gregoras provides the most extensive political if not geographic information; within this smaller circle, Italy occupies an important place for obvious reasons. Keeping away from the obvious, it is better to concentrate on the particularities of Gregoras' presentation of Italy and Italian affairs. First of all, a note on geography and terminology. Gregoras uses the term "Italy" to refer almost exclusively to the kingdom of Naples, i.e., Pachymeres' Apulia.[92] Only in the discussion of religious matters are "Italy" and "Italians" sometimes used in the sense of Catholic.[93] The other parts of Italy are designated specifically, and often are given short descriptions. Lombardy is the other large province as far as Gregoras is concerned: Montferrat and Savoy are both presented as part of Lombardy.[94] In a curious passage, which aims to explain the various titles of Western rulers as having derived from titles held by imperial officials in the great days of the Roman Empire, he refers to Lombardy and Montferrat (which is unnamed) as though they were the same thing, and this "province" as having a ruler with the title of *markesios*.

[90] Gregoras, I, 106 ff.
[91] Gregoras, II, 683–89. Ihor Ševčenko has pointed out that all this (except the Smyrna crusade) points to Genoese ships as transmitters of information; cf. I. Ševčenko, "The Zealot Revolution and the Supposed Genoese Colony in Thessalonica," Προσφορὰ εἰς Στίλπωνα Π. Κυριακίδην (Thessalonike, 1953), 611–12 (Ἑλληνικά 4, supp.). Stella mentions all this: RISS, 107SE, 1078D (Muslim attack on Spain); 1080C (Genoese vs. Golden Horde); 1087A (French-English war in Flanders).
[92] See, for example, Gregoras, I, 123 ff, 193, 523; where the use might be generic, i.e., in the characterization of Barlaam as being from Italy, the reference turns out to be for the geographic area of the kingdom of Naples, i.e., Barlaam was from Calabria: Gregoras, I, 555; II, 901.
[93] Gregoras, I, 501–20, on papal initiatives for church union in 1334.
[94] Gregoras, I, 26, 383–84.

He places it "somewhere between the Alps and lower Iberia," and says it is small and insignificant.[95] Milan he does not specifically situate in Lombardy, but he does give a geographic description of it on the occasion of the surrender of Genoa to Giovanni Visconti, in 1353. Milan is an old city, placed in the middle of the Alps, and surrounded by mountains on all sides so that it is impregnable.[96]

Sicily, too, appears in Gregoras' history, primarily because of Manfred, and thus, through Pachymeres, and merits a geographic description: it is a large and populous island, whose distance from Scyllaeum, the Italian promontory, to Messina is no more than 30 *milia*.[97] Sardinia comes in for a description, because of the role it played in the later stages of the War of the Straits. "There is a large and populous island lying in the Tyrrhenian Sea, which has long mountains and a number of rivers, and many cities, both on the coast and in the interior. All around there are coasts and harbors and gulfs."[98] To round off the discussion of Italy, it is perhaps worth noting that the geography of the area is effortlessly used as a reference—for example, to make an argument by analogy. In trying to argue that one should judge men's virtue by their intention and not by their final actions, Gregoras produces the analogy that this is similar to what would happen if someone started from Sicily and wanted to sail to the ports of Sardinia and Corsica (due west), but a violent western wind pushed him to Crete. The analogy is never completed, but he presumably means that the observer should keep in mind the original intent, not the final and accidental end of the journey.[99]

Italy then is a very familiar place, but still one that merits description, not unlike Cyprus, Rhodes, or Crete in other instances: a place that is important to know, foreign enough for geographic description, but not sufficiently foreign for ethnographic description (not that Gregoras is much given to that). In any case, similarly, he finds it necessary—or perhaps just fun, and a way to show off—to provide the translation of important terms. Specifically, he gives us the Greek equivalents of the terms for the most important officials of the Italian colonies in Constantinople: the *bailo*, he says, is an "epitropos," the Pisan consul an "ephoros," and the Genoese *podestà* an "exousiastes."[100]

In terms of political importance, it is, of course, Venice and Genoa that retain pride of place, with Genoa far outdistancing Venice. Gregoras has an interest in the internal affairs of these places, and, most particularly, in their colonial policies. His knowledge of the internal affairs of Genoa is actually quite impressive.[101] The tumultuous events of Genoese history are presented, quite correctly from a fourteenth-century observer's point of view, as a long struggle between Guelphs and Ghibellines. The first mention of this struggle is preceded, in a typical manner, by a brief positioning of Genoa on the map: "Genoa is a maritime Italian city in the West, lying between the Alps and the

---

[95] Gregoras, I, 237. But cf. I, 13, where he names the marquis of Montferrat who became king of Thessalonica, and I, 167–68, where Irene of Montferrat is identified as a descendant of that first marquis of Montferrat, even though Montferrat is not expressly named.
[96] Gregoras, III, 193.
[97] Gregoras, I, 217.
[98] Gregoras, III, 190.
[99] Gregoras, II, 589.
[100] Gregoras, I, 97–98; cf. I, 268, on the Genoese *podestà*.
[101] Here I differ with Origone, *Bisanzio e Genova*, 253, and "Genova," 488, who finds that Gregoras' discussion of Genoese affairs simply falls within his preconceived ideas of democracy and tyranny.

Tyrrhenian sea."[102] It was inhabited, he says, by two γένη, families or factions, the Guelphs and the Ghibellines. He mentions the unseating and exile of the Ghibellines in the early 1320s, and the fact that the unrest spread to the Genoese colonies, which the exiles attacked with mercenary forces. The confusion of the late 1330s and early 1340s is telescoped: He talks of the rise in power of Simone Boccanegra, who is called by the title "touzos," i.e., doge, without details, saying simply that he was raised from a butcher to doge. The reason for that rebellion had been that the nobles (he mentions Spinola and "Sertorio," i.e., D'Oria) had been behaving in a tyrannical manner; they were therefore exiled. Later, they were allowed back into the city; they formed a conspiracy against Boccanegra, and soon began to behave like tyrants again. The people then rose against them once again, and exiled them from the city, electing another doge who also sprang from a lowly class.[103] This is quite accurate. He also has a circumstantial description of the battle of Alghero, longer than Stella's and more detailed.[104]

On the other hand, Gregoras is quite wrong in his description of the composition of the mahona of Chios. He confuses the original aim of the mahona—opposition to the exiles of Monaco—with the participants of the mahona, and says, wrongly, that the mahona was made up of Genoese exiles. Cantacuzenus is much more accurate in this respect.[105] Equally, his discussion of the effect of the War of the Straits on Genoese internal affairs is exiguous. Whereas he gives a proper explanation of the participation of the "Catalans," that is, of the king of Aragon, against the Genoese (Genoa had taken a part of Sardinia, which belonged to Aragon), he has very little to say of the fate of Pagano Doria, so much bemoaned by Cantacuzenus. He simply says that the Genoese feared lest they be conquered by Venice, there was civil disorder, and "in a short time they overturned the ancient institutions of their Republic," and gave themselves up to Milan. The overlordship of Milan he considers to have been divine punishment for Genoa's arrogance and faithlessness, and most particularly for the way it had behaved toward the Byzantines. A true case of *hubris* is presented here: having dreamt of the mastery of all the seas, from Tana and the Sea of Azov to Gadeira and the Heracleian columns, the Genoese even lost their own country; having unjustly appropriated common property, they justly lost even what belonged to them (τὸ κοινὸν ἀδίκως ἰδιοποιούμενοι, ἔλαθον καὶ τὸ ἴδιον ἐνδίκως . . . ἀπολωλεκότες).[106]

This brings us to the most interesting part of Gregoras' treatment of the Italians. His most insightful moments—which, one must admit, are not many—come when he discusses the commercial and colonial policy of the Italians, especially the Genoese, and, to a lesser extent, the Venetians. The establishment of Genoese power he attributes, unsur-

---

[102] Gregoras, I, 286.

[103] "Touzos" must be a transliteration of the Genoese "düxe." Gregoras, I, 286–87; I, 548: they elected ἡγεμόνα τῆς πολιτείας ἕνα τοῦ δήμου, κατὰ τὸ ἀρχαῖον τῆς ὑπατείας τὼν Ῥωμαίων ἀξίωμα, ἢ μᾶλλον κατὰ τὴν τῶν Βενετικῶν πολιτείαν (1339). Cf. II, 687–88, and Origone, *Bisanzio e Genova*, 253. In fact, Giovanni di Murta, who succeeded Boccanegra, was a noble, but a moderate man; and there *was*, also, a rebellion, which made the council a preserve of the popular class.

[104] Gregoras, III, 190 ff. Cf. Stella, RISS, 152.

[105] Gregoras, II, 765–66, and cf. Cantacuzenus, II, 583; cf. Balard, *La Romanie génoise*, 122–24.

[106] Gregoras, III, 193–94. Actually this is fairly close to Stella's explanation of the cession of Genoa to Milan; he attributes it to the fear of an explosion of civil conflict: RISS, 152.

prisingly, to the privileges granted by Michael VIII.[107] But as far as the increase in their power is concerned, his analysis is almost subtle, or in any case subtler than that of Cantacuzenus. He attributes it in part to the decline of the Byzantine navy, and to the service of Byzantine sailors on Genoese ships; he attributes it, too, to the incessant civil wars of the Byzantines, and to the fact that their rulers paid no attention to the political or economic affairs of the state, while the Genoese of Pera, on the other hand, gave close attention to such matters. As a result, he says in a well-known passage, the Genoese expected to have the mastery of these seas, took over not only the commercial wealth but also the money collected from commercial duties, and opposed any effort of the Byzantines to sail and trade in the Black Sea.[108]

Virtually his whole discussion of the Genoese in the Levant revolves around the idea that they wanted "thalassocracy"—by which he means essentially mastery of the northern Aegean and the Black Sea. And it is he who provides the classic model of Genoese expansion in these parts in another well-known passage that discusses the origins of their colony in Caffa and their relations with the Mongols, down to the war of 1343 and the expulsion of the Genoese. There are enough parallels between the concepts in this passage and in two passages in Pachymeres to suggest that Gregoras acquired his understanding of Genoese commercial and colonial policy from that older and much better historian.[109] However, he does contribute his own observations, from his own time, such as his understanding of the international aspect of the grain trade, and of the effects of the expulsion of the Genoese from Caffa both on that area and on their compatriots in Trebizond. He understands, too, that the War of the Straits was an all-out war between Venice and Genoa, fought all over the Mediterranean, although he does not seem to understand why.[110] He understands the mechanics of it, however, and sees it as a war between two powers with colonies, in which the colonies (including Crete) participate fully in the hostilities.[111] He also understands something of Venice's way of doing business. He reports that the Venetians try to buy peace, which is essential for the conduct of trade, from which they garner great profits; they go to war only when they are forced to, and then they buy off their neighbors and others, make them into allies, and even get armies from them.[112]

It is time to look at our three historians together. Between the time of Pachymeres and that of Gregoras and Cantacuzenus, a period of almost fifty years, great changes had taken place. As far as our topic is concerned, two of these changes are of importance: the loss of Asia Minor to the Turks and the firm establishment of the Genoese presence in the eastern Mediterranean and the Black Sea in a supremacy that was already greatly disputed at the time the histories of Gregoras and Cantacuzenus were written. As a result of these developments, the relative weight of Italy and the Italians increased, as one may

[107]Gregoras, I, 526–27.
[108]Gregoras, I, 526–27; II, 841–45.
[109]Gregoras, II, 683–87, and Failler, 535; Pachymeres, (Bonn), II, 448–50.
[110]Gregoras, II, 880.
[111]See, e.g., Gregoras, III, 39.
[112]Gregoras, III, 189–90. It should be noted that he also mentions very briefly the efforts toward an anti-Turkish league, spearheaded by Venice: I, 525; cf. A. E. Laiou, "Marino Sanudo Torsello, Byzantium and the Turks: The Background to the Anti-Turkish League of 1332–34," *Speculum* 45 (1970), 374–92.

see in the accounts of the two later historians. Their knowledge of Italian affairs may not be greater than that of Pachymeres, but it lies closer to the surface. At the same time, in terms of analysis, Pachymeres is exceptional, for he understood the causes and eventual effects of Genoese supremacy, and Gregoras is at his best when he follows in the steps of this analysis. If Pachymeres was still very much writing within the atmosphere created by 1204 and then by the Union of Lyons, and thus used a terminology that defined the Italians in religious terms, he was also a man who had a concept of the Mediterranean and the complex interrelationships of politics in that basin. His successors had much closer contact with the Italians; they counted some among their friends, they used terminology that reflects their knowledge of both the institutions and, to some degree, the language of Italy. All of this is attended by more detailed discussion of geography (in the case of Gregoras) and more detailed attention to the internal politics and policies of Italian states by both. Italy and the Italian colonies in the Mediterranean are very much at center stage by the middle of the fourteenth century.

The role of the Italians as perceived by our three historians may be seen in their discussion of the effects of the dissolution of the Byzantine navy in 1285. Pachymeres describes at length and bitterly the counsel of those who urged the dissolution of the expensive fleet on the illusion that it was not needed since the Venetians and the Genoese were newly at peace, and Charles of Anjou had no power anymore (he died in 1285). He laments the decision, for he sees the impossibility of preserving the security of the Byzantine Empire, Constantinople, and the islands without a navy, especially since the Italians were eager to recapture Constantinople. He notes the fact that some of the sailors became pirates, and the unpleasant effects of that development. He then shows how that action made hostilities on the part of the Venetians possible, in 1302, and how, at the time of the Catalan campaign, Andronicus II was bitterly berated by the people at Constantinople, who said that they never would be secure without a fleet.[113] Cantacuzenus mentions the fleet, yes, but primarily to attack the merchants of Constantinople for not having given him the money he wanted to build a fleet until it was almost too late and the Genoese were causing trouble: a case, once again, of Cantacuzenus' mistreatment by the people of Constantinople. Note also that here the effects of the destruction of the fleet have shrunk, to the defense of the city itself.[114] Gregoras returns to Pachymeres' analysis and makes the destruction of the fleet a major step in the decline of the Byzantine Empire: he can now add to Pachymeres' fear of Italian attacks by sea the fear and reality of Turkish piratical expeditions and Turkish armies arriving in Europe on Turkish ships without the Byzantines being able to do much about it.[115] He can also expand, as we have already noted, on the many and multiple effects of the quest of the Genoese for mastery of the seas. Interestingly, one of the remedies the Byzantines took, in 1343, he describes in terms that Cantacuzenus clearly and Gregoras less clearly had used for an Italian—a Genoese—action: when the rich people of Constantinople, in 1348, became persuaded of the need to build a fleet, "they built and armed men-of-war and small ships at their own expense" (λέμβους στρατιώτιδας καὶ ἀκάτια συνεσκευάσαντό τε καὶ ἐξώπλισαν ἐξ

---

[113] Pachymeres, (Bonn), II, 69–71, 322–24, 530–33. Cf. Laiou, *Constantinople*, 74–75, 110, 114–15.

[114] Cantacuzenus, III, 68 ff, and to the same effect Gregoras, II, 854 ff.

[115] Gregoras, I, 174–76, 208–9, 841 ff, 866–67. "The Latins would not have grown so arrogant toward the Romans, nor would the Turks ever have gazed upon the sands of the sea . . .": Laiou, *Constantinople*, 115.

οἰκείας δαπάνης).[116] The words "ἐξ οἰκείας δαπάνης" are the exact equivalent of Cantacuzenus' words—"οἰκείοις ἀναλώμασι"—with which he describes the arming of the mahona, the fleet of Vignoso that took Chios.[117] Thus, our Byzantine historians saw similarities even in institutions that were rather particular to, in this case, Genoa.

As Constantinople became the center of a vanishing state, in the mid-fourteenth century, interest in Italy and the Italians increased, for the very fate of the city seemed to
depend on them. The broad interest in Italy is a measure of the weakness of the Byzantines and a measure of the colonization of the old Byzantine Empire; to put it euphemisti-
cally, it is a measure of the inclusion of Byzantium into a broader Mediterranean world
whose center of gravity was in Italy, and whose motor was the policies of the great Italian
maritime republics. It was an unequal world; the ties that bound Byzantines and Italians
did not bind them with equal force.

---

[116]Gregoras, II, 857.
[117]Cantacuzenus, II, 583.

Monopoly and privilege: the Byzantine reaction to the Genoese presence in the Black Sea

The Genoese expansion in the Black Sea area took place with the connivance and support of the restored Palaeologan state, which opened up these areas to the Genoese, in part as payment for presumed naval-military support at a time when relations between Byzantium and Venice were generally hostile[1]. The subsequent political and economic developments in the Black Sea area are well-known, having formed the object of many important studies[2]. The effects on Byzantine merchants have also been examined by several scholars[3]. While there was much collaboration between native merchants and the Genoese and the Venetians, there was also considerable resent-

---

[1] See M. BALARD, *La Romanie génoise (XIIe-début du XVe siècle)*, Rome, 1978, vol. I, 42 ff.

[2] The bibliography is too immense to append here. See, as examples, L. BALLETTO, *Genova, Mediterraneo, Mar Nero (secoli XIII-XV)*, Genova, 1976; M. BALARD cit.; G. PISTARINO, *Genovesi d'Oriente*, Genova, 1990; M. BALARD, *Byzance et les régions septentrionales de la mer Noire (XIIIe-XVe siècles)*, in «Revue historique», 288, 1993, pp. 19-38.

[3] See, for example, K.-P. MATSCHKE, *Zum Charakter des byzantinischen Schwartzmeerhandels im 13. bis 15. Jahrhundert*, in «Wissenschaftliche Zeitschrift, Karl-Marx-Universität, Gesch. und sprach. Wiss.», 19/3, 1970; N. OIKONOMIDÈS, *Hommes d'affaires grecs et latins en Constantinople (XIIIe-XVe siècles)*, Montreal, 1979; A.E. LAIOU-THOMADAKIS, *The Byzantine Economy in the Mediterranean Trade System. Thirteenth-Fifteenth Centuries*, in «Dumbarton Oaks Papers», 34-35, 1980-1981, pp. 177-222; EAD., *The Greek Merchant of the Palaeologan Period: A Collective Portrait*, in «Πρακτικὰ τῆς Ἀκαδημίας Ἀθηνῶν», 1982, pp. 96-132.

ment among segments of Byzantine society towards the expansion of the maritime Italian cities which, in this period as opposed to the period before 1204, was territorial as well as economic. Here, I should like to focus on the major manifestations of resentment, and to examine briefly the extent to which the Byzantine government responded to the issues raised. The starting-point will be a document which illustrates some of the concerns at a moment which chronologically belongs to the early phase of the Genoese presence in the Black Sea.

The document is a letter of Gregorios Kyprios to the «protosevastos and protovestiarites», that is, Theodore Mouzalon. It dates from the period of Gregorios's patriarchate, i.e., from the years 1283-1289[4]. No closer identification of the date is possible, unless one were to imagine that the Emperor, Andronikos II, and his officials did in fact take the action recommended by the Patriarch. In such a case, it would be possible to suggest that the complaints addressed to the Emperor by a Genoese embassy, led by Jacopo D'Oria, in 1285, refer to these actions, undertaken as deliberate imperial policy, and that therefore Gregorios's letter dates to the early part of his patriarchate[5]. In this letter, there is both a description of conditions in the Black Sea, as set out by the Patriarch, and some measures which he recommends to the Emperor.

With regard to conditions in the Black Sea, the Patriarch's information is provided by a relatively recent acquaintance and friend, a man called Symeon, who was a «Syrian» from Acre. He was both a shipcaptain and a merchant, who seems to have been travelling between Acre and the Black Sea, and who became friendly with Gregory because they felt an affinity towards each other

---

[4] SOPHRONIOS EUSTRATIADES, Γρηγορίου τοῦ Κυπρίου οἰκουμενικοῦ Πατριάρχου ἐπιστολαὶ καὶ μῦθοι, Ἐκκλησιαστικὸς φάρος, 4, 1909, letter 164; cf. A. LAIOU, The Greek Merchant of the Palaeologan Period: A Collective Portrait, in EAD., Gender, Society and Economic Life in Byzantium, London, Variorum Reprints, 1992, Study VIII, pp. 101-102, and EAD., The Correspondence of Gregorios Kyprios as a Source for the History of Social and Political Behavior in Byzantium, or On Government by Rhetoric, in press.

[5] On this embassy and the Genoese complaints, see A.E. LAIOU, Constantinople and the Latins: The Foreign Policy of Andronicus II, 1281-1328, Cambridge, Massachusetts, 1972, pp. 70-73, and M. BALARD, La Romanie génoise cit., vol. I, 56 ff. On Mouzalon, see Prosopographisches Lexikon der Palaiologenzeit, 8, Vienna, 1986, no. 19439.

because of the proximity of their native lands. He also, undoubtedly, sought the Patriarch's patronage[6]. The general complaint has to do with the Genoese disregard for treaties and with the fact that their activities in the Black Sea are out of control. They sail there «not as in the olden days, that is, as the Emperor allowed them», but at will, meaning that they did as they liked.

One set of complaints is on behalf of Byzantine merchants, among whom we must include Syemon who, although from Palestine, was treated by the Patriarch as his own man. The Genoese «jump inside the ships (ἔνδον τῶν νεῶν) and seize the merchants who wish to sail on them. «They push the merchants into their own galleys (τριήρεις), as if they were the masters of everything, [...] so that the freight charges (πορθμεῖα) and the profits accrue to them alone». The Genoese, then, were using force to make Byzantine merchants sail on Genoese ships. That they made money off the freight charges, to the detriment of Byzantine shipowners, is clear. In what manner they also managed to turn a profit from the trade of the Greek merchants is less clear, unless they bought the merchandise for their own account, at a low price, and then resold it. In any case, their reported actions are an effort to establish, even at this early date, a monopoly of the Black Sea trade.

The second set of complaints is of a different nature, more political than economic, at least at first glance. There was, apparently, in the Black Sea, an imperial fleet, presumably to patrol it. According to the Patriarch, the Genoese were harboring evil designs against this fleet, which was too frightened to do its job properly. There were already, at that moment, enough Genoese to arm at least six ships, probably a greater number, and they were behaving in a way which was insulting to the Emperor and contemptuous of his authority: πολλὰ μὲν πρὸς τὸν βασιλέως στόλον ἐπιβουλῆς ἔργα, πολλὰ δὲ καὶ ὕβρεως ἐνδείκνυνται καὶ περιφρονήσεως. They were, in fact, ready to engage the fleet in battle. Thus, the Genoese are guilty of two sins: one is the insult to the Emperor, and the other is their non-observance of the treaties. The Patriarch urges the Emperor to put an end to Genoese activities against the fleet and against the

---

[6] Symeon is described as ἔμπορος in this letter, and as a both a merchant and a shipowner (ἔμπορος, νεὼς κύριος) in another letter of Gregorios Kyprios, addressed to Theodora Raoulaina: Cod. Vat. Gr. 1085, no. 202 (fol. 260 ro).

merchants, by sending the appropriate orders to them, and also by eliciting letters from «the powerful among them in our parts» (presumably the consuls of Pera). In his own letter, Gregory of Cyprus accuses the Genoese of showing ingratitude toward the Empire, and of being a disloyal, haughty and malicious people (ἄπιστον...εἰς φιλίαν, καὶ ὑπεροπτικὸν ἄλλως καὶ βάσκανον). These are traditional attitudes, applied to the Venetians by the Byzantine sources of the twelfth century, and to the Genoese throughout the fourteenth century[7].

The two sets of complaints in the Patriarch's letter address two issues, one traditional (protecting imperial dignity) and one, I think, new (concern for safeguarding the activities of the Byzantine merchant). The first of these we can trace both back and forward in time. It is very much in evidence in the discussion of the Venetians by the authors of the twelfth century. Particularly clear in the condemnation of the Venetians for the contempt shown to Manuel I at Corfu, when Venetian sailors parodied him, it also appears in more general invective against the Venetians. The accusation of contemptuous and insulting behaviour is usually associated with a statement deploring the ingratitude toward those (the Byzantines, and especially the Emperors) who raised the Venetians from the swamps into the ranks of rich and powerful nations[8]. Similarly, in the fourteenth century, Alexios Makrembolites traces the «effrontery» (ἰταμότης) of the Genoese to the privileged position given them by Michael VIII, which made them change into «horses, from the donkeys they were, as the proverb goes». They showed themselves to be a people «murderous and ungrateful to their benefactors», and eventually attacked the Empire from which they had enriched themselves[9]. Nikephoros Gregoras described both the expansion, the

---

[7] See, for example, ALEXIOS MAKREMBOLITES, Λόγος ἱστορικὸς περιέχων τὴν τῶν Γεννουιτῶν ἀσθένειαν..., in A. PAPADOPOULOS-KERAMEUS, Ἀνάλεκτα Ἱεροσολυμιτικῆς Σταχυολογίας, I, vol. I, 1891, 144 ff, and GREGORAS, Bonn, vol. I, p. 527; II, pp. 684-687; PACHYMERES, vol. II, pp. 70, 449.

[8] See, for example, KINNAMOS, Bonn, 170, 280 ff; CHONIATES, ed. VAN DIETEN, 86, pp. 171-172; EUSTATHIOS OF THESSALONIKI, in W.V. REGEL, Fontes Rerum Byzantinarum, I.1, Petersburg, 1892, p. 36; cf. A. LAIOU, L'interprétation byzantine de l'expansion occidentale (11e - 12e siècle), in press.

[9] A. MAKREMBOLITES cit., pp. 144-145.

enrichment and the «ingratitude» of the Genoese in the same vein [10]. All of this is perfectly understandable. It reflects, on the one hand, the reaction of a society where privileges were considered to be reciprocal, being granted in return for something in the case of Venetians and Genoese, alliance with and military help to the Empire. When the bargain was not kept, charges of ingratitude were natural. On the other hand, it reflects also the envy of an urban population which was faced with the increasing and visible wealth of foreigners. Given the equally traditional Byzantine concern with rank and hierarchy, both internal and international, and an age long commonplace that merchants are engaged in a business that entails lying, the survival of the traditional posture is to be expected.

On the other hand, Gregorios's concern with the plight of the Byzantine merchant seems to herald a new trend. To some extent, this was undoubtedly a personal interest of the Patriarch, who counted merchants among his friends, and who was, perhaps, involved in some kind of mercantile activity himself, using the offices of an Athanasios Chatzykes, in all probability a merchant [11]. Probably on behalf of this same Chatzykes, Gregorios had sought and obtained from the Emperor an exemption from the *kommerkion* [12]. He intervened, too, in the case of the merchants of Adramyttion, who were being run out of business by the tax collectors who, instead of levying the normal tax on commercial transactions, behaved in an arbitrary manner. In that instance, the Patriarch sought the intervention of the Emperor, pointing out that such practices make it impossible for merchants to continue their trade, since their merchandise is eaten up by the taxes, which we may interpret to mean that instead of a profit they were operating at a loss [13]. Even his metaphors reflect a world in which trade is important enough to become part of the system of reference. In a letter to Theodora Raoulaina, he talks about a gift of mulberries, and describes it as a forced loan, similar to trade in a buyer's market (δυναστικὴ

---

[10] GREGORAS, vol. II, 834, 841 ff; A. FAILLER, *Georges Pachymérès, Relations historiques*, vol. II, Paris, 1984, p. 595.

[11] See A.E. LAIOU, *The Correspondence of Gregorios Kyprios* cit.

[12] EUSTRATIADES, letter 128.

[13] EUSTRATIADES, letter 134 (early January, 1285).

ἐμπορία). The situation he describes is one where merchants buy the produce of poor peasants against a very low price. This is, he says, not a real sale, because the peasants do not freely agree to the price, but, the implication is, are forced to give up their produce by necessity, while the merchants go off with more than their money is worth [14]. I think he is talking of the advance purchase of agriculturals products, which he shrewdly equates to a consumption loan; indeed, we know that such transactions are a form of concealed loan, present in the sources since the late Roman period, and typically carry a very high, though concealed, interest rate [15]. So the Patriarch understands the practice perfectly well. Perhaps his Cypriot upbringing, or his residence in the great commercial port of Acre, had something to do with his interest in mercantile activity and his special concerns with merchants. But if he was especially conversant with the language of the marketplace, he was not alone. Theodoros Mouzalon, the Grand Logothete, an imperial official and intellectual who in other times would have eschewed all references to trade, also has recourse to trade metaphors when he writes to the Patriarch. In a very important letter, in which he agrees, somewhat reluctantly, to return provisionally Gregorios's letters to him so that they can be included in a collection, he says the following: «I wish to have in return, in the manner of a great merchant, my merchandise with its profit; or, to use a different imagery, I would like to have my loan returned with the highest interest, along with the capital», that is to say, he wishes to have both the originals themselves and the collected letters, which he will copy and return [16]. There is, then, both a personal interest of the Patriarch which explains his interventions, and, possibly, a more pervasive acquaintance with merchants and mercantile activity.

If the latter is the case, we have a changed attitude toward the merchants on the part of those who ruled the Byzantine state, mani-

---

[14] EUSTRATIADES, letter 189; Cod. Vat. Gr. 1085, no. 223; Cod. Mutin. 82 (III C3), no. 211.

[15] On such loans, see A. LAIOU, *The Church, Economic Thought and Economic Practice*, in press.

[16] EUSTRATIADES, letter 156: «Ὥσπερ τις οὐκ ἀδόκιμος ἔμπορος σὺν κέρδει τὰ τῆς ἐμπορίας ἀπολήψεσθαι βούλομαι. ἢ κατ' ἄλλην εἰκόνα, τὸ δάνειον σὺν δαψιλεστάτῳ τῷ τόκῳ καὶ πρὸς αὐτοῖς τοῖς κεφαλαίοις [...]».

fested in a new, sporadic to be sure, but nevertheless real, interest in their economic well-being. Looking to the past, we can say that the Comnenian state can certainly not be accused of showering great attention on the merchants. The granting or withholding of privileges to Venetians, Genoese and Pisans seems to have been motivated primarily by political factors: the need for assistance, or the pressure of hostile activity. Nowhere is there any indication that imperial policies were dictated by a concern for the Byzantine merchant. There is, possibly, one exception: the expulsion of the Venetians from the Empire by Manuel Comnenus, in 1171, may have been an effort to reverse the negative effects of their presence on the mercantile activity of the Byzantines, effects which by that time should have become evident. Nevertheless, it must be said that the reported motivation of Manuel had little to do with trade; it is presented as a desire to punish the Venetians for their arrogance, that is to say, as a political and ideological stance [17]. At the end of the twelfth century, Isaakios II Angelos protested to the governments of Genoa and Pisa about an act of piracy in the course of which the property of some Byzantine merchants was lost. But the ship attacked by the pirates had also carried presents sent by Saladin to the Emperor, as well as Byzantine and Egyptian ambassadors, and this certainly was a major reason for Isaakios's protest [18].

By contrast, in the Palaeologan period Emperors did make representations to the governments of Venice and Genoa for damages suffered by Byzantine merchants. The negotiations with Genoa in 1300-1302 include the complaints of the Byzantine government on behalf of their subjects [19], while in 1319 Andronikos II asked Venice for reparations for the seizure of the ships and merchandise of merchants from all over the Empire, to the tune of 29,300 *hyperpyra* [20]. To some extent, undoubtedly, the Byzantines were simply responding to the practice already followed by Italian merchants who had

---

[17] KINNAMOS, pp. 284-285; CHONIATES, pp. 171-172.

[18] F. MIKLOSICH-J. MULLER, *Acta et Diplomata Graeca medii Aevi*, vol. III, pp. 37-40 (1192).

[19] M. BALARD, *La Romanie génoise* cit., vol. I, pp. 61-62.

[20] G.M. THOMAS, *Diplomatarium Veneto-Levantinum, sive acta et diplomata res Venetas Graecas atque Levantis illustrantia, a. 1300*, vol. I, Venice, 1880, no. 72. Cf. A.E. LAIOU-THOMADAKIS, *The Byzantine Economy* cit., pp. 205-206.

claimed reparations for damages done to their subjects ever since the twelfth century. Thus, the list of Byzantine complaints in 1300-1302 parallels the complaints of the Genoese, and the same is true about the negotiations with Venice in 1319-1320. At the same time, a new reality is being addressed: both the increase of contact between Italian and Byzantine merchants in the Black Sea and the Aegean, and a heightened interest of the Byzantine state for its own merchants. It may be argued that the matter was a fiscal one, that is, that the Byzantine state simply was interested in the revenues it would collect from the duties paid by Byzantine merchants, which would be lost if their merchandise fell into the hands of the Italians. Certainly, the collection of duties remained a concern of the state, even as it was being undermined by the privileges granted to the Italian merchants; indeed, as early as 1285, the specious arguments made for the destruction of the imperial fleet included the statement that the sailors would then turn to trade and increase state revenues[21]. But it was not only a fiscal matter, as is shown by the fact that during this same early Palaeologan period the state began to issue duty exemptions to some of its own subjects. Chatzykes, the friend of Gregory of Cyprus, had received such an exemption from the *kommerkion*, even though imperial officials subsequently rescinded it. The privileges to the merchants of Monemvasia, originally issued by Michael VIII, and then extended by Andronikos II and Andronikos III, are a much more important indication of this position. Since the merchants of Monemvasia (first the ones resident at Pegai and then also those of the city itself) were granted the right to trade without paying the *kommerkion* in most of the Empire, and paying reduced duties (1% or 2%) in Constantinople and Thrace, what the government was doing was to reduce the adverse effects of Italian privileges for at least some of the Byzantine merchants[22].

The final act of this new state effort to support the activities of the Byzantine merchants, whom it had placed in an uncompetitive position, came with the policies of John VI Kantakouzenos in the late 1340's. Alexios Makremvolites speaks of the «benefaction accord-

---

[21] This is how I understand PACHYMERES, vol. II, p.70.2-4; GREGORAS, vol. I, p. 174, says only that the Treasury would save money from the expenses of the fleet.

[22] On the privileges, see A.E. LAIOIU-THOMADAKIS, *The Byzantine Economy* cit., pp. 206-208.

ed to the Romans by chrysobull», which must refer to the reduction of the *kommerkion* in Constantinople to two percent[23]. That this policy foundered in the defeat during the War of the Straights does not detract from its importance as the last in a series of measures that sought to reduce the competitive edge the Byzantine Emperors had given to the Italians. It must be stressed that we are talking not of a monopoly (sought by the Genoese) versus a free competitive market, but rather of a situation in which the Genoese were, indeed, seeking a monopoly based on privilege. The Byzantine state could not respond by establishing equal conditions for all merchants, but rather, in a way perfectly appropriate to the Middle Ages, by giving privileges to some of its own merchants. Such an action would tend to equalize the terms of trade, but they were terms founded on privileges which were granted by the state. Nor were the privileges of the Byzantine merchants ever equal to those of the Italians. By the late fourteenth century, the absence of a monopoly is to be attributed more to the competition between Venice and Genoa, and to the role the Byzantine merchant was called to play in this system, than to the policies of the Byzantine government.

Returning to the letter of Gregory of Cyprus, we may say that, although the two issues it raises were to remain abiding concerns of the Byzantine state, until it ceased to function in the 1350's, the most interesting of the two, because of its novelty, is the protection of the Byzantine merchant. Indeed, it seems to me that the Patriarch made reference to the more traditional idea of Byzantine sovereignty and honor primarily in order to elicit imperial action on behalf of the merchants. Be that as it may, his letter is an important witness to the fact that already in the 1280's, at a time of firm political alliance with Genoa, a certain reaction was setting in.

Twenty years later, another Patriarch, Athanasios I, would bring up one more aspect of the Genoese presence in the Black Sea that would also become a matter of constant discussion between the Byzantine state and the Italian maritime cities. This was the provisioning of Constantinople, especially in wheat. With their control of the Black Sea, the Genoese, followed eventually by the Venetians, had access to one of the most important sources of grain. The Genoese were also buying wheat from Thrace, especially the great

---

[23] A. MAKREMBOLITES cit., p. 146.

granary of Rodosto, where, in the 1280's, grain was sold them by the emperor [24]. They did not have a monopoly of the grain trade, as the correspondence of Athanasios I makes abundantly clear. Indeed, the Patriarch was as opposed to the practices of Byzantine merchants and officials, who were stockpiling grain at a time of grave difficulties and reselling it at famine prices, as he was to the fact that the Genoese were following similar practices [25]. However, the Italian merchants were, according to him, contributing to the famine conditions in two ways: first by selling grain in Constantinople at very high prices, and secondly by exporting grain, thus further reducing the supply available in the capital [26]. While he might be referring here both to Venetians and to Genoese, the likelihood is that the Genoese were the real object of his attack, because the Venetian trade in wheat, both within the Byzantine Empire and outside it, were still controlled at this time, whereas that of the Genoese seems to have been free [27]. The Patriarch was a traditionalist whose driving concern was the care, both physical and spiritual, of the poor and the people in general. He considered himself, and the Emperor, responsible for dispensing justice impartially, and, at another level, for ensuring the supply of the people with basic foodstuffs. With regard to the grain trade, his remedy was also traditional, consisting in the re-establishment, for a brief period of time, of imperial control over the supply of bread, as well as the direct sale to the consumer of grain imported from the Black Sea [28]. Thus, unlike Gregorios Kyprios, Athanasios was interested in the plight of the consumer, and much less in that of the merchant. Indeed, a little earlier, he had

---

[24] Cf. A.E. LAIOU, *Constantinople* cit., 72 ff.

[25] A.M. MAFFREY TALBOT, *The Correspondence of Athanasius I Patriarch of Constantinople*, Washington, D.C., 1975, letters 72, 73, 74, 93, 100, 106, and PACHYMERES, vol. II, pp. 460-461.

[26] A.M. MAFFREY TALBOT cit., letter 72. It is not explicitly stated in this letter that the people who exported grain were Italians; however, it must be taken in conjunction with letter no. 93, which does say that, because of the famine, «the Romans' fortune, both gold and silver, has almost all ended up in the hands of the Latins». In combination, the two letters suggest that the exporters were Italian rather than Byzantine.

[27] A.E. LAIOU, *Constantinople* cit., pp. 65, 73.

[28] A.M. MAFFREY TALBOT cit., letter 100.

been accused of having caused a fire in which the properties of the merchants and the aristocracy were burned. In the course of the night, after the fire, shops were looted; the merchants lost not only their goods, but also the contracts they kept in their establishments. A number of court cases were occasioned by these events [29]. The discussion of the incident by Pachymeres is a little curious: he says that the Patriarch had held one of his frequent litanies, with the participation of monks, clerics, and a great mob of people, and that later it was said that the litany caused the fire. This can only mean that the Patriarch was accused of having incited the people to burn the merchants' establishments along with the houses of the rich. Whatever the truth of the story, the measures Athanasios advocated, and was apparently able to enforce for a while, went contrary to the interests of the Genoese: both the prohibition of exports of grain from Constantinople and the control over the supply and price of grain were good for the consumer and bad for the merchant. These measures were a response to acute famine conditions, and may not be regarded as normal. However, the provisioning of Constantinople with cheap grain was one of the questions which continued to engage the interest of the Byzantine authorities. The matter comes up again and again, in negotiations with the Genoese and the Venetians. The Byzantine state tried to keep grain prices down by forbidding the export of Byzantine wheat when its price in Constantinople was above a certain level (fixed at 1 hyperpyron per centenarium). While this restriction was not always observed, its purpose is clear. The state also undertook a measure with a different tenor, which was to try to either forbid the sale of Black Sea grain by Italian merchants, or allow it only with the payment of a tax, and in areas outside Constantinople [30]. The aim here is to protect the Byzantine producer, and perhaps the Byzantine merchant, assuming the latter was able to sell Black Sea grain in Constantinople. In both cases, the net effect is an effort to hinder the Genoese and the Venetians from acquiring a monopoly of the grain trade, cornering the market, and controlling the supply of grain into Constantinople, and therefore its price.

---

[29] PACHYMERES, vol. II, pp. 581-583.

[30] On these measures, see A.E. LAIOU-THOMADAKIS, *The Byzantine Economy* cit., 212 ff.

Indeed, all of the combined concerns of Gregorios Kyprios and Athanasios I meet at this point. Both the traditional concepts (the preservation of imperial prerogative, the guarantee of cheap grain for the people of Constantinople), and the new ones (the protection of the Byzantine merchant from the worst effects of the privileged position of Italian merchants) can be interpreted as opposition to the establishment of a monopoly in the hands of the Italians [31]. The measures advocated and followed were very different, indeed Athanasios I's measures harmed all merchants. And in the end, they were only partially successful, for, while some Byzantine merchants thrived, the conditions of trade remained unfavorable to them. As for the grain market, it was never totally controlled by the Italians, but by the end of the Byzantine period it was an open market in which the Italians had very much the upper hand.

What emerges from the texts we have discussed above is the fact that quite early in the process of the establishment of the Genoese in the Black Sea, there were Byzantines in high positions of authority who could perceive quite well what was happening. We have here not a general negative reaction to the presence of Italians, based on xenophobia, but a reaction to the economic realities that were developing. The fact that what appeared first were the problems of the Byzantine merchants and that the question of the provisioning of Constantinople was raised only years later may be due in part to accident: to the fact that Gregorios Kyprios was less public-minded than Athanasios I, and more prone to seek benefactions for his friends, the fact of the famine in the capital during the years of the Catalan campaign. But it may also signal the progress of Genoese economic activity in the Black Sea and in Constantinople. It was an activity which met with opposition from the beginning, although it was an ineffective opposition.

---

[31] On this monopoly, as perceived by the Byzantines, see also PACHYMERES (Bonn), vol. II, pp. 448-50; PACHYMERES (Failler), p. 535; CANTACUZENUS, vol. III, p. 69; GREGORAS, vol. II, pp. 683-687.

XII

Monopoly and Privileged Free Trade
in the Eastern Mediterranean (8th-14th century)

After the eleventh century, the eastern Mediterranean was a busy sea. International trade was on an upward curve which continued until about 1350. Venetian, Pisan and Genoese ships and, with time, those of other western states sailed to Egypt, the Byzantine Empire, Syria and eventually to the Black Sea. Teeming markets, busy ports, a developing international culture: such was the eastern Mediterranean during this period. These new conditions necessitated new mechanisms and institutional arrangements, which, in turn, facilitated the further development of international trade. My purpose here is to trace some aspects of this process, namely, monopoly, privilege and free trade as they evolved through the dialectic relationship of Italian merchants and the Byzantine state. I will try to show the interplay between monopoly, protected trade, free trade, and the liberalization of the conditions of trade, in a period that extends from the eighth through the late fourteenth century. The focus will be on the Byzantine Empire. However, since for much of the period the role of Byzantium and especially, but not only, Constantinople, was pivotal, the case of Byzantium is not parochial but, rather, paradigmatic for the eastern Mediterranean. My argument is that, whereas in the beginning of the period envisaged here, Mediterranean exchange in the East took place in conditions where the restrictiveness imposed by political entities (in our paradigmatic case, the Byzantine state) played an important role, there occurred a liberalization in the terms of trade, brought about by state action among other factors. As more players entered the field, the exercise of national sovereignty in economic matters changed, as did the dynamic between political and economic factors in exchange.

The Byzantine economy was never fully controlled or directed by the state. The state did, however, until some time in the eleventh century, act as a restraining agent, placing restrictions on processes such as the untrammeled accumulation of wealth in private hands, or the exploitation of the weakest members of society.[1]

Foreign trade is the economic sector in which state intervention can be seen in its strongest manifestation. In our case, we are dealing with an environment where international exchange took place between states, and therefore state policies were important. That the Byzantine state had a powerful voice in the exercise of foreign trade and in establishing the terms in which exchange would take place is very easy to show, for the period through the tenth century. The very fact that terms of trade were often included in political treaties with outsiders is characteristic: the

---

1. N. OIKONOMIDES, The Role of the Byzantine State in the Economy, *EHB*, 3, p. 973-974.

512

treaties with the Bulgarians (716) and the Rus (907) established restrictive terms: the kind and value of Byzantine merchandise that might be bought by foreigners was fixed and, in the case of the Bulgarians, official places of exchange (Mesembria, Develtos) were specified; the merchandise was to be stamped or sealed by Byzantine officials.[2] This is a port of trade situation. The restrictions upon foreign merchants or on any outsiders who went to Constantinople for trade, set out in the Book of the Prefect, are too well known to be rehearsed again. All of these phenomena, the special treatment of merchants of varying nationalities, the existence of ports of trade, the differential treatment afforded to Constantinople, where the terms of foreign and even domestic trade were much more closely regulated than in the provinces until the eleventh century,[3] suggest that exchange was a complex of political, strategic, economic and even psychological factors.

The philosophy underlying the terms in which foreign trade was conducted, the normative role of the government and the intended restrictions upon practice can be seen with clarity in the category of goods whose export was forbidden by the Byzantine state, sometimes on pain of death. These were the *kolyomena* or *kekolymena*, the forbidden items, a category of goods considered to be outside normal commercial exchange with the outside world. The category of *kekolymena* was a legal one, and appears in the legislation already between the fourth and the sixth century. It included precious metals (gold), iron, arms, wheat, wine,[4] olive oil, salt, garum and best-quality silks. The prohibitions remained in the law books at least through the tenth century.[5]

The export of gold had been forbidden since the fourth century. An edict of Gratian (374 AD ?) had stated that traders, trading in foreign lands, must not pay in gold, but rather in goods. "For one should not only not give gold to the barbarians, but even take the gold that they have."[6] Barter was thereby encouraged, if commercial transactions in cash did not result in a positive balance for the Romans. The purpose of this prohibition is self-evident: it keeps the monetary system functioning, even if it forms an impediment to trade. In the tenth century, the provisions in the Book of the Prefect, that if a goldsmith (*argyroprates*) was offered gold, silver or precious stones by a woman he was to declare them to the Prefect "so that they may not be exported to foreigners" (ἵνα μὴ τοῖς ἔθνεσι παραπέμπωνται) (*EB* 2.4), and that if anyone coming into Constantinople from the outside sold gold or silver, he should be questioned as to where he had found it, suggest that the prohibition was still in place at the time.[7] However, it is not easy to see how it can have been fully implemented, since in all the discussion of

2. A. E. Laiou, Exchange and Trade, Seventh-Twelfth Centuries, *EHB*, 2, p. 704, 724.
3. N. Oikonomides, The Economic Region of Constantinople: From Directed Economy to Free Economy, and the Role of the Italians, *Europa medievale e mondo bizantino. Contatti effettivi e possibilità di studi comparati*, ed. G. Arnaldi, G. Cavallo, Rome 1997, p. 221-338.
4. É. Patlagean, Byzance et les marchés du grand commerce, vers 830-vers 1030 ; entre Pirenne et Polanyi, *Mercati e mercanti nell' alto medioevo: l'area euroasiatica e l'area mediterranea*, Spoleto 1993, p. 623. The author states that wheat and salt were added in the second half of the 10th c., in the *Synopsis Basilicorum*. That, however, is not the case, for they appear already in the Digest and the Basilics.
5. *Synopsis Basilicorum*, I. and P. Zepos, *Jus Graecoromanum* (hereafter, *JGR*), 5, Athens 1931, (K. X.), p. 346.
6. B 56.1.8 = CJ IV.63.2: Οἱ πραγματευταὶ ὑπὲρ ὧν ἀγοράζουσιν ἐν τῷ βαρβαρικῷ φορτίων μὴ παρεχέτωσαν χρυσόν, ἀλλ᾽ ἕτερα εἴδη διδότωσαν . . . Χρὴ γὰρ μὴ μόνον μὴ διδόναι χρυσὸν τοῖς βαρβάροις, ἀλλὰ καὶ τὸν ὄντα παρ᾽ αὐτοῖς ἀφαιρεῖν.
7. J. Koder, *Das Eparchenbuch Leons des Weisen*, Vienna 1991 (CFHB 33) (hereafter, *EB*), 2.4, 2.6.

foreign merchants in Constantinople barter is mentioned only once, and it affected Bulgarian merchants, at a time when, we know, the Bulgarian economy was not yet truly monetised.[8] For the prohibition to have been effective, even in Constantinople, the foreign merchants must have bought merchandise of higher value than what they sold. But it is not clear that such was the case.

The reason for the prohibition of the export of strategic commodities is also self-evident: arms and iron were not to be exported, on pain of death and the confiscation of the property of the guilty party.[9] In the tenth century, the export of timber to Syria and Egypt was also forbidden, on pain of death. The emperor Leo VI, on the other hand, reduced the punishment of those who exported to the enemies "those things which help them" (ἅ συγκροτεῖν αὐτοὺς μέλλει), and who had been subject to the death penalty. He retained severe property and corporal punishments, but considered the death penalty disproportionate to the crime.[10]

What obtained, therefore, was a boycott of particular enemy countries, as well as a general prohibition of the export of certain strategic commodities.

Foodstuffs form another category of *kekolymena*. Since the time of Valentinian (370-375), it had been forbidden to export to "barbarian lands" wine or olive oil or garum.[11] Merchants were forbidden to carry these foodstuffs abroad even for their own use, let alone allow the foreigners to taste or buy them. One can understand the prohibition of the export of oil and wine as a sort of protection of the internal market, that is, of the consumer of what after all are primary elements of the Mediterranean diet. The prohibition that bore on garum is harder to interpret.

The export of grain, along with that of arms, iron and salt, had been prohibited in the late third century upon pain of death.[12] We shall deal with grain at some length. Here, I note that, while the reasons for prohibiting the export of foodstuffs is obvious, the first explicit justification of which I am aware dates from the early thirteenth century. A privilege granted by Manuel Angelos (1230-1240: emperor and then despot of Thessaloniki) to the Ragusans in 1234, allowed them to trade everywhere in his domains and to export all commodities, except for crops in time of dearth. At such times, he wrote, crops were not to be exported, since the first obligation was to feed the native population.[13]

The prohibition of the export of high quality silks is Byzantine, not late Roman.[14] The purpose of the prohibition was political and psychological rather than economic. Silks were imbued with a high degree of symbolism, which made

---

8. *EB* 9.6.

9. B 19.86 (87) = CJ IV.41.2 (Marcian, 455-457).

10. P. NOAILLES, A. DAIN, *Les novelles de Léon VI le Sage*, Paris 1944, Novel 63. It seems to refer to B 60.36.4 = D XLVIII.4.4, i.e. the statements of the jurist Scaevola on those who are punished by death: among them, according to the jurist, is the man who helps the enemy with men, arms or money, or in any other way, or who arranges to provide to the enemy hostages, money, beasts of transport etc.

11. B 19.85 (86) = CJ IV.41.1.

12. Paulus: B 56.1.11 = D 39.4.11.

13. MM, 3, p. 66-67.

14. There is a late fourth-century prohibition on the use of murex as a colorant, and on the sale of murex-dyed cloth. It is an edict of Valentinianus Theodosius (383-392) and Arcadius (395-408): CJ IV.40.1: *Fucandae atque distrahendae purpurae vel in serico vel in lana, quae blatta vel oxyblatta atque hyacinthina dicitur, facultatem nullus possit habere privatus sin autem aliquis supra dicti muricis vellus vendiderit, fortunarum se suarum et capitis sciat subiturum esse discrimen.* Cf. B 19.1.82: μηδεὶς βαπτέτω ἢ πιπρασκέτω πορφύραν μήτε ἐν μετάξῃ μήτε ἐν ἐρίῳ. Ὁ δὲ πωλήσας καὶ δημεύεται καὶ κεφαλικῶς τιμωρεῖται.

of them an expression of the majesty of the state. The famous statements of Constantine VII, about imperial garments having been given to Constantine the Great by an angel and therefore carrying a very powerful export prohibition, point out the symbolic importance of such items.[15]

Similarly, when Leo VI allowed the sale of small pieces of purple (ἀλουργόν), i.e. imperial, silk to the residents of Constantinople, he did so, as he himself owned, in order to associate them, even in a small way, in the luxury and the glories of the Empire.[16] Still, in the same period, in the Book of the Prefect issued by the same emperor, it was forbidden for Jewish merchants to purchase from the *metaxopratai* (merchants in raw silk) raw silk in Constantinople, presumably because the Jews were engaged in long-distance trade involving both the Far East and western Europe, and therefore might be expected to re-export it outside the frontiers of the Empire.[17] The same regulation prohibited the sale of raw silk to any merchant (Jews included) whose purpose was to resell it outside the Empire. Any silk clothes (*himatia*) worth above 10 *nomismata* were to be declared to the Prefect,[18] for these were not to be sold to outsiders.[19] This last provision is to be noted, for it shows that the prohibition is broader than the imperial silks (*vlattia kekolymena*) defined in *EB* 8.1. The *vestiopratai* (clothes merchants) were also prohibited to sell *kekolymena* to outsiders who bought them to resell to foreigners.[20] The tenor of the prohibition of the export of raw silk is different, for its purpose was the protection of the native industry rather than that of imperial prestige.

The prohibitions seem to have been breaking down in practice in the course of the tenth century, at least if one is to believe Liutprand of Cremona[21] who stated that forbidden purple silks were available in the markets of western Europe through the mediation of Venetian merchants. The Byzantine treaty with Aleppo, in 969-970, shows fine silk and silk brocades, as well as gold, silver, precious stones and jewels being sold in Aleppo which, however, was virtually imperial territory at this point.[22] The prohibition was slowly dissolving through the combined action of merchants and the Byzantine government, although the process was still at a very early phase, and is of interest mostly as a forerunner of later developments.

15. *Constantine Porphyrogenitus, De Administrando Imperio*, ed. G. MORAVCSIK, R. J. H. JENKINS, Washington 1967 (CFHB 1), ch 13, p. 66-68. PATLAGEAN, Byzance et les marchés du grand commerce (as in n. 4), p. 600, notes that silk represents administered trade par excellence.

16. NOAILLES - DAIN, *Novelles* (as in n. 10), Novel 80: σεμνοπρεπείας μοίραν παρεχόμενοι τοῖς ὑπηκόοις.

17. *EB* 6.16; cf. D. JACOBY, Les juifs à Byzance: une communauté marginalisée, Οι περιθωριακοί στο Βυζάντιο, Athens 1993, p. 135-136.

18. *EB* 8.1, on the *serikarioi*; cf 8.5 which punishes them with the confiscation of their property in the contrary case.

19. *EB* 8.3.

20. *EB* 4.1.

21. J. BECKER, *Die Werke Liudprands von Cremona*, Hanover-Leipzig 1915³ (MGH, Script. rer. Germ.), ch. 53-55. Byzantine officials confiscated some purple silks (*pretiosissimas purpuras*), that Liutprand had acquired, because they were "prohibited to all nations except for us Romans."

22. M. CANARD, *Histoire de la dynastie des H'amdanides de Jazira et de Syrie*, Algiers 1951, 1, p. 831-836, clause 20; PATLAGEAN, Byzance et les marchés du grand commerce (as in n. 4), p. 606, says that the Arab *Livre de la perspicacité* (second half of the ninth century) mentions imports from the Byzantine Empire: gold and silver vessels, *nomismata* ("dinars qaysarani"), silks, etc. Byzantine silks are also mentioned in the Cairo Geniza documents.

Expensive and perhaps forbidden silks were one of the major items of what I have termed non-economic exchange,[23] that is, gift exchange or quasi-gift exchange, including ransom payments, as well as diplomatic gifts and payments. In the eighth, ninth and tenth centuries, silks hold pride of place in the gifts exchanged with Muslim potentates and others; silks and gold. Gold, whose export in the course of commercial activity was strictly forbidden,[24] was used for gifts or ransom. Large sums of money occasionally left the empire, especially toward the east, whether to the Persians during the reign of Justinian I, or to the Arabs; the largest reported such exports of gold are a gift of 1000 *kentenaria* of gold (7,200,000 gold coins) sent by Theophilos to the Caliph (Theophilos also offered 200 *kentenaria*, along with silks, as ransom payment, but it was not accepted, being found too low), the 216,000 gold coins and 200,000 dinars sent to the caliph by Constantine IX in 1046 (2.23 tons of gold), and the 500,000 *hyperpyra* given to the crusaders in 1203.[25] One hopes that the figures are exaggerated, although the case of Theophilos is reported not by an Arab source but by a Byzantine one.[26]

The silks sent to western Europe or to the Slavs are important, although it cannot be assumed that they were of first quality.[27] One imagines that the 2500 silk garments sent to the Slavs by Constantine V for ransoming prisoners (in 768) were not first quality.[28] Some silks meant for lesser Arab potentates ("noble foreigners") when the emperor went on campaign were clearly not imperial, for they were bought in the marketplace of Constantinople.[29] Those meant as gifts for caliphs, on the other hand, may be assumed to have been of very high quality, of imperial manufacture and of the forbidden variety, as was certainly the case with some silks given to the *protospatharios* Epiphanios, on embassy to Hugh of Provence.[30] The Emperor Romanos I, we are told, sent to the Arabs brocades, cut velvet and other splendid silks, while Leo VI sent garments of purple (furfur) brocade, and brocades woven with gold, each valued at the vast sum of 2000 dinars.[31] Even allowing for the expected degree of exaggeration, these were items of extremely high quality, and must be assumed to have been imperial silks. In any case, the philosophy behind gift-giving between Byzantines and Arabs hinged precisely on the exchange of rare and highly valued items. Both Arab and Byzantine sources state unambiguously that important gifts impress upon the recipient state the magnifence

23. See A. E. LAIOU, Economic and Non-economic Exchange, *EHB*, 2, p. 681-696.
24. On this, see M. HENDY, *Studies in the Byzantine Monetary Economy c. 300-1450*, Cambridge 1985, p. 257-258, who says that the first formal lifting of the prohibition was in 1261 (Treaty of Nymphaeum).
25. *EHB*, 2, p. 716, 738; HENDY, *Studies* (as in n. 24), p. 266.
26. *Theophanes Continuatus*, ed. B. G. NIEBUHR, Bonn 1838 (CSHB), p. 96-97, 131.
27. On this, see A. MUTHESIUS, Silken Diplomacy, *Byzantine Diplomacy*, ed. J. SHEPARD, S. FRANKLIN, Cambridge 1990. Muthesius says that *some* imperial silks sent west were dyed with inferior, i.e. non-murex dyes. She connects this with the "fact" that imperial silks were not only woven in the imperial workshop but also commissioned by the emperor to the *serikarioi*. It is possible that some imperial silks were commissioned to be dyed with madder (*ibid.*, p 246-247). According to D. JACOBY, Silk in western Byzantium before the Fourth Crusade, *BZ* 84-85, 1991-1992, p. 456-457, however, what matters is not the type of dye, but the color purple.
28. *EHB*, 2, p. 699.
29. *Three Treatises on Imperial Military Expeditions*, ed. J. F. HALDON, Vienna 1990 (CFHB 28), p. 112.
30. In 935: HENDY, *Studies*, p. 268. Other cases are mentioned *ibid.*, p. 269.
31. LAIOU, Exchange and Trade (as in n. 2), p. 717.

and wealth of the gift-offering ruler;[32] or, as imperial officials told Liutprand of Cremona, "as we surpass all other nations in wealth and wisdom, so it is right that we should surpass them in dress."[33]

In other words, as some items were taken out of the normal market exchange, so they played another, and most important role, in the political relations between the Byzantine Empire and foreign powers.

As late as the eleventh and twelfth centuries, this political role of high quality silks remains visible in the treaties between the Byzantine Empire and western powers. A striking example of this phenomenon is the chrysobull composed by Michael Psellos and issued by Michael VII (1071-1078) for Robert Guiscard. This was a highly political document, and highly unusual in its form, since it incorporated for the first time an oath by the emperor; in any case, the emperor was seeking to form a firm alliance with Robert Guiscard, cemented with a marriage alliance.[34] There is, here, a veritable hierarchy of offices granted to Robert to distribute at will, and with them an annual distribution of 100 pieces of silk cloth (*vlattia, pallia*) specifically mentioned, that includes both the silks appropriate to the various offices and a supplement as an extra gift. In the late twelfth century, expensive silk cloth was given as a (forced) present to Frederick Barbarossa to buy peace, while an annual gift of 40 pieces of Theban silk was promised to the Sultan of Iconium.[35]

The privileges granted to the maritime cities of Italy in the course of the eleventh and twelfth centuries incorporated gifts of money and silks. The latter had no immense economic value, but did carry the usual symbolic value. The privilege to the Venetians issued by Alexios I in 1082 and its subsequent confirmations do not explicitly mention silks, but these may be subsumed in the *roga* accruing to the office of *protosevastos*, promised to the Doge.[36] Alexios I's privilege to the Pisans in 1111, and Manuel's to the Genoese in 1155 specifically mentioned annual gifts of gold coins (400 *hyperpyra*) and two *pallia* to the church of Pisa, as well as 60 *hyperpyra* and one *pallium* to the archbishop of Pisa during Alexios' and John's lifetime in the first case,[37] with similar arrangements (500 *hyperpyra* to the church) in the case of Genoa.[38] Gifts of silks and cash are mentioned in imperial chrysobulls throughout the twelfth century. Almost none of the imperial privileges of the thirteenth or fourteenth century, that is, after the fall of Constantinople in

---

32. *Theophanes Continuatus*, p. 96: on a gift of 4 *kentenaria* of gold: εἰ γὰρ ἄμμου δίκην ὁ ἀποσταλεὶς τὸ χρυσίον ἔχει σπείρειν ὡς βούλεται, πολλῷ δήπου μᾶλλον τὸν ἀποστείλαντα ἐπὶ πλούτου θημῶνας θαυμάζεσθαι χρή.

33. *Legatio*, in BECKER, *Werke* (as in n. 21), ch. 54 (transl. by F. A. WRIGHT).

34. On this document see, in the last instance, A. E. LAIOU, The Emperor's Word: Chrysobulls, Oaths and Synallagmatic Relations in Byzantium (11th-12th c.), *TM* 14 (= *Mélanges Gilbert Dagron*), 2002, p. 348-351.

35. *Nicetae Choniatae Historia*, ed. J. A. VAN DIETEN , Berlin 1975 (CFHB 11), p. 461: five *kentenaria* of silver coins once, as well as three *kentenaria* of silver and 40 pieces of cloth every year: σηρικοῖς νήμασιν, ἅπερ ἐκ Θηβῶν βασιλεύς ... κεχορήγηται. On this cloth, see JACOBY, Silk in Western Byzantium (as in n. 27), *passim*.

36. *JGR*, 1, Athens 1931, p. 369: *honoravit autem et nobilem Ducam...protosebasti dignitate cum roga etiam sua plenissima*. Cf. Isaac II's confirming chrysobull, 1187: *cum salario ejus plenissimo*. Note that Romanos IV still paid his officials both in cash and in silk cloth (E. Th. TSOLAKES, Ἡ συνέχεια τῆς χρονογραφίας τοῦ Ἰωάννου Σκυλίτση [Ioannes Skylitzes Continuatus], Thessaloniki 1968, p. 142), and that Alexios I gave Gregorios Pakourianos imperial garments as gifts.

37. The gifts were renewed and increased by Manuel I and by Isaac II in 1192: *JGR*, 1, p. 457 ff; Latin version in MM, 3, p. 3 ff.

38. *JGR*, 1, p. 417 (1170).

1204, mentions such gifts. An exception is the chrysobull to the Genoese, issued by Michael VIII in 1265, which does retain the gifts promised by Manuel I, although this may be just formulaic.[39] This change is remarkable for several reasons. For one thing, it signals the end of anything that might resemble the prohibition of the export of imperial silks, and so, also, of the usefulness of these silks in political relations. Secondly, it is a marker of the different conditions that prevailed in Mediterranean commerce in the thirteenth century and after, conditions that resemble an international market, where economic forces played a much greater role than before as integrating mechanisms, and also conditions in which the intervention of the state played a different role than before.

I have taken silk as an example of the role of the *kekolymena* in the trade and exchange of the Byzantine Empire with its neighbors, in the Mediterranean and the Middle East. It is one of the two most interesting items on the list of forbidden commodities of international commercial exchange, in part because the prohibition seems to have been in force longer than for wheat. It was, of course, easier to enforce this prohibition, since the manufacture of highest quality purple silk was controlled, indeed almost an imperial monopoly, in the tenth century. It is also interesting because highest-quality silk is the item that most clearly shows the interrelationship between political and economic factors and interests in a Mediterranean in which the expansion of trade had not yet broken down state policies that had been meant to safeguard the interests of the state, political primarily and economic in the second instance. The active economic exchange which had been developing in the Mediterranean since the eleventh century may have reduced, relatively speaking, the importance of items of high prestige; after all, one could always make substitutes, cheaper and thus affordable by a larger number of clients, as the Venetians did with some objects of the minor arts. It is well known that in the thirteenth century Venetians manufactured semi-luxury products, such as glass medallions of saints, emulating Byzantine cameos, or miniatures under crystal, which mimicked Byzantine enamels and found customers in the unified market that the Mediterranean was becoming. There was, thus, commodification of artistic production.[40] It could be that a similar case of economic, not physical, substitution occurred in the case of silk too. Good quality silks were, in the eleventh-twelfth centuries, produced in Thebes, Corinth, Andros and elsewhere, and were exported by Venetians and Genoese, primarily the Venetians.[41] In the tenth century, restrictions on the export of silk from Constantinople applied not only to imperial silks but also to high-quality ones. The prestige value of imperial vestments no doubt remained in the eleventh and twelfth centuries, but the larger market could be satisfied with products where monopoly no longer obtained. This is even more clearly the case

---

39. *Ibid.*, p. 490.
40. A. E. LAIOU, Venice as a Center of Trade and of Artistic Production in the Thirteenth Century, *Atti del XXIV Congresso del Comitato Internazionale di storia del' Arte*, sez. 2, Bologna 1982, p. 20-25.
41. JACOBY, Silk in western Byzantium, p. 466, 490-492. Gold brocade was captured in Thebes by Roger II. ID., Italian Privileges and Trade in Byzantium before the Fourth Crusade, *Annuario de estudios medievales*, 14, 1994, p. 349-368, says that the Genoese and the Pisans could not buy high-quality silks in Thebes, though "no source mentions it." He bases this on the Genoese request of 1171, by which the Genoese asked to be allowed to trade in silk cloth in Thebes as "the Venetians do." Cf. A. LAIOU, Byzantine Traders and Seafarers, *Byzantium and the Sea*, ed. Sp. VRYONIS, New York 1993, p. 87 ff. But this request may refer to a desire for lower customs, or permission to establish themselves there, or be a response to a quasi-monopoly of the Venetians who had, since 1082, been allowed to settle in Thebes and Corinth, and deal in *species universas: JGR*, I, p. 370.

518

with the commodification of silk in the thirteenth century, when Venice developed its own silk industry, producing silks along a spectrum of quality.[42]

How was the liberalization, if this is the right word, of the silk trade of the Byzantine Empire come about ? Liutprand of Cremona gives us a first clue: through the activities of individual merchants, in his text Venetian and Amalfitan merchants, who managed to export forbidden silks and sell them in the market-places of Italy. An economic process, therefore: there is a market, and the entre-preneur finds ways of meeting the demand, at least up to a point. But the Byzantine state itself facilitated the process. None of the privileges granted to Italians in the eleventh and twelfth centuries mentions the prohibition of the export of imperial or high quality silks, or any restriction on silk exports, such as those that had been in place at earlier times, in the treaties with the Bulgarians and the Rus. It might be argued that this was so because the state still controlled the supply of highest quality silks in any case, although I do not think there is sufficient or compelling evidence for such an argument.[43] It seems more plausible that the tacit lifting of restrictions regarding the export of silks in general was due to the increase of pro-duction and the general opening of the Mediterranean markets.

Thus, the liberalization of the silk market which, I argue, occurred in the twelfth century, marked an important change in the economics of the silk trade. Byzantine governmental control and monopoly ended, through a combination of market forces (the pressure of western merchants – as I believe the Genoese request of 1171 must be understood) and imperial decision, that is, the privileges. After 1204, the entire situation changed, since the presence of western merchants on Byzantine soil became massive and the opening of Central Asia to Italians with the Pax Mongolica led to importations of Asian silks and since the Byzantine silk industry declined, and was partly replaced by the silk industry of Latin-occupied Greece in the thirteenth century and less so in the fourteenth.[44] Imperial monopoly was no longer an issue.

As for the prohibition of the export of gold, that was problematic anyway. Occasionally, it was remembered: in 1261, the chrysobull of Michael VIII to the Genoese prohibited the export of gold and silver, save by imperial permission, except for minted Tatar or Seljuk dinars whose export was allowed.[45] Occasionally, too, an effort was made not to impose the prohibition, but rather to

---

42. D. JACOBY, Dalla material prima ai drappi tra Bisanzio, il Levante e Venezia: La prima fase dell' industria serica Veneziana, *La seta in Italia dal Medioevo al Seicento*, ed. L. MOLÀ, R. C. MUELLER, Cl. ZANIER, Venice 2000, p. 266.

43. JACOBY, Silk in Western Byzantium, makes an argument for partial government control, on the basis of the Genoese request of 1171 (only Venetians were allowed to trade in Theban silks, according to Jacoby) and the gift of 1195. The argumentation is not persuasive. In any case, it would almost be sufficient for my own argument if even the Venetians alone were allowed to export imperial silks.

44. M. BALARD, *La Romanie génoise : XIIIe-début du XVe siècle*, Rome 1978, p. 723 ff. Exports of Romania silks to Genoa in the 13th c. (from Smyrna, Chios, Sea of Marmora etc.); Cathay silks start arriving in 1258, become abundant after 1276. Cf. D. JACOBY, The Production of Silk Textiles in Latin Greece, *Τεχνογνωσία στη Λατινοκρατούμενη Ελλάδα*, Athens 2000, p. 22-35.

45. HENDY, *Studies*, p. 259, states that this is the first formal breach of the prohibition, reading the privilege as: *yperperos aureos et Turchifaros licet eis extrahere ad eorum voluntate et deferre* (*JGR*, 1, p. 494), and understanding that Michael VIII permitted the export of both gold *hyperpyra* and "Turchifaros." If Hendy is right, then Michael recognised the need to allow commercial coin to leave the realm, and forbade only the export of unminted gold and silver. However, the editor of the document wisely suggests that the "et" is unnecessary. If it is deleted, the meaning of the text would be that the emperor permitted only the export of foreign coin.

facilitate the importation of precious metals: in the privilege to the city of Pisa, Alexios I established a *kommerkion* of 4%; but no *kommerkion* was to be paid on the gold and silver that Pisan merchants brought into the Empire.[46]

Let us now look at what happened to other items whose export had been legally forbidden. The most important such category consists of foodstuffs, mostly bulk products: olive oil, wine, cereals and garum.

Although the pertinent legislation remained in the lawbooks, I know of no instance, in the middle Byzantine period, where there is any mention of its being enforced. For a long time, until perhaps the eleventh century, the conditions probably did not exist for massive exports of foodstuffs. On the supply side, the Byzantine agrarian economy was not yet so developed as to produce sufficient foodstuffs for extensive exports. True, the agrarian economy had entered a virtuous cycle probably in the early ninth century, as conditions of relative safety were slowly re-established in various areas. But the increase in agricultural production went hand in hand with a population increase,[47] as it did in western medieval Europe; and that means that increases in production were absorbed by the rising population. Surpluses did exist; but concomitantly, the urban population rose, thus creating a higher internal demand that had to be met and was successfully met, as is testified by the fact that cereal prices remained relatively stable in the middle Byzantine period, except, always, for momentary crises when extreme natural phenomena or some other calamity created famine conditions.[48] Thus, on the supply side, there was no great surplus becoming available for export because it could not be absorbed by the internal market . On the demand side, there was no effective market, for various reasons. It does not seem that the Arab world had great need of Byzantine alimentary products, at least not on a large scale, and except for specific situations (for example, when cities were under siege). In western Europe, the same phenomena of increased production and perhaps productivity along with a rising population existed. The European economy had not yet become sufficiently differentiated to have need of relatively small suppliers, such as the Byzantine ones might potentially be. Most importantly, there was not yet an integrated Mediterranean market, with product specialization, or with those trade mechanisms that would make it economically sensible to exploit all available and potential sources of supply, that is, create conditions that would match the supply to the demand across regions.

Export prohibitions of foodstuffs were part of a protectionist policy. Such a policy was predicated on an integrated internal market coupled with the possibility of occasional purchases of foodstuffs from abroad, as need arose. It is not by chance that in the middle period, until the 12th century, we have much more information about merchandise and foodstuffs in particular coming *into* the Byzantine Empire than about exports. The purpose of the policy was to safeguard the interests of the consumer in times of high demand for foodstuffs; the interests of the merchant did not enter into the calculation, nor, in fact, did those of the native grower, who might, *caeteris paribus*, have found a higher price in an export market. The purpose of this protectionist policy was met until the twelfth century, but almost by default, for the reasons I have detailed.

46. MM, 3, p. 3 ff.
47. J. Lefort, The Rural Economy, Seventh-Twelfth Centuries, *EHB*, 1, ch. 14, *passim*.
48. C. Morrisson, J.-Cl. Cheynet, Prices and Wages in the Byzantine World, *EHB*, 2, p. 822-830; in the 9th-11th c., the normal price of wheat in Constantinople was 1/12 *nomisma* per *modios*.

In the ninth, tenth and I think the eleventh centuries, the interest of the Byzantine government to safeguard the provisioning of cities, most particularly Constantinople, would have severely discouraged exports of grain especially, even had conditions for massive exports existed. But this is speculation. In point of fact, we know of no instance where such prohibition occurred in reality. We do, on the contrary, know of a few cases where foodstuffs were exported by that little known group, the Byzantine provincial merchant, whose activities do not seem to have been regulated by the government.[49]

In the twelfth century, indications for the free circulation of foodstuffs proliferate, as bulk products enter the Mediterranean trade. Italian merchants, Venetians, Pisans and Genoese, bought wheat in Halmyros, which had become a major center for the grain of Thessaly and western Greece.[50] The Venetians bought olive oil and wine in the Peloponnese, Sparta and Corinth being important trade centers for these commodities.[51] In part, this signals the participation of foreigners (Italians) in the internal, domestic Byzantine market, a recent phenomenon.[52] There is also, however, clear evidence of the export of such commodities: olive oil was exported by the Venetians from Sparta not only to Constantinople, but also to Alexandria and Venice; from Thebes, Venetian merchants traveled to Constantinople, Greece and Venice. In the eleventh and twelfth centuries, Byzantine lands exported wheat, oil, wine, silk, mastic.[53] As far as I know, there was no official complaint on the Byzantine side regarding the export of these theoretically forbidden commodities, nor any effort to restrict it. Here, again, it was the foreign merchants, the Venetians, the Genoese and others who bought and resold merchandise, the Byzantine merchants who may have cooperated with them, and the Byzantine producers through their commercial activities who opened up the trade in these foodstuffs. But the Byzantine government provided the legal basis for such activity.

The privileges granted to Italian merchants, starting with the chrysobull of Alexios I for the Venetians in 1082, differed from earlier trade treaties, such as those with the Bulgarians and the Rus, in that they were not restrictive as to the commodities exchanged or, with one exception, as to the places in which trade could be carried out.[54] The chrysobull of 1082, while making mention of specific cities in which the Venetians could trade (a list that became much larger in the late twelfth century with the chrysobull of 1198), nevertheless made it clear that the list was not restrictive, for the Venetians were allowed to trade in all merchandise

49. On them see N. OIKONOMIDES, Le marchand byzantin des provinces (IXᵉ-XIᵉ s.), *Mercati e mercanti nell' alto medioevo: l'area euroasiatica e l'area mediterranea*, Spoleto 1993 (Settimane di studio del Centro italiano sull'alto medioevo 40), p. 633-665.

50. JACOBY, Italian Privileges (as in n. 41), p. 366: the Pisans were in Halmyros already in the 1150's, and the Genoese in the early 1160's.

51. LAIOU, Exchange and Trade, p. 752; BALARD, *La Romanie génoise* (as in n. 44), p. 30; AL-IDRISI, *La géographie d'Edrisi*, ed. J.-A. JAUBERT, 2, Paris 1840, p. 291, 296; *The Itinerary of Benjamin of Tudela*, trans. M. ADLER, A. ASHER, Malibu, California 1993, p. 69.

52. LAIOU, Byzantine Traders (as in n. 41), *passim*. Silk, too, was traded within the empire: *Ibid.*, p. 87; R. MOROZZO DELLA ROCCA, A. LOMBARDO, *Documenti del commercio veneziano nei secoli XI-XIII*, Torino 1940, no. 308 (1179).

53. R.-J. LILIE, *Handel und Politik zwischen dem byzantinischen Reich und den italienischen Kommunen Venedig, Pisa und Genua in der Epoche der Komnenen und der Angeloi (1081-1204)*, Amsterdam 1984, p. 272-276.

54. On privileges, see JACOBY, Italian Privileges, p. 349-368, and J. CHRYSOSTOMIDES, Venetian Commercial Privileges under the Paleologi, *Studi Veneziani* 12, 1970, p. 267-356.

everywhere in the Empire.[55] The chrysobull given to Pisa in 1111 permitted the Pisans to buy Byzantine products on the same terms (i.e., paying the same duties) as the emperor's subjects; they also paid the *kommerkion* on exports from the Byzantine Empire.[56] This shows that restrictions on buying Byzantine products no longer applied. Only the chrysobull of 1169 to the Genoese excluded Rossia and Matracha from the list of places where the Genoese ships could sail, unless they received special and specific imperial permission.[57] There was no total or formal ban on the Italians engaging in Black Sea trade, but on the other hand there was little presence there of Venetians or Genoese merchants.[58] So, although there was, in the legal/political foundation of their privileges, no effort by the Byzantine government to either limit or control the export of grain generally, it is likely that neither Venetians nor Genoese traded in the Black Sea area which was wheat-producing par excellence. Byzantine monopoly on the import of grain from this area continued in practice.

The explanation of the somewhat surprising formal liberality of the Byzantine government in the matter of grain exports is to be found in a combination of domestic and international economic factors. In the eleventh and twelfth centuries, trade within the Byzantine Empire was very active, and, while there was govern-ment involvement since the state exacted a transactions tax and various other duties, there was no state intervention. The last state intervention in the grain trade was the effort of Nikephoritzes, in the 1070's, to centralize the great grain market of Rodosto so that the state could be sure to exact its *kommerkion*, that is to say, for fiscal reasons. The measure failed, and no state intervention in the grain trade, even in Constantinople, is attested in the twelfth century. Nevertheless, we hear of no particular problems in provisioning, and the price of grain seems to have remained stable; at a time of increasing urbanization, this suggests both increased production and improved mechanisms of distribution. In the absence of shortages, there was also no pressing need to forbid the export of grain. Indeed, the presence of privileged Italian merchants both gave greater impetus to the already active trade and, in turn, further promoted freer and cheaper trade conditions; at least insofar as the Venetians were concerned, those Byzantines who traded with them were also exempted from the transactions tax. Finally, it is also probable that grain exports were not yet significant enough to worry the Byzantine state.

This liberal attitude insofar as trade in foodstuffs is concerned underlines an important development that should be stressed. Although it was in the late thir-teenth and fourteenth centuries that privileges to western merchants in Byzantine lands proliferated, the structures that support a free and active commerce, the

---

55. *JGR*, 1, p. 368-371.

56. JACOBY, Italian Privileges, p. 357.

57. *JGR*, 1, p. 420 = MM, 3, p. 35: ἄνευ τῆς Ρωσίας καὶ τῶν Ματράχων. Conditions for Genoese trade had worsened with the privilege of 1169, since the goods they imported and sold in the provinces paid the full *kommerkion*. In 1192, the duties they paid everywhere and on domestic goods were lowered to 4%, as the Pisans' had just been. Exports still paid a 10% duty: JACOBY, Italian Privileges, p. 362.

58. LILIE, *Handel* (as in n. 53), p. 272-273, and BALARD, *La Romanie génoise*, p. 28, n. 44, argue that the Black Sea was closed to foreign merchants. JACOBY, Italian Privileges, p. 360, suggests that there was no total ban: it affected Genoese ships, but not Genoese merchants. M. E. MARTIN, The First Venetians in the Black Sea, Ἀρχεῖον Πόντου 35, 1978, p. 111-122, says that both Venetians and Genoese had access to the Black Sea in 12th c., but it did not interest them yet.

mechanisms that lower the transaction cost to the merchant, were really set in place during the twelfth and thirteenth centuries, and that not only in the Byzantine empire but all over the eastern Mediterranean.[59] One can see such mechanisms in the development of a common law of the sea that affected shipwrecks and salvage; in the reparations offered for goods seized (already in the Pisan privilege of 1111); in the progressive lowering of duties; and in the guarantees progressively given to merchants dying in foreign lands as to the disposition of their property. We can see them too in the special provisions made for the resolution of disputes involving foreign merchants. All of these mechanisms developed in the entire eastern Mediterranean region and North Africa, and created the conditions for the efficient exchange between trade regions. We can also see these mechanisms in the relaxation, indeed the absence, of controls regarding the export of foodstuffs and other forbidden commodities. This last point can be made for the Byzantine Empire; it is for others to say whether it holds for other parts of the eastern Mediterranean.

Only with the reestablishment of the Byzantine Empire in Constantinople in 1261 did the Byzantine state try to establish a measure of control over the export of grain grown on its territories. With the treaty of Nymphaeum, in 1261, Michael VIII allowed the Genoese to buy and export freely and without paying any duty all commodities (except gold and silver), specifically including foodstuffs and grain.[60] But by 1265, restrictions were put into place. It seems almost as though there was a residual eminent domain of the state over the grain trade (and over salt, another old imperial monopoly), which the state chose to exercise, starting in 1265, with Michael VIII's treaty with Venice. The emperor allowed the Venetians to export Byzantine wheat (except to enemy lands) only when its price in Constantinople was below 50 *hyperpyra* per *kentenarion* (that is, in times of plenty, when wheat was cheap), a price which in 1277 became 100 *hyperpyra* per *kentenarion*, there to remain throughout the Palaeologan period.[61] This meant that the Venetians could not export wheat in times of grave shortages and very high prices. In 1304, in a moment of great dearth, the Genoese were not allowed to export any Byzantine cereals at all – a prohibition lifted in 1317.[62] The export prohibition when the price in Constantinople reached a certain level remained in force, theoretically, throughout the fourteenth century, and it was even extended, in 1310, to the purchase, not just the export, of Byzantine grain by foreigners when the price in Constantinople

59. A. E. LAIOU, Byzantine Trade with Christians and Muslims and the Crusade, *The Crusades from the Perspective of Byzantium and the Muslim World*, ed. A. E. LAIOU, R. P. MOTTAHEDEH, Washington 2001, p. 186; EAD., Institutional Mechanisms of Integration, *Studies on the Internal Diaspora of the Byzantine Empire*, ed. H. AHRWEILER, A. E. LAIOU, Washington 1998, p. 171-178; M. MARTIN, The Venetians in the Byzantine Empire before 1204, *Byzantium and the West, c. 850-c. 1200*, ed. J. D. HOWARD-JOHNSTON, Amsterdam 1988, p. 212.

60. *JGR*, 1, p. 488 ff. On these matters, cf. BALARD, *La Romanie génoise*, p. 755; A. E. LAIOU, *Constantinople and the Latins; The Foreign Policy of Andronicus II, 1281-1328*, Cambridge, Mass. 1972, p. 148-150.

61. In 1265: *JGR*, 1, p. 499. In the confirmation of 1268, they were permitted to export the wheat, but only with imperial permission. On this, cf. CHRYSOSTOMIDES, Venetian Commercial Privileges under the Palaiologi (as in n. 54), p. 312. A *kentenarion* is equivalent to 100 *modioi*.

62. *JGR*, 1, p. 532. The text says can buy and *extrahere* all *victualia, preter furmentum et alia semina.* On the other hand, the Genoese may export grain from areas *que sunt in mare majori nec sunt subjecte imperio nostro.*

was at 100 *hyperpyra* per *kentenarion*, that is, in times of great scarcity.[63] However, none of these measures were effective. Venetians, Genoese, eventually Ragusans, bought and exported Byzantine wheat even when its price was higher than that established in 1277. In fact, the grain trade within the Byzantine Empire and outside it was quite free. Byzantium had become an exporter of wheat to the west, certainly until the 1340's, but also in the late fourteenth and early fifteenth century.[64]

What led to the recrudescence of interest in controlling the export of foodstuffs was on the one hand the renewed interest of the Byzantine state in protecting the consumer, especially in Constantinople, against high prices of essential commodities. At times, after the late thirteenth century, there were points of acute crisis, indeed famine conditions, which undoubtedly influenced some of these measures. Furthermore, the international grain market had changed, as the Byzantine territories and the Black Sea had become a prime source of provisioning for Italy. Grain of this provenance became important for the ever-needy Genoese market after 1258, while in 1268, when there was severe scarcity in Italy, the Venetians were able to buy sizeable quantities of wheat form the Black Sea area and import it to the west, realizing high profits.[65] The grain trade had become internationalized, and the Byzantine Empire and the Black Sea areas played a major role in it, even through the late fourteenth century, despite important political setbacks from time to time.[66] Italian merchants controlled this grain market to an ever-greater degree. It was impossible for a weak Byzantine state to impose true controls; there remained the protectionist intent, in a situation where international trade was much less regulated than in the past.

In their treaties with the Venetians, renewed every few years until 1325, the issue of the export of Byzantine grain appeared again and again, as did the question of the sale of Black Sea grain in the Byzantine Empire. Here, the protection of the consumer, the protection of the Byzantine producer and the protection of the Byzantine merchant came up against the two principles which governed the policies of Italian merchants, that is, the people who had integrated the Mediterranean market: they desired freedom of trade for themselves, and adverse conditions of trade for everyone else. That is to say, on the one hand there were efforts to impose monopolies, and on the other hand these monopolies were based on privileges which established freedom of trade for particular groups of merchants. The trade of the eastern Mediterranean in the thirteenth to the mid-fifteenth century was greatly influenced by these two demands, obviously in conflict when more than one state was involved. The two demands can be seen in the efforts of the Venetians and the Genoese to acquire trade monopoly in the Byzantine Empire, and especially in the Black Sea area.

---

63. In 1317, the accord with Genoa forbade the sale of wheat from Varna and Anchialos (while these cities remained under Bulgarian control) in the Byzantine Empire. It was permitted to export it, and no restrictions were placed on the export of Byzantine wheat either: BALARD, *La Romanie génoise*, p. 757.
64. A. LAIOU-THOMADAKIS, The Byzantine Economy in the Mediterranean Trade System, Thirteenth to Fifteenth Centuries, *DOP* 35, 1980-1981, p. 217-222.
65. BALARD, *La Romanie génoise*, p. 749; CHRYSOSTOMIDES, Venetian Commercial Privileges (as in n. 61), p. 316.
66. For the export of Thracian wheat in the late fourteenth century, see LAIOU-THOMADAKIS, The Byzantine Economy (as in n. 64), p. 218 ff.

In order to achieve these aims, Venetians and Genoese relied on war, but also on privileges issued by the Byzantine state. Thus, for example, the treaty of Nymphaeum, as well as that of 1267, granted the Genoese quasi-monopoly in the trade of the Byzantine Empire (although Pisan merchants were also allowed to operate), including the Black Sea area.[67] In different political conditions, the same emperor in 1265, in his treaty with the Venetians, excluded the Genoese, because they were enemies of the Venetians, from Byzantine territories, although the possibility of a future change of this policy was envisaged.[68] These provisions were changed by later treaties, after 1268 (in the ratification of the treaty with Venice, the Emperor retained the right to ally himself with both Venice and Genoa), which allowed the merchants of both states access to the Black Sea. At the other end of the Pontic area, in 1319, the emperor of Trebizond Alexios I gave the Venetians the same privileges enjoyed by the Genoese.[69] After 1269, it became a matter of policy for the Genoese to try to stop the Venetians from sailing into the Black Sea: *quod non iretur ad Tanam*. On the other side, the Venetians argued for the freedom of the seas, a statement not in favor of free trade generally, this is not the World Trade Organization, but rather for freedom for themselves to trade in this area. So did the Doge Andrea Dandolo say that he wanted to preserve *libertatem maris* in 1350, at a time of acute conflict between Venice and Genoa; the Pope also supported the principle of the open seas.[70] The Byzantines also traded in the Black Sea in the 1340's, which caused Genoese reaction. At the end of the war of the Straits, there was an effort on the part of the Genoese to limit the access of both Venetians and Byzantines to Tana and the Sea of Azov.[71] Eventually, the relative freedom of the seas was reasserted, whether officially or unofficially, and both Byzantines and Venetians were allowed to sail there, although the Genoese had a clear preponderance in the Black Sea. What is of interest is the internationalization of these markets, as well as the rivalries and efforts to establish monopolies, and, finally, the role of privileges issued by the states of the area.

In effect, the Byzantine quasi-monopoly in the Black Sea, which we have seen operating through the twelfth century, disappeared, and was replaced by rivalries and by the efforts of Genoese to establish monopolies, while merchants of Venice and Byzantium tried, for a while successfully, to participate in the grain trade of the Black Sea. One may say that those who were well established in the area aimed toward monopoly, the others toward more competitive, which means freer, trade. A measure of protectionism (both of the Byzantine consumer and of the Byzantine merchant) remained where possible, as with the ceiling price established by the Byzantine government for the export of grain by the Venetians. To what extent this was implemented is a different question.[72]

67. *JGR*, 1, p. 491; BALARD, *La Romanie génoise*, p. 44.
68. *Ibid.*, p. 49: MM, 3, p. 76-84, especially p. 79.
69. *Ibid.*, p. 130 ff.: confirmation by Alexios III in 1364; cf. S. KARPOV, Venezia e Genova, rivalità e collaborazione a Trebisonda e Tana, secoli XIII-XV, *Genova. Venezia, il Levante nei secoli XII-XIV*, Genoa-Venice 2000, p. 261.
70. *Ibid.*, p. 260-261.
71. LAIOU-THOMADAKIS, The Byzantine Economy, p. 194-195.
72. *Ibid.*, p. 212 ff.

The realities of Mediterranean exchange in this late period include conflicts between trading powers and between merchants of different states, as well as cooperation among merchants who realized that war was detrimental to their collective commercial interests. They are also characterised by a very clear erosion of the sovereign rights of the recipient state, the Byzantine Empire in our example, which were undercut by the rights claimed by privileged free trade. This fact may be seen very clearly in the negotiations between Byzantium and Venice regarding the "right" of the Venetians to sell Black Sea grain within the Byzantine Empire without paying duties. The dispute is clearly one between sovereign rights (the right of the Byzantine state to tax the sale of foreign imports within its frontiers) versus the right claimed by the Venetians to trade freely in all commodities, except for a few that had been explicitly excluded in the treaties.[73] In this respect, the situation in the eastern Mediterranean of the late Middle Ages is, indeed, paradigmatic, for similar situations were reproduced later, in the Ottoman Empire and in China, and are even present today.

The prohibition of the export of a certain number of commodities had been effective in a period in which the domestic Byzantine market was coherent, and a time when there was more interest in the import rather than in the export of commodities. The prohibitions had a markedly political character: from safeguarding the interests of the fisc, to ensuring those of the consumer, to protecting the image of wealth, luxury and power of the Byzantine state through the exclusive right to disseminate gold coins and commodities such as imperial silks. It is, indeed, significant that there was no prohibition of imports, only of exports. With the liberalization of the silk market, political concerns and control melt into the economics of free trade; and a larger international market emerges, where there may be substitution of demand from imperial silks to high quality silks.

With grain exports, we see first what seems to be a full liberalization of the grain trade in the twelfth century, and subsequently efforts to reestablish controls in the late thirteenth and fourteenth centuries, primarily for the protection of the consumer, of local growers and of the fisc. But this was at a time when the grain trade had changed, the market had become liberalized, and the imposition and implementation of controls had become correspondingly difficult.

In the liberalization of the market, the granting of privileges by the Byzantine state (but also by all states of the eastern Mediterranean) to Italian traders played a primary role. The Constantinopolitan market became much freer, and lost its privileged status in the course of the twelfth century, partly because of the privileges granted to the Italians (especially the Venetians) and to those Byzantines who traded with them.[74] Thus a privileged-nation situation developed into a more general freedom of trade, which in turn was to lead to rivalries and conflicts between Italian city-states and other states of the area. Once the ball started rolling, there was no stopping it. Thus there was a continuous lowering of the transaction costs, through the regulation of the terms in which foreign merchants traded in Byzantine markets. This is a general phenomenon in the eastern Mediterranean.

---

73. On this, see LAIOU, *Andronicus II* (as in n. 60), p. 274-275.
74. OIKONOMIDES, The Economic Region of Constantinople (as in n. 3), and LAIOU, Byzantine Traders and Seafarers, *passim*. Cf. K.-P. MATSCHKE, Commerce, Trade, Markets, and Money, Thirteenth-Fifteenth Centuries, *EHB*, 2, p. 771-772.

Connected with the lowering of the transaction costs and the greater freedom of trade was the partial dissolution of national sovereignty into the larger regulations necessary for the efficient functioning of an international market – a situation quite reminiscent of the creation of large economic and political units today: the European Union is one such example, to avoid going into other, similar examples from the globalised economy of our times. I am, still, speaking of the Byzantine Empire, and perhaps other states of the eastern Mediterranean. In western Europe, even in Venice, protectionist measures remained. But in the exchange system of the eastern Mediterranean, raison d'état in international economic matters was over-taken, to a significant degree, by raisons du marché, certainly so in the territories and former territories of the Byzantine Empire. Raisons du marché, fuelled by the interests and exigencies of Italian maritime cities and their merchants.

It is in the framework of the assertion of economic factors that one must inscribe the commodification of luxury objects: the large trade in artifacts and art objects made for the market in the thirteenth century and after, whether these were silks produced in Venice and the rest of Italy, or objects of glass and crystal or gold produced in Venice, or icons produced on Crete and Cyprus.[75] Art historians have noticed and examined this phenomenon for some decades now. It may be said that even the fusion of artistic elements, the *koine*, also noticed by art historians long ago, mirrors the fusion of commercial practices in the eastern Mediterranean. The implications of economics are broad indeed.

---

75. LAIOU, Venice as a Center of Trade (as in n. 40), p. 11-26.

XIII

Regional Networks in the Balkans in the Middle and Late Byzantine Period*

[125] Let me say at the outset how pleasant and comforting it is to me to see the revived interest in Byzantine trade that has developed over the past few years – maybe a couple of decades. It signals considerable progress in the study of Byzantine economic history. A number of factors have contributed to this development, and I will signal only two, which in my view are the most significant. One is, undoubtedly, the advances in archaeology, which is now carried out with sophistication and with a view toward uncovering and studying not only elite products but also more humble ones. The other is the liberation of Byzantine economic history from the primitivist models, the outcropping of the Finley-Jones views, as Sean Kingsley and Michael Decker have called them,[1] a liberation that, while not yet complete, is very much in evidence, as a number of the papers in this Symposium show. Such views had for some considerable time informed the study not only of the late antique and early Byzantine period but of subsequent periods as well.[2]

---

* This article is also published in *Trade and Markets in Byzantium*, ed. C. Morrisson (Washington, D.C.: Dumbarton Oaks, 2012). Used with permission. The original page numbers are given in square brackets within the text. For the purposes of this volume the images accompanying the original article have not been reproduced.

This draft was communicated to Peter Temin in advance of the Symposium, in April 2008. It has been edited minimally here by Cécile Morrisson, completing the references indicated by the author with the help of Demetra Papanikola-Bakirtzi, Johannes Koder, and Rowan Dorin. When there was some doubt as to which publication Laiou had in mind, the reference has been inserted between square brackets. The few sentences where the style was adapted to the oral presentation have been left unchanged.

[1] S. Kingsley and M. Decker, introduction to *Economy and Exchange in the East Mediterranean during Late Antiquity: Proceedings of a Conference at Somerville College, Oxford, 29th May, 1999*, ed. S. Kingsley and M. Decker (Oxford, 2001), 3.

[2] E.g., M.F. Hendy, [*Studies in the Byzantine Monetary Economy, 300–1450* (Cambridge, 1985)]; J. Haldon, ["Production, Distribution and Demand in the Byzantine World, c. 660–840," in *The Long Eighth Century: Production, Distribution and Demand*, ed. I.L. Hansen and C. Wickham (Leiden, 2000), 225–64]; C. Wickham, ["Overview: Production, Distribution and Demand," ibid., 345–77]; M. Angold, [*Byzantine Government in Exile: Government and Society under the Laskarids of Nicaea, 1204–1261* (London, 1975)].

The study of international exchange had suffered less than that of regional and interregional exchange, and for good reason.[3] The export (or import) of luxury items, thought to constitute the objects of international trade, can easily fit the model of an economy based on status and embedded in politics, in which exchange is controlled in one way or the other, and where one or two large centers of demand and production are sufficient. Regional and interregional trade engage different productive forces and different modes of distribution.

What does one mean by regional trade? The definitions depend partly on distance and partly on **[126]** function. One concept based on distance calls long-distance trade, as opposed to regional trade, that which extends over 100 kilometers by land, or covers the distance from Egypt to Africa by sea.[4] The borderline between local and regional trade would be 50 kilometers by land or one day's sailing.[5] Distance, of course, is not the only factor, and perhaps not the primary one, since its role can vary, depending on more functional aspects, such as the purpose of the transactions and the pull of major centers of consumption. For regional trade, I use the definition that locates it within a radius of 50 to 300 kilometers. In terms of function, it would implicate transactions that were more large-scale than those of local trade, and goods that were produced and consumed within the region; and the merchants would be professionals, not the producers who would frequent local markets. The types of product exchanged are usually thought to be more expensive and lighter than those of local trade, but not luxury items, which are thought to form the commodities of interregional and international trade, but I do not think that this is a good distinguishing factor.[6]

---

[3]   E.g., É. Patlagean, "Byzance et les marchés du grand commerce vers 830–vers 1030: Entre Pirenne et Polanyi," in *Mercati e mercanti nell'alto medioevo: L'area Euroasiatica e l'area Mediterranea*, Settimane di studi del Centro italiano di studi sull'alto medioevo 40 (Spoleto, 1993), 587–632. Some scholars, however, have stressed the role of non-economic international circulation of goods and money: P. Grierson, "Commerce in the Dark Ages: A Critique of the Evidence," *Transactions of the Royal Historical Society*, 5th ser., 9 (1959): 123–40 (repr. in idem, *Dark Age Numismatics* [London, 1979], art. II).

[4]   J. Durliat, *De la ville antique à la ville byzantine: Le problème des subsistances*, Collection de l'École française de Rome 136 (Rome, 1990), 513–14; A.E. Laiou, "Exchange and Trade, Seventh–Twelfth Century," in *EHB*, 2:705.

[5]   A. E. Laiou and C. Morrisson, *The Byzantine Economy* (Cambridge, 2007), 81; J.H. Pryor, *Geography, Technology and War: Studies in the Maritime History of the Mediterranean, 649–1571* (Cambridge, 1988), 139–52.

[6]   The above is an adaptation of de Ligt's definitions for fairs: L. de Ligt, *Fairs and Markets in the Roman Empire: Economic and Social Aspects of Periodic Trade in a Pre-industrial Society*, Dutch

It is necessary to introduce nuances and amplifications into this definition. Some distinctions do not hold: regional trade is not necessarily domestic, as it can also take place across frontiers – John Haldon has already noted this in connection with Cyprus, the southern coast of Asia Minor, and Syria-Palestine, and the recently completed dissertation of my student, Koray Durak,[7] makes the same point for a period that extends to the late eleventh century. Trade between the Byzantine Empire and Bulgaria is both regional and international in the sense that it implicates two different political entities. Trade between Crete and Egypt, which in the tenth century and after included herbs and cheeses from Crete and spices from Egypt to Crete, implicates commodities that are semiluxury on one leg and luxury on the other. Indeed, in terms of commodities, the same commodity can be the object of regional transactions as well as long-distance, international ones, as will be argued in the case of eleventh- to twelfth-century ceramics. A real difference exists in the conditions in which international trade takes place: it is subject to strictures, limitations, and bilateral arrangements, such as, for example, affected the Bulgarian trade. The treaty of 716 had permitted the export to Bulgaria of "garments and red leather of a price up to 30 pounds of gold," and it has plausibly been suggested that this exchange would have taken place in Mesembria, which would then have functioned as a port of trade.[8] In the early tenth century, the *Book of the Prefect* set down specific terms regarding the exchange of silks for the linen and honey brought by the Bulgarians.[9] In other words, there is an institutional component to international trade that is absent from regional and interregional trade within the Byzantine Empire. The distinction between the products exchanged in regional and in interregional/long-distance trade is also not a stable one, but changes with time and economic conditions: thus, in the thirteenth century and after, exchange between the Black Sea area and the northern Aegean, on the one hand, and Venice and Genoa, on the other, was not limited to the luxuries that in the first instance one associates with long-distance trade, but very much involved bulk products, primarily wheat

---

Monographs on Ancient History and Archaeology 11 (Amsterdam, 1993), 15, 82–3, 88–9.

    [7]   K. Durak, "Commerce and Networks of Exchange between the Byzantine Empire and the Islamic Near East from the Early Ninth Century to the Arrival of the Crusaders" (Ph.D. diss., Harvard University, 2008).

    [8]   See Theophanes the Confessor, *Theophanis Chronographia*, ed. C. de Boor, 2 vols (Leipzig, 1883–85), 1:497–9; N. Oikonomides, "Tribute or Trade? The Byzantine-Bulgarian Treaty of 716," in *Studies on the Slavo-Byzantine and West-European Middle Ages: In memoriam Ivan Dujčev*, Studia Slavico-byzantina et Medievalia Europensia 1 (Sofia, 1988), 29–31.

    [9]   *Eparchenbuch* 9.6.

and alum. Thus the various categories of trade are not clear-cut; they become blurred at the boundaries, as the same commodities (grain, for instance) at times circulate between contiguous areas and at other times travel over long distances. I use the term "regional trade" here to refer to exchanges within a limited geographic range (the geographic component) that involve commodities which are produced within that area. When the exchange involves the resale of **[127]** commodities from or to greater distances, this will be noted.

If the existence of local trade may be assumed except in the most extreme of circumstances, that of regional networks is not self-evident. It is their development that we are concerned with here, and for that there are certain preconditions. There has to be a level of effective demand that cannot be adequately met by local exchange either because it is too large or because it involves specialty products. Large, concentrated demand for alimentary products, typically associated with the existence of large cities (but which could also be the result of the presence of an army in a particular location), cannot be met by the production of the immediate hinterland: it has been estimated that in medieval societies an urban population of ten to twenty thousand could not be provisioned from the immediate hinterland, which necessarily means regional or interregional trade in foodstuffs.[10] In the Balkans, Constantinople is the obvious case in point, but it is, of course, far from a unique case: Thessalonike and, after the tenth century, certainly in the eleventh–twelfth, Corinth, Monemvasia, and other cities[11] were large enough to depend on regional and perhaps interregional trade. The second point, specialty products, is exemplified by the sale of Bulgarian honey in Thessalonike or the dispersion of pottery from Thessalonike and Serres in the Palaiologan period. Channels of distribution are important and require good communications, which are not simply a given: effective demand helps develop good communications, and is reinforced by them.

Let us look at the development of regional trade networks in Thrace and Macedonia. These are privileged areas, since Thrace has the strong magnet of the great consumption center that was Constantinople, and Macedonia has the equally important magnet of Thessalonike, not only a major consumption and production center but also a port. At times, both areas were very insecure: Thrace in the seventh and eighth centuries, and from time to time afterward, and Macedonia whenever there were troubles with the Bulgarians. These areas

---

[10]   J. Landers, *The Field and the Forge: Population, Production and Power in the Pre-industrial West* (Oxford, 2003), 114.

[11]   W. Treadgold, *A History of the Byzantine State and Society* (Stanford, 1997), 702.

also had, since Roman times and throughout much of the Byzantine period, a good network of roads, doubtless built for military reasons but also able to serve peaceful ones: the two major such roads were the Via Egnatia and the so-called Military or Imperial Road (Via Militaris or Regia, *basilikē hodos*), traversing the Balkans diagonally, from Belgrade to Braničevo and Niš, then to Philippopolis, Adrianople, and Constantinople.[12] The Via Egnatia, difficult of access in the late seventh century, began to be reopened toward the end of that century, and seems to be functioning partly in the 830s and fully by the late ninth century, at least in times of peace. Alternatively, communications along the southern shore of Thrace were carried out by sea, also a dangerous but, it seems, not unusual enterprise.[13] By the end of the ninth century, people could travel along the entire length of the Via Egnatia.[14] The way inland would have followed the rivers or the river valleys of Axios, Strymon, and Nestos.[15] The lower part of the Via Regia, as far north as Philippopolis, seems to have been recently reopened in the late eighth century, when the empress Eirene [128] visited the city and rebuilt Veroe (Stara Zagora) and Anchialos, in 784.[16]

---

[12]   K. Belke, "Roads and Travel in Macedonia and Thrace in the Middle and Late Byzantine Period," in *Travel in the Byzantine World*, ed. R. Macrides (Aldershot, 2002), 73–90.

[13]   Despite grave dangers posed by Slavs such as those "Slavic robbers" who, in the 830s, robbed ships that tried to cross the Strymon River: G. Makris, ed., *Ignatios Diakonos und die vita des Hl. Gregorios Dekapolites*, ByzArch 17 (Stuttgart, 1997), 86; or those of a "sklavinia" in the hinterland of Thessalonike who rebelled against imperial authority or, at the very least, launched a destructive expedition in the surrounding area (ibid., 110). On his first trip, St. Gregory went to Thessalonike from Constantinople by sea from Ainos to Christopolis (Kavalla), and then to Thessalonike by land, having persuaded the Slavic "robbers" to let him cross the Strymon. Interestingly, he was then able to go, in the service of a monk, from Thessalonike to Corinth overland, and then on board ship, braving the Arab pirates, to Rhegion and then to Rome (86–88). Travel between Thessalonike and Constantinople took place both by land (though Anastasios and George the *protokangelarios* took a ship at Maroneia) and by sea (112–16).

[14]   As did Anastasius Bibliothecarius in 870: Belke, "Roads and Travel," 78–9. [N. Oikonomides, "The Medieval Via Egnatia," in *The Via Egnatia under Ottoman Rule (1380–1699): Halcyon Days in Crete II*, ed. E. Zachariadou (Rethymnon, 1996), 9–16 (repr. in idem, *Social and Economic Life in Byzantium* [Aldershot, 2004], art. XXIII)]; A.E. Laiou, "Η Θεσσαλονίκη, η ενδοχώρα της και ο οικονομικός της χώρος στην εποχή των Παλαιολόγων" (Thessalonike, its hinterland and its economic space), in *Διεθνές Συμπόσιο Βυζαντινή Μακεδονία 324–1430 μ. Χ., Θεσσαλονίκη, 29–31 Οκτωβρίου 1992*, Πρακτικά Μακεδονική Βιβλιοθήκη 82 (Thessalonike, 1995), 183–94, at 184.

[15]   N. Oikonomidès, "Le kommerkion d'Abydos: Thessalonique et le commerce bulgare au IXᵉ siècle," in *Hommes et richesses dans l'Empire byzantin*, vol. 2, *VIIIe–XVe siècle*, ed. V. Kravari, J. Lefort, and C. Morrisson (Paris, 1991), 241–8, at 245–7.

[16]   Theophanes, ad 6276, *The Chronicle of Theophanes Confessor: Byzantine and Near Eastern History, AD 284–813*, trans. C. Mango and R. Scott (Oxford, 1997), 142–3.

If Theophanes' account of the travels is accurate, Eirene went first to Veroe, then to Anchialos, and finally to Philippopolis, from where she returned to Constantinople. Whatever the reason for this somewhat crisscross journey, it is clear that not only was the southern part of the main route open at this time but there were roads connecting Veroe to Anchialos, a fairish long way away, and Veroe to Philippopolis. At the same time, communications by sea between Constantinople and the Black Sea coast must have been open at least since the Byzantine-Bulgarian treaty of 716; in any case, the Black Sea was controlled by Byzantine ships.

For the commercial networks of Thrace in the period down to the eleventh century, the available information is primarily Constantinopolitan or connected to Constantinople. It has been established, on the basis primarily of Arab sources of the eighth and ninth centuries, that Constantinople was provisioned in agricultural products from the Thracian hinterland, first the area adjacent to the city and then further inland. By the tenth century, Raidestos, to the south of Constantinople, had become a major center of agricultural production and diffusion, and so it remained throughout the Byzantine era. Mesembria, Anchialos, and in the ninth century Develtos (which replaced Mesembria) also functioned as export centers for the trade of the Bulgarian hinterland, that is, agricultural products.[17] It has also been argued, on the basis of texts and the seals of *kommerkiarioi*, that in the late ninth century the products of the Bulgarian hinterland reached Constantinople by land as well, along the Via Regia, which led from Sofia to Constantinople.[18] Independent evidence supports the idea that commerce with parts of the Bulgarian hinterland increased over time. The Bulgarian merchants in the *Book of the Prefect* sold linen and honey and they bought Byzantine and Syrian silks. In 969, the Russian Prince Svetoslav described Presthlavitza as a commercial center where, along with products from Hungary, Bohemia, and the Rus, one could find gold, silks, fruit, and wine "from Greece."[19] Indeed, archaeological finds

---

[17]   Oikonomidès, "Le kommerkion d'Abydos," 247–8.

[18]   Ibid., 247. By this time, the *kommerkiarioi* were imperial officials who controlled imports and exports and collected the customs duties: N. Oikonomides, "Silk Trade and Production in Byzantium from the Sixth to the Ninth Century: The Seals of Kommerkiarioi," *DOP* 40 (1986): 50 (repr. in idem, *Social and Economic Life in Byzantium*, art. VIII). In the seventh and eighth centuries, according to this scholar, the kommerkiarioi had been important merchants dealing primarily in silk, who received from the emperor official rights in their province (33–53).

[19]   Reported in the *Russian Primary Chronicle*: N. Oikonomides, "Presthlavitza, the Little Preslav," *Südost-Forschungen* 42 (1983): 1–19.

include fine White Ware ceramics and objects in high-quality glass.[20] While the jewelry of the Preslav treasure might be there as a gift from Byzantium, the other objects, especially those mentioned by Svetoslav, seem to belong best to the context of commercial exchange. The Byzantine products sold here would be luxury products (silks), but also semiluxury commodities (fruit and wine).

The expansion of regional trade inland, intensifying in the eleventh and twelfth centuries, is a natural function of the rise in demand, which one may plausibly suggest developed with the revival of cities and city functions, as it seems to have occurred since the early ninth century; it continued, as an overall pattern, through the twelfth century at least. The demand of the capital for agricultural goods and raw materials, as well as for Bulgarian linen, would have been a particular stimulus for exchange involving the northern part of the region.

This, then, was the situation in the ninth to tenth centuries with regard to Thrace. The southern and easternmost part of Thrace had connections with centers of trade – mostly with Constantinople is what we hear about, but perhaps with other centers of consumption as well. For the products to reach the distribution centers, there must have been smaller networks, whose composition we cannot know. The question that arises naturally, and especially given the debate about the nature of the Byzantine economy, is the degree to which the commodities involved were exchanged through commercial channels or were inscribed in a system of non-economic exchange, primarily that of (tribute or) tax. Secondarily, there is the question of the medium through which these transactions were conducted.

Starting from the geographic north, to the extent that exchanges involved Bulgarian-ruled territories and given that these territories were independent until 1018, there is no question of a fiscally driven **[129]** exchange. Nor did the Bulgarians pay tribute to the Byzantines. From early on, the exchange seems to have involved merchants: the treaty of 716 mentions the *emporeuomenoi* of both states, who were required to have their merchandise stamped with an official stamp.[21] In 893, two Byzantine merchants with friends in high places tried to divert the trade of the Bulgarian hinterland from Constantinople to Thessalonike – these were commercial exchanges, involving merchants, on whom our two Byzantines also imposed higher customs duties, which they

---

[20]   I. Jordanov, "Preslav," in *EHB*, 2:669.
[21]   Theophanes, ed. De Boor, 1:497; Laiou, "Exchange and Trade," 704.

collected. The complaints of the Bulgarian merchants provoked the attacks of Tsar Symeon.[22] The Bulgarian merchants in the *Book of the Prefect* are just that.

Further south, within Byzantine Thrace, fiscal grain must have ceased being significant in the second half of the eighth century: since 769, when Constantine V forced the collection of taxes in cash rather than in kind, there was a fiscally driven commercialization of production, with all that means for monetization. What does raise a question is the fact that the area had a number of large estates, especially well documented in the eleventh and twelfth centuries; so one would have to address the question of whether the products of the region – primarily, of course, agricultural ones – were sold to merchants who then resold them to centers of concentrated demand, including Constantinople, or whether important landlords collected their rents (in kind, in such a scenario) and transferred them to their urban dwellings, thus taking a considerable proportion of urban demand (Constantinopolitan in the case of Thrace, Thessalonian in the case of Macedonia and perhaps western Thrace) out of the commercial circuit. In the tenth and eleventh centuries, the seals of the *horreiarioi* mark the presence of warehouses that stored grain from imperial estates, perhaps for consumption in Constantinople. In Thrace, these were in Herakleia and Philippopolis, so that some of the production of the area probably moved outside the regional commercial network.[23] In the *Book of the Prefect* there is no hint that any of the commodities entering Constantinople did so in any conditions other than market ones; the question still remains, however, as to the proportion of the goods that did so.

Finally, we must consider the issue of the medium of payment. For Byzantine Thrace, especially its southern regions, there is no reason to believe that transactions were carried out in any medium other than cash in the ninth to tenth centuries. On the other hand, the first Bulgarian empire (680–971) issued no coinage of its own, and it is assumed that it was mostly a barter economy. Certainly, the Bulgarian merchants in Constantinople in the early tenth century bartered their products, whether because they found Byzantine

---

[22]   Theophanes Continuatus, ed. I. Bekker (Bonn, 1838), 357–8: (ἀνδράσιν ἐμπορικοῖς καὶ φιλοκερδέσι καὶ φιλοχρύσοις); *Ioannis Scylitzae synopsis historiarum*, ed. I. Thurn (Berlin, 1973), 175–6: ἀνδράσιν ἐμπορικοῖς καὶ φιλοκερδέσι; Oikonomidès, "Le kommerkion d'Abydos," 246ff.; Laiou, "Exchange and Trade," 726. Skylitzes' phrasing suggests that Constantinople would no longer import the Bulgarian trade directly. So the enterprise would also involve a further exchange, from Thessalonike to Constantinople.

[23]   J.-C. Cheynet, "Un aspect du ravitaillement de Constantinople aux Xe–XIe siècles d'après quelques sceaux d'*hôrreiarioi*," in *Studies in Byzantine Sigillography*, ed. N. Oikonomidès, vol. 6 (Washington, D.C., 1999), 1–26 [repr. in idem, *La société byzantine: L'apport des sceaux* (Paris, 2008), 209–36].

silks more serviceable than money or because the Byzantines themselves preferred to barter with them rather than export their own coinage (but commission fees between the Byzantines themselves were paid in cash).[24] Coin finds from the area of Preslav show that some Byzantine money circulated, and also that the quantity of Byzantine coins increased very considerably, almost doubling, during the period of Byzantine rule (971–1185).[25] The decision of the emperor Michael IV (1034–41) to demand the Bulgarian taxes in cash must have played a role in the monetization of exchange.[26] **[130]**

In the eleventh and twelfth centuries, a period in which the Byzantine economy was in a virtuous cycle, regional exchange networks are visible throughout the empire. Cities thrived, commercial exchanges intensified, and manufactured products, not only luxury ones but pottery, glass, and perhaps others, circulated. In Thrace, given the relative peace in the region and the demand generated from increased urban populations, the hinterland seems to have been integrated more fully into the commercial networks. The well-known example of Raidestos, a very important center of grain collection and export to Constantinople, shows the impeccable workings of a market that functioned on market principles, where prices were formed freely on the ground.[27] This fact is so well known that there is no reason to dwell on

---

[24]   [*Eparchenbuch* 1.13, 1.14, 1.19 (*synetheiai* due to the *primmikerios* or the *grapheus* by the new *didaskalos* or the new *taboullarios*); 4.5 (6 *nomismata* due to the guild by the new *vestioprates*); 6.4 (*kankelarion*); 6.11, 22.1 (*arrabona*); 6.9, 6.13 (fine to pay to the guild); 7.2, 8.1 (price of silk textiles); 1.4, 1.5, 1.9ff., 2.8, 11.5, 11.7, 12.1, etc. (fines); 21.2 (profit of the *bothroi*); 21.9 (fees due to the *prostates* of the *bothroi*); 1.6ff., 1.25, 22.3 (various *misthoi*).]

[25]   Jordanov, "Preslav," 670.

[26]   One hopes that the hoarding of coins in Matak near Nim (1 *solidus* and 7 *histamena*), which has been connected with this policy, is an isolated instance: I. Touratsoglou, "Από τα νομισματικά πράγματα στα Βαλκάνια των Μακεδόνων: Με αφορμή το 'θησαυρό' Ισταμένων Θεσσαλονίκη 2000," in *Βυζαντιό Κράτος και Κοινωνία, μνήμη Ν. Οικονομίδη*, ed. Α. Avramea, A.E. Laiou, and E. Chrysos (Athens, 2003), 523–41, at 526. [Laiou's "hopes" are confirmed by the context of this find: it belongs with a series of Dalmatian hoards formerly connected by D. M. Metcalf to the wreck of a ship loaded with 10 *kentēnaria* of gold recovered by Stephen of Dioclea (*Coinage in the Balkans* [Thessalonike, 1975], 48–9). I. Mirnik ("The Coinage of Romanos III Argyros in the Archaeological Museum of Split," *Vjesnik za Arheologiju i historiju Dalmatinsku* 87–9 [1998–99]: 305–60) connects them to the increasing Ragusan trade at that time. See in this volume R.W. Dorin, "Adriatic Trade Networks in the Twelfth and Early Thirteenth Centuries," 235–79 C.M.]

[27]   See G. Bratianu, "Une expérience d'économie dirigée: Le monopole du blé à Byzance au XIe siècle," *Byz* 9 (1934): 643–62 [repr. in idem, *Études byzantines d'histoire économique et sociale* (Paris, 1938), 129–81]; A. Harvey, *Economic Expansion in the Byzantine Empire, 900–1200* (Cambridge, 1989), 236–8; M. Kaplan, *Les hommes et la terre à Byzance du VIe au XIe siècle: Propriété et exploitation du sol* (Paris, 1992), 468–70; P. Magdalino, "The Grain Supply of Constantinople,

XIII

it here. Philippopolis and its hinterland must have become a major producer of agricultural products in the eleventh century, as also the hinterland of Mosynopolis, in the south (see below); Veroe and the Hebros Delta were also important in the twelfth century.[28] All of these towns or, increasingly, cities were, in terms of distance, situated within a radius of less than 300 kilometers from Constantinople, the only exception being Philippopolis (372 km).[29] All were situated along major land or sea routes (see **fig. 1**). The products of their hinterland would, presumably, have arrived at the centers of distribution, if I may call them that, on the large number of smaller roads about which we have information from a much later period, and which seem to have been ubiquitous.[30]

Trade networks in the interior of the Balkans are not easy to determine with great precision. Here, we have a valuable source of information, the foundation charter of the monastery of the Theotokos, in Petritzos, south of the city of Philippopolis, dated 1083 (see **fig. 2**). Its founder was a Georgian noble, Gregory Pakourianos, a great soldier in the service of the Byzantine Empire and a man who, only two years earlier, had been an emperor maker.[31] He endowed his monastery with very considerable properties that had been given him by imperial decrees as reward for his services, as well as with those that had been given to his late brother, Apasios. The properties were in three

Ninth–Twelfth Centuries," in *Constantinople and Its Hinterland*, ed. C. Mango and G. Dagron (Aldershot, 1995), 40–43.

[28]   C. Asdracha, *La région des Rhodopes aux XIIIe et XIVe siècles: Étude de géographie historique* (Athens, 1976), 180–219 (production), 219–31 (trade and monetary circulation); J.L. Teall, "The Grain Supply of the Byzantine Empire, 330–1025," *DOP* 13 (1959): 87–190; A.E. Laiou, "Introversion and Extroversion, Autarky and Trade: Urban and Rural Economy in Thrace During the Byzantine Period," in *4th International Symposium on Thracian Studies Byzantine Thrace: Evidence and Remains (Komotini, 18–22 April 2007)*, forthcoming. At the time of the Third Crusade, a large part of Frederick Barbarossa's army was sent to take and plunder the *civitas opulentissima* of Veroe (= Stara Zagora): Ansbert, "Historia de Expeditione Friderici Imperatoris," in *Quellen zur Geschichte des Kreuzzuges Kaiser Friedrichs I.*, ed. A. Chroust (Berlin, 1928), 44, 45. The city can have become "very rich" only through trade, and that regional trade.

[29]   Varna lies at a distance of 260 km. The distance of Great Preslav to Constantinople would be about the same.

[30]   Belke, "Roads and Travel," 86ff.

[31]   See P. Lemerle, *Cinq études sur le XIe siècle byzantin* (Paris, 1977); A.E. Laiou, "L'étranger de passage et l'étranger privilégié à Byzance, XIème–XIIème siècles," in *Identité et droit de l'Autre*, ed. L. Mayali (Berkeley, 1994), 69–88; and eadem, "Introversion and Extroversion"; I have used the Petit edition of the *typikon* (L. Petit, "Typikon de Grégoire Pacourianos pour le monastère de Petritzos (Bačkovo) en Bulgarie, texte original," *VizVrem* 9, supp. 1 [St. Petersburg, 1904]), hereafter cited as Petit.

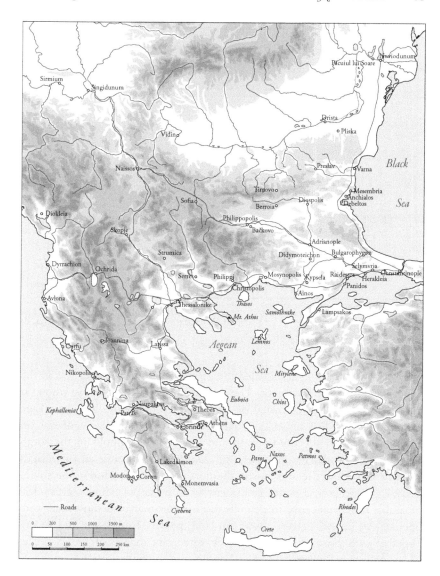

Figure 1. Map of the Balkans in the Middle and Late Byzantine Periods (from *Le monde byzantin*, vol. 2, *L'Empire byzantin, 641–1204*, ed. J.-C. Cheynet, Nouvelle Clio [Paris, 2006], courtesy CNRS, UMR 8167)

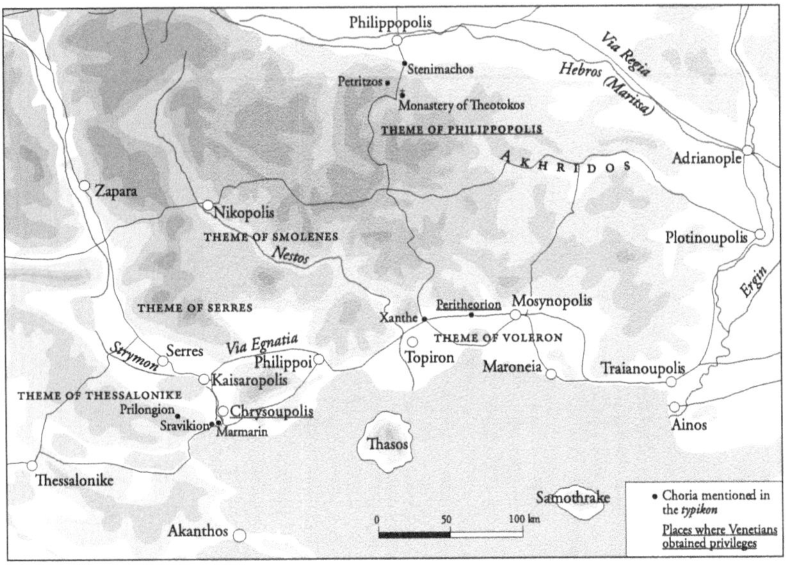

Figure 2. Venetian privileges in and around Pakourianos's estates (after C. Asdracha, in Lemerle, Cinq études, facing 176)

solid blocks: the one that included the properties of his brother was in the eastern part of the theme of Thessalonike/western part of Strymon, at the Strymon Delta. It consisted of the city of Kaisaropolis and the village communities of Prilongion and Sravikion. The second was centered on Philippopolis, and the third was in and around Mosynopolis in the south on the Via Egnatia, Peritheorion, and Xanthe. They consisted of villages and towns, such as Stenimachos in the north and Peritheorion in the south, houses and other real estate in the city of Mosynopolis, and a great deal of arable land, vineyards, trees, mills (both water mills and those that were operated by animal power), mountain land, pasture land, lakes, and so on. Together with those of his brother, they were in the themes of Thessalonike, Voleron, Serres, Philippopolis, and Xanthe, and in the region of Komotene. They were, **[132]** he tells us, functioning and income-producing.[32] The properties he gave to his monastery were going concerns and in the past had yielded very considerable revenues, according to Pakourianos.[33] In his

---

[32]   On the domains, see Petit, paras. 2, 14; Lemerle, *Cinq études*, 180, 190–91.

[33]   Lemerle, *Cinq études*, 166–8. Cf. Petit, para. 14.

praktikon (foundation charter), Pakourianos provides rather generously for subsidies for the *hēgoumenos* and the monks, as well as for commemorative services. Just these two expenses, paid in good coin (*histamenon trachy*), add up to about 14 pounds of gold a year. It has been estimated that the total outlay in cash would be about 20 pounds of gold a year, and the value of expenses in kind about 79 pounds of gold. Ten pounds of gold were to be kept as a reserve at all times, and the rest of the money would be invested in land.[34] He also expected that revenues would increase in time, as he and his successors effected land improvements, and perhaps as he constructed towers, doubtless for defensive purposes. He obtained privileges from the emperor to ensure that in such a case these increased revenues would also be free of taxes.[35] A hundred years later, according to an elegant study by Michael Hendy, the abbot buried the sum of 10 pounds of gold in order to protect it from the marauding crusaders of Frederick Barbarossa. Of the 786 coins, 239 date from the reign of Alexios I (1081–1118); they had been in the monastic reserves almost from the beginning.[36]

The ubiquity of coins on the estates of Pakourianos, even before these were turned over to the **[133]** monastery, presupposes the sale of a considerable part of the production of the monastery.[37] One has to remember, of course, that there was a Byzantine army stationed in Philippopolis, so it is possible that some of the production of the monastery was sold to the state, and was thus taken out of regional trade. But there was also an imperial grain storehouse, with state grain from imperial estates, which might have been used for the army.[38] In any case, the position of the three hostels built by Pakourianos, as

---

[34]   C. Morrisson, "Byzantine Money: Its Production and Circulation," in *EHB* 3:949.

[35]   Petit, para. 55.

[36]   M.F. Hendy, "The Gornoslav Hoard, the Emperor Frederick I, and the Monastery of Bachkovo," in *Studies in Numismatic Method Presented to Philip Grierson*, ed. C.N.L. Brooke, J.G. Pollard, B.H.I.H Stewart, and T.R. Volk (Cambridge, 1983), 179–91 (repr. in idem, *The Economy, Fiscal Administration and Coinage of Byzantium* [Northampton, 1989], art. XI).

[37]   Michael Hendy thinks that there was a dearth of coin in the interior, even in the twelfth century. He believes that the coin mentioned in the typikon came from revenues gained in the monastery's properties in the themes of Voleron and Thessalonike and transferred to Petritzos, thus from the coast to the interior: M.F. Hendy, in *DOC* 4:277. Paul Lemerle, on the other hand, believes that the cash was collected from the dues of the *paroikoi*. I have no problem with Hendy's interpretation, as long as it means that the production of Petritzos was marketed in these coastal cities and towns, and not that the cash revenues came from the production of the southern estates.

[38]   Asdracha, *La région des Rhodopes*, 154–62; Cheynet, "Quelques sceaux d'*hôrreiarioi*," 12, cites Leon, horreiarios of Philippopolis in the tenth century.

well as the content of the Venetian commercial privileges (on which more below), makes it very likely that his production, or considerable parts of it, was commercialized. If the cash mentioned in the *typikon* came from the rents of the peasantry, then we are looking at local trade, which, I suspect, would have been unlikely to satisfy the demands of the two important cities and other smaller ones, unless we posit the existence of merchants who bought the crops from the peasants and then sold them both to the cities of the immediate area and elsewhere along a regional network. If the peasants paid their rent in kind, on the other hand, then the monastery itself was involved in the cash-producing trade. The monastery also had an unusually large domanial reserve, which would have meant concentrated production that could, again, be channeled to regional trade. Through his own holdings and those of his brother, Gregory Pakourianos had access to important markets: Philippopolis, for one, and also Mosynopolis on the Via Egnatia in the south, not far from Xanthe, and Peritheorion by the sea.[39] Pakourianos built three hostels on his property, apart from the preexisting ones: one was at a crossroads near the large village of Stenimachos, southeast of Philippopolis, where an (annual?) fair also took place. Of the other two hostels, one (Marmarin, Sravikion) was located at the Strymon Delta, near a bridge, and the other in Prilongion, to the west of Marmarin near the sea (see fig. 5.2). Marmarin is mentioned by al-Idrīsī as a river flowing outside the walls of Chrysoupolis (the editor says that al-Idrīsī is mistaken and the river is the Maritsa),[40] a city renowned for "the beauty of its markets and the importance of its commerce."[41] All three were

---

[39]   On Mosynopolis, Xanthe, and Peritheorion, see Asdracha, *La région des Rhodopes*, 104–9, 93–96, and 98–104, respectively. Asdracha says that Mosynopolis was destroyed in 1206 and never recovered (106); she thinks it is the Messene mentioned by Kantakouzenos.

[40]   In fact, al-Idrīsī is quite correct as to the location of Marmarin at the Strymon Delta. He is wrong in thinking it a river, and clearly confuses it with the Strymon; see *La Géographie d'Édrisi: Traduite de l'arabe d'après deux manuscrits de la Bibliothèque Nationale*, by P.-A. Jaubert, 2 vols (1836–40; repr. Amsterdam, 1975), 2:297 (hereafter cited as al-Idrīsī): "Cette dernière ville ['Akhrisoboli la Maritime'] est agréable et remarquable par la beauté de ses marchés et par l'importance de son commerce. Auprès de ses murs coule une rivière connue sous le nom de Marmari." On Marmari(o)n (bandon of Zabalta, theme of Serres), see Asdracha, *La région des Rhodopes*, 184, 200. See also P. Gautier, "Le typikon du sébaste Grégoire Pakourianos," *REB* 42 (1984): 112–13.

[41]   Al-Idrīsī, 2:297. Chrysoupolis is near the ancient Amphipolis on the Strymon Delta: see A. Dunn, "The Rise and Fall of Towns, Loci of Maritime Traffic, and Silk Production: The Problem of Thisvi-Kastorion," in *Byzantine Style, Religion, and Civilization: In Honour of Sir Steven Runciman*, ed. Elizabeth Jeffreys (Cambridge, 2006), 38–71; idem, "Loci of Maritime Traffic in the Strymon Delta (IV–XVIII cc.): Commercial, Fiscal, and Manorial," in Οι Σέρρες και η περιοχή τους από την αρχαία στην μεταβυζαντινή κοινωνία: Σέρρες, 29 Σεπτ.-3 Οκτ. 1993, Πρακτικά,

for the use of travelers, which very much suggests that they were built and maintained for merchants or people moving commodities. The two coastal places are accessible from Philippopolis by road and they are, of course, very much accessible from Mosynopolis. Philippopolis had access to the sea through four networks of roads. A circuitous route could lead, south of the Via Regia, to the valley of the Nestos, down to Xanthe and Peritheorion. A second, eastern route would follow the Hebros Valley (and so the Via Regia) to Adrianople and eventually to the Via Egnatia. More interesting for us are the vertical routes: the route Philippopolis-Stenimachos-Achridos-Mosynopolis and the route from Philippopolis-Stenimachos, crossing the Arda, to Xanthe and Peritheorion. This last route is **[134]** thought to be the one mentioned in the typikon of Pakourianos.[42]

The chronicles of the first three crusades attest that the production of agricultural goods was very high in the areas along the Via Regia from Serdica (Sofia) southward, and suggest the existence of regional trade and the underlying monetization of the area. It should be remembered that the forces of the crusaders were very large, and they certainly must have taxed the resources of the areas through which they passed, especially Thrace.[43] Most destructive was the army of Frederick Barbarossa, which spent eight and a half to nine months on Byzantine soil, most of the time in Thrace.[44] The fact that the participants of the First Crusade were expected to buy their provisions along the way, and that money changers seem to have been present, indicates that such was the case in Thrace already in the eleventh century. Better information from the twelfth century (Second Crusade: 1147–49; Third Crusade: 1187–92) allows us to be more specific. In Sofia, the French members of the Second Crusade were able to get provisions from the governor. In Philippopolis, there was a Latin settlement outside the walls of

---

2 vols (Thessalonike, 1998), 2:343, 345–6; idem, "From *polis* to *kastron* in Southern Macedonia: Amphipolis, Khrysoupolis, and the Strymon Delta," in *Archéologie des espaces agraires méditerranéens au Moyen Âge*, ed. A. Bazzana, Castrum 5 (Madrid, 1999), 408, 411f.

[42]   Asdracha, *La région des Rhodopes*, 34–39.

[43]   The First Crusade, including that of 1100–1101, must have numbered in toto 150,000–200,000 people; the Second Crusade may well have numbered 100,000, while for the Third Crusade we have the figure of 100,000 men.

[44]   A.E. Laiou, "Byzantine Trade with Christians and Muslims and the Crusade," in *The Crusades from the Perspective of Byzantium and the Muslim World*, ed. A.E. Laiou and R.P. Mottahedeh (Washington, D.C., 2001), 157–96, at 161–2. The First Crusade spent two to two and a half months on Byzantine soil in the Balkans, the Second Crusade two and a half to three months.

the city, "who sold a great many supplies to travellers."[45] The existence of a settlement of western merchants in Philippopolis in the middle of the twelfth century is proof positive that at this time, and doubtless for some time before, the city was a center of concentration and, it follows, of dissemination of agricultural products. The list of cities where the crusaders were permitted to buy and sell in 1100–1101 is enlightening. It includes Philippopolis, Adrianople, and Didymoteichon, all three on the Via Regia, as well as Panidos (= Panion, near Raidestos), Raidestos, and Selymbria, in the vicinity of Constantinople.[46] Panidos and Raidestos were very active in the grain trade, we have seen that Philippopolis was also, and so must the others have been; al-Idrīsī mentions Chrysoupolis, Christopolis, Panidos, Raidestos, Herakleia, and Selymbria as rich commercial cities.[47] Part of Frederick Barbarossa's army stayed in Philippopolis for about five months, while he traveled south and stayed in Adrianople for three and a half months.[48] The resources of both areas as well as the distribution system collapsed during this time; it is a wonder that they did not do so during the earlier crusades, which suggests a well-functioning regional network in the area (see fig. 5.1).

The chrysobulls with commercial privileges issued to the Venetians are a good source for the expansion of trade networks in inland Thrace in the eleventh to twelfth centuries. I do quite recognize that since 1082, Venetian merchants possessed the right and privilege to trade everywhere in the empire, and thus the fact that a place is not specifically mentioned in the grant does not indicate that it was not important as a commercial center. On the other hand, I assume that when places or cities *are* specifically mentioned, this suggests that the Venetians had specifically asked that they be, presumably because they thought them particularly important.

In Thrace, the Venetians had requested and received, in 1082, the right to trade along the shore from Thessalonike to Constantinople (including Chrysoupolis and Peritheorion, where the Pakourianoi had properties), and

---

[45]   Odo of Deuil, *De Profectione Ludovici VII in Orientem: The Journey of Louis VII to the East*, ed. V.G. Berry (New York, 1948), 45, 43. On the issue of the provisioning of the crusaders, see Laiou, "Byzantine Trade," 163ff. For Philippopolis in the Third Crusade, see *Nicetae Choniatae Historia*, ed. J. L. van Dieten, CFHB 11.1 (Berlin, 1975), 403.

[46]   Albert of Aix, *Historia Hierosolymitana*, RHC HOcc 4 (Paris, 1879), 559; Laiou, "Byzantine Trade," 165. Hendy, "Gornoslav Hoard," 180, thinks "Rusa" is Rus Koy (= Kosan), not Xanthe or Komotene, and he is doubtless correct.

[47]   Al-Idrīsī, 2:120–21, 297–8.

[48]   Hendy, "Gornoslav Hoard," 180.

Adrianople on the Maritsa River.[49] We have already seen that at the time of the Second Crusade there was an active "Italian" colony of merchants just outside the walls of Constantinople. By the end of the twelfth century, the Venetians requested privileges in the entire "provinces" (themes) of Strymon, Voleron, and Thessalonike, and in a host of areas in the interior: the provinces of Thrace and Macedonia, Adrianople and Didymoteichon, as well as the provinces of Philippopolis, Veroe, Morra and Achridos – that is, exactly where **[135]** one concentrated part of the estates of the monastery lay – and the "episkepseis" (large estates, perhaps imperial) of Tzouroulos, Theodoroupolis, Arkadiopolis (Lule-Burgas), Messene (between Arkadiopolis and Tzouroulos), and Boulgarophygon. This attests to the expansion of Venetian interest and activities in the Byzantine Empire, but also confirms what we know from other sources: that these inland areas had grown rich, one assumes through the sale of their products in regional exchange. And it also reminds us that there are points where regional and interregional/international networks meet, when commercial activity intensifies, and the market is greatly enlarged. Of course, this change cannot necessarily be credited to the Venetians, who may well have replaced Byzantine merchants in internal trade.

The composition of the estates of Pakourianos and the routes linking them suggest, among other things, that Philippopolis and its production can be thought as belonging to both trade regions: the eastern, Thracian one, with Constantinople as one of the major centers, and the western, Macedonian one. The products of the hinterland that arrived at the Strymon Delta might then travel east or west.

The border between the economic regions of Thrace and Macedonia lies along the Strymon or the Nestos River, a fact that is supported by the evidence of monetary circulation. If we look at the areas of circulation of bronze coins in the fifth to the mid-seventh century, we find two neatly differentiated zones: coinage from the mint of Constantinople circulated in Moesia Secunda, Thracia, Haemimons, and Rhodope (= the diocese of Thrace), while coins from the mint of Thessalonike circulated in (today's Greek province of) Macedonia and the two Dacias; that would make the Nestos River the frontier.[50] Between the late eleventh and the thirteenth

---

[49]   M. Pozza and G. Ravegnani, eds, *I trattati con Bisanzio, 992–1198* (Venice, 1993), 40.

[50]   C. Morrisson, "La diffusion de la monnaie de Constantinople: Routes commerciales ou routes politiques?" in *Constantinople and Its Hinterland*, ed. C. Mango and G. Dagron (Aldershot, 1995), 79; C. Morrisson, V. Popović, and V. Ivanišević, with P. Culerrier et al., *Les trésors monétaires byzantins des Balkans et d'Asie Mineure (491–717)* (Paris, 2006), 62–3.

centuries, another numismatic division delineates two broad zones. The Balkan regions north of the Rhodope mountains and to the east used as petty coin the billon trachy (the *stamenon* of western sources); this is the eastern zone. In the western zone, in Greece and the Peloponnese, the lower-value copper *tetarteron* predominated. Thessalonike primarily used the tetarteron, but it served both zones of numismatic circulation: in the twelfth century, its mint issued both billon trachea and tetartera.[51]

The regional trade of Macedonia is connected with the great city of Thessalonike, which serves as a magnet, given its large market and the variety of products that it could send to the interior. I will not discuss this network in any detail; in any case, I have already indicated how I think regional trade networks developed and functioned. Here I will simply make a few supplementary points that emerge from the study of Macedonian trade. The first point is the obvious one that regional networks can change direction. Thus, in the late seventh century, the city of Thessalonike sought its grain, when it did not come by sea from the east, in southern parts: in Thessaly and particularly in the region of Demetrias and Phthiotid Thebes.[52] Its hinterland to the west, its natural hinterland, was, apparently, too unruly for much exchange to take place there. The situation to the east was also difficult for some time. When St. Gregory the Decapolite tried to reach Thessalonike from Constantinople (before 841), he went by sea up to Christopolis and then, when he tried to cross the Strymon, he was attacked by Slav robbers who apparently made a habit of attacking travelers. Since he was a saint, he managed to leave and continue his journey by foot. On the other hand, he seems to have been able to travel by land from Thessalonike to the south, as far as Corinth, without mishap, at least not of the kind he met earlier.[53] A while later, another monk, along with a Byzantine official who was in disgrace, managed to reach Constantinople by land; the saint himself preferred the sea route.[54] The commercial network of Thessalonike that included Thessaly, particularly Demetrias, continued in the later ninth century.

---

[51]   Hendy, *Studies*, 434–7, 601–2; *DOC* 4:1, 129–30; Morrisson, "Byzantine Money," 935–6, 960.

[52]   P. Lemerle, *Les plus anciens recueils des miracles de Saint Démétrius et la pénétration des Slaves dans les Balkans*, 2 vols (Paris, 1978–80), 1:211, 218, miracle 2.4, §§254, 268; on this affair, see Durliat, *De la ville antique*, 401ff. Demetrias was an important center in the late ninth century (Laiou, "Exchange and Trade," 727).

[53]   Makris, ed., *Ignatios Diakonos*, 86, 88.

[54]   Ibid., 114–16.

By the second half of the ninth century, trade became active between Thessalonike and lands to the west, at least as far as the city of Veroia (63 km [136] away). Furthermore, the Axios, a navigable river, became an avenue of exchange with the interior; it is explicitly stated that in the late ninth and early tenth century, ships sailed up the river, carrying merchandise and increasing the wealth of the city.[55] The source that describes all this new activity claims that it was due to the fact that the Bulgarians had converted to Christianity (in 865), and that therefore peaceful relations were possible, and goods circulated by land and sea.[56] Thus there was a regional network, extending to the west and north of Thessalonike, that also involved areas of the state of Bulgaria; we see again that regional trade need not be confined within national boundaries. In the tenth century, Thessalonike was apparently a gateway to the interior as far as Belgrade, a distance of 507 kilometers, which Constantine VII pronounced to be a leisurely eight-day journey.[57] However, there is no indication of significant commercial activity anywhere near this far north at this time.

It is the part of this network that included "Bulgaria" that two merchants from Greece (who were also imperial officials?) tried to expand in the 890s. The "Bulgaria" in question is not the Black Sea coast but the hinterland – around Philippopolis, for instance. The effort to divert the Bulgarian trade from Constantinople to Thessalonike (with a considerable increase of the

---

[55] Kameniates, *De expugnatione Thessalonicae* 6.8. For a discussion of this, see A.E. Laiou, "The Byzantine City: Parasitic or Productive?" in *Byzantium: The Economic Turn*, ed. M. Whittow (Oxford, forthcoming). The most recent study of Thessalonike in this period is by Ch. Bakirtzis: "Imports, Exports and Autarky in Byzantine Thessalonike from the Seventh to the Tenth Century," in *Post-Roman Towns, Trade and Settlement in Europe and Byzantium*, ed. J. Henning, vol. 2, *Byzantium, Pliska, and the Balkans*, Millennium-Studien zu Kultur und Geschichte des ersten Jahrtausends n. Chr. 5.2 (Berlin, 2007), 89–118.

[56] Kameniates, *De expugnatione Thessalonicae* 9.2–4, ed. G. Böhlig, CFHB 4 (Berlin, 1973): ἐξ ὅτου γὰρ ἡ κολυμβήθρα τοῦ θείου βαπτίσματος τὸ τῶν Σκυθῶν ἔθνος τῷ χριστωνύμῳ λαῷ συνεμόρφωσε καὶ τὸ τῆς εὐσεβείας γάλα κοινῶς ἀμφοτέροις διείλετο, πέπαυτο μὲν ἡ τῶν πολέμων στάσις, . . . ἔνθεν αἱ τῆς γεωργίας ἀφθονίαι, ἐκεῖθεν αἱ τῆς ἐμπορίας χορηγίαι. (4.) γῆ γὰρ καὶ θάλασσα λειτουργεῖν ἡμῖν ἐξ ἀρχῆς ταχθεῖσαι πλουσίαν καὶ ἀδάπανον τὴν περὶ ἕκαστον ἐδωροφόρουν. "The Bulgarian trade with Thessalonike coming down the Nestos-Strymon-Axios rivers seems to have increased ever since the peace with the Bulgarians in 815; indications from the seals of *kommerkiarioi*, of the second half of the ninth century, attest to this importance. The new customs officials in Thessalonike had jurisdiction over Thessaly, Kephallonia, the theme of Thessalonike and the West of Greece" (Laiou, "Exchange and Trade," 726; citing Oikonomidès, "Le kommerkion d'Abydos," 241–8).

[57] Constantine Porphyrogennetos, *De administrando imperio*, ed. G. Moravcsik, trans. R.J.H. Jenkins (Washington, D.C., 1967), chap. 42.

duties paid by the Bulgarians) has been interpreted as an effort to decentralize trade and help the economy of Thessalonike.[58] It is a plausible assumption that the two merchants might have had commercial interests in the network that linked Thessalonike to parts south, and were trying to establish an interregional network from the Bulgarian interior to some parts of Greece.[59]

The regional network of Thessalonike, insofar as it included Bulgaria, still at a low level of monetization and with no coins of its own, was probably in part an exchange of commodities, although precious metals in some form may have been used, as well as Byzantine coins. The city produced pottery; glass; metal objects made of copper, iron, tin, and lead; and perhaps silk.[60] Presumably, this is what was sold to the interior, in exchange for foodstuffs, and possibly linen. The text mentions in Thessalonike a profusion of linen cloth, very thin and of excellent quality, and some of this may have come from Bulgaria, as it did in Constantinople. In this period, there is no identifiable pottery from Thessalonike with dispersion anywhere else. On the other hand, Constantinopolitan Polychrome Ware and Glazed White Ware dating from the late tenth to the late eleventh century [137] have been found in Thessalonike, confirming the links between these two cities.[61]

---

[58]   Oikonomidès, "Le kommerkion d'Abydos," 246–8.

[59]   Interestingly, although this endeavor failed in the tenth century, one of the permanent markets of the city was called the "Sthlavomese," the "market of the Slavs," presumably referring to those west of Thessalonike: N. Oikonomidès, ed., *Actes de Docheiariou*, 2 vols (Paris, 1984), no. 4, l. 27.

[60]   Kameniates 9.8–9 (ed. Böhlig, 499–501): ἐντεῦθεν χρυσίου καὶ ἀργυρίου καὶ λίθων τιμίων παμπληθεῖς θησαυροὶ τοῖς πολλοῖς ἐγίνοντο, καὶ τὰ ἐκ Σηρῶν ὑφάσματα ὡς τὰ ἐξ ἐρίων τοῖς ἄλλοις ἐπινενόητο. περὶ γὰρ τῶν ἄλλων ὑλῶν, χαλκοῦ καὶ σιδήρου κασσιτέρου τε καὶ μολύβδου καὶ ὑέλου, οἷς αἱ διὰ πυρὸς τέχναι τὸν βίον συνέχουσι, καὶ μνησθῆναι μόνον παρέλκον ἡγοῦμαι, τοσούτων ὄντων ὡς ἄλλην τινὰ δύνασθαι πόλιν δι' αὐτῶν δομεῖσθαίτε καὶ ἀπαρτίζεσθαι. 58.7–8 (568–69): ἐτελεῖτο δὲ ταῦτα ἐφ' ὅλοις νυχθημέροις δέκα, τῆς πληθύος ἀεὶ τῶν χρημάτων εὐφορουμένης ἀπὸ τῆς πόλεως, τῆς τε λοιπῆς ἀναγκαίας ὕλης, ὅση διὰ σηρικῆς ἐσθῆτος εὐπρεπὴς ἦν καὶ ὅση διὰ λίνου τοῖς ἀραχνείοις ἤριζεν ὑφάσμασιν, ὡς ὄρη καὶ βουνοὺς ἐκτελεῖσθαι τὰς τούτων σωρείας, ἄλλων ἐπ' ἄλλοις ἐπιτιθεμένων καὶ τὸν ὑποκείμενον τόπον πληρούντων. χαλκῶν γὰρ καὶ σιδηρέων σκευῶν ἢ τῶν ἐξ ἐρίων ἐσθημάτων οὐμενοῦν οὐδ' ὅλως ἐφρόντισαν, περιττὴν ἡγούμενοι τὴν κτῆσιν αὐτῶν. For the archaeological information regarding such activities (except for silk, very difficult to attest archaeologically), see Bakirtzis, "Imports, Exports," 108, on pottery; 111, on glass; 99–100, on metalwork, but referring to an earlier period.

[61]   I. Kanonides, "Μεσοβυζαντινή εφυαλωμένη κεραμική με λευκό πηλό από ανασκαφές οικοπέδων στη Θεσσαλονίκη," in *VIIe Congrès international sur la Céramique Médiévale en Méditerranée, Thessaloniki, 11–16 octobre 1999: Actes*, ed. Ch. Bakirtzis (Thessalonike, 2003), 71–6.

The commercial activity of Thessalonike by land and by sea appears to have been substantial in the tenth century. Monetary finds do not, however, seem to confirm this. Of the 285 bronze coins found recently, only 15 belong to the period between the seventh and the tenth century.[62] The dissonance between monetary finds and other sources is, unfortunately, not rare.

In the eleventh and twelfth centuries the relative peace in the western Balkans, following the victories of Basil II over the Bulgarians, doubtless played a role in the evident flourishing of Thessalonike. The greatly expanded hinterland to the northwest – that is, Serbia – begins to enter the commercial networks. The regional trade network is partly deduced from the Venetian privileges of 1198. The provinces of Kastoria, Servia, Veroia, Skopje, Strumica, Prilep, Pelagonia, and Moglena are an enlarged regional market trading with Thessalonike. In the documentation, the themes of Strymon and Voleron are mentioned in geographic proximity to Thessalonike rather than to the east.[63] Thessalonike produced, among other things, silk, as attested by Benjamin of Tudela; and it produced pottery that was disseminated widely, in places that included northern Greece, Serbia, and Bulgaria.[64] The presence in Prilep, Skopje, and Niš of pottery that may have originated in Thessalonike and Constantinople clearly indicates that there were, indeed, trade relations with the northwestern Balkans in the twelfth and early thirteenth centuries. In the early thirteenth century, local imitative production begins.[65] Pottery may easily have been one of the items exchanged for the agricultural products of Macedonia. Pottery production is also attested in the city of Veroia and the town of Kitros, to the south of Veroia.[66] I take this conjunction of production for diffusion into a large area along with the existence of more centers of production in smaller cities as an indication of hierarchization of both production and trade, regional and interregional.

Some information may be gleaned about the regional and interregional trade that found its way to Thessalonike in the twelfth century from the description of the great fair that took place on the feast of St. Demetrios.

[62]   Bakirtzis, "Imports, Exports," 112.

[63]   Pozza and Ravegnani, eds, *Trattati*, 130.

[64]   Benjamin of Tudela, *The Itinerary of Benjamin of Tudela: Travels in the Middle Ages*, trans. M.N. Adler (Malibu, 1983), 10; J. Vroom, *Byzantine to Modern Pottery in the Aegean: 7th to 20th Century; An Introduction and Field Guide* (Utrecht, 2005), 87 (Painted Fine Sgraffito Ware).

[65]   M. Bajalović-Hadzi-Pesić, "Ornamentation of Medieval Serbian Tableware – Byzantine Heritage," in Bakirtzis, ed., *VIIe Congrès international sur la céramique médiévale en Méditerranée*, 90.

66 Laiou and Morrisson, *The Byzantine Economy*, 118, with references and map, 120. Al-Idrīsī (2:296) describes Kitros as "a considerable city, strong, commercial, and well populated."

Apart from the Italian, Spanish, French, Egyptian, and Syrian merchants – all, it seems, bringing cloth – there are the Byzantine merchants. They come "from everywhere," says the source, but it mentions specifically those from the south, Boeotia and the Peloponnese, who trade in textiles (doubtless silks). There is no mention of specific products from western Macedonia or the western Balkans: the fair seems to have specialized in textiles and cattle, and we do not know of commercialized production of textiles in areas west of Thessalonike. On the other hand, merchandise does come to the fair from Bulgaria and the Black Sea: it comes by way of Constantinople, and by land, carried on the backs of "numerous" horses and mules, although we do not know what it was.[67]

Thessalonike had a mint that produced both gold and copper coins in the eleventh century. The "dramatic" increase of issues in 1081–85 has been attributed by Michael Hendy to the presence of Alexios I and his army, on campaign against the Normans. The mint continued to produce gold, electrum, and copper coins after the monetary reform of Alexios I. The bulk of the issues was in copper tetartera. A recent discovery brought to light a hoard of fourteen gold *histamena* of the period 976–1055. They were found in the port, and Ioannis Touratsoglou suggests that they may have belonged to a sea captain/merchant.[68]

Let us look at our third region, Greece and the Peloponnese. A differentiating characteristic of these areas is that there are no cities of the size and concentration of Constantinople or Thessalonike to act as magnets for regional and interregional trade. [138] This statement needs to be nuanced. Thessaly, specifically Demetrias, had traded with Thessalonike since at least the seventh century, and seems to have done so in the early ninth century,[69] exporting agricultural products. And Corinth developed into a major center of regional and interregional trade. Its industrial production as well as its size (15,000–20,000 people in the late eleventh and twelfth centuries)[70] of necessity posit regional trade, as does the existence of other important cities in the region (Halmyros, Larissa, Patras, Sparta, Athens, Thebes); these formed as many foci of trade of one kind or another, unless one were to argue that urban effective demand was kept down by the local large landlords feeding their urban households on the products of their estates. But even that extremely conservative and choleric landlord Kekaumenos, a great advocate

---

67   Pseudo-Lucian, *Timarione*, ed. R. Romano (Naples, 1974), 53–5.
68   *DOC* 4:129–30; Touratsoglou, "Από τα νομισματικά πράγματα," 527–8.
69   *AASS* 4:666, vita of Blasios of Amorion.
70   G.D.R. Sanders, "Corinth," in *EHB* 2:653–4.

of living off one's land, could not escape the fact that there were merchants around and that his autarkic ideal was far from realistic.[71]

One important difference with the earlier period should be noted. The city of Halmyros replaced Demetrias as a center of collection and export of the agricultural production of Thessaly, as is well known. But this trade seems to have been reoriented in the twelfth century. Thessalonike no longer looks like an important trade partner. The connections of Halmyros are with its hinterland to the west, from where came agricultural products. According to the Venetian documents, Halmyros is linked with commercial links to Corinth, and also to Constantinople by sea; in fact, this second route appears to be well established ("taxegio de Armiro"). There even seem to be people trading from Halmyros to Syria, Palestine, and Egypt, but not to Thessalonike.[72] This shift in regional trade patterns should be further investigated.

It has long been recognized, and so I will not insist upon it, that rising demand led to increased productivity or at least production, and to the sale of agricultural commodities locally, regionally, and interregionally.[73] Halmyros, as we have just seen, was a center where the products of the hinterland were concentrated and then exported. The area around Thebes had rich agricultural production and animal husbandry in the eleventh and twelfth centuries, and some of the wealth of the city certainly came from the commercialization of this production. Sparta and its area grew rich on the sale of olive oil.[74] When the study of unglazed ceramics is further advanced, it will doubtless provide precious information about the specificities of the movement of agricultural goods and of the ceramic containers themselves. In the area under discussion, for example, specifically in Boeotia, unglazed ware, especially amphorae of the Günsenin 3/Saraçhane 61 type, proliferated in this period, with finds concentrated in rural sites.[75] The amphorae, which can be used for the transport of liquids – wine, oil, and honey, all produced in

---

[71]   Kekaumenos: G. G. Litavrin, *Sovety i rasskazy Kekavmena* (Moscow, 1972), 188–90; see also A.E. Laiou, "Economic Thought and Ideology," in *EHB* 3:1127.

[72]   *DCV*, nos. 35 (1112), 108 (1142), 151 (1161), 152 (1191), 202 (1168), 212 (1169), 236 (1170), 238 (1171); *NDCV*, nos. 21 (1168), 190 (1169).

[73]   On central Greece, see A. Harvey, "Economic Expansion in Central Greece in the Eleventh Century," *BMGS* 8 (1982–83): 21–9.

[74]   Harvey, *Economic Expansion*, 145, 147; A. Dunn, "Historical and Archaeological Indications of Economic Change in Middle Byzantine Boeotia and Their Problems," in *B´ Diethnes Synedrio Voiotikon Meleton* (Athens, 1955), 755–74. See the elegant churches of twelfth-century Mani.

[75]   J. Vroom, *After Antiquity: Ceramics and Society in the Aegean from the 7th to the 20th Century A.C.: A Case Study from Boeotia, Central Greece* (Leiden, 2003), 153–5.

Boeotia – bespeak trade in agricultural products but also in unglazed pottery: all of which in turn means considerable product specialization. Günsenin 3 amphorae have also been found in Sparta, a famous exporter of olive oil.[76] As places of production of this pottery, northeastern Turkey and central Greece, Boeotia, and Athens have been variously suggested.[77] The detailed study of regional and interregional trade in unglazed ceramics of the middle Byzantine period would have a lot to teach us. It is, in any case, clear that centers of consumption and distribution of agricultural products also both produced ceramics **[139]** and traded them within the region, as is the case in Sparta and Larissa, for example.[78]

The Peloponnese seems to have encompassed a set of regional markets, as well as having trade relations with Thebes and doubtless Athens.[79] As we will see, there is a very active subsystem around the Corinthian Gulf that encompasses Athens, Thebes, Corinth, and perhaps Euripos (Nigroponte). In 1082, the Venetians specifically requested access to Nauplion and Corinth, but we know that Venetian merchants were in Sparta already in the tenth century; they maintained an active trade in Sparta throughout the twelfth century. In 1198, they also got access to the regions of Patras and Argos as well as Modon.[80] al-Idrīsī speaks of about fifty "cities" in the Peloponnese,

---

[76]   G.D.R. Sanders, "Excavations at Sparta: The Roman Stoa, 1988–91," *BSA* 88 (1993): 283.

[77]   J.W. Hayes, *Excavations at Saraçhane in Istanbul*, vol. 2, *The Pottery* (Princeton, N.J., 1992), 76 (Boeotia or Athens); J.F. Cherry, J.L. Davis, and E. Mantzourani, with J.W. Hayes, "Introduction to the Archaeology of Post-Roman Keos," in J.F. Cherry, J.L. Davis, and E. Mantzourani, *Landscape Archaeology as Long-term History: Northern Keos in the Cycladic Islands*, Monumenta Archaeologica 16 (Los Angeles, 2001), 351–64, at 354–5; Vroom, *Byzantine to Modern Greek Pottery in the Aegean*, 97–9.

[78]   For Sparta, see notes 74 and 76, above, and A. Bakourou, E. Katsara, and P. Kalamara, "Argos and Sparta: Pottery of the 12th and 13th Centuries," in Bakirtzis, ed., *VIIe Congrès International sur la Céramique Médiévale en Méditerranée*, 233–6; J. Dimopoulos, "Byzantine Graffito Wares Excavated in Sparta (12th–13th Centuries)," in *Çanak: Late Antique and Medieval Pottery and Tiles in Mediterranean Archaeological Contexts*, ed. B. Böhlendorf-Arslan, A. Osman Uysal, and J. Witte-Orr, Byzas 7 (Istanbul, 2007), 336–41. For Larissa as a possible center of the production of glazed ceramics in the late twelfth to early thirteenth century, see D. Papanikola-Bakirtzi, "Εργαστήρια εφυαλωμένης κεραμικής στο Βυζαντινό κόσμο," in Bakirtzis, ed., *VIIe Congrès International sur la Céramique Médiévale en Méditerranée*, 53.

[79]   The distance from Thebes to Corinth is 54 km as the crow flies. The vita of St. Loukas Stereiotes shows how easy and common communications were between Boeotia and Corinth: D. Sofianos, Όσιος Λουκάς: Ο βίος του Οσίου Λουκά του Στειριώτη: Προλεγόμενα - μετάφραση - κριτική έκδοση του κειμένου (Athens, 1989), paras. 41, 42.

[80]   Pozza and Ravegnani, eds, *Trattati*, 40, 130.

sixteen of which are important and renowned. Among them is, of course, Corinth, but also Sparta ("an important and flourishing city"), Patras, Argos, and others.[81] A number of Venetian commercial contracts have Corinth as their destination or as the starting point for trade to Constantinople, Halmyros, southern Greece, and the rest of the Peloponnese.[82] This, of course, is both regional and interregional trade. What is more interesting is a look at some of the commodities that we know were exported from Corinth: I will speak first of the products of the Peloponnese and then of the manufactured products of the city itself. Corinth exported olive oil, presumably from the region around it; for the Venetians to pick it up in Corinth, merchants – originally certainly Byzantines, then probably Venetians as well – had to bring it there. From Corinth, good-quality cotton was exported (4,000 light lbs., valued at 64 "old" *hyperpyra* – the place of production is not known, although it could be the area around Lake Kopais, that is, the Theban hinterland; this cotton was exported to Constantinople).[83] There is some indication that Corinth also served as a point of collection and export of olive oil from Sparta.[84] Together with the contracts that mention Corinth as a point of departure for trade in southern Greece and the Peloponnese, it is clear that Corinth was one of the important centers of regional trade (and interregional and international, of course).

Let us now turn to the trade in manufactured products and raw materials. In the twelfth century, Athens and Thebes were linked through the silk industry. Thebes had become one of the great centers of silk production, as we know from narrative sources, both Byzantine and other.[85] Its great workshops produced purple silk cloth, one supposes together with silk textiles of lower quality.[86] Great silk manufacturing operations and the demand for their products do not develop from one day to the next, and so the fact that our information starts around the mid-twelfth century (with Niketas Choniates' description of the raid of Roger II of Sicily in 1147) does not mean that this is when the silk industry began. Besides, Venetians are attested there since 1071,[87]

---

[81]   Al-Idrīsī, 2:124–6.

[82]   *DCV*, nos. 35 (1112), 65 (1135), 67 (1135), 68 (1136), 69 (1136), 80 (1142), 97 (1150), 145–7 (1161), 185 (1167), 192 (1168), 202 (1168), 314 (1179), 336 (1183), 451 (1200).

[83]   Ibid., no. 192 (1168) [concerning a shipment of cotton from Corinth to Constantinople].

[84]   Ibid., no. 65 (1135). Of course, the Venetians also collected oil from Sparta itself.

[85]   *Nicetae Choniatae Historia*, 74; Benjamin of Tudela, *The Itinerary*, 10.

[86]   Benjamin of Tudela, *The Itinerary*, 10; *DCV*, no. 243 (1171) ("pro samito uno ulati").

[87]   D. Jacoby, "Silk in Western Byzantium before the Fourth Crusade," *BZ* 84–5 (1991–92): 494 (repr. in idem, *Trade, Commodities and Shipping in the Medieval Mediterranean* [Aldershot, 1997], art. VII).

and the Venetian privilege of 1082 already mentions Thebes as a place where the Venetians wished to trade; the only commodity specifically associated with Thebes in the Venetian documentation is silk, which does not mean that nothing else was exported, but nevertheless points up the importance of the city's silk industry.[88] The **[140]** remnants of dye workshops have been found in the city, but otherwise the archaeological record is thin and, as has been pointed out, the evidence for the silk industry is primarily documentary or narrative.[89] Despite the valuable archaeological work undertaken in the area, the archaeological record does not, at the moment, provide many answers.[90] We do all remember, of course, that medieval textile industries do not easily leave an archaeological record, and that Thebes, like Corinth and other cities with continuous habitation, has not been and cannot be properly excavated.

Athens was a great producer of murex shells, from which the dye came that gave the best and most expensive purple color. That production, or part of it, was sold, we assume, to the silk works of Thebes, as was the soap that was needed to clean the silk.[91] Possibly, Thebes also got murex from Kastorion/Thisbe, on the Corinthian Gulf; heaps of murex shells have been found here and are clearly related to the production of purple dye, but, unfortunately, they have not been dated and Archibald Dunn uses them as evidence for both the early and the middle Byzantine period.[92] It also received murex from its closest port, Chalkis (Euripos = Nigroponte).[93] Thus both the area close to Thebes and Athens sent this important and expensive item to the city. In the case of Athens, this may be considered regional trade, of a somewhat different kind from what we have seen until now, since the product that we know was sent to Thebes from Athens was an expensive one. What Athens got from Thebes we do not know – possibly silks or simply money. It is no wonder that both Athens and Thebes prospered during the eleventh and twelfth centuries, when Athens enjoyed a building boom as seen in a number

---

[88]   Pozza and Ravegnani, eds, *Trattati*, 40.

[89]   Ch. Koilakou, "Βυζαντινά εργαστήρια (βαφής) στη Θήβα," *Technologia* 3 (1989): 23–4; Dunn, "The Problem of Thisvi-Kastorion," 38–71.

[90]   There are two archaeological projects, the Boeotian Archaeological-Geological Expedition (directed by A. Snodgrass and J. Bintliff), and the Thisbe Basin Survey, directed by T. Gregory.

[91]   M. Kazanaki-Lappa, "Medieval Athens," in *EHB* 2:644–5.

[92]   Dunn, "The Problem of Thisvi-Kastorion," 46, 53–8. Al-Idrīsī, 2:125, calls the gulf between Naupaktos and Corinth the "port of the dyers," "Sabbughun" or "Mers' al-Sabbughun," and says that it was navigable by small ships only. All others had to circumnavigate the Peloponnese.

[93]   J. Koder, F. Hild, and P. Soustal, *Hellas und Thessalia*, TIB 1 (1993), 164.

of churches built at the time.[94] The catchment area for Athenian trade seems to extend to the north as well; its metropolitan, Michael Choniates, was informed of the excellence of the makers of agricultural implements of the town of Gardiki in Thessaly, and requested that cart makers be sent there from Athens.[95]

The end product of the Theban silk industry was sold in Constantinople or reached it through noncommercial means, that is, in the form of tax, if Benjamin of Tudela is to be believed on this point.[96] It is also probable that some of it, and of varying qualities, was the object of regional trade, in an economy that was flourishing, with cities increasing in size and demand becoming differentiated and moving down the socioeconomic scale.[97] A Venetian document dated August 1159 and redacted in Thebes is a quittance for a *colleganza* (total: 150 hyperpyra "paleokenurgos" – new, but of "old" weight)[98] whereby the merchants would travel by land to all of "Catodica" (southern Greece or the theme of Hellas) and the Peloponnese, back to Thebes, "and from Thebes up to Thessalonike." The journey lasted for three to four months, beginning in May 1159.[99] A number of other documents show that Thebes was the starting point for commercial trips to southern Greece and the Peloponnese.[100] For the trip to **[141]** the southern parts of Greece, the Peloponnese, and Thessalonike and back to Thebes to have taken only

---

[94]   Kazanaki-Lappa, "Medieval Athens," 642.

[95]   *Michaelis Choniatae Epistulae*, ed. F. Kolovou, CFHB 41 (Berlin, 2001), no. 43. For the location, see A. Avramea, *Η Βυζαντινή Θεσσαλία μέχρι του 1204: συμβολή εις την ιστορικήν γεωγραφία* (Athens, 1974), 162–3. Unfortunately, the destination of the soap, olive oil, and ecclesiastical vestments cut and dyed and sewn in Athens and carried on Monemvasiot ships (Kolovou, no. 84) cannot be determined. The statement of Michael Choniates that Athens did not produce silk as other places did (no. 60) should be taken as a comparative claim: Athens did not produce as much silk as Thebes.

[96]   Benjamin of Tudela, *The Itinerary*, 15; Jacoby, "Silk in Western Byzantium," 489–90.

[97]   The fact that there was social stratification in the period and that demand was boosted even by rich peasants has been recognized by M. F. Hendy, "'Byzantium, 1081–1204': The Economy Revisited, Twenty Years On," in *The Economy*, art. III, 9.

[98]   *DOC* 4:1, 56 and n. 85 with references.

[99]   *DCV*, no. 137 (1159).

[100]   Ibid., nos. 235 (1170), 239 (1171), 426 (1195). A document dated 1185 shows a contract redacted in Thebes for the merchant (Pietro Morosini) to go to Durazzo by land, then to Venice; from Venice he was to go to Corinth by sea and then, by land, to reach the investor (Vitale Voltani) in Thebes, and clear the accounts (the contract was for 250 "old-new" hyperpyra); or, depending on political conditions, Morosini was to go from Venice to Constantinople, either directly (by sea) or indirectly (docking at Durazzo and traveling by land to Constantinople). In either case, the accounts would be cleared in Constantinople: no. 353 (1185).

three to four months indicates that there were well-established routes, with inns and other necessary infrastructure, and with either commercial agents with whom the merchants dealt or other good information about markets. I find it hard to believe that the Venetians developed these inland markets and suggest therefore that they represent preexisting networks of regional trade.

The entire Corinthian Gulf and places inland formed an industrial triangle with very active trade between Thebes, Athens, Corinth, and Euripos. Pottery was implicated in this trade, as it was with regional trade within the Peloponnese. As is well known, pottery is something of a guide for the movement of other goods as well, whereas it has also been pointed out that the movement of other consumer goods can point to the direction in which pottery moved.[101]

Glazed White Ware, found more or less everywhere, and Polychrome Ware are elite pottery from Constantinople. In the tenth to eleventh centuries, they are found in Thebes and the Boeotian countryside, but in small quantities. They are also found in Sparta, Lakonia, Milos, Xanthos, Crete, and elsewhere.[102] This is of no interest to us except as an indicator for other things, and that is the size of provincial demand. It has been pointed out that in Corinth the importation of Constantinopolitan White Ware and Polychrome Ware increased greatly through the eleventh century; indeed, the overall peak of demand for this luxury pottery is thought to be the third quarter of the eleventh century.[103] Regional trade it is not, but indication of constantly and significantly rising demand it is.

Corinth and Sparta produced good glazed pottery in this period; Argos is a smaller center of production in the Peloponnese in the twelfth century and subsequently. Both cities also imported glazed ceramics, both from Byzantine centers of production and, in the thirteenth century, from Italy.[104] For Boeotia, we have good information resulting from the intensive surveys conducted

---

[101] Vroom, *After Antiquity*, 241.

[102] P. Armstrong, "From Constantinople to Lakedaimon: Impressed White Wares," in *Mosaic: Festschrift for A.H.S. Megaw*, ed. J. Herrin, M. Mullett, and C. Otten-Froux (Athens, 2001), 57–8; G.D.R. Sanders, "Byzantine Polychrome Pottery," ibid., 89–103.

[103] Hayes, *Excavations at Saraçhane*, 2:35–7, G.D.R. Sanders, "An Overview of the New Chronology for 9th- to 13th-Century Pottery at Corinth," in Bakirtzis, ed., *VIIe Congrès International sur la Céramique Médiévale en Méditerranée*, 37 (he thinks Polychrome Ware is an exclusively eleventh-century production); G.D.R. Sanders, "New Relative and Absolute Chronologies for the 9th- to 13th-Century Glazed Wares at Corinth: Methodology and Social Conclusions," in *Byzanz als Raum: Zu Methoden und Inhalten der historischen Geographie des östlichen Mittelmeerraumes im Mittelalter*, ed. K. Belke, F. Hild, J. Koder, and P. Soustal (Vienna, 2000), 164.

[104] Bakourou, Katsara, and Kalamara, "Argos and Sparta," 233–6.

in the framework of the Boeotia Project. The data come from various sites, including Thebes itself, although the fact that Thebes has had continuous habitation and is still an important city means that the archaeological **[142]** information is quite sporadic and incidental to rescue excavations. It shows the existence of plain glazed ware in Boeotia since the late ninth century.[105] In the same period, petty coins reappear, as they do elsewhere in the Byzantine Empire, pointing to a livelier trade.[106] Between the tenth and early thirteenth centuries, glazed ware of types common in central Greece increase in number, to the extent that Joanita Vroom speaks of a boom in the number of ceramics, especially in the different types of decorated ware, and especially in rural sites; in Thebes itself, the number of sherds recovered is doubtless limited by the obstacles to archaeological work that I have already mentioned. The ceramics in question include Slip-Painted Ware (eleventh–twelfth century), Green and Brown Painted Ware (late eleventh–twelfth century [Morgan] or mid-twelfth to early thirteenth century [Sanders]), Fine Sgraffito Ware (twelfth century), Painted Fine Sgraffito Ware (mid-twelfth century) and Incised Sgraffito Ware (second half of the twelfth century to early thirteenth century).[107] The place of production of a number of these wares appears to be somewhere in central Greece: Corinth and Thebes itself have been proposed as possibilities, although no kilns have been found in Thebes;[108] I have a theory that Athens (where kilns have been found) is a good candidate for large production of ceramics, but any proof or disproof of this must await the forthcoming study of Charalambos Bouras on medieval Athens.[109]

The proliferation of pottery types and the quantity of pottery in Thebes and its hinterland in the middle Byzantine period are sure signs of the increase in demand, not only here but more generally in central Greece and the

---

[105] Vroom, *After Antiquity*, 121.

[106] For this, and for the high degree of monetization in the twelfth century, see Hendy, *Studies*, 310–12, 424–8, 435–7; Dunn, "Economic Change in Middle Byzantine Boeotia," 765–6; M. Galani-Krikou, "Thebes: 6th–15th c," in *Επετηρίς Εταιρείας Βοιωτικών Μελετών IIIA*, ed. V. Aravantinos (Athens, 2000), 901.

[107] Vroom, *After Antiquity*, 150–53, 163–4, 285–6; also Aegean Ware and Zeuxippus Ware (late twelfth–thirteenth century), and Zeuxippus derivatives, probably of local production, middle–third quarter of the thirteenth century: P. Armstrong, "Byzantine Thebes: Excavations on the Kadmeia, 1980," *BSA* 88 (1993): 295–335, here 306–13, 328.

[108] Wasters of unglazed pottery and of uncertain date have been found in the Kadmeia: Armstrong, "Byzantine Thebes," 335.

[109] Ch. Bouras, *Βυζαντινή Αθήνα, 10ος, 11ος, 12ος αι.* (Athens, 2010), 112, 113, nn. 919–41; Laiou and Morrisson, *The Byzantine Economy*, 118; Vroom, in *After Antiquity*, 363, mentions workshops of the early Turkish period in Athens.

XIII

Peloponnese. They are also signs that production responded to demand, with differentiated wares. The increase of demand in the countryside, exemplified by the glazed ceramics from an undetermined Greek center in eastern Phokis,[110] is underwritten by the prosperity of the **[143]** peasantry, itself resulting from a rise in population, rise in urban population, and increase in production. And the fact that very similar types of glazed pottery – Fine Sgraffito Ware, Green and Brown Painted Ware, Slip-Painted Ware, Incised Sgraffito Ware – circulated widely in central Greece, the Peloponnese, Thessalonike, and elsewhere, combined with the existence of many centers of production (Corinth, Athens, Sparta, Argos, and in all probability Thebes), shows very active trade at the regional level. Let me explain. Corinth, of course, is the best known of the production centers of pottery (and also of glass, but glass is not very useful for our purposes because its study is still in its infancy), thanks to the exemplary excavations of the American School of Classical Studies at Athens. The first, and still the major, publication by Charles H. Morgan II established the typology and the chronology of the ceramics.[111] The chronology has since been disputed, primarily by G. D. R. Sanders, who has pushed it forward by a hundred years or so, carrying with it the chronology of much of the other ceramics production, which has frequently been established on the basis of comparison with the Corinthian one.[112] The numerous publications on the ceramics production of the Peloponnese can help us with the question of regional trade. I repeat first of all the fact that we find both concentrated production in Corinth and production in other centers. Second, and importantly, a particular type of pottery, commonly known as Measles Ware, was produced only in the Peloponnese, namely, in

---

[110] P. Armstrong, "Some Byzantine and Later Settlements in Eastern Phokis," *BSA* 84 (1989): 1–47. These are rural sites near Atalanti and Orchomenos. The (unsystematically collected) finds include Green and Brown Painted Ware, Slip-Painted Ware, Sgraffito, Aegean Ware, and Zeuxippus derivatives. The author thinks that Fine Sgraffito Ware from these sites is close both in decoration and in form to Corinth examples and those found on the Pelagonessos shipwreck, though in terms of fabric they show similarities to those of Pelagonessos, Constantinople, and Athens but not to those of Corinth (43). There is also some evidence of production of glazed pottery in a village (46).

[111] C.H. Morgan, *The Byzantine Pottery*, Corinth 11 (Cambridge, Mass., 1942).

[112] See, for example, Sanders, "An Overview of the New Chronology," 35–44; idem, "Corinth Workshop Production," in *Byzantine Glazed Ceramics: The Art of Sgraffito*, ed. D. Papanikola-Bakirtzi (Athens, 1999), 159–64; idem, "New Relative and Absolute Chronologies," 153–73; and idem, "Recent Developments in the Chronology of Byzantine Corinth," in *Corinth: The Centenary, 1896–1996*, ed. C.K. Williams and N. Bookidis, Corinth 20 ([Princeton, N.J.], 2003), 385–99.

Corinth and Sparta. Morgan has established that some of the Measles Ware of Sparta were imported from Corinth, while others were made locally, imitating Corinthian wares.[113] Measles Ware is found only in a few sites other than Sparta and Corinth, but also in Albania and Italy, including Padua and Venice.[114] We have already seen a commercial connection between Corinth and Sparta, involving olive oil. The presence of Corinthian pottery in Sparta and also its local imitation strengthen the idea that there was regional trade involving these two cities and the Lakonian hinterland. Further, the export of both Corinthian and Spartan ware to Italy[115] ties in very well with the relations of these two cities with Venice. Among the other finds in Sparta are champlevé pottery (a type of Aegean Ware or Incised Ware, late twelfth century) and locally made Sgraffito Ware.[116] **[144]** Champlevé pottery may in fact have originated in Corinth and Sparta (or the eastern Mediterranean), but has wide dissemination, as does Sgraffito Ware.[117] Indeed, one of the best known of champlevé ceramics is the so-called Digenes and the Girl, from Corinth. Sparta (along with Corinth) has also been proposed as the origin of Green and Brown Painted Ware, which is found mostly in the Peloponnese, but also elsewhere in the eastern Mediterranean, Cherson, the Balkans, and Venice.[118] The connection between regional trade, production, and interregional trade becomes obvious.

A phantom "leading undetermined site"[119] of large and organized production in the late twelfth century and early thirteenth century floats over ceramics and trade in ceramics. It produced excellent-quality Incised Sgraffito Ware (Aegean Ware), the pottery found in the Kastellorizo shipwreck[120] and

---

[113]   Morgan, *The Byzantine Pottery*, 95ff.

[114]   Sanders, "Excavations at Sparta," 267; Vroom, *Byzantine to Modern Pottery in the Aegean*, 89.

[115]   S. Gelichi, "La ceramica bizantina in Italia e la ceramica italiana nel Mediterraneo orientale tra XII e XIII secolo: Stato degli studi e proposte di ricerca," in *La ceramica nel mondo bizantino tra XI e XV secolo e i suoi rapporti con l'Italia: Atti del Seminario, Certosa di Pontignano (Siena), 11–13 marzo 1991*, ed. idem (Florence, 1993), 9–46; V. François, "Sur la circulation des céramiques byzantines en Méditerranée orientale et occidentale," in *La céramique médiévale en Méditerranée: Actes du VIe Congrès de l'AIECM2, Aix-en-Provence, 13–18 Novembre 1995* (Aix-en-Provence, 1997), 231–3; Laiou and Morrisson, *The Byzantine Economy*, 118.

[116]   Sanders, "Excavations at Sparta," 260, 264.

[117]   See Vroom, *Byzantine to Modern Pottery in the Aegean*, 84–93.

[118]   Vroom, *After Antiquity*, 151–2, with reference to Vroom, *Byzantine to Modern Pottery*, 83.

[119]   Morgan, *The Byzantine Pottery*, 127.

[120]   G. Filotheou and M. Michailidou, "Βυζαντινά πινάκια από το φορτίου ναυαγισμένου πλοίου κοντά στο Καστελλόριζο," *Αρχ.Δελτ.* 41 (1986): 271–330.

the Skopelos shipwreck (in the Northern Sporades Islands).[121] In the middle of the twelfth century, a ship that foundered off Pelagonisi (also in the Northern Sporades) carried beautifully made Fine Sgraffito Ware that seems to ceramicists to be close to the production of Corinth; 1,500 pieces have been recovered, but neither the place of production of the pottery nor the destination of the ship has been fully determined.[122] Demetra Bakirtzi has, however, pointed out that the pottery on these shipwrecks as well as that securely attributable to Constantinople and Corinth was manufactured in large and well-organized workshops, with division of labor.[123] Clearly, the ships carried objects of interregional and international trade, which must also have been highly organized, although we do not **[145]** know any of the details.[124] What I have tried to do here is show the earlier step: regional trade, which we should think of as both riding on the coattails of interregional trade and feeding it.

The evidence from coins is helpful to our inquiry up to a point. Coin finds in Corinth increase abruptly beginning with the reign of Basil I (867–86), rising dramatically after 970 or so.[125] The problem is that the vast majority of the twelfth-century coins are tetartera or half-tetartera, the copper coin of small-scale transactions. Only a few gold and electrum coins, and a smaller number of silver *miliaresia*, have been found. During the reign of Alexios I (1081–1118) and again from 1143 to 1195 a "Balkan" mint, other than those of Thessalonike and Constantinople, is attested; Michael Hendy considers it very likely that it was established in either Corinth or Thebes, for the administrative reason that Thebes was the capital of the themes of Hellas and Peloponnesos, while Corinth had earlier been the capital of the theme of Peloponnesos.[126]

---

[121]   P. Armstrong, "A Group of Byzantine Bowls from Skopelos," *Oxford Journal of Archaeology* 10.3 (1991): 335–45. The author thinks that a group of glazed bowls from the Ashmolean Museum similar to those of the Kastellorizo shipwreck come from a shipwreck off the island of Skopelos.

[122]   Ch. Kritzas, "Το βυζαντινόν ναυάγιον Πελαγοννήσου Αλοννήσου," *Ἀρχαιολογικά Ἀνάλεκτα εξ Ἀθηνών* 4.2 (1971): 176–82; E. Ioannidaki-Dostoglu, "Les vases de l'épave byzantine de Pélagonnèse-Halonnèse," in *Recherches sur la céramique byzantine*, ed. V. Déroche and J.-M. Spieser, BCH supp. 18 (Athens, 1989), 157–71. A.H.S. Megaw and R.E. Jones have found similarities in the clay of Red Sgraffito Ware found in Constantinople and the Pelagonisi ceramics: "Byzantine and Allied Pottery: A Contribution by Chemical Analysis to Problems of Origin and Distribution," *BSA* 78 (1983): 235–65, at 237.

[123]   Papanikola-Bakirtzi, "Εργαστήρια εφυαλωμένης κεραμικής," 63–4.

[124]   François, "Circulation des céramiques byzantines," 235.

[125]   Morrisson, "Byzantine Money," graph 6.9; Sanders, "Corinth," 649; V. Penna, "Numismatic Circulation in Corinth from 976 to 1204," in *EHB* 2:655–8.

[126]   *DOC* 4:9, 131.

This mint, wherever it was based, produced tetartera and half-tetartera. The coins are perfectly adequate for small, everyday transactions, but they do not reflect either regional trade or the interregional/international trade of both Thebes and Corinth; notably, the Venetian documents register their transactions in gold coins, which are not money of account since specific types of coin are mentioned. Actually, the dearth of precious metal coins in the archaeological record is a generalized phenomenon in central and southern Greece. I know of no persuasive explanation for this disjunction between the numismatic evidence and the rest of the archaeological, documentary, and historical evidence. In any case, the increase in copper coins is rightly interpreted as an indicator of the high level of monetization in the area.

Conclusion

It is evident that regional trade during the long period we have been examining took different forms. In Thrace and Macedonia, it was considerably affected by the needs of the two great centers of consumption. At first, the centers of exchange were along the coasts of the northern Aegean and the Black Sea. The extension of trade networks into the hinterland went hand in hand with the establishment of more or less normal military and political conditions, and with the upward demographic curve that began some time in the second half of the eighth century. It must have been hindered by the low monetization of the interior, which, however, I do not think was acute starting after the middle of the eleventh century. The multiplication of smaller cities, both along the coast and inland, is a witness to the well-functioning trade activities of the twelfth century. The agricultural production of that part of the Balkans was doubtless exchanged not only for money but also for some of the manufactured products of the cities: this is clear for the tenth century, and clear in the twelfth century, with the dissemination of Thessalonian pottery in the interior. Until the end of the period, the hinterland's part in regional exchange remained heavily dependent on agricultural products.

Central and southern Greece and the Peloponnese exhibit a different pattern. The general demographic trend and the effects of a virtuous cycle are not much different from in the rest of the empire. But when documentation of various kinds becomes more abundant, in the ninth century, and especially [146] in the eleventh and twelfth centuries, an important difference from the northern areas is evident: there is much more trading activity *within* the region, involving both agricultural products and manufactured items. One explanation of this phenomenon may lie in the fact that the regional products

XIII

were specialized: olive oil comes in different qualities, as does wine; silk cloth and pottery also were manufactured in different qualities, and these industries need raw materials, available in the region. We can therefore see quite clearly the differentiated production, which doubtless reflects differentiated demand, as well as the greater wealth of virtually all segments of the population that made it possible.

The increase in effective demand in these southern areas may well have been influenced by interregional trade, in the sense that imports from other areas had an impact on people's decision to invest in the kind of goods to which they had been exposed as consumers. Constantinopolitan silks were known to the upper class and the church. Pottery from the Arab world may have influenced some designs of Peloponnesian pottery. The White Ware and Polychrome Ware of Constantinople were relatively abundant in the eleventh and twelfth centuries, but had been imported in smaller quantities earlier. Significantly, the form of mid-tenth-century Corinthian chafing dishes imitate the form of Constantinopolitan ones.[127] I understand the impact of interregional trade to be the following: people are exposed to imported items used by the upper class; as the population becomes wealthier, its taste for some type of similar product becomes demand; local production responds, producing items that are similar to the imported ones, but cheaper and more affordable; because tastes differ, pottery, for example, is produced in many centers, and is also diffused within the region through trade. The pattern is reproduced on a regional scale, as when the production of pottery in Sparta imitates "imported" Corinthian wares. And it is reproduced for a time in the northern areas, when Serbian potters start making imitative ware, in the thirteenth century.

This brings me to my final point. Trade networks develop and function in complex and interrelated ways. While local, regional, and interregional trade have distinguishing characteristics, and broadly speaking respond to different kinds and levels of demand, nevertheless they meet at several points, and the existence of one exerts varying, multidimensional, and multidirectional influences on the other. In this context, I think that regional trade occupies a nodal place in a society's economic development. It is the point where both demand and production become differentiated and specialization sets in; where the productive forces of a large segment of the population become active; where demography, urbanization, and monetization meet and reinforce each other; it is the point at which products become commodities. This is how the market expands, and the economy with it. I do not want to

---

[127]   See, for example, Sanders, "New Relative and Absolute Chronologies," 165.

be misunderstood. Long-distance trade, whether domestic or foreign, is very important to an economy. I hope I have demonstrated the effects of the pull of demand from outside the region on regional economies. And I have long argued that it was the virtual monopolization of Mediterranean trade by Italian merchants of foreign markets that played a seminal role in altering the structure of demand for Byzantine products, in the eventual demise of Byzantine industries, and in profound changes in regional patterns of trade. But international trade has always received scholarly attention; the story of *regional* trade in the Byzantine Empire, its structures and its conjunction with foreign trade, has yet to be told.

Abbreviations used:

AASS	*Acta sanctorum* (Paris, 1863–1940)
BMGS	*Byzantine and Modern Greek Studies*
BSA	*The Annual of the British School at Athens*
Byz	*Byzantion*
ByzArch	Byzantinisches Archiv
BZ	*Byzantinische Zeitschrift*
CFHB	Corpus fontium historiae byzantinae
DCV	R. Morozzo della Rocca and A. Lombardo, eds., *Documenti del commercio veneziano nei secoli XI–XIII*, 2 vols (Rome, 1940)
DOC	A.R. Bellinger, P. Grierson, and M.F. Hendy, *Catalogue of the Byzantine Coins in the Dumbarton Oaks Collection and in the Whittemore Collection* (Washington, D.C., 1966–99)
DOP	*Dumbarton Oaks Papers*
EHB	*The Economic History of Byzantium: From the Seventh through the Fifteenth Century*, ed. A.E. Laiou, Dumbarton Oaks Studies 39, 3 vols (Washington, D.C., 2002)
Eparchenbuch	*Das Eparchenbuch des Leons des Weisen*, ed. J. Koder (Vienna, 1991)
NDCV	A. Lombardo and R. Morozzo della Rocca, eds, *Nuovi documenti del commercio veneto dei secoli XI–XIII*, Monumenti storici, n.s., 7 (Venice, 1953)
RHC HOcc	Recueils des historiens des Croisades, Historiens occidentaux (Paris, 1844–95)
TIB	*Tabula imperii byzantini*, ed. H. Hunger (Vienna, 1976–)
VizVrem	*Vizantiiskii vremennik*

XIV

Byzantium and the Neighboring Powers:
Small-State Policies and Complexities

[42] The region of and around the Byzantine Empire in the Palaiologan period was a world of small powers, with all the complexities and instabilities inherent in such systems (**fig. 1**).[1] The dynamics of the relations between various political powers is the topic of this essay.

Maps help to remind us of the first basic and well-known point: the progressive fragmentation of the geographic space of the twelfth-century Byzantine Empire. Until 1340 there was a Byzantine state with more or less discernible boundaries, and so it is with Serbia and even Bulgaria. There were efforts, both before and after 1340, by several powers, whether Byzantium, Bulgaria, or Serbia, to unify large segments of this space. But by the end of the fourteenth century, the fragmentation was so advanced, so many lords and "kings" or "emperors" ruled – if that is not a euphemism – tiny areas with ever-shifting borders, that it would be virtually impossible to construct a political map of the area.

The fragmentation of the Byzantine space had begun in the late twelfth century and had certainly been accelerated by the Fourth Crusade (1202–1204). After the Byzantine restoration in 1261 there were about eighty years during which a certain amount of reconcentration occurred, primarily as a result of the first three Palaiologan emperors. But under the surface, or even on it, the breakup of relatively large units progressed, in ways that augured the future. Some examples will illuminate the process.

In 1299 Andronikos II accepted the annexation of part of Byzantine western Macedonia by Stefan Uroš II Milutin of Serbia, although the

---

* From *Byzantium: Faith and Power (1261–1557), Perspectives on Late Byzantine Art and Culture*, ed. S.T. Brooks. © 2006 by the Metropolitan Museum of Art, New York. Reprinted by permission. Original page numbers are given in square brackets within the text.

[1]   See, for example, Alvin M. Saperstein, "The Prediction of Unpredictability: Applications of the New Paradigm of Chaos in Dynamical Systems to the Old Problem of the Stability of a System in Hostile Nations," in *Chaos Theory in the Social Sciences: Foundations and Applications*, eds L. Douglas Kiel and Euel Elliott (Ann Arbor, 1996), pp. 139ff.

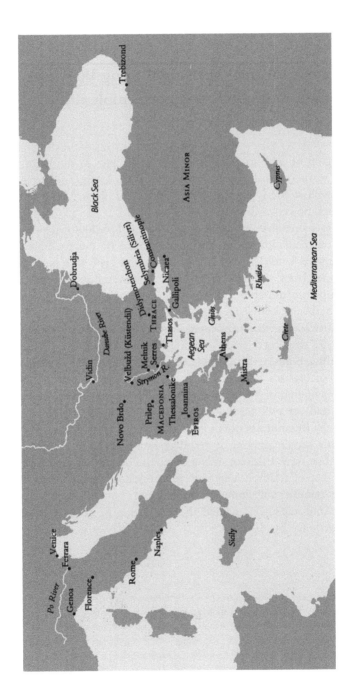

Fig. 1. Cities and Regions of the Balkans, Italy, and Asia Minor in the Palaeologan period.

recognition was disguised as the granting of a dowry.[2] The event is significant in view of future developments regarding the acceptance of rights established by conquest. In other Balkan states, the disaggregating effects of hostilities and conquests are apparent. In 1330 the battle of Velbužd (Küstendil) between the Serbs and the Bulgarians brought about the fragmentation of the Bulgarian state, which proceeded despite the efforts of Ivan Alexander (r. 1331–71). The brigand Momčilo established a tiny and short-lived principality in the Merope region of Thrace from 1343 to 1345; a little later, Dobrotitsa, the best known of a number of semi-independent rulers, governed the Dobrudja, the region between the lower Danube and the Black Sea. In Serbia, the battle of Velbužd resulted in the accession of Stefan Dušan (r. 1331–55), who was to undertake his own efforts at restructuring the territories and becoming "Emperor of the Romans."[3] In 1334 Stefan Dušan and Andronikos III made an agreement that firmly and formally recognized Dušan's rights to some of the Macedonian lands he had conquered.[4] This was an important step in the process of establishing the rights of conquest de jure, and not simply de facto.

Need one say more? Need one perhaps mention that even the conquest of territories in the process of consolidation no longer had the same meaning as in the Middle Byzantine period? As witness one example will **[44]** suffice, although more could be produced. That is the surrender of the city of Ioannina to Andronikos II in 1319. Its inhabitants gave up the city only upon receipt of extensive privileges, forming with the emperor a relationship that was certainly bilateral and synallagmatic, very different from the Middle Byzantine concept of sovereignty.[5]

These few examples from the period before midcentury serve as reminders that both the principles and the forms of fragmentation that became

[2] Angeliki E. Laiou, *Constantinople and the Latins: The Foreign Policy of Andronicus II (1282–1328)* (Cambridge, Mass., 1972), pp. 228–32, 282 [hereafter *Andronicus II*]; Lj. Maksimović, "Ē anaptuxē centrophugōn ropōn stis politikes scheseis Byzantiou kai Serbias ton 14. aiōna [The development of centrifugal tendencies in the political relations of Byzantium and Serbia in the 14th century]," in *Byzantio kai Servia kata ton 14. aiōna* [Byzantium and Serbia in the fourteenth century] (Athens, 1996), p. 60.

[3] Nicolaï Todorov, *A Short History of Bulgaria* (Sofia, 1975), pp. 30–31; George Christos Soulis, *The Serbs and Byzantium during the Reign of Tsar Stephen Dušan (1331–1355) and His Successors* (Athens, 1995), p. 60; M.C. Bartusis, "Chrelja and Momčilo: Occasional Servants of Byzantium in Fourteenth Century Macedonia," *Byzantinoslavica* 41, no. 2 (1980), pp. 201–21.

[4] Soulis, *The Serbs and Byzantium*, pp. 37–42.

[5] Angeliki Laiou, "The Emperor's Word: Chrysobulls, Oaths and Synallagmatic Relations in Byzantium (11th–12th C.)," *Mélanges Gilbert Dagron, Travaux et Mémoires* 14 (2002), pp. 360–61; Laiou, *Andronicus II*, p. 258.

common after it were present earlier. With the midcentury, the process of disaggregation became rapid: Serbia after the death of Dušan, Byzantium after the second civil war, the end of which may be placed in 1354 but which continued to have repercussions until the end of the empire, Bulgaria after the death of Ivan Alexander, all dissolved into small or smaller states or rulerships.[6] Noteworthy, and typical of the **[45]** sort of disaggregation that occurred, is the existence of multiple capitals during a considerable part of the Palaiologan period. Constantinople was, by its history, location, and ideological weight, the capital of the Byzantine Empire, but Thessalonike served as almost an alternative capital under the Byzantine Empress Yolanda/Irene, who resided there between 1303 and 1317 and carried out her own foreign policy: an indirect and unintended consequence of the marriage of her daughter Simonis to Stefan Uroš II.[7] Thessalonike performed the same function during the second civil war and later still under Manuel II, while Didymoteichon was the capital of John VI Kantakouzenos for a few years after his investiture as emperor in October 1341. In 1382 there were three Byzantine capitals: Selymbria (modern Silivri), ruled by Andronikos IV Palaiologos and his son John VII; Thessalonike, ruled by Manuel; and Constantinople, where the emperor John V held court. In Bulgaria, Tŭrnovo and Vidin alternated as capitals. During the reign of Dušan, Prilep was a second capital.[8] After Dušan's death in 1355, Serres became another Serbian capital. Trebizond, of course, remained a capital city. Mistra may perhaps not be considered a capital in the same sense, but it was certainly a center of power alternative to Constantinople.

Similarly, one could point to the proliferation of people bearing the title *basileus*, once jealously held and guarded by the *basileus ton Romaion*, the Orthodox, Greek-speaking **[46]** emperor ruling in Constantinople, who recognized it with the greatest difficulty in a few other monarchs. In the early thirteenth century, the participle *basileusas* was used by Niketas Choniates to describe the rule of Henry of Flanders.[9] The narrative of Laonikos Chalkokondyles, written in the 1480s, is peppered with *basileis*, including the βασιλεὺς βυζαντίου (*basileus Byzantiou*).[10]

---

[6]   On Ivan Alexander, see Ivan Bozhilov, *Familiiata na Asenevtsi (1186–1460)* (Sofia, 1985), no. 33; on Michael Šišman, see ibid., no. 30.

[7]   See below, p.9; Laiou, *Andronicus II*, pp. 93ff., 228–33.

[8]   Soulis, *The Serbs and Byzantium*, pp. 42–3.

[9]   *Nicetae Choniatae Historia*, ed. Immanuel Bekker (Bonn, 1835), p. 852.

[10]   Laonikos Chalkokondyles, *Historiarum libri decem*, ed. Immanuel Bekker (Bonn, 1843), p. 462. The appearance of the term *emperor of Byzantium* predates by almost eighty years its use by

What is exhibited here is multipolarity, which increases the areas of instability in the system and makes it more prone to warfare.[11] The question then arises whether and how these states functioned and, subsequently, what were the dynamics of their relations. The early fragmentary states, formed just before or just after the fall of Constantinople in 1204, gave evidence of viability. Some, like Serbia and Bulgaria, had a certain coherence already before 1204. The states of Epiros and Nicaea, although certainly smaller than the Komnenian Empire, were economically viable, having both the essentials of self-sufficiency and enough of a surplus to trade. Given the secular trend for trade to increase, a large tax base was no longer as essential as before and, in any case, small-scale politics are sufficiently served by small-scale resources – except, of course, when other factors, or the logic of the system, intervene and destroy the proportionality, as will be shown below. Thus, in the thirteenth century, Bulgaria, Serbia, Epiros, and Nicaea were able to sustain economic growth (where evidence exists, it is clear) and to provide for defense, while Epiros and Nicaea, far from Constantinople, were able to create viable political institutions. The reconquest of Constantinople in 1261 brought with it the impetus for the reconsolidation of territories.

These early fragmentary states, however, operated under various impediments. Or, to put it differently, there were factors that, unless checked, would make the existence of these states problematic. For one thing, the creation of several political units in what had been the Byzantine Empire necessarily increased the possibility (and the reality) of warfare, at the same time increasing the cost [47] of government.[12] It is true that government was not nearly as ostentatious or as expensive in the successor states as it had been in the Komnenian Empire. On the other hand, the tax base was not changed much overall, so that the same resources had to support a number of smaller governments and smaller armies. The spectacular rise in the importance of Serbia in the fourteenth century must be partly ascribed to the fact that it commanded new resources, unavailable to others in the area, that is, the silver mines at Novo Brdo and elsewhere.

Hieronymus Wolf in 1557. See Helen C. Evans, "Byzantium: Faith and Power (1261–1557)," in *Byzantium: Faith and Power (1261–1557)*, ed. Helen C. Evans, exh. cat., The Metropolitan Museum of Art (New York, 2004), pp. 5, 15; the date provided the end point of the exhibition.

[11]   Saperstein, "Prediction of Unpredictability," pp. 140, 153–5.

[12]   Ibid., passim. For a general and theoretical discussion from a different viewpoint, see Alberto Alesina and Enrico Spolaore, *The Size of Nations* (Cambridge, Mass., 2003), pp. 95ff. The authors point out that as states proliferate so do the frontiers that have to be defended, and the likelihood of conflict increases.

This interesting book was brought to my attention by my student Aslihan Akisik.

Multipolarity and increased conflict create interesting dynamics. With small states, warfare was also small-scale, not only in the size of the armies involved but also in its aims. Michael VIII and to some extent Andronikos II had before them the large task of recovering imperial territories. Soon **[48]** enough, however, even during the reign of Andronikos II, the conflicts were over small areas, towns, and forts, as, for instance, those along the Serbian frontier. In these circumstances, border lords or warlords flourished and added to the instability of the system. Any number of examples could be cited of these people, who had typically participated in warfare between states and who then tried to become independent rulers. One could mention the Serbian warlord Hrelja, one of the lieutenants of Stefan Dečanski and Stefan Dušan, who, in the 1330s, built his own independent statelet in the region around the Strymon River and sought to assert his overlordship of the fort town of Melnik. Hrelja's loyalties were transferred from Dušan to Andronikos III and John Kantakouzenos and back to Dušan, as occasion warranted.[13] Another example is Momčilo, the Bulgarian who served the rivals John VI and John V successively and built his own statelet.[14] In the 1350s two brothers, the grand *stratopedarches* Alexios and the grand *primikerios* John fought against the Serbs of Serres and, as a reward, were granted by Emperor John V the coastal area of eastern Macedonia as well as Thasos to rule as hereditary possessions – in other words, exercising full powers, including state power.[15] How any of these possessions might be represented on a map showing political frontiers beggars the imagination.

One result of the shattered power structure is the fact that small events, or events that seem peripheral to the area, could lead to major upheavals: a situation that has been termed "crisis instability."[16] Such was the case with the Catalan mercenaries, released from their obligations in Sicily after the Peace of Caltabelotta (1302), who offered their services to the Byzantine emperor Andronikos II.[17] They were engaged to fight, as mercenaries, for the Byzantines and against the Turks in Asia Minor. But this band of perhaps sixty-five hundred men, of whom fifteen hundred were cavalry, brought considerable changes to several parts of the Balkans that were certainly disproportionate

---

[13]   Bartusis, "Chrelja and Momčilo," pp. 201–6.

[14]   Ibid., pp. 206–10.

[15]   Soulis, *The Serbs and Byzantium*, pp. 159, 189; *Actes du Pantocrator*, ed. Vassiliki Kravari, Archives de l'Athos, 17 (Paris, 1991), pp. 7ff.; Paul Lemerle, *Philippes et la Macédoine orientale à l'époque chrétienne et byzantine* (Paris, 1945), pp. 205ff.

[16]   Saperstein, "Prediction of Unpredictability," p. 149.

[17]   On the Catalans, see Laiou, *Andronicus II*, pp. 130ff.

to both their strength and the role they had initially been meant to play. Not only did they engage in the plunder type of warfare that was becoming a structural element of war in the Balkans in this period. They also threatened Constantinople itself, and eventually Thessalonike; as they moved south, they ended up establishing the Catalan duchy of Athens in 1311. Fearsome pirates, they became one more element of instability, especially at sea. Their presence and the threat they posed had moved Byzantium and the Genoese much closer in their alliance. In 1305, as part of this alliance, Benedetto Zaccaria took over and subsequently received from the emperor the rich island of Chios.

Meanwhile, another upheaval had occurred. The Catalans had had with them a group of Turks, possibly Ottomans, under a leader named Chalil. This group, numbering perhaps twenty-one hundred men, left the Catalans in the spring of 1309 and subsequently captured a fort in Gallipoli, received reinforcements from Asia Minor, and looted the surrounding area in Thrace. It took the help of the Serbians to root them out; as a result, Stefan Uroš II received, for the monastery of Chilandar, certain possessions in the Strymon Valley.[18] In the *Histories* of Chalkokondyles, written in the late fifteenth century, this incident is given surprising prominence, perhaps because it was, after all, the first settlement of Turks in Europe and involved the peninsula of Gallipoli, the launching pad of Ottoman invasions after 1352.[19]

In sum, the activities of a small band of mercenaries had broad consequences for the relations of the Byzantine Empire with its neighbors as well as with outside powers such as Genoa and Aragon. Furthermore, they hastened the fragmentation of power and authority: as the central government was seen to be incapable of resisting the Catalans, other actors, such as the Zaccaria in Chios, the Knights Hospitaller in Rhodes, and the inhabitants of the Byzantine walled towns, took matters into their own hands.[20] While not quite the Butterfly Effect,[21] it does very **[49]** much characterize a complex system in which small inputs can have very considerable outputs. This is, of course, the very definition of chaos, and to observe such outcomes is virtually

---

[18]   Ibid., pp. 232–3; M. Živojinović, "La frontière serbo-byzantine dans les premières décennies du XIVe siècle," in *Byzantio kai Servia*, pp. 60–61; Nicolas Oikonomides, "The Turks in Europe (1305–13) and the Serbs in Asia Minor (1313)," in *The Ottoman Emirate (1300–1389): Halcyon Days in Crete I*, ed. Elizabeth Zachariadou (Rethymnon, 1993), pp. 161–8.

[19]   Chalkokondyles, *Historiarum libri decem*, pp. 16–17, says that the Turks numbered eight thousand and that they were defeated not by the Serbs, but by the Tatars.

[20]   Laiou, *Andronicus II*, pp. 228–9.

[21]   This is the idea that a butterfly stirring the air in Beijing can have a profound effect on the weather in New York a month down the line: James Gleick, *Chaos: Making a New Science* (New York, 1987), p. 8.

to state that the politics of the period follow the rules of chaos theory.[22] Equally predictable by chaos theory is the fact that some major events may have disproportionately small consequences. Thus, in 1402 the battle of Ankyra, which one might consider a major event, neither reversed the disunity of Balkan Christians nor stopped the eventual unification of the area under the Ottomans.[23]

After the second half of the fourteenth century, the system became atomized as disintegration followed its own dynamic. Theoretically, the high costs of increased warfare and government, with a decreasing revenue base – the result, among other things, of constant warfare and the Black Death – should have led to efforts to create larger states, more capable of providing for defense.[24] In fact, it took a long time for such a process to begin. Perhaps this was because of the nature of warfare. Border warfare as practiced by the Byzantines, Bulgarians, Serbs, Albanians, and others in the first half of the century usually consisted of looting wars: wars for the redistribution of income, which was the reward of the warrior. Although frequently involving fairly low-level violence, looting wars arise from and contribute to fragmentation of power and authority. Conflict becomes a way of life and gives rise to smaller and smaller political units.

From time to time, the wars became larger, more extensive, and meant to redistribute resources rather than income: thus the Byzantine civil wars, the wars of Michael Šišman, and eventually the expansion of Serbia under Stefan Dušan.[25] However, these larger wars, which may be seen as centripetal efforts, did not create long-lived large states and were not repeated after Dušan's death. There was, therefore, a downward spiral that may be considered irrational except in terms of the redistribution of income among many suitors. Eventually, the system became too burdened with small-scale units of power,

---

[22]   Saperstein, "Prediction of Unpredictability," pp. 139–40, 149 (definition of chaos: "small disturbances of a deterministic mathematical system lead to disproportionately large changes in the system and the consequent loss of control"). Cf. Thad A. Brown, "Nonlinear Politics," in Kiel and Elliott, *Chaos Theory*, p. 128.

[23]   It should perhaps be noted that similar chaotic conditions prevailed in Asia Minor after the dissolution of the Seljuk Empire. Throughout this essay the Ottomans are mentioned *only* in connection with the Balkans, that is, after they had achieved a certain consolidation of power in Asia Minor.

[24]   As in Alesina and Spolaore, *The Size of Nations*, p. III.

[25]   On this, see Angeliki E. Laiou, "In the Medieval Balkans: Economic Pressures and Conflicts in the Fourteenth Century," in *Byzantine Studies, in Honor of Milton V. Anastos*, ed. Speros Vryonis, Jr. (Malibu, 1985), pp. 148ff.

fighting small-scale wars, to be sustainable. The imperative to centralize was then carried out by the Ottomans.

Part of the dynamic characterizing the relationship between the numerous actors in the political scene during the Palaiologan period is the effort not so much to centralize but rather to form networks that would provide for their members a modicum of security and more power than each one alone could command. Perhaps the most common form this dynamic assumed was the formation of marriage alliances among the various actors, large or small and growing smaller as disintegration advanced. A glance at the genealogical tables of the ruling and/or powerful Balkan families easily makes the point. There were "royal" alliances; for example, the marriage of the five-year-old Simonis, daughter of Andronikos II, to Stefan Uroš II Milutin, kral of Serbia, then about forty years old. Its purpose was to stop Serbian incursions into Macedonia as a *quid pro quo* for the quasi-recognition of Milutin's conquests in the form of Simonis's dowry. The end result was mixed, as has already been mentioned.

Other royal alliances include the marriage of Constantine Tich Asen of Bulgaria to a niece of Michael VIII in 1270 or 1272 and that of Irene, Michael's daughter, to John Asen III in 1278, both not particularly effective efforts to cement alliances with Bulgaria.[26] Following in his father's footsteps, Andronikos II married off his granddaughter Theodora to Theodore Svetoslav, king of Bulgaria, in a marriage alliance that did further its purpose in a peculiar and unanticipated way: after the death of Theodore Svetoslav, Michael Šišman, who became king in 1323, was hostile toward the Byzantine state until he married the widow Theodora, the sister of Andronikos III, who was in full rebellion against his grandfather.[27]

All these alliances eventually created complex and murky situations as competing **[50]** and conflicting political groupings formed around them. At the time of the first civil war between Andronikos II and Andronikos III in the 1320s, Michael Šišman asked for a part of the Byzantine Empire in the form of a dowry because of his marriage to the Byzantine princess.[28] Šišman's

---

[26]   Averkios Th. Papadopulos, *Versuch einer Genealogie der Palaiologen, 1259–1453* (Speyer, 1938), no. 133.

[27]   Laiou, *Andronicus II*, p. 291.

[28]   *Ioannis Cantacuzeni Eximperatoris Historiarum libri IV*, ed. Ludwig Schopen, 3 vols (Bonn, 1829–32), vol. I, pp. 325–9 [hereafter Cantacuzenus]; S. Ćirković, "Between Kingdom and Empire: Dushan's State 1346–1355 Reconsidered," in *Byzantio kai Servia*, p. 118.

request was made in order to legitimize his attacks on that area.[29] During the same war, the Serbs were more or less allied to the old emperor and the Bulgarians to the young one, following the lines of the existing marriage alliances, which, in the case of Serbia, were reinforced by yet another marriage, that between Stefan III Dečanski and an imperial princess. However, after the destruction of Bulgarian power in 1330, Stefan Dušan, the son of Stefan Dečanski, married the sister of Ivan Alexander, nephew and successor of Michael Šišman. This alliance in effect replaced an earlier "lost" alliance, which had united Michael Šišman to Anna-Neda, sister of Stefan Dečanski, before Šišman repudiated the marriage and contracted a Byzantine one.[30]

"Royal" marriage alliances could be discussed at great length and tedium. There is no reason to do so. Suffice it to say that by the late fourteenth century the royal houses (of every persuasion) of the Byzantine state, the Serbs, the Bulgarians, and Trebizond, of course, were connected among themselves in intricate matrimonial patterns. These did not impede the fragmentation but simply furnished a palliative in the form of temporary and shifting alliances.

The nonroyal marriage alliances would be more interesting to trace: although the task is so complex that the rewards would not perhaps repay the effort expended. As the fragmentation of power turned into the pulverization thereof, political marriage alliances took place among various small-time powermongers. Thus, Dobrotitsa married off his daughter to a son of the Byzantine emperor John V Palaiologos. The grand *primikerios* John married Anna Asenina, cousin of John V's wife, Helena, who was the daughter of John VI Kantakouzenos and Irene Asenina. Albanian and Serbian local rulers intermarried. And the last Byzantine ruler, Constantine XI, was the son of Manuel II and Helena, daughter of a lateral descendant of Dušan, who was a local ruler in eastern Macedonia.[31]

Marriage alliances created a nexus of relationships but did not provide a counterweight either to fragmentation or to local warfare. Did any other mechanism or institution function centripetally? It might be thought that Constantinople, with all the burden of imperial tradition behind it, could exercise a centripetal pull. In fact, this was hardly the case, at least after the first three Palaiologoi, although even earlier its monopoly on imperial authority had been lost. The fact of the existence of alternative capitals for much of

[29] Nicephorus Gregoras, *Nicephori Gregorae Byzantina historia*, eds Ludwig Schopen and Immanuel Bekker, 3 vols. Corpus scriptorum historiae byzantinae (Bonn, 1829–55), vol. I, p. 325 [hereafter Gregoras].

[30] Soulis, *The Serbs and Byzantium*, pp. 32ff.

[31] Ibid., pp. 189ff.

the Palaiologan period undermined the role the city might have played. What remained was that the city still, and for a long time, was considered to convey legitimacy to a ruler who wanted to be seen as the heir to the Byzantine past.

It is for this reason that the reconquest of Constantinople by Michael VIII in 1261 had both a real significance and a profoundly symbolic one. For the same reason, John Kantakouzenos could not be content with his holdings in Macedonia and Thrace; he wanted to be crowned emperor in Constantinople. Similarly, Stefan Dušan, who used the title Emperor of Serbia and Romania after being crowned emperor in the spring of 1346 did not consider his ascendancy complete until he had conquered Constantinople – which, of course, he never did. It is just as important to note, however, that the claims Dušan considered to have on the Byzantine imperial throne originated with the act of conquest of Byzantine lands, which he wanted to solidify further through the conquest of Constantinople. This is made crystal clear in his letter to Venice in 1346, in which he announced that he, the emperor, already held "ten parts of the Roman Constantinopolitan Empire," with the exception of the city of **[51]** Constantinople.[32] Ruling in Constantinople, therefore, did not by itself serve to unite fractured rulership, it was only meant to give additional legitimation to the victor of war or civil war. Eventually, it did that for Mehmed II the Conqueror as well.

Aside from the legitimation given by conquest, there were other legitimizing authorities or mechanisms in the Palaiologan period. Most of them were located outside of the area. In the early thirteenth century, the pope had legitimized the rule of both Bulgarian (1204) and Serbian (1217) rulers by crowning them kings. Stefan Dušan twice sought the aid of Venice in his quest to conquer Constantinople and become emperor not only of the Romania but also of the Romans: once just after his coronation in 1346, and a second time in 1350. The fact that Venice did not accede to this request does not negate the perception, on the part of Dušan, that the city could act as a legitimizing factor. It is notable in this context that in its reply to the Serbian ambassador Venice called Dušan "serenissimus dominus Imperator

---

[32] Cantacuzenus, vol. 2, p. 552; Gregoras, p. 747. Josephi Valentini, *Acta Albaniae Veneta saeculorum XIV et XV*, vol. I, part I (Palermo, 1967), p. 130: "dominus imperator per gratiam Dei acquisiverit...decem partes Romani imperii Constantinopolitani, preter civitatem ipsam Constantinopolis, quam expugnare et subiugare nequit" (With the Grace of God, the lord emperor acquired...ten parts of the Roman Constantinopolitan Empire, except for the city of Constantinople, which he was unable to take and subjugate). Cf. Ćirković, "Between Kingdom and Empire," pp. 118–19; N. Oikonomides, "Emperor of the Romans – Emperor of the Romania," in *Byzantio kai Servia*, pp. 121–8.

Grecorum et Raxie."[33] Finally, in the petty Byzantine civil wars of the 1370s, the Venetians and the Genoese shared that function, which was soon to be taken over by the Ottomans. None of these agencies of legitimation worked against fragmentation – quite the opposite, in fact.

There was perhaps another legitimizing mechanism indigenous to the area, the one celebrated in the exhibition "Byzantium: Faith and Power." Art in the Byzantine style undoubtedly contributed to the self-image and self-esteem of the various rulers, great and small, who shared among them the diminishing political power left to the Christian populations of the area. Here, at least, the regional or local rulers substituted their own patronage for that of Constantinople. Similarly, and equally obviously, dress similar to the Byzantine imperial one was a symbol of legitimacy, as the historian Nikephoros Gregoras realized. After Dušan conquered Serres, Gregoras wrote, he had himself proclaimed Emperor of the Romans and changed his barbarous ways into Roman ones, disporting all the ceremonial clothing appropriate to the imperial office.[34] In the cultural sphere there were, indeed, some unifying elements.

The developments briefly presented here did not take place in a vacuum, but within a larger, correspondingly more complex and unstable system of political and economic relations in which Western powers and, increasingly, the Ottomans also participated. I have argued elsewhere[35] that the political decline of the Byzantine Empire and the atomization of power in its former territories coincided with the economic integration of **[52]** the area, which functioned as an international market – at least insofar as this was possible in medieval conditions – organized by and for the benefit of Western economic powers, primarily Venice and Genoa. It is possible that the coincidence was more than chronological. Without necessarily positing a cause-and-effect relationship, one may nevertheless suggest that the system of small political units was able to survive partly because the international market had no use for large, internally self-sufficient political units. Indeed, to the extent that such units tended to be protectionist, their interests would be opposed to those of the major economic players. Thus, as far as the surrounding economic

---

[33] Valentini, *Acta*, pp. 133–6.

[34] Gregoras, vol. 2, pp. 746–7.

[35] See, in the first instance, Angeliki E. Laiou–Thomadakis, "The Byzantine Economy in the Mediterranean Trade System, Thirteenth-Fifteenth Centuries," *Dumbarton Oaks Papers* 34–35 (1980–81), pp. 177–222, and, in the last instance, Angeliki E. Laiou, ed., *The Economic History of Byzantium from the Seventh through the Fifteenth Century*, 3 vols (Washington, D.C., 2002), vol. 3, pp. 1156–61.

circumstances were concerned, there was nothing to impose, elicit, or create favorable conditions for consolidation as opposed to fragmentation of political power.[36] A case in point is Venice's refusal to help Stefan Dušan take Constantinople, perhaps precisely in order to inhibit the creation of a large state. Similarly, when the Ottomans united the political space and conquered Constantinople, they established a protectionist state much like that of the Byzantine Empire in its middle period and destroyed the already fractured international market that had existed since the mid-thirteenth century.

The fact that there was a dialectic relationship between political fragmentation and economic unification poses with some urgency a final question. Small states are not necessarily unviable. There are benefits to these more cohesive entities, which are perhaps easier to govern. The question is, when are the benefits overwhelmed by the costs, political and/or economic? When does disaggregation reach a fatal point, after which the units are too small to function at all effectively? The nodal points, which are different from area to area and from unit to unit, can be traced chronologically. Analyzing the process is more difficult. Perhaps the point of nonfunctionality comes when statelets no longer have the resources or the institutions to provide elementary public services, such as the defense of their subjects, let alone the preservation of infrastructures or the assurance of provisioning. At that point also the rivalry for fragments of power and resources becomes so ubiquitous that it negates the possibility of acting in a larger common interest – in putting up a common defense, for example. It is then that the need for political reconcentration becomes overwhelming.[37] But it was the Ottomans, an outside power with a very considerable reservoir of human resources, and increasingly of economic resources, who carried out that imperative and fused the fragments of political power floating adrift in the geographic space of the former Byzantine Empire.

---

[36]   This argument is almost the reverse of that made by Alesina and Spolaore, *The Size of Nations*, pp. 81ff.

[37]   John Kantakouzenos seems to have realized, in 1341, that the point had been reached. He had a vision of reuniting to Byzantium the Latin parts of the Peloponnesos as well as the duchy of Athens, so that the power of the empire would be restored to what "it used to be in the old days." After that, he thought, it would be easy to defeat the Serbs and "the other neighboring barbarians" (Cantacuzenus, vol. 2, p. 80). For a theoretical view of nonequilibrium conditions leading a system to cross a critical threshold, see Kenyon B. De Greene, "Field Theoretic Framework for the Interpretation of the Evolution, Instability; Structural Change, and Management of Complex Systems," in Kiel and Elliott, *Chaos Theory*, p. 276.

INDEX

Terms that recur frequently in the texts, such as *Byzantium, Byzantines, Greeks, Romans, Mediterranean*, have not been included in the index. Emperors and other rulers are listed by their first name; other persons (where possible) by their last.

For Product Safety Concerns and Information please contact our EU
representative GPSR@taylorandfrancis.com Taylor & Francis Verlag GmbH,
Kaufingerstraße 24, 80331 München, Germany

Printed and bound by CPI Group (UK) Ltd, Croydon, CR0 4YY
08/05/2025
01864327-0003